TEACHING LEADERSHIP

"*Teaching Leadership* is a wonderful guide to becoming a wise and effective teacher and facilitator of leadership development, embracing the fact that leadership contexts are becoming more relational and collaborative and thus require the integration of diverse disciplines and worldviews."

—**Charles J. Palus**, Center for Creative Leadership, USA

"In a brilliant move, Crosby calls attention to an unspoken truth: teaching leadership demands soul searching about one's own leadership work. This book is memorable in an important way—it is scholarly grounded, and yet quite inspirational and profound."

—**Sonia M. Ospina**, New York University, USA

"Barbara Crosby explains and exemplifies the passion, smarts, and action (heart, head, and hands) of leadership and teaching for it. The book will serve as a wonderful introduction to those entering the field of teaching leadership, a metric for those who have been at it for a while, and a capstone for those finishing a program in leadership."

—**Richard A. Couto**, Union Institute and University, USA

Teaching Leadership provides guidance for leadership educators in a variety of organizational and community contexts and across academic disciplines. An experienced leadership educator, Crosby promotes an inclusive vision of leadership that recognizes the inherent leadership potential in everyone. Featuring interviews with numerous respected leadership educators, *Teaching Leadership* complicates and enriches the leader-follower dichotomy to advance a holistic and practice-oriented model of leadership education. Using the metaphor of "heart, head, and hands," Crosby shows how authentic leadership is an embodied practice based equally in emotional, intellectual, and experiential learning.

Barbara C. Crosby is Associate Professor at the Hubert H. Humphrey School of Public Affairs at the University of Minnesota, USA.

LEADERSHIP: Research and Practice Series
A James MacGregor Burns Academy of Leadership Collaboration

SERIES EDITORS
Georgia Sorenson, Ph.D, Møller Leadership Scholar and Møller By-Fellow, Churchill College, University of Cambridge, Founder of the James MacGregor Academy of Leadership at the University of Maryland, and co-founder of the International Leadership Association.
Ronald E. Riggio, Ph.D, Henry R. Kravis Professor of Leadership and Organizational Psychology and former Director of the Kravis Leadership Institute at Claremont McKenna College.

Aneil Mishra and Karen E. Mishra
Becoming a Trustworthy Leader: Psychology and Practice

Ronald E. Riggio and Sherylle J. Tan (Eds.)
Leader Interpersonal and Influence Skills: The Soft Skills of Leadership

Dinesh Sharma and Uwe P. Gielen (Eds.)
The Global Obama: Crossroads of Leadership in the 21st Century

Nathan W. Harter
Leadership and Coherence: A Cognitive Approach

George R. Goethals
Presidential Leadership and African Americans: "An American Dilemma" from Slavery to the White House

Michael Genovese
The Future of Leadership: Leveraging Leadership in an Age of Hyper-Change

Al Bolea and Leanne Atwater
Applied Leadership Development

Barbara C. Crosby
Teaching Leadership: An Integrative Approach

Dinesh Sharma (Ed.)
The Global Hillary: Women's Political Leadership in Contemporary Contexts

TEACHING LEADERSHIP

An Integrative Approach

Barbara C. Crosby

Routledge
Taylor & Francis Group

NEW YORK AND LONDON

First published 2017
by Routledge
711 Third Avenue, New York, NY 10017

and by Routledge
2 Park Square, Milton Park, Abingdon, Oxon, OX14 4RN

Routledge is an imprint of the Taylor & Francis Group, an informa business

Library of Congress Cataloging-in-Publication Data
Names: Crosby, Barbara C., 1946– author.
Title: Teaching leadership : an integrative approach / Barbara C. Crosby.
Description: New York, NY : Routledge, 2016. | Series: Leadership:
    research and practice series | Includes bibliographical references and index.
Identifiers: LCCN 2016000789 | ISBN 9781138825031 (hardcover : alk. paper) |
    ISBN 9781138825048 (pbk. : alk. paper) | ISBN 9781315740188 (ebook)
Subjects: LCSH: Leadership—Study and teaching.
Classification: LCC HD57.7 .C7533 2016 | DDC 658.4/092—dc23
LC record available at http://lccn.loc.gov/2016000789

ISBN: 978-1-138–82503-1 (hbk)
ISBN: 978-1-138-82504-8 (pbk)
ISBN: 978-1-315-74018-8 (ebk)

Typeset in Bembo
by Apex CoVantage, LLC

This book is dedicated to my grandson Benjamin Kai Sooja,
my daughter Jessica Ah-Reum Crosby Bryson, and
my son John Kee Sooja.

CONTENTS

SERIES EDITORS' FOREWORD

While tens of thousands of books have been written about leadership, only a handful focus on how to teach leadership to others. Why is this the case? Leadership is fantastically complex, involving leaders, followers, context, and timing, and while there is a large and growing body of literature on leadership and leadership theories, teaching leadership is about developing leaders—not only teaching about leadership, but teaching *how* to be an effective leader. *Teaching Leadership: An Integrative Approach* is the only book to our knowledge that relies on solid research in order to derive best practices for teaching leadership, both about leadership and about how to lead.

Rather than hearing just the voice of the author—Barbara Crosby, who has had an entire career teaching leadership—you will hear the voices of two dozen leadership educators, across a wide range of disciplines and perspectives. Collectively, they offer a wealth of information about how to better understand and teach leadership.

As you can imagine, we are quite happy to have this book in our series, *Leadership: Research and Practice*. It takes the series in a new direction—toward leadership education—but using a scientific approach to better understand how to teach leadership effectively.

For teachers and professors of leadership, as well as leadership trainers and developers, there is no resource available that has the breadth and depth of this volume. You will need this book in your back pocket as you go forth with the awesome task of developing the next generation of leaders.

Georgia Sorenson
Ronald E. Riggio

PREFACE

Great teachers understand that all serious thinking starts with wonder. To be educated, they insist, is to develop a sense of wonder, to imagine, to think differently, to reexamine one's principles, and to qualify what one says with the word perhaps. They help us to realize it is a mistake to be afraid of making mistakes; new challenges and risk taking have a genius, power, and magic in them for those who are unafraid of a life of continuous learning.

Effective leaders share these same qualities: unlocking our imaginations, defining our central challenges, urging us to look at our longer-term horizons, and clarifying our choices for both the short and longer terms.

Thomas Cronin and Michael Genovese (2012)

For almost 30 years I regularly have stood in front of professionals, graduate or undergraduate students, community activists, political officials, and artists from a variety of countries and proposed that together we can improve their leadership practice. In many cases, this means that I also am proposing that people in the audience start thinking of themselves as leaders, something they may not be accustomed to. It's often an audacious venture, raising questions about tampering with personal identity, distinguishing between good and bad practice, and making consequential—albeit unpredictable—interventions in organizational and community life.

I never intended to become a teacher of leadership, and that's true of most people teaching leadership today around the world. Most of us prepared to work or teach in some other field—such as business management, entrepreneurship, public affairs, nonprofit management, or the arts. The good news these days is that anyone who is called or called upon to teach leadership in any of these fields can easily find an array of exercises, techniques, and workshop or course designs that are candidates for her tool kit. However, relatively little research-based advice is available for how to prepare oneself to teach leadership (or develop leaders) or how to choose among and adaptively deploy tools and designs.

The primary aim of Teaching Leadership *is to help teachers or developers of leadership better prepare themselves to foster integrative leadership—the work of bringing diverse groups of people together across multiple boundaries to develop their own leadership and build better organizations and communities.* You, the reader, will be prompted to integrate your multiple intelligences and other assets in order to bring renewed commitment and your full self—heart, head, and hands—to your leadership work. You will be introduced to a comprehensive framework for leadership development and practical tools for classroom and workshop settings.

Why does leadership development matter? Obviously, the acts of leaders are consequential. Societies around the world are affected tremendously by the quality of the people who fill formal leadership positions and by the decisions they make. (This point is easy to support when we consider the impact of someone like President Obama or Angela Merkel, or the CEO of Ford Motor Co.; but it also applies to the nonprofit program manager who is deciding whether to start or jettison a legal aid program, or the entrepreneur who is convincing a small staff to keep plugging away at a new technology.) Societies also are benefited or harmed by informal leaders who gain a substantial followership by promoting new ideas or new solutions to organizational and community problems. (I think, for example, of Jody Williams's tireless efforts to ban the use of antipersonnel land mines or Julian Assange's controversial founding of WikiLeaks.) Leaders' damaging behavior or toxic effects have been tellingly delineated by Kellerman (2004), Lipman-Blumen (2005), Helms (2012), Capriles (2012), and Lemergaard and Muhr (2013). Meanwhile, problems often fester because no one seems prepared to exercise the leadership that would help citizens or employees focus on the problem and decide what to do about it.

Moreover, leadership inherently requires attention to followership, which makes leadership possible (Riggio, Chaleff, and Lipman-Blumen, 2008; Popper, 2012). When followers fail to keep a check on leaders' power, or when they fail to carry out their responsibilities in a leadership endeavor, the results can be disastrous (Kellerman, 2008). As people like me prepare to teach leadership or develop leaders, we would thus be wise to explore the work of followers, who are such a vital part of the leadership equation. Yet, few leadership development programs and little writing about leadership education focus on good followership as a prerequisite for excellence in leadership.

The vision of leadership development that infuses this book sees leaders and followers as exerting mutual influence and moving in and out of leader and follower roles. It is an *inclusive, relational* vision that recognizes leadership potential in just about everyone, yet also acknowledges that some people are much more adept leaders than others, or face more demands to exercise wise leadership. The vision rests on a firm conviction that leadership involves continual learning about self and others, experimenting with new behaviors, and questing for the common good (Crosby and Bryson, 2005). You will find a more thorough presentation of leadership and followership theories (especially those grounded in a relational perspective) in upcoming chapters.

Some people continue to question whether leadership can be taught. They argue that in the real world, leaders emerge naturally and learn their lessons and hone their skills mainly in the hurly-burly of teamwork, organizational life, or the political arena. These leadership education skeptics sometimes argue that leadership is really an idiosyncratic art, and therefore, hardly a subject that can be captured or conveyed through training or classroom instruction. Sharon Daloz Parks took on these skeptics in *Leadership Can Be Taught* (2005), which focuses on courses taught by Ron Heifetz on the Harvard faculty. She presented evidence that Heifetz's "case-in-point" method helps course participants intervene creatively in complex social systems. Additionally, the Multi-Institutional Study of Leadership has documented the effectiveness (and limitations) of undergraduate leadership development instruction and experiences (Komives et al., 2011). Several researchers have found that formal leadership development experiences can improve commitment to leadership work and effectiveness, especially among motivated participants (Bono, Shen, and Snyder, 2010; Day and Sin, 2011).

Certainly, leadership cannot be taught in a codified or formalized manner, no more than good painting, sculpture, physical therapy, or childcare can be taught this way. All of these endeavors are actually practices, in which principles about how to influence people, use materials, or care for human beings are applied (or not) by people with varying motives and competencies in specific contexts and circumstances. At the same time, most people would agree that being schooled in the principles and insights from others' experience can help guide behavior in real situations. Leadership educators or developers also can provide safe environments or laboratories that allow participants to try out or refine skills, reflect on their own practice, and make plans for change.

Leadership also can be taught badly, and journalists as well as respected scholars (e.g., Barbara Kellerman, 2004) have criticized the "leadership industry" for ill-conceived, over-marketed, and poorly assessed programs. Especially harmful is any promise that simply identifying and playing to one's strengths or mastering a particular set of skills will make a person an effective leader.

Teaching leadership is definitely a dicey business, more like conducting a cooking class than explaining the history and tenets of political science. Leadership instructors bring to our kitchen (or teaching lab) knowledge of basic skills and measurement tools. Ideally, we use tacit knowledge, drawn from our own training and experience, to match that knowledge to the conditions at hand, and we emphasize—much as a cooking instructor warns cooking novices—that best practices must be adapted to particular conditions (in the case of baking, the type of oven, for example). Yet teaching leadership is more complicated than teaching cooking, since recipes don't really exist. In the case of leadership, pursuing the analogy further, those who teach certainly should know how to cook, but we also must examine the effects of our cooking and the ambiguities and uncertainties involved. If we are pushing the people in our courses and workshops toward authentic practice, we have to engage in some of the same soul-searching we expect them to do. Yet, so far no one has written a book that comprehensively considers how leadership educators can develop their own leadership as they also design leadership learning experiences for others.

Fortunately, over the last four decades a broad community of leadership educators has formed across sectors, across academic and practitioner lines, and across geographic boundaries to explore and document the effectiveness of practice-based, context-sensitive, and morally aware leadership education. As one respected leadership scholar, Morgan McCall (2010), has noted, these educators see leadership development as being as much about "being" as "doing." In other words, any development experience must include opportunities for participants to attend to their own (and others') character, their motivations, and their identities as leaders as well as to gain new knowledge about effective communication or coalition building. Leadership education, in other words, will integrate heart, head, and hands.

Much of what affects whether and how an individual moves into formal or informal leadership roles stems from that person's genetic makeup and early formative experiences (Riggio and Mumford, 2011), and many leadership educators might do well to shift their attention to youth development. For those of us who continue to be called or called upon to help adults be better leaders, the good news is that human beings do have the capacity for further development, particularly at life transition points (McCall, 2010). Our challenge is to develop learning experiences that build upon individuals' varied innate and learned capacities.

Where This Book Is Headed

Teaching Leadership is designed to help people prepare themselves to teach leadership in a variety of organizational and community contexts. It is for the faculty member who has little background in leadership education but has been called on to teach leadership for majors in his department. It is for the seasoned leadership educator who seeks to deepen his practice. It is for the student affairs professional who wants to ensure that co-curricular programming helps develop student leaders and complements for-credit leadership courses. It is for teachers in community leadership programs and for consultants inside and outside organizations seeking to develop a cadre of leaders to sustain a business, nonprofit, or government enterprise. It is for community organizers and reformers inside the academy and out who realize that participants in their change initiatives sorely need to develop effective leadership practices. Many people for whom this book is written are unlikely to think of themselves as leaders; this book is aimed at helping them acknowledge and analyze their own experiences and aspirations as leaders and followers, precisely so that they are better prepared to help others do so.

This book will offer insights from more than two dozen highly respected leadership educators, as well as some relative newcomers to the field, who have been at the forefront of developing a holistic, practice-oriented approach to leadership education. We have taught in university, organizational, and community settings. (Several of us are University of Minnesota faculty and staff who have built the Center for Integrative Leadership, founded in 2006 to help leaders and followers work across sector, cultural, and geographic boundaries to tackle grand challenges and achieve the common good. The center sponsors research, teaching, and outreach activities aimed at understanding and fostering individual and group capacities to think and work in an integrative fashion.) These educators are leaders, because indeed we do leadership work as we build the legitimacy of leadership development in our organizations and communities, as we mine our own practice for lessons that inform our teaching, as we conduct field-shaping research, and as we offer a model of leaders who value feedback about the impacts of their work and are continuously innovating. These educators may or may not have held public office, been CEO of a company, served as a university president, or been a nonprofit executive director, but we all have a record of inspiring and mobilizing others to tackle shared problems and become better leaders and followers.

The book is in five parts, each focusing on a key practice of leadership education, distilled from the experiences of leadership educators who take a holistic or integrated approach to leadership development. The practices are: *using personal narrative, hosting and hospitality, tackling organizational and societal problems, strengthening citizenship,* and *assessing, coaching, and mentoring.* The first practice allows aspiring and seasoned leaders to probe their formative experiences and cultivate deeper understanding and commitment to leadership work. Hosting and hospitality are crucial for convening diverse human beings to develop mutual understanding and the ability to work together. Tackling organizational and societal problems requires cultivating socio-emotional, cognitive, and behavioral complexity and engaging diverse groups in defining shared problems and implementing solutions. The fourth practice links leadership and the responsibilities of citizenship in one's community and beyond. The final practice is the way that leadership educators help aspiring and seasoned leaders assess their growth as leaders and continue along a development track. Of course, assessing is also the way we educators understand the effectiveness of the learning experiences we design.

The exploration of each practice will cover three dimensions: Heart, Head, and Hands. *Heart* refers to the passion and energy at the core of this work, among educators and learners alike. It requires attention to emotion, spirit, intuition, and ethical purpose (see Hickman and Sorenson, 2013). The heart of leadership also summons the toughest and most intriguing questions about why leadership education is needed, how to achieve personal authenticity, how to discern right and wrong, and how to confront failure and evil. For each practice, the Heart section will include leadership educators' personal narratives, as well as compelling reasons to include attention to this practice, major ethical questions it evokes, and lessons educators have "taken to heart" about power and authenticity.

Head refers to aspects of leadership education that spring to mind as leadership educators think about the content of a leadership course or workshop: theories of leadership, readings, and research literature. The Head sections will draw upon and integrate major theories and scholarly evidence, in order to highlight the research literatures and traditions at the bedrock of our endeavor. These sections will include a wealth of books and articles that might be assigned as readings in leadership courses or workshops.

Finally, *Hands* point to the actual in-the-world work of teaching leadership. Some of that work goes on in classrooms and workshop settings, but also in virtual spaces and the "just in time" experiences of group projects and active learning analysis. The Hands sections will focus on the design of learning experiences and offer specific exercises, agendas, assignments, visual aids, and web-based activities that have proven effective in helping people respond to their own leadership calling and build their leadership capacity. I encourage readers to complete many of the exercises themselves—both to develop stronger insights into their own leadership and to better understand what participants in our courses and workshops are likely to experience as they complete these exercises.

My use of bodily metaphors is intentional. Leadership and leadership education are embodied practices (Ladkin, 2010). People's animated bodies carry meaning and harbor power. They exude energy and occupy space. Full-fledged leadership only occurs when we use our whole selves—our bodies with their various strengths, bruises, and scars—and show up where we are needed. While often leadership discussions become a "head trip," a distanced analysis of foibles and faults of people in visible positions or critical roles in history, I assert that leadership education must move beyond the political or social critique. Leadership is at least as much an affair of the heart and work of hands as it is a head trip. *Teaching Leadership* is an invitation to walk the talk, to practice a deeper approach to leadership education, and to proceed in the face of uncertainty and imperfection (Nielsen, Ferraro, and Marrone, 2013). No one can be, or needs to be, perfect to practice leadership or teach it.

Outline of the Book

Part I, Using Personal Narrative, explores how crafting life narratives helps learners discern their core commitments and strengths, and then integrate these with personal failures and weaknesses. Chapter 1, the Heart section, presents leadership educators' narratives as examples and considers how writing and discussing one's personal narrative builds the self-awareness that fosters mindful leadership. The chapter highlights the power of telling one's story and asks why some people get to tell their story and others don't. Chapter 2, the Head section, describes key thinkers and theories that undergird the use of personal narrative in leadership development programs. Chapter 3, the Hands section, highlights a few methods of using autobiography and biography in leadership programs. The chapter explains how to use the methods (such as the Narrative of Commitment and

Outlining and Constructing Personal Visions) effectively and adapt them to different audiences.

Part II, Hosting and Hospitality, describes the ways in which hospitality and hosting are necessary for leadership education that fosters inclusive leadership. In Chapter 4, the Heart section, other leadership educators and I reflect on what separates and connects us to other people and describe our experiences with hosting. Chapter 5, the Head section, draws attention to authors and approaches that influence how we think about hosting oneself and hosting others, and holding "crucial conversations" (Patterson, Grenny, McMillan, and Switzler, 2011). Chapter 6, the Hands section, offers exercises for exploring commonalities and differences and covers details such as food, room setup, and pacing of the learning experience.

Part III, Tackling Organizational and Societal Problems: Leadership Praxis, delves into leadership theory in action, with special attention to organizational and societal leadership as an ongoing (and changeable) practice that shapes and is shaped by implicit and explicit leadership theories. Chapter 7 focuses on the heart of leadership praxis. Leadership educators tell personal stories of being called to lead in our families, organizations, communities and, through these stories, explore compassion, courage, and embodiment—what it takes to work in community (whether that refers to teams, organizations, or inter-organizational networks). Chapter 8, the Head section, describes frameworks and theories which more fully develop relational leadership and communities of practice; these theories form the foundation of what it takes to lead and sustain leadership on knotty, public challenges. The chapter gives special attention to development of social, cognitive, and behavioral complexity, which are crucial for relational leadership practice. Chapter 9, the Hands section, describes the use of reflection on practice in leadership education, and emphasizes the Action Learning Project and other techniques that help create learning communities of practice.

Part IV, Strengthening Citizenship, links leadership, citizenship, governance, and the common good. In Chapter 10, the Heart section, leadership educators explain how we see our work as helping people increase their efficacy as citizens of their communities, their countries, and the world. We educators trace our own economic and political histories and how we came to understand ourselves as citizens or "public people."

We will describe our encounters with educational experiences and how we came to see leadership development and, indeed, education as emancipating forces that are essential to robust citizenship and vibrant democracy. Chapter 11, the Head section, explores theories of leadership that connect to citizenship, democracy, governance, and policy assessment; these frameworks help us to direct our action as educators. Chapter 12, the Hands section, focuses on participatory learning environments, power balancing methods, action learning groups, and use of technology-enhanced learning as a way to build new democratic experiences and improve pedagogies for the current era.

Part V, Assessing, Coaching, Mentoring, explores the delicate work of providing individualized assistance to learners while not doing the work for them. In Chapter 13, the Heart section, leadership educators describe the ways in which we have been mentored and coached (including by the people we teach), and we note what we have learned as we sought to coach and mentor others. Chapter 14, the Head section, presents research on coaching, mentoring, feedback, leadership assessment, and assessment of learning. Chapter 15, the Hands section, suggests methods of incorporating assessment, coaching, and mentoring into leadership development programs.

The *Conclusion* of the book proposes design principles for courses, seminars, and workshops to enable readers to develop programs that foster relational, context-sensitive, and morally aware leadership practices. The chapter also summarizes leading educators' thinking about how one can better prepare oneself to engage fully in the sacred, scary, and ultimately rewarding work of leadership education.

Conversation Partners

As preparation for this book I talked with numerous leadership educators who have a lot of experience with, and insight about, relational, context-sensitive, and morally aware approaches to leadership development. Most are academics with strong connections to the world of practice outside the academy, but some have done most of their leadership development in community programs or as consultants. Many have been leaders in building the contemporary field of leadership studies. In many cases, my conversation partners graciously gave me two hours or more of their time to explore the book's themes. Regardless of the length of our conversations, I deeply appreciate their contributions to leadership education and to this book. Here they are with their professional titles. You will get to know them better as we go along.

Kimberly Boal, Rawls Professor of Management at the Rawls College of Business, Texas Tech University

Ronnie Brooks, founding director of the James P. Shannon Leadership Institute, Amherst H. Wilder Foundation, St. Paul, Minnesota

Yvonne Cheek, president of Millennium Consulting Group

Richard Couto, distinguished senior scholar, Union Institute and University

Gary DeCramer, senior fellow, Humphrey School of Public Affairs, University of Minnesota

Janet Denhardt, Chester A. Newland Professor of Public Administration and director of the Sol Price School of Public Policy in Sacramento at the University of Southern California

Robert Denhardt, professor and director of leadership programs in the Sol Price School of Public Policy at the University of Southern California

Kevin Gerdes, director of the Masters of Public Affairs degree program, Humphrey School of Public Affairs, University of Minnesota

Jonathan Gosling, emeritus professor of leadership, University of Exeter

Gill Hickman, professor emerita of leadership studies in the Jepson School of Leadership Studies at the University of Richmond

Brad Jackson, head of School of Government and professor of public and community leadership at Victoria University of Wellington

Lars Leafblad, co-founder and principal of Ballinger | Leafblad, Inc. a St. Paul–based executive search and selection consulting firm serving civic clients

Tracey Manning, former senior scholar at the James MacGregor Burns Academy of Leadership, and faculty for healthcare leadership and communications in the School of Public Health at the University of Maryland College Park

Ricardo Morse, associate professor of public administration and government, University of North Carolina School of Government

June Nobbe, director of the Office for Leadership Education & Development—Undergraduate Programs, University of Minnesota

Sonia Ospina, professor of public management and policy at the New York University Wagner Graduate School of Public Service

Charles J. (Chuck) Palus, senior faculty member in Research, Innovation & Product Development at the Center for Creative Leadership

Carol Pearson, former executive vice president/provost and president of Pacifica Graduate Institute

Kathryn Quick, assistant professor, Humphrey School of Public Affairs, University of Minnesota

Ronald Riggio, Henry R. Kravis Professor of Leadership and Organizational Psychology and former director of the Kravis Leadership Institute at Claremont McKenna College

Betty Robinson, associate professor emerita and co-founder of the Master in Leadership Studies program, University of Southern Maine

Jodi Sandfort, professor, Humphrey School of Public Affairs, University of Minnesota

Valerie Shangreaux, director of leadership programs for the Blandin Foundation in Grand Rapids, Minnesota

Georgia Sorenson, leadership scholar, Cambridge University, Churchill College

Sharon Turnbull, head of research, The Leadership Trust, U.K.

Mary Uhl-Bien, professor of management, Texas Christian University

Montgomery Van Wart, professor, California State University San Bernardino

This group has lived and worked mostly in the United States, United Kingdom, and New Zealand, though some were born or lived for extended periods in other countries. Some are near retirement and others are much younger. They come from diverse academic, ethnic, and religious backgrounds. More biographical information is in Leadership Educator Biographies, following this Preface; my methodology for conducting research for this book is in Appendix A.

Throughout *Teaching Leadership*, you will hear stories and examples from my own practice most frequently—after all, I am my most accessible conversation partner. Some of the other educators will be featured more prominently than others, because I was able to gather more information from them.

Two of my Humphrey School colleagues, Gary DeCramer and Jodi Sandfort, have contributed greatly to conceptualizing this book. Their experiences and insights are incorporated in most chapters. Sadly, I no longer have Gary as a conversation partner, since he passed away in March 2012. He continues to speak in this book, however, and I am grateful for that.

Further Acknowledgments

In addition to the conversation partners I already have named, I acknowledge with limitless gratitude the partnership of John M. Bryson, who has been my co-teacher, co-author, and co-conspirator in a variety of leadership programs and projects. He has been a cherished adviser as this book evolved over several years. I also am grateful to Ariel Kaufman, a leadership educator based at the University of Wisconsin-Madison, for her careful critique of every chapter.

I have learned about leadership education from many other co-teachers: Sharon Anderson, Bob Terry, Zbig Bochniarz, Susan Atwood, Katherine Fennelly, Verna Price, Art Harkins, Byron Schneider, Paul Vaaler, and Karen Zentner Bacig. During his time as the Humphrey School's associate dean, Greg Lindsey encouraged this project and introduced me to Ken Bain's book, *What the Best College Teachers Do* (2004). I offer thanks also to Milne Kintner for insightful conversations about coaching and to Lonnie Helgeson and Gayle McPherson for their counsel as this project took shape. The International Leadership Association has given me a rich network of connections with people who see the entire world through the leadership lens.

Jean Lipman-Blumen, a scholar who is deeply committed to leadership for the common good, gave me welcome encouragement as I was developing this book. I also deeply appreciate the support of Georgia Sorenson and Ron Riggio, who are co-editors of the Routledge series *Leadership: Research and Practice*, of which this book is a part.

My own leadership practice has been influenced by the patience and kindness of my mother, Louse McGoldrick Crosby, by the adventurousness and fond regard of my father, Irving Crosby, and by the support of my sister, Marilyn Crosby Pavliscsak. Two other important early influences are Tom Lawrence and Frye Gaillard, cherished friends and partners in leadership at Vanderbilt University. Skeet Muncie was a stalwart supporter during my reporting years.

Finally, I acknowledge all the people who have signed up for my courses and workshops over the years. We have learned together and you have kept me committed to this daunting, complex, and rewarding endeavor of teaching leadership.

References

Bain, K. (2004). *What the best college teachers do*. Cambridge, MA: Harvard University Press.

Bono, J. E., Shen, W., & Snyder, M. (2010). Fostering integrative community leadership. *Leadership Quarterly, 21*(2), 324–335.

Capriles, R. (2012). *Leadership by resentment: From ressentiment to redemption*. Cheltenham, UK: Edward Elgar.

Cronin, T., & Genovese, M. (2012). *Leadership matters*. Boulder, CO: Paradigm.

Crosby, B. C., & Bryson, J. M. (2005). *Leadership for the common good: Tackling public problems in a shared-power world* (2nd ed.). San Francisco: Jossey-Bass.

Day, D.V., & Sin, H. (2011). Longitudinal tests of an integrative model of leader development: From childhood through adulthood. *Leadership Quarterly, 22*(3), 545–560.

Helms, L. (2012). *Poor Leadership and bad governance: Reassessing Presidents and Prime Ministers in North America, Europe and Japan*. Cheltenham, UK: Edward Elgar.

Hickman, G. R., & Sorenson, G. J. (2013). *The power of invisible leadership*. Thousand Oaks, CA: SAGE.

Kellerman, B. (2004). *Bad leadership: What it is, how it happens, why it matters*. Boston, MA: Harvard Business School Press.

Kellerman, B. (2008). *Followership: How followers are creating change and changing leaders*. Boston: Harvard Business School Press.

Komives, S., Dugan, J. P., Owen, J. E., Slack, C., Wagner, W., & Associates. (2011). *Handbook for student leadership development* (2nd ed.). San Francisco: Jossey-Bass.

Ladkin, D. (2010). *Rethinking leadership*. Cheltenham, UK: Edward Elgar.

Lemergaard, J., & Muhr, S. L. (Eds.). (2013). *Critical perspectives on leadership: Emotion, toxicity, and dysfunction*. Cheltenham, UK: Edward Elgar.

Lipman-Blumen, J. (2005). *The allure of toxic leaders: Why we follow destructive bosses and corrupt politicians—And how we can survive them*. New York: Oxford University Press.

McCall, M. W. (2010). The experience conundrum. In N. Nohria, & R. Khurana (Eds.), *Handbook of leadership theory and practice: A Harvard business school centennial colloquium* (pp. 679–708). Boston, MA: Harvard Business School Press.

Nielsen, R., Ferraro, H. S., & Marrone, J. A. (2013). *Leading with humility*. New York: Routledge.

Parks, S. D. (2005). *Leadership can be taught*. Boston, MA: Harvard Business School Press.

Patterson, K., Grenny, J., McMillan, R., & Switzler, A. (2002). *Crucial conversations: Tools for talking when stakes are high*. New York: McGraw-Hill.

Popper, M. (2012). *Fact and fantasy about leadership*. Cheltenham, UK: Edward Elgar.

Riggio, R. E., Chaleff, I., & Lipman-Blumen, J. (2008). *The art of followership*. San Francisco: Jossey-Bass.

Riggio, R. E., & Mumford, M. D. (2011). Introduction to the special issue: Longitudinal studies of leadership development. *Leadership Quarterly, 22*(3), 453–456.

LEADERSHIP EDUCATOR BIOGRAPHIES

Kimberly B. Boal (Ph.D., University of Wisconsin) is the Rawls Professor of Management at the Rawls College of Business, Texas Tech University. Kim was book review editor for *Organization Studies* (2007–2012) and was co-editor-in-chief of the *Journal of Management Inquiry* from 1997–2006. He served on the Board of Governors of the Academy of Management from 2001–2004, and as president of the Western Academy of Management in 1999–2000. He was twice awarded the Joan G. Dahl Presidential Award by the Western Academy of Management. His work has covered such managerial topics as worker attitudes and motivation, strategic leadership, organizational change and learning, strategic planning, mergers and acquisitions, and corporate social responsibility. He is published in leading academic journals such as: *Academy of Management Executive, Academy of Management Review, Administrative Science Quarterly, Journal of Business Venturing, Journal of Management, Leadership Quarterly, Organizational Behavior and Human Performance, Strategic Management Journal*, as well as other journals and numerous book chapters.

Ronnie Brooks is the founding director of the James P. Shannon Leadership Institute, a program that provides a year-long renewal experience for foundation and nonprofit organization leaders. She recently stepped down as the director of the Amherst Wilder Foundation Center for Communities where she oversaw the foundation's leadership development and stakeholder engagement programs.

Ronnie also consults on strategic planning, leadership development, and nonprofit organization governance and management. In the past several years she has worked with a variety of performing arts and higher education organizations to help them elucidate their core values and to use those values to anchor their planning work.

Ronnie has extensive experience in both the public and private sectors in Minnesota. She served as special assistant to the governor of Minnesota and as director of majority research for the Minnesota State Senate, and has managed development projects for the mayors of both Minneapolis and St. Paul. Ronnie was also vice president of the Keystone Center, a Colorado-based public policy organization; executive director of the St. Paul Downtown Council; and manager of community development and policy planning for the Dayton-Hudson (now Target) Corporation.

Ronnie has played a leadership role in several Minnesota civic and professional organizations. She was president of both the Citizens League and the Mediation Center and a board member of the Voyager Outward Bound School, the Minnesota Museum of Art, the David Preus Leadership Council, the Civic Leadership Foundation, MAP for Nonprofits, and Graywolf Press. Currently she serves on the boards of the Friends of the Mississippi River and the Minnesota Center for Book Arts and on the National Advisory Council for both the Servant Leadership Program at Gustavus Adolphus College and the Great Plains Institute.

Ronnie did her undergraduate work at the University of Michigan and received her master of arts degree in political science from Michigan State University. She has been on the faculty of the Legislative Staff Management Institute of the University of Minnesota's Hubert H. Humphrey School of Public Affairs and the University of St. Thomas Center for Nonprofit Leadership where she focused on leadership and management in the nonprofit sector.

Ronnie was a McKnight Fellow at the Salzburg Seminar and an International Business Fellow. Additionally, she is a recipient of the Lloyd Short Award for Distinguished Public Service and the YWCA Outstanding Leadership Award.

H. Yvonne Cheek is president of the Millennium Consulting Group, founded in 1993. With her multiethnic team of associates, she works with private, public, and nonprofit organizations to accelerate intentional change. National and local projects in which the firm is engaged include launching bold initiatives, employee engagement, community engagement, strategic planning, diversity and inclusion initiatives, team alignment, training, assessments, meeting/retreat design and facilitation, board governance, and cross-sector collaboration.

The firm is often invited to expand organizations' thinking about being more inclusive in policies and practices, and creating a more productive work environment that benefits all of the stakeholders. Results-oriented and client-specific, all of the firm's work is issue-based. Helping clients solve problems, manage polarities, and reduce problem creation are a primary focus.

One of the highlights of Yvonne's career was co-designing and facilitating a White House conference on Women and Leadership. Yvonne's background includes teaching at the University of North Carolina at Greensboro and the University of Puget Sound, directing the citizen education program at the University of Minnesota's Humphrey School of Public Affairs, and being a manager in corporate marketing at Control Data Corporation.

Her past civic involvement includes being a trustee of the Jerome Foundation, being a board member of the United Way of Minneapolis, Women Venture, KFAI Radio, Vocal Essence, and the Minnesota Orchestra. Currently she is a trustee with the Blandin Foundation and the Sundance Family Foundation, and a board member of Gillette Children's Specialty Healthcare. She is a member of the Association of Black Foundation Executives and an associate of Human Systems Dynamics. Yvonne's bachelor's and master's degrees are from the University of North Carolina Greensboro and her Ph.D. in music education is from the University of Michigan.

Richard A. Couto has a background of practice and scholarship in community leadership. At Vanderbilt University from 1975 to 1988, he pioneered campus and community collaborative programs that connected the student movement of the 1960s; community leadership in Appalachia and in rural, predominantly African American counties of western Tennessee; and the current programs of civic engagement in higher education. He won several national awards for this work including a Kellogg National Fellowship. He has been a founding faculty member of undergraduate and Ph.D. programs in leadership and a senior fellow at several programs, including the James MacGregor Burns Academy at the University of Maryland. Five of his 14 authored or edited books have won national awards. This includes his most recent edited work, the two-volume *Political and Civic Leadership Reference Handbook* (SAGE). He has a Ph.D. from the University of Kentucky.

Barbara C. Crosby has been a part of the global community of scholars seeking to understand leadership and good practice in leadership education since the mid-1980s. During that time she has been based at the Hubert H. Humphrey School of Public Affairs at the University of Minnesota, where she has taught graduate and undergraduate courses, organized professional development programs, and directed leadership centers.

In 1992, she and co-author John M. Bryson published *Leadership for the Common Good: Tackling Public Problems in a Shared-Power World* and a second edition in 2005. She also is the author of *Leadership for Global Citizenship* (1999) as well as numerous articles on integrative leadership, cross-sector collaboration, and public value. Along with John Bryson and Laura Bloomberg, she edited two recent books on public value: *Creating Public Value in Practice* (2015) and *Public Value and Public Administration* (2015). For many years she has served on the editorial boards of *The Leadership Quarterly* and the *Journal of Public Affairs Education*.

Before focusing on leadership studies, Barbara was a news reporter and editor. After graduating from Vanderbilt University in 1968 with a degree in political science, she went to work for the *Augusta (Georgia) Herald* and subsequently edited weekly newspapers in Baltimore, Maryland. She moved to Madison, Wisconsin, in 1974 to pursue a master's degree in journalism and mass communication, and in 1975 joined the press office of Wisconsin Gov. Patrick Lucey and subsequently became his press secretary.

In 1977, Barbara moved to Minneapolis and became a speechwriter for Gov. Rudy Perpich of Minnesota. After that she was vice president for communications at The Minnesota Project, a nonprofit focusing on public policy and community development, while finishing research for her master's degree (completed in 1980).

During her three decades at the University of Minnesota, Barbara has been a prime organizer of the Humphrey School's midcareer master's degree program, the university's leadership minor, and the Center for Integrative Leadership. She is also part of the Public and Nonprofit Leadership Center at the Humphrey School. In 1990, Barbara began her work on a Ph.D. in leadership studies with Union Institute and University and completed that degree in 1996. Her dissertation focused on leadership in and by Amnesty International and the International Women's Rights Action Watch. Also in the early 1990s, she was coordinator of the Humphrey School's International Fellows Program.

Some of Barbara's leadership research and teaching has been conducted outside the U.S., especially during the four separate years that she and her spouse, John Bryson, have lived in the United Kingdom. In addition to teaching in the U.K., she has taught in Poland and Ukraine. She is a fellow of The Leadership Trust in the U.K. You can follow her on Twitter @crosb002.

Janet V. Denhardt is Chester A. Newland Professor of Public Administration and director of the University of Southern California Price School in Sacramento. She was previously professor and director of the doctoral program in the School of Public Affairs at Arizona State University. Janet is a member of the prestigious National Academy of Public Administration, the field's equivalent of the National Academy of Sciences. She is the 2013 recipient of the Charles Levine Award, given by American Society for Public Administration and the National Association of Schools of Public Affairs and Administration (NASPAA) to recognize a public administration faculty member who has demonstrated excellence in three major areas of the field of teaching, research, and service to the wider community.

Janet has published five books, including *The Dance of Leadership*, *The New Public Service*, *Managing Human Behavior in Public and Nonprofit Organizations*, *Public Administration: An Action Orientation*, and *Street Level Leadership*. Several of these are in multiple editions and translations. She has also published numerous articles in professional journals, primarily in the areas of citizen engagement, leadership, and governance. She is a native of Seattle, Washington, and she earned her doctorate in public administration from the University of Southern California.

Robert B. Denhardt is a central figure in leadership education nationally and internationally and currently is professor and director of leadership programs (including the Executive Master's of Leadership) in the Sol Price School of Public Policy at the University of Southern California. He was previously ASU Regents Professor and director of the School of Public Affairs at Arizona State University. He is also a distinguished visiting scholar at the University of Delaware and heads a consulting and publishing firm, Denhardt Leadership (http://denhardtleadership.com/).

Bob is a past president of the American Society for Public Administration (ASPA), a nationwide organization of academics and practitioners in the field of public administration at all levels of government. He is also a member of the prestigious National Academy of Public Administration, the field's equivalent of the National Academy of Sciences. He was the 2004 recipient of ASPA's Dwight Waldo Award, celebrating lifetime achievement in scholarship in public administration. He was the founding chair of the Arts and Leadership Group of the International Leadership Association. His holds a bachelor's degree from Western Kentucky University and master's and Ph.D. degrees from the University of Kentucky, all in political science.

Bob has published over a dozen books, including *The Dance of Leadership, The New Public Service, Managing Human Behavior in Public and Nonprofit Organizations, The Pursuit of Significance, In the Shadow of Organization, Theories of Public Organization, Public Administration: An Action Orientation, Executive Leadership in the Public Service, The Revitalization of the Public Service*, and *Pollution and Public Policy*. Many of these are in multiple editions and translations. He has published well over one hundred articles in professional journals, primarily in the areas of leadership and organizational change.

In addition to his academic work, Bob has strong practical experience in leadership positions, including time as vice-provost at the University of Missouri—Columbia, as well as those positions mentioned above. Bob's combination of practical and academic experience in leadership gives him a unique perspective on leadership, one truly bridging the gap between theory and practice.

Speaking of practice, Bob's latest book is *Just Plain Good Management (JPGM)*, a mini-book filled with the best practical advice available for those wishing to succeed in the art of managing. JPGM is being used for management and leadership development in many companies and public agencies, including Cambria Consultants, Working in Harmony, the City of Los Angeles, the City of San Antonio, the County of Los Angeles, Los Angeles Metro, various Chambers of Commerce, and the State of California.

Kevin Gerdes is the director of the Masters of Public Affairs (M.P.A.) degree program, capstone programs, and the Public Safety Leadership Program at the Humphrey School. Prior to his assignment at the University of Minnesota, Kevin served 33 years with the Minnesota National Guard in a variety of leadership positions, including commander at the company, battalion, and brigade levels. He culminated his full-time career with the National Guard as the adjutant general's chief of staff and retired in July 2012 as deputy commanding general of the 34th "Red Bull" Infantry Division. He completed a tour of duty in Iraq as commander and returned in 2006 to help establish Minnesota's "Beyond the Yellow Ribbon" reintegration program—a cross-sector, community-based collaboration—as a national model.

Kevin attended St. John's University where he completed ROTC, and received a bachelor's degree in management from Upper Iowa University. He received a master's degree in strategic studies at the United States Army War College and an educational doctorate in leadership from the University of St. Thomas. His dissertation focused on the interaction of converging cultures as new immigrants become residents in small, rural communities. His recent research involved working with a state agency to identify government service delivery redesign opportunities. Kevin brings a practitioner approach to leadership and policy analysis in the public sector.

Jonathan Gosling is an independent academic with a number of roles, including professor of organization and leadership development at IEDC Bled School of Management, Slovenia; and emeritus professor at the University of Exeter, U.K., where he directed the Centre for Leadership Studies for 12 years. Jonathan brings a philosophical turn of mind to a range of topics. Recently he was researching the leadership of malaria elimination programs, of sustainable supply chains in China, of large systems change, and of professional organizations (universities, healthcare, etc.). He has written a series of papers on the relevance of philosophy to leading and managing. His work is published in journals such as *Leadership, Harvard Business Review, Organization, AMLE*, and *Social Epistemology*. His most recent book is *Napoleonic Leadership: A Study in Power* (with Stephanie Jones; 2015), examining various modes of "doing power." He was an early instigator of the critical management studies movement, and now plays a significant role in the "greening" of management education worldwide, including co-founding the One Planet M.B.A. He worked for many years as a mediator and on other interventions inspired by psychodynamic perspectives on power and organizing. He has served as visiting professor at INSEAD, McGill, Copenhagen Business School, and Renmin University of China (lecturing on the philosophy of leadership at the School of Philosophy). He is co-founder of Coachingourselves.com and is a keen sailor.

Gill Robinson Hickman is currently professor emerita of leadership studies in the Jepson School of Leadership Studies at the University of Richmond. Her career has involved both administrative and academic appointments. Her expertise is in management, with an underpinning of organizational behavior, organizational theory, and human resource management. As an inaugural faculty member of the Jepson School, Gill participated in the early structuring and formation of the program, a role for which her background as dean in the School of Health at California State University, acting associate dean in the School of Community and Public Affairs at Virginia Commonwealth University, and professor of public administration prepared her.

Gill has presented at the China Executive Leadership Academy Pudong (CELAP), Shanghai, China; the Leadership in Central Europe Conference at Palacky University in Olomouc, Czech Republic; the Salzburg Seminar in Salzburg, Austria; and the University of the Western Cape in South Africa. She has presented at international conferences in Amsterdam, the Netherlands; Guadalajara, Mexico; and Vancouver and Toronto, Canada.

She is the author or editor of several books, including: *Leading Organizations: Perspectives for a New Era; The Power of Invisible Leadership* (with Georgia Sorenson); *Leading Change in Multiple Contexts; Leadership for Transformation* (with JoAnn Barbour); and *Managing Personnel in the Public Sector: A Shared Responsibility* (with Dalton Lee). She has also authored multiple articles and book chapters.

Gill has served as vice president and board member of the International Leadership Association and a member of several other professional, scholarly, and community organizations. She is the recipient of several awards, including the University of Richmond Distinguished Educator Award.

Her Ph.D. in public administration is from the University of Southern California and she has an M.P.A. in public administration from University of California Los Angeles. Her bachelor's degree in political science is from the University of Denver.

Brad Jackson is the head of the School of Government and professor of public and community leadership at Victoria University of Wellington. He has also been the head of the School of Management and director of the Centre for the Study of Leadership at Victoria. More recently he has been the Fletcher Building Education Trust Chair in Leadership and co-director of the New Zealand Leadership Institute at The University of Auckland Business School. He also was an associate professor of continuing education at the University of Calgary in Canada.

Brad has spoken to academic and practitioner audiences throughout the world and has published five books—*Management Gurus and Management Fashions; The Hero Manager; Organisational Behaviour in New Zealand; A Very Short, Fairly Interesting and Reasonably Cheap Book About Studying Leadership*; and *Demystifying Business Celebrity*—and edited the *Sage Handbook of Leadership* and *Major Works in Leadership*.

He is a former co-editor of the journal, *Leadership*; the former vice-chair of the International Leadership Association; and a fellow of the Australian and New Zealand Academy of Management, The Leadership Trust, and the Lancaster Leadership Centre. He serves on the boards of the Akina Foundation, the Australian and New Zealand School of Government, and Toi Whakaari New Zealand Drama School.

He obtained a B.Sc. in geography from Bristol University, a master of arts also in geography from the University of British Columbia, and a Ph.D. in management from Lancaster University.

Lars Leafblad is co-founder and principal of Ballinger | Leafblad, Inc. a St. Paul–based executive search and selection consulting firm serving civic clients (foundations, nonprofits, higher education institutions, and associations).

Prior to co-founding Ballinger | Leafblad, Inc., he was leadership and engagement director at the St. Paul–based Bush Foundation, where he directed the Bush Fellowship leadership programs.

He was formerly a partner at KeyStone Search, a Minneapolis-based executive search firm where he co-chaired the firm's civic practice. He is also founder and publisher emeritus of PollenMidwest.org, a Minnesota-based nonprofit whose mission is to build better-connected communities through digital storytelling.

Lars earned a B.A. in economics from St. Olaf College, an M.B.A. from the Carlson School of Management, and was a Humphrey policy fellow in 2008–2009. He also spent two summers in college on the National Touring BBQ Team for Famous Dave's of America, competing in barbecue competitions across the U.S.

Lars serves on the advisory boards for MinnPost.com and the Public and Nonprofit Leadership Center at the University of Minnesota, and is a former board member of CaringBridge.org. He is also a former member of the membership committee of the Minnesota Council on Foundations.

He lives in the Twin Cities with his wife, Maren, and their four children. In his free time, he enjoys spending time with his family, reading, coaching soccer, playing poker, and is a novice rock hound who loves hunting for Minnesota's state gemstone, Lake Superior agate.

He encourages you to connect with him directly on Twitter via @larsleafblad or on LinkedIn at http://www.linkedin.com/in/larsleafblad.

Tracey Manning began her career as a personality and social psychologist teaching at the College of Notre Dame of Maryland (now Notre Dame of Maryland University), after receiving her Ph.D. from The Catholic University of Maryland, Washington, D.C.

Intrigued by the impact of leadership as highlighted in *The Pursuit of Excellence* (Collins and Porras, 1982), Tracey embarked upon what became a lifelong commitment to the study and development of leadership, both as a graduate and undergraduate leadership educator and as an organizational consultant. She has now focused on transformational leadership development and leadership education for over 30 years, with a particular emphasis on nontraditional leaders, e.g., women as leaders, non-positional leaders, and volunteers.

While at Notre Dame College, as well as teaching psychology courses, Tracey coordinated and taught graduate leadership courses in the Management Program, the Nonprofit Management Program, and the undergraduate Certificate Program in Leadership and Social Change. Her teaching excellence was honored with the Mullan Distinguished Teacher Award.

In 2001, she began a research sabbatical at the James MacGregor Burns Academy of Leadership at the University of Maryland College Park, after which she left Notre Dame to take a position as senior scholar at the Academy, researching transformational leadership in adolescents. She also created and has taught graduate healthcare leadership and communications in the School of Public Health at the University of Maryland College Park for most of the last decade.

While at the Academy of Leadership, Tracey was recruited by the University of Maryland's Center on Aging to help develop what became Legacy Leadership Institutes, a national award-winning leadership development model for equipping baby boomer retirees for non-positional leadership in high impact volunteer roles. She was responsible for teaching and evaluating the impact of leadership development in those programs, and continues this work in the Legacy Leadership Institute for the Environment she has helped to create in central Maryland. She also has worked extensively in leadership development of older adult volunteers in other settings, both directly and through aging agencies.

Tracey has facilitated leadership development of women in nontraditional fields, particularly women faculty in higher education at several institutions through the National Science Foundation's WELI (Women in Engineering Leadership Institute) and ADVANCE programs. Her leadership research has appeared in *Women in Management Review*, the *American Psychologist*, the *Journal of Leadership and Organizational Studies*, and the *Journal of Leadership Education*, among others. She also contributed a invited chapter on leadership and civic engagement through the life span to *Civic Engagement and the Baby Boomer Generation*, edited by Laura Wilson and Sharon Simson.

Ricardo S. (Rick) Morse is associate professor of public administration and government at the University of North Carolina (UNC) School of Government in Chapel Hill, North Carolina, where he has been on the faculty since 2006. Prior to joining the UNC faculty he was an assistant professor at Iowa State University from 2004–2006 and project manager at the Institute for Policy Outreach (now called the Institute for Policy and Governance) at Virginia Tech, from 2000–2004.

Rick's work has long focused on the practice of collaborative governance in communities and regions. He has led community visioning efforts in Virginia and North Carolina and consulted with a variety of organizations—principally local governments—on issues related to collaboration, community engagement, and leadership.

Rick's entryway into leadership studies was principally through his interest in and experience with collaborative governance and community engagement. He found that successful partnerships were always leaderful, but that traditional models of leadership (hierarchical, in terms of leaders and followers) did not fit the kind of leadership he was seeing. His research and teaching in leadership studies have therefore had a strong focus on nonhierarchical, integrative, or collaborative leadership.

Working with Terry Buss, who at the time was at the National Academy of Public Administration, Rick edited a collection of essays by public administration scholars and practitioners on leadership. *Transforming Public Leadership for the 21st Century* was lauded by Montgomery Van Wart as "the most sophisticated volume of new essays to appear on administrative leadership in several decades—perhaps ever." The follow-up volume *Innovations in Public Leadership Development* also received positive reviews and offers a distinctively public administration–focused approach to leadership development.

At the School of Government Rick is an integral part of the leadership development of M.P.A. students as well as in-service practitioners. He is a core faculty member of the school's flagship leadership program for local government managers, the Public Executive Leadership Academy. He also has taught leadership workshops for many other groups of public servants, including judges, local government clerks, newly elected sheriffs, state government administrators, and county and municipal elected officials. Rick really enjoys the "pracademic" mission of the School of Government, where he spends equal time in the worlds of academia and the "real world" of community practice.

Rick was born in Brazil and is a dual citizen of the United States and Brazil. He was raised in Virginia and attended Brigham Young University in Provo, Utah, where he received bachelor's and master's degrees in public policy. He did his doctoral work in public administration at Virginia Tech's Center for Public Administration and Policy, where he received a Ph.D. in 2004. You can follow Rick on Twitter @MorseSOG.

June Nobbe serves as director of the Office for Leadership Education and Development—Undergraduate Programs at the University of Minnesota. She provides oversight for the academic undergraduate leadership minor, co-curricular leadership development programs, and central career and internship services. She has worked at the University of Minnesota-Twin Cities for over 30 years in several capacities in the Division of Student Affairs and is a key player in efforts to internationalize student affairs on the Twin Cities campus. June has extensive experience in global program and course development, integrating student development theory, leadership, intercultural engagement, authentic community engagement, and reflective practice. She has led short-term global seminars in Northern Ireland, Istanbul, and Buenos Aires; collaborated on the development of semester courses in Rome, Montpellier, Istanbul, and Tanzania; led faculty training on experiential learning, reflection, and student development theory for global seminar leaders and on-site providers and faculty abroad; and taught the leadership minor capstone course. She also developed a "glocal" leadership minor practicum course in an East African immigrant community proximate to the university. June is a qualified administrator of the Intercultural Development

Inventory and integrates the IDI in the capstone leadership minor course and short-term global seminars. In addition to her administrative roles, June completed her Ph.D. in educational policy and administration. Her research topic is the civic mission of U.S. public higher education.

Sonia M. Ospina, professor of public management and policy at the New York University (NYU) Wagner Graduate School of Public Service, is a sociologist by training. Her interest in the participatory, inclusive, and collaborative dynamics of democratic governance has produced research on social change leadership, social innovation, and accountability in communities and in public systems. An expert in qualitative research, she works in the U.S. and Latin America, and has been a visiting scholar in many Latin American and European countries.

In 2014 Sonia and Erica Foldy convened an international network of leadership scholars, *Co-Lead Net*, sponsored by the NYU Leadership Initiative. Its two annual meetings aimed to continue the conversation started in her 2012 co-edited book with Mary Uhl-Bien, *Advancing Relational Leadership Research: A Dialogue Among Perspectives.*

In 2015 Sonia joined the Scientific Council of CLAD, a United Nations consulting body on state reform in Latin America. She is a fellow of the U.S. National Academy of Public Administration since 2012. She is co-editor of the *Journal of Public Administration Research and Theory* since 2010, and member of several journal editorial boards, including *Public Administration Review*. Sonia was president of the Inter-American Network of Public Administration Education from 2008 to 2010.

Sonia co-founded the Research Center for Leadership in Action with Ellen Schall in 2003, and was faculty co-director until 2015. From 2001 to 2009 Sonia led a national research project exploring, among others, the relationship between leadership and social change, social identity, capacity building, power, collaboration, paradox, and action research. During this period, she also did comparative research in Latin America and in 2008 co-authored, with Nuria Cunill Grau, *Strengthening Monitoring and Evaluation Systems in Latin America: Analysis of 12 Countries* (in Spanish).

Sonia directed Wagner's management specialization in 2002 and its doctoral program in 1998. She has been a member of the executive councils of the National Association of Schools of Public Affairs and Administration (1996–1999) and the Association of Public Policy and Management (1999–2002).

Attaining a sociology Ph.D. in 1989 and a Policy M.S. in 1985 from Stonybrook University (SUNY), Sonia joined the Wagner school in 1989. Her dissertation developed into the book *Illusions of Opportunity: Employee Expectations and Workplace Inequality*, published in 1996.

Born in the United States to Colombian parents, Sonia grew up in urban Bogotá, where she got a B.A. in education in 1976 and worked in this field until 1981, when she returned to the United States. She has now lived more than half her life in another great urban space, New York City, where she and her husband raised their son. Sonia's bicultural experience and her strong ties to both countries are embodied in her transnational and multicultural approach to life.

Charles J. (Chuck) Palus is a senior fellow and faculty member in research, innovation, and product development at the Center for Creative Leadership (CCL). As a collaborator in several cross-disciplinary research groups he studies, teaches, and develops leadership as a collective social process, with the key question: *In what ways does a shift in perspective—from leadership as the capacity and actions of individuals, to leadership as a collective social process—yield better results for leaders, groups, teams, organizations, partnerships, coalitions, and communities?*

He is co-founder and global director of CCL Labs, a community-based innovation laboratory with a long line of products including: Visual Explorer; Leadership Essentials; Transformations; and the Early Leadership Toolkit.

Chuck is a designer, facilitator, and researcher in the CCL Organizational Leadership practice and is one of its co-founders. He has co-designed numerous development programs and experiences including: Leading Creatively; Edge-Work; Facing and Solving Complex Challenges; Transforming Your Organization; Boundary Spanning Leadership; and Leadership for Societal Impact. He is a passionate contributor to the Leadership Beyond Boundaries initiative for democratizing leadership for societal impact and has worked extensively in Africa from the grass roots with students to senior levels at the African Union.

He is co-author of the award-winning book *The Leader's Edge*; and the influential essays "Making Common Sense: Leadership as Meaning-Making in a Community of Practice" and "Evolving Leaders." He has been published in *Leadership Quarterly*, *Harvard Business Review*, the *Harvard Business School Handbook for Teaching Leadership*, the *CCL Handbook of Leadership Development*, the *CCL Handbook of Coaching*, the *Handbook of Action Research*, and the *Change Handbook*.

Prior to coming to the Center for Creative Leadership, Chuck was an R&D engineer in polymers with DuPont; a water purification engineer with Vaponics; an instructor and designer with the Hurricane Island Outward Bound School; and he taught social psychology and statistics at Boston College. He received a B.S. in chemical engineering from Pennsylvania State University and a Ph.D. in social psychology from Boston College.

Chuck and his colleagues blog at:

Interdependent Leadership	www.ccl.org/interdependent
Leadership Explorer	www.ccl.org/explorer
Leadership Beyond Boundaries	www.leadbeyond.org
CCL Labs	www.ccl.org/labs
Insights	insights.ccl.org/blog

Carol S. Pearson is an internationally known authority on archetypes and their application to leadership and organizational development, best known for books such as *The Hero Within: Six Archetypes We Live By*; *Awakening the Heroes Within: Twelve Archetypes To Help Us Find Ourselves and Transform Our World*; *The Hero and the Outlaw: Building Extraordinary Brands Through the Power of Archetypes* (co-authored by Margaret Mark); *Mapping the Organizational Psyche: A Jungian Theory of Organizational Dynamics and Change* (co-authored by John Corlett); and *The Transforming Leader: New Approaches to Leadership for the Twenty-First Century* (ed.), which grew out of a three-year project with the Fetzer Institute that she co-led. Her newest book is *Persephone Rising: Awakening the Heroine Within*.

A scholar and higher education administrator, Carol served most recently as executive vice president/provost and then president of Pacifica Graduate Institute. Previously, she was professor of leadership studies in the School of Public Policy at the University of Maryland and the director of the James MacGregor Burns Academy of Leadership. During her tenure, the academy was the incubator of the International Leadership Association (ILA), and Carol was a member of ILA's Board of Directors. She obtained her M.A. and Ph.D. from Rice University in English. Website: www.herowithin.com

Kathryn Quick is an associate professor at the Humphrey School of Public Affairs and academic co-director of the Center for Integrative Leadership at the University of Minnesota. Her research, teaching, and community service are all oriented to integrative, boundary-spanning efforts to address complex public problems and build community resilience. She is especially interested in inclusive leadership and management practices for engaging diverse stakeholders in defining problems, generating solutions, and collaborating on implementation. These commitments grow out of her professional practice. She worked as an environmental advocate and planner in Indonesia for eight years and then a community development manager for two California cities for six years.

Kathy returned to graduate school for a Ph.D. because she wanted to be part of training graduate students to be effective, collaborative problem-solvers. She teaches graduate courses and executive education workshops on integrative leadership, facilitating democratic decision-making, public and nonprofit management, and public affairs scholarship. Her research intersects the public and nonprofit management, urban planning, and public policy fields. Her research settings involve a wide range of policy content areas (often but not exclusively transportation, urban planning, and environmental management). The common thread is analysis of how decision-making is done, with what consequences for policy outcomes and democratic capacity-building. She is committed to engaged scholarship and the mission of public land-grant universities to provide leadership and address critical community concerns, and thus often collaborates with city, county, and tribal governments in her research. The products have been published in *Leadership, Public Administration Review*, the *Journal of Public Administration Research and Theory*, the *Journal of Planning Education and Research*, and *International Public Management Journal*.

Kathy holds a Ph.D. in planning, policy, and design from the University of California, Irvine, a master's degree in city and regional planning from the University of California, Berkeley, and a bachelor's degree in biology from Swarthmore College.

Ronald E. Riggio is the Henry R. Kravis Professor of Leadership and Organizational Psychology and former director of the Kravis Leadership Institute at Claremont McKenna College. His undergraduate degree in psychology is from Santa Clara University. His master's and Ph.D. graduate degrees are in social psychology, and his initial research interests were in the area of emotional communication, nonverbal communication, and communication skill. This led him to begin studying charisma (in social interaction), which then led to interest in leadership, particularly charismatic and transformational leadership. He is the author of a well-known textbook, *Introduction to Industrial/Organizational Psychology* (now in its 7th edition) and co-author, along with Bernard Bass of *Transformational Leadership* (2nd edition).

Ron is a psychologist and leadership scholar with over a dozen authored or edited books and more than 150 articles and book chapters. In addition to teaching leadership and organizational psychology, he has been very active in leadership development efforts at Claremont McKenna College. He is a member of the International Leadership Association, the Academy of Management, the Society of Industrial and Organizational Psychology, and the American Psychological Association.

Ron worked for several years as both an industrial-organizational psychology consultant and a trial strategy consultant on product liability cases. He is the father of two girls, and is a researcher involved in the Fullerton Longitudinal Study which is attempting to look at leadership development across the lifespan (beginning at one year of age and continuing through adulthood). Besides research on leadership development, he has been actively involved in training young (and not so young) leaders at the college level, and beyond.

Betty Robinson graduated with degrees in sociology from Colby College, University of Maryland, and Boston University where she earned her Ph.D. During these years, she also worked in the Massachusetts legislature as a legislative aide and as the administrator of the Massachusetts Battered Women's Coalition. Her dissertation research on the formation of nurses' labor unions took her into the trade union world.

Before returning to academia full-time in 1988, Betty spent seven years working as an analyst and arbitration advocate for labor unions in Massachusetts and Maine. She came to the University of Southern Maine's (USM) Lewiston Auburn College (LAC) attracted by the innovative interdisciplinary concept of the new college, as well as its close affiliation with the local community and commitment to nontraditional students in a former mill town.

For six years, Betty served as assistant professor of leadership and organizational studies (LOS), a curriculum she developed with colleague Dr. Marvin Druker. Soon after her promotion to associate professor, she was selected as LAC dean, a position she held for seven years. During this time this interdisciplinary college was known as the fastest growing part of the University of Maine System.

In July 2003, prior to stepping back into the faculty ranks, Betty worked with Druker to develop USM's master in leadership studies program. She taught the first master's level leadership theory course and worked to increase the "world-mindedness" components of both the bachelor's and master's programs. In 2004, she led the first LAC international student trip to universities in Botswana and South Africa, initiating the ongoing Leadership Study Abroad courses and developing the graduate course in cultural contexts.

During these years, her research and publications covered such areas as the scholarship of teaching, innovations in public sector retrenchment, grievance mediation, and social capital across the U.S. and in her local Maine community. Betty was also an active participant and presenter in the International Leadership Association (ILA) annual meetings and a co-developer of the ILA Guidelines for Leadership Study Programs.

Over the next several years, her interest shifted to increasing faculty capacity to offer leadership programs online and in a blended fashion, while maintaining the highest standards of quality. She participated in the Sloan-C Institute and was a founding member of the New Century Learning Consortium, a coalition of nine public comprehensive universities across the U.S. that shared courses and best pedagogical practices using enhanced technology.

Betty served on numerous boards of Lewiston-Auburn community organizations and a number of statewide entities including: Maine Coalition for Excellence in Education, the Compact for Maine's Future (concerning the promotion of higher education in Maine), Androscoggin Chamber of Commerce, L-A Excels (community and economic development), Androscoggin Home Care and Hospice, Maine Community Foundation, and Maine's Board of Arbitration and Conciliation. She currently serves as board chair for Tree Street Youth, a K–12 after-school and summer program for students at risk (70% from refugee families) in Lewiston.

Jodi Sandfort is a professor at the University of Minnesota's Humphrey School of Public Affairs, and chair of the school's management and leadership area. Her research, teaching, and practice all focus on improving the implementation of social policy, particularly those policies designed to support low-income children and their families. She is passionate about leadership development because of how critical leaders are in improving public investments and assuring they create desirable results.

Jodi has spent her career moving back and forth between professional practice and academic posts. She was a senior fellow at the Minnesota Council of Nonprofits and directed the human service program at the McKnight Foundation in Minneapolis, where she managed a portfolio of $20 million in annual giving directed to the human service system in Minnesota. She has worked as senior strategy consultant with the Bush Foundation and special assistant to the University of Minnesota's president. She is a Family Self-Sufficiency Scholar funded by the U.S. Department of Health and Human Services, Office of Planning, Research and Evaluation. She is also the academic director of the Hubert Project, a global initiative promoting interactive teaching and learning through use of multimedia learning materials in public affairs education (see http://www.hubertproject.org).

Jodi is currently engaged in a multiyear partnership with the Minnesota Department of Human Services focused on improving welfare service delivery for families in 20 counties. Her research focuses more broadly on the organizations and fields involved in social policy delivery, such as human services, early childhood, and welfare. She is the author of a recent book *Effective Implementation in Practice: Integrating Public Policy and Management* with Stephanie Moulton. She has published articles in numerous academic journals and contributed chapters to books on public management, service networks, systems redesign, and research methodology. She also has authored numerous reports for policy makers and practitioners in philanthropy, early childhood education, welfare reform, and workforce development, as well as numerous award-winning teaching case studies, and most recently, multimedia learning objects.

Her interest in public policy was sparked by her earlier professional experience as a case manager for the AIDS Care Connection in Detroit and as a program assistant at the Children's Defense Fund in Washington, D.C. She was also an assistant professor of public administration at the Maxwell School at Syracuse University. She regularly consults with national and statewide foundations, think tanks, and other nonprofit human service organizations, offering leadership coaching and organizational development services. Jodi also is passionate about professional education and has built trainings and training programs for philanthropists, midlevel public managers, nonprofit leaders, and master's, midcareer master's, and doctoral students.

Jodi received a Ph.D. in political science and social work in 1997 from the University of Michigan. She also holds a master's degree in social work from the University of Michigan and a B.A. from Vassar College. She is a member of Phi Beta Kappa. Originally from Menomonie, Wisconsin, Jodi lives with her husband and two sons in St. Paul, Minnesota, where she likes to swim and garden.

Valerie Shangreaux is the director of the Blandin Leadership Programs for the Blandin Foundation in Grand Rapids, Minnesota.

Previously she worked as the program manager and the campus coordinator for the Louis Stokes Oklahoma Alliance for Minority Participation in Science, Technology, Engineering, and Mathematics (LS-OKAMP STEM) Program at Oklahoma State University. Valerie was also on the faculty of the Department of Family Relations and Child Development at Oklahoma State University.

Valerie holds a Ph.D. from Oklahoma State University in educational psychology. Her research topic was resiliency in a Native American community. Her master's degree, also in educational psychology, and bachelor's degree in home economics are from the University of Nebraska.

Valerie's volunteer involvement includes serving on the Board of Directors for the Heartland Center for Leadership Development, Lincoln, Nebraska, and the Board of Directors for the YMCA in Grand Rapids, Minnesota.

Valerie is a member of the Oglala Sioux Tribe and originally from Pine Ridge, South Dakota.

Georgia Sorenson founded the James MacGregor Burns Academy of Leadership at the University of Maryland, U.S.A., where she was distinguished research professor, before coming to Churchill College's Møller Centre, University of Cambridge. She is also co-founder of the International Leadership Association. In addition, Georgia has served as senior policy analyst to President Jimmy Carter in the White House, inaugural chair and professor of transformational leadership of the U.S. Army War College, and visiting senior scholar at the University of Richmond's Jepson School of Leadership Studies as well as the University of Maryland Carey School of Law.

An architect of the leadership studies field, she was awarded the 2015 International Leadership Association's Lifetime Achievement Award, an award that "honors an individual's accomplishments in the development and enhancement of the field of leadership over his or her lifetime."

Georgia is co-editor (with George Goethals and James MacGregor Burns) of the four-volume multi-award-winning *Encyclopedia of Leadership*, and *The Quest for a General Theory of Leadership*. She was co-author of *Dead Center* (with James MacGregor Burns), an analysis of the Clinton presidency. Her latest book, *The Power of Invisible Leadership* (with Gill Hickman), is on business leadership. Georgia serves on the editorial board of numerous refereed journals including *Leadership* (U.S. editor), *Leadership Quarterly* (associate editor, 2007–2014), and *Leadership Review*. She is co-editor (with Ronald Riggio) of a series, *Leadership: Research and Practice*, for Routledge. Her upcoming book is on the business leadership philosophy of Béla Hatvany.

Sharon Turnbull is a cycle director of the International Masters Programme in Practicing Management. Sharon is an independent academic who specializes in leadership, executive education, and organizational development. She works with a number of business schools and other clients to provide program development, doctoral and master's level supervision, executive teaching, and leadership development and research. She teaches and researches in the fields of "worldly" and global leadership, leadership wisdoms in ancient and indigenous societies, responsible leadership, organizational culture and values, organizational change and development, and leadership.

Sharon is also associate head of research at The Leadership Trust, an educational charity that specializes in leadership and leadership development. Prior to joining The Leadership Trust in 2003, she directed M.B.A. and executive programs, and taught and researched at Lancaster University Management School for almost 10 years, following a successful corporate career in human resources and management development.

Sharon has a Ph.D. in management and an M.B.A., both from Lancaster. She is a chartered fellow of the Chartered Institute of Personnel and Development. She is visiting professor at the Universities of Gloucestershire, University of West of England, and Worcester, and a visiting senior research fellow and fellow of the Lancaster Leadership Centre at the University of Lancaster.

Sharon has published in many journals and management publications. She co-edited *Worldly Leadership: Alternative Wisdoms for a Complex World*, co-authored *Your MBA With Distinction: Developing a Systematic Approach to Succeeding in Your Business Degree*, and co-edited *Critical Thinking in Human Resource Development*.

Mary Uhl-Bien is the BNSF Endowed Professor of Leadership in the Neeley School of Business at Texas Christian University. Prior to that she was professor and Howard Hawks Chair in Business Ethics and Leadership at the University of Nebraska. She has been a visiting scholar in Australia, Sweden, Portugal, and Spain.

Mary's research focuses on complexity leadership, relational leadership, and followership, and has appeared in such journals as *Academy of Management Journal, Journal of Applied Psychology, Journal of Management*, and *The Leadership Quarterly*. Her papers on complexity leadership theory and followership theory have been recognized with best paper awards, and her research has been conducted in partnership with Lockheed Martin, Bank of America, Disney, the U.S. Fish and Wildlife Service, and Stryker. She is senior editor of the Leadership Horizons series for Information Age Publishing, and is currently on or has served on the editorial boards of *Academy of Management Review* and *The Leadership Quarterly*. She is a founder of the Network of Leadership Scholars in the Academy of Management, and currently serving as division chair for the OB Division in the Academy.

Mary is active in executive education nationally and internationally, teaching for the Brookings Institute, the Gallup Organization, and universities in the U.S., Australia, and Europe. She served as the executive consultant for State Farm Insurance Co. from 1998–2004. She participated in a Fulbright-Hays grant to Mexico during the summer of 2003, trained Russian businesspeople for the American Russian Center at the University of Alaska Anchorage from 1993–1996, and worked on a USAID grant at the Magadan Pedagogical Institute in Magadan, Russia, from 1995–1996. Her Ph.D., M.B.A., and bachelor's degrees are from the University of Cincinnati.

Montgomery (Monty) Van Wart received his Ph.D. from Arizona State University. Mostly Monty has worked in higher education in various capacities for over 25 years, nearly always in administrative roles. He served as the interim dean of the College of Business and Public Administration at California State University San Bernardino, where he was also a longtime chair of the Department of Public Administration. He was also a senior research fellow at KU Leuven (formerly Catholic University) in Belgium (2012–2013) and a visiting professor at Rutgers (2013). He is currently a visiting professor at the University of Hong Kong.

Monty taught his first leadership class in 1990. He was appalled at the lack of quality materials and materials appropriate to the public sector. It has been a lifetime goal to help the field develop and mature.

As a scholar, Monty conducts research in administrative leadership, human resource management, training and development, administrative values and ethics, organization behavior, and general management. His primary research frequently appears in the best journals in the field; for example, he has eight refereed articles in *Public Administration Review*. His 11 books include *Dynamics of Leadership, Leadership in Public Organizations, Human Resource Management in Public Service* (with Berman, Bowman, and West), *Changing Public Sector Values, Leadership and Culture: Comparative Models of Top Civil Servant Training* (with Hondeghem and Schwella), *and Leadership Across the Globe* (with Gupta). He has well over 2,000 Google Scholar citations. Monty received his university's inaugural award for outstanding research and the Van Riper Award from ASPA. He serves as associate editor for *Public Productivity and Management Review*, and serves on numerous editorial boards. He is active in community affairs, serving on a variety of official City of Riverside, California, advisory boards.

Reference

Collins, J. C., & Porras, J. I. (1982). *Built to last*. New York: HarperCollins.

PART I

Using Personal Narrative to Foster Self-Understanding and Commitment

While personal narratives are woven throughout this book, this part focuses specifically on the creation of such narratives as a foundation of leadership development. By leadership development I mean achieving a more mature view of oneself as a (sometime) leader and (frequent) follower and becoming more skilled in helping others achieve the common good.

In the first chapter, several leadership educators join me in describing the "heart" of leadership development. How did we become committed to leadership development work? How were we influenced by family, gender, race/ethnicity, economic circumstances, religion, education, professional paths, and culture? I hope that these stories will prompt you to start responding to these questions yourself.

The second chapter is more "heady." Why is personal narrative so important in leadership development? What are some of the major theories of adult development and leadership that shed light on important components and uses of these narratives? The third chapter describes specific tried-and-true narrative exercises that can help you and the participants in your classes and workshops deepen their understanding of themselves as leaders (and followers) and strengthen their commitment to leadership work.

In *Leadership for the Common Good* (2005) John Bryson and I emphasize two starting places for leadership—first, understanding one's self and others and, second, understanding the context that summons you to leadership. Part I of the current book focuses on the first of these; subsequent parts will focus on diagnosing context and using your personal assets to lead in that context.

My Commitment to Leadership Development

I am a child of the 1950s, 1960s American South, and I never intended to be a teacher, much less a teacher of leadership. My only career aim was to get out—get out of my parents' house and out of Augusta, Georgia. College was my ticket and I settled on Vanderbilt University because it offered me the best scholarship. My four years at Vanderbilt are still vivid four decades later. They gave me the opening to the larger worlds I sought, helped me see that the South and its inhabitants could break the hold of segregation, revealed new heroes, and gave me the conviction that my contemporaries and I could alter the course of our society. This conviction persisted despite the blows of Martin Luther King Jr.'s assassination in April of my senior year, followed in June by the assassination of Robert F. Kennedy Jr.

My conviction about the impact of organized citizens pursuing just causes has persisted despite many other blows since. It has been a consistent thread through my years as a newspaper reporter and editor, my volunteer work, my time in governors' offices, my work for a Minnesota nonprofit, and my three decades teaching and writing about leadership and public affairs. I've seen triumphs and setbacks, breakthroughs and shenanigans. One question has become central for me and has led to my commitment to excellence in teaching leadership: How do individuals and groups become committed to beneficial social change and how do they achieve it? This question led me to leave my job with the Minnesota Project in 1984 and devote substantial time to developing the book that eventually became *Leadership for the Common Good* (1992), co-written with John Bryson.

In 1984 I also enrolled in the Leadership and Social Policy seminar being conducted by Dr. Robert Terry at the Humphrey Institute (now School) of Public Affairs. I wanted to gain a more solid academic base for my analysis of major social and political change efforts. Bob's great assets were a relentless curiosity and great intellectual generosity. Moreover, he was a shameless extrovert who never encountered someone he couldn't talk to. He loved messing with participants in his Humphrey School seminars, in order to shake us out of our habitual ways of thinking and seeing. He did so with considerable humor, however, and usually had participants appreciating his repartee if not becoming acolytes. Occasionally, though, seminar participants were skeptical, if not downright offended, by his pushing various boundaries and sometimes stepping over them without permission.

Bob was a generous colleague and a frustrating one. He invited me to help staff the seminars and programs at the Reflective Leadership Center. He helped me move from a nervous novice at leading seminars to a seasoned vet and showed by example what it was like to bring one's whole

(*Continued on p. 4*)

1

USING PERSONAL NARRATIVE AND THE HEART

So where do we leadership educators begin? With ourselves, of course; with self-examination.

Why do we care about developing leaders and leadership? What do we bring to this work in the way of inheritances, skills, experience, and vulnerabilities? What story are we crafting of ourselves at this point in the early 21st century on Planet Earth?

On the opposite page is a story in which I answer these questions. Other leadership educators have their own unique stories to tell. Most of the people you will meet in this book teach leadership courses or coordinate leadership programs; some mix leadership into consulting or coaching work. For example, Yvonne Cheek, a veteran facilitator and organizational development consultant, says, "I infuse leadership development in all the work I do." These educators' academic degrees are in psychology, political science, organizational behavior, public administration, sociology, business administration, engineering, music, and other fields. (My own are in political science, journalism and mass communication, and leadership studies.) Of those with Ph.D.s, some had practical experience after their undergraduate education and others pursued advanced degrees right away.

What seems to matter most are some key formative experiences. They range from finding oneself on stage with a reggae band, to attending boarding school, to experiencing injustice, to finding a guru, to enduring family difficulties and loss.

Formation

Chuck Palus grew up in Johnstown, Pennsylvania, in a Catholic, blue-collar middle-class family. He felt smothered by Catholicism, and was happier being self to the task of teaching. At the same time, he was not an easy man to hold accountable and to keep on the right side of boundaries. His charisma was an asset but also shielded him from some of the usual constraints on an academic administrator.

During the 1980s, I gained clearer understanding that my mission as a writer and activist was to comprehend leadership and followership. Thanks to Bob Terry, I became part of a thinking circle that tried to get a handle on what leadership was all about. We were teaching seminars about leadership at the same time, so this was definitely a case of building the bridge as we walked on it. What an exhilarating endeavor! This, of course, was in the days before leadership studies had developed as an academic field. (Only later did we realize we were helping to build the field.) We invited several insightful scholars from elsewhere to join our thinking circle, people like James MacGregor Burns, Barbara Kellerman, Ron Heifetz, and Harold Prince. From our work emerged the frameworks and exercises we tried out in our seminar sessions. Some worked like a charm, others bombed, and some required reworking.

My commitment to excellence in leadership teaching emerged from my desire to help other people find their leadership calling and succeed in bringing diverse groups of people together to tackle complex problems. Plus, I had found even as a master's candidate teaching news writing well before my time at the Humphrey School that I got a kick out of teaching. Teaching—whether in a classroom, a workshop setting, a discussion circle, or in an auditorium full of people—is at once what I live for and about the scariest thing I ever do. It's scary because leadership is a serious subject. People who summon the courage to tackle inequities, shake up the status quo, and confront abusive power mongers are putting themselves on the line. There's also the need to practice what I preach—I can't just talk about leadership, I have to practice it in my own context. Yikes!

Perhaps the biggest barrier for me, though, has been nearly debilitating anxiety about speaking to more than a few people at a time. I have spent years getting to the bottom of this anxiety and training myself to manage it so that I can do what I am called to do. In the late 1980s, in a seminar on women and leadership that I had helped organize, I heard with empathy the story of an accomplished woman leader, who said she threw up before every major talk. I never lost my dinner over an upcoming presentation, but I often lay awake the night before convinced that I would forget every line and wind up a miserable failure. I envisioned a firing squad sitting in the front row.

Being female has had its disadvantages as well, as has being a nontraditional academic. For a long time, I had an exceptionalist perspective on

(*Continued on p. 6*)

a Boy Scout. "I was tinkering and figuring the world out," he says. "I was the first person in my extended family to go to college. I got a bit of money to go to Penn State." There he studied engineering. One evening he showed up for a campus reggae concert and suddenly found himself caught up in the band that was playing that night. The band leader coaxed him onto the stage to introduce the group. "I'd never done anything like this, but I went ahead and introduced the group, and realized I could do things I'd never contemplated." From Penn State he went to work for DuPont. "It was five years of figuring things out. That's what I do." He was assigned a role in quality assurance, and became intrigued by the human side of engineering projects. He decided to study psychology and human systems at Boston College, where he would receive a Ph.D. in developmental psychology. While in graduate school, he was an instructor with Outward Bound, an organization that focuses on character development through outdoor experiences. "It was fun and exciting." It also allowed him to see the potential for personal transformation when people are offered challenging assignments in a supportive environment. "I started working with young people in Outward Bound and transitioned to working with adults in organizations with the Center for Creative Leadership."

Gill Hickman grew up in Birmingham, Alabama, in the segregated American South. At that time in the African American community, "if you had capabilities you were volunteered. Teachers, ministers, and parents volunteered you for leadership roles. I was always put in leadership positions in church, Girl Scouts, and clubs."

> *In Sunday school, the minister said because we are preparing you to be leaders, I am going to turn Sunday School classes over to the youth. Gill, I want you to teach the adult class. I said I can't, my mother is in that class. He insisted so I really prepared, I drew on many sources, I thought about how to get people interested. I was 15. It turned out to be an incredible experience.*
>
> —Gill Hickman

"My teachers and my parents reinforced the message that I could do anything I wanted to do. They said, 'Look, there are barriers to you as an African American, but so what.'" Her mother was a role model. "She was a first lieutenant in World War II, an army nurse with the Tuskegee airmen. She became evening coordinator, which made her head of the whole VA hospital for the evening shift, before she retired. She was always pushing and encouraging me to take leadership roles."

Hickman also was caught up in the civil rights movement as a young person. "Children were involved in the movement. I saw that anyone could be a leader. I saw that you can make a difference at all levels of society from the family to the highest level. You can engage."

being female in various male preserves like journalism in the 1960s—that is, I assumed that if I was smart enough and worked hard enough I would be able to achieve what I wanted. Experience taught me about the shortcomings of this view; feminist analysis gave me a lens through which to critique my own attitudes and build solider connections to other women.

I am sustained by a marvelous partnership with John Bryson that is now in its fifth decade; by my children John Kee Sooja and Jessica Ah-Reum Crosby Bryson, who have become sharp analysts and generous human beings; and by my many hardworking colleagues and reliable (if often quirky) friends. I also have the pleasure of contemplating the growth of leadership studies, the strengthening of the leadership centers with which I am associated, and my fellow scholars' growing attention to the questions that animate my own commitment to leadership education. Finally, I get a thrill from each and every person who comes up to me after taking one of my classes or reading something I've written and says, I've been using the ideas and tools you taught me and they actually work!

As a teenager Hickman won a scholarship to attend a college prep school in Massachusetts.

> *Going to boarding school gave me the academic background for college but also exposed me to so many things I wouldn't have had in the South. We were exposed to libraries and plays and art museums—those things would mainly have been off limits in Alabama. Teachers challenged us to be critical thinkers and make up our own minds. It was very democratic. Students really set rules of the school. I did a lot that shapes me today. It was really a critical point in my development.*

After graduating from the University of Denver, Hickman began a career as a university administrator in California. "I was asked to do some teaching, so I did. Later the dean came up and said, do you realize you've been teaching for free? You must like it, he said. I realized I did. I fell in love with college teaching." She later became part of the core faculty at the Jepson School of Leadership Studies, University of Richmond.

Unlike Gill Hickman, Sonia Ospina sensed from a very early age that she was destined to be a teacher. As a child in Colombia, she found herself playing school, teaching, helping her brother learn. "When I had to choose my first career it was so obvious that I had to be a teacher. It wasn't necessarily what my parents wanted."

She never thought of herself as a leader, but rather simply wanted to contribute, to serve. "In high school, for example, there was a hurricane in Central America. I collected money to send, because I felt we needed to do something. It was quite successful. I was in charge of the senior yearbook, and that involved lots of responsibility." She saw herself as "more of a nerd," compared to more visible, popular people. Later, friends from that time would describe her as having been a role model, but she didn't think of herself that way.

When Ospina went to university in Bogotá, she became involved in extracurricular service projects that opened her eyes to poverty in her country. She remembers, in particular, working with a Catholic charity. One night she was planning activities with a group of nuns at a convent when a kid knocked on the door. "The kid was hollering, screaming, asking to be let in, but the nuns said this happens every night. At that moment I said this doesn't make sense. I thought, this is ridiculous. It has stuck in my mind forever: That people can become so callous. It marked me. I disconnected from the group, and never went back. It made me a little bit more political."

Later Ospina left Colombia to study in the United States and decided to settle there. Having to master English as a second language has made her think carefully about communicating her ideas. "I have to be very careful, less spontaneous about my preparation. I have to do more work prior. I have to be on top of conversations." After obtaining a Ph.D. in sociology she joined the faculty of the Wagner School of Public Affairs, where she became deeply involved with leadership education as co-founder of the innovative Research Center for Leadership in Action, which focuses on the leadership of diverse grassroots groups.

Gary DeCramer, like Ospina, traced his teaching career back to his childhood. He grew up on a farm in southwestern Minnesota in a family that expected him to go into the Catholic priesthood.

Gary De Cramer's Earliest Recollection of Being Inspired to Teach

In about Grade 3, I recall crawling over the wood fence next to the barn and into the barnyard where I found my 4-H calf foaming at the mouth. Frisky was a Holstein heifer born from one of our best milk cows. She was to be my first 4-H project with one of our farm animals.

I told my dad about finding Frisky in a bad state. He asked, "Did you put your hand in her mouth?" (She loved to suck on my fingers—it was a way to get her to come close so I could pet her and curry her white and black hair). I said no. I then learned that Dad was concerned she had rabies. He had shot a rabid skunk a few days before. Apparently Frisky was a victim of a bite before Dad blew that skunk away. Dad called our vet, Doc Merritt, and asked him come out to look at the calf. When he saw her, he put her down with a lethal injection.

I was astonished by all this: Rabies, a dreaded evil in our midst. I told my teacher Sr. Mary Vita about this incident with Frisky. She was my third grade teacher at St Eloi's elementary in Ghent. She said, "That is quite a story, Gary. You should go to the other classrooms and tell this story." I said, yes, I will. So, I told our class of third and fourth graders, then went to the first and second grade room (there were four rooms in the school), then to the fifth and sixth. Then to Sr. Mary Cannon's dreaded seventh and eighth grade room. I knocked on her door, and this red-faced nun asked, "What do you want?" I said I had a story, an important lesson for all to hear. To these 15 or 16 giant upper classmates, I told my story. They did not laugh at me. They smiled, nodded. And I left trembling. The whole world now knew: Stay away from rabid skunks.

Mary Uhl-Bien was a freshman in high school, where she had a math teacher who struggled with teaching. She began to help him and later, in college, she had an engaging teacher who gave her a role model to follow. She was recruited into a doctoral program by George Graen, the foremost proponent of leader-member exchange research. The result, she says, was an enduring understanding of leadership as relational. "I always thought of leadership as social exchange and interaction. I paid attention to the follower role and leadership embedded in context." She traces her drive to be a leader in leadership studies in part to growing up in a family of nine children. Money was tight, and she knew she would have to work hard to achieve professional success and financial security.

Ron Riggio was from a medical family and planned to study pre-med in college. "My adviser was very discouraging, so I went into psychology. I decided I liked the academic lifestyle." He went on to graduate school and became intrigued by the study of emotions, charisma, and interpersonal communication. Becoming director of the Kravis Leadership Institute at Claremont McKenna College gave him the chance to "really pursue my passion," continuing research into the social psychology of leadership, developing leaders, and building the field of leadership studies. Taking on the director job also prompted him to take on a stronger leader identity. "There can be a labeling effect, and I think that happened to me. Being labeled a leader caused me to undertake self-examination and want to be better."

Rick Morse grew up Mormon, middle class. He took advantage of opportunities for youth leadership in the church and when he went on the traditional mission as a young man, he was given a supervisory role. "I was pretty privileged and unreflectively moderate-conservative as a high school student. I saw myself as a Reagan Republican. As a missionary though, I saw a different world when I worked in the projects in California. This opened my eyes to the real world. I spent a lot of time with people who were really struggling in life. I went about 180 degrees. I asked, am I a Republican? Was I ever?"

At Brigham Young University Morse took public policy courses that helped him develop a communitarian ethic. "Personal responsibility toward the community and the nobility of public service—that was the biggest driver for me." He developed a strong sense of stewardship for the earth and the communities in which people live, and his interest in leadership stems from that. "I see leadership as incumbent for all who care about community and environment." Today, as a faculty member at the University of North Carolina, he offers leadership development for public affairs students and local government practitioners.

Lars Leafblad, a lifelong Minnesotan, says that his understanding of leadership was shaped by his college experience and before that by his mother's example.

> *My mother spent lots of time on the phone thanking people, writing notes to people. She conveyed the importance of relationships, of work done together. She modeled an approach to connectivity—showing her children connectedness through action.*
>
> —Lars Leafblad

He subscribed early in life to a pay-it-forward philosophy, which was reinforced by one professor in particular who encouraged him as a freshman at St. Olaf College to implement his idea for a group that would link students with alumni. "The effort to start the organization met with skepticism from some faculty, but other faculty encouraged it, and fellow students were supportive." Leafblad and his supporters succeeded in launching the organization, and now it is a fixture at the college. This early success is a key contributor to his commitment to developing leaders in his work with public and nonprofit organizations.

Leafblad is among those who cited difficult family dynamics as an important influence. His parents divorced when he was seven. "They had a pretty progressive arrangement; I stayed with each one a week at a time. How I coped was to be the list maker, organizer, while my sister was a free spirit. I learned to be flexible, able to adjust."

Georgia Sorenson spent nine years living in Japan as a child. "That profoundly affected me—the culture, the arts, the countryside, the smells." She was attracted to Zen Buddhism, and Buddhist practice continues to infuse her life. As a college student Sorenson gravitated toward humanities and the arts, but then she heard Jean Lipman-Blumen, at the National Institute for Education, give a talk on women's equality and the achievement-oriented research she was doing. "I wrote to her saying I want to work with you. I didn't hear from her for about a year, but then she invited me to Washington, D.C." Sorenson went and became intensely involved in the women's movement there. Later she would become a psychotherapist, and was working on a dissertation exploring charisma. Someone suggested she call James MacGregor Burns, who had written the field-altering book *Leadership* a few years before, to talk about her resistance to the idea of solo leadership. "I called him and he said, 'I agree. Charisma is important but not enough. We've got to figure this out.' He was so welcoming and affirming, and agreed to be on my dissertation committee." The association with Burns would turn into a lifelong friendship, and Sorenson would found the James MacGregor Burns Academy of Leadership at the University of Maryland.

Crucible Experiences

Some of the formation stories you've just read about fit the definition of "crucible experiences" (Thomas and Bennis, 2002), trying situations that change us in some fundamental way. There are others. Gary DeCramer and Richard Couto felt called as young men to serve within a religious order. A crucible experience for them was making the difficult decision to leave; they would find other ways to serve.

Still others entered the crucible as young professionals. For me, it was being a 20-something, female newspaper reporter in the South during the late 1960s and early 1970s when the white establishment was still resisting integration and the antiwar movement was swirling through the nation. I believed my conservative newspaper should be reporting on the various social upheavals that were going on all around us. As the education reporter, I confronted the local school superintendent over his resistance to integrating teaching staff. I created a poverty beat, and wrote stories about people, black and white, from the poorer parts of town who were organizing themselves and taking advantage of Lyndon Johnson's Great Society programs. I won some battles with my editors and lost some. I emerged with some humility about my own limitations, but also pride in having used my writing to tell stories that brought issues of social justice to the fore.

Rick Morse didn't know it right away, but his first job just after graduate school—teaching in the Master of Public Administration Program (M.P.A.) at Iowa State—would be his crucible experience. "I was so excited to be there. We had a young faculty and were developing great partnerships in the community. About a year in, it was if the floor was pulled out from under me. The politics of the university changed. There was a new provost, and the commitment to the M.P.A. program evaporated. As exciting as things were that first year, at the end of it I felt I was on a sinking ship. At the time I was shattered—I had three little kids, had bought a house."

> *About a year in, it was if the floor was pulled out from under me.*
> —Rick Morse

Morse knew he had to leave and found a new position at University of North Carolina (UNC), where he has been ever since. What was at the time a terrible trial became in retrospect an impetus for personal development. "It didn't take long to see the challenge as good for all of us. Other young faculty also found new and better jobs. I learned regardless of the situation there are opportunities for learning and growth. At Iowa State I had a lot of professional opportunities that prepared me for the UNC job. This helps me when I try to help local officials as they face challenges. I note we can't predict the future but we can make choices about what we do here and now to shape it."

Mary Uhl-Bien was challenged when, as a young associate professor at the University of Central Florida, she was assigned to teach executives. She realized she couldn't match the experience of the people in her classroom and could hardly teach a whole class based on her leader-member exchange research. So she turned to *Harvard Business Review* cases and learned from the students. "Doing executive education really changed me." It prompted her to expand beyond her focus on leaders' relationship with their followers. "I set out to find a leadership model that had rigor and practical usefulness. Complexity was it."

Setting out to understand leadership in complex adaptive systems was an exciting, bruising adventure. Along with colleagues Russ Marion and Michael Arena, she began a research network including academics and practitioners. They were part of a growing number of scholars in the 1990s who were questioning traditional leader-centric views. They argued that leadership scholars needed to know more about recent developments in complexity science—that is, the investigation of complex natural and social systems—and rethink what leadership might mean in a world of multiple feedback loops and contextual influences, a world where no person or group could really be in charge.

Early on this was really embraced by people in leadership studies because they said we need something different. Then we got pushback when we tried to refine it. We got beat up, and that actually helped us refine the theory further. People felt threatened because they didn't understand this approach. The post-positivists were worried because it wasn't in their skill set. They wanted to hold onto their view of science. The field of leadership studies has now tipped in favor of complexity. It's been a hard journey but a fun one.

At 24, Gill Hickman went to work as an entry-level manager in a California city. "When I started in administration, women were just starting to be in management roles. I was often the first woman and first African American in a role. I had experienced overt racism but now I was facing institutional racism." As a young minority woman, she had three counts against her, and even some other women sought to undermine her.

Some of the women who typed my work weren't comfortable with my appointment. I'd give them work and wouldn't get it back. I told my boss about not getting my work back and he had to direct them to do my typing. These women started documenting everything I did.

—Gill Hickman

Pushback also came from some superiors.

I had a project that was very dependent on the sanitation department, and the supervisor was very dismissive. When I came to see him, he put his feet on the desk, reared back and acted as if I weren't there. It took perseverance and lots of Pepto Bismol to overcome this kind of resistance. As time went on I learned how to develop relationships and get people on my side. The Pepto Bismol went away. Women even came to my side when I had my first baby. They said, 'She's a woman!'

I began to change rules that were completely out of line—for example, the requirement that women leave in the seventh month of pregnancy. Most people really appreciated the changes. This built a lot of my strength and practical knowledge in leadership studies.

Some of us have experienced the pain of divorce and the loss of parents. Rick Morse's mother recently died from cancer. "It was a year-long process. On the other end, I learned a lot about empathy. It was a real in-your-face opportunity to understand key principles I teach in leadership. I emphasize that regardless of the situation we can control only what we do."

Georgia Sorenson became the chief caretaker for her parents and her brother, who was schizophrenic. "I'm glad I did this, but it was very hard," she says. An enduring effect of caring for her brother has been a commitment to speaking up for people who are disenfranchised by virtue of their disability, income level, race, or gender.

Some of us have had to deal with significant mental or emotional barriers to carrying out our life's work. At the beginning of this chapter, I described my struggles with public speaking. Georgia Sorenson went through a period of wanting to withdraw from the world. Instead she listened to her Buddhist teacher. "When I wanted to pack up and to give away all my possessions, he suggested instead to put them in the attic. He said, 'Stay in the world. Stay at the University of Maryland.'" Lars Leafblad has been on a journey of recovery since undergoing outpatient treatment for alcoholism a few years ago. "The 12-step program has been vital. Admit the problem, ask for help, be humble—all of this shapes how I now live my life."

> *I realized my relationships were at risk if I didn't take action. For me it's been a willingness to humble myself, ask for help, and help others. I've met some of the most remarkable individuals, who stand out not by demonstrating their power. When I think of humility and courage, I see them in these people. I want to transfer these qualities as I talk to fellows in the Bush Foundation leadership program.*
>
> —Lars Leafblad

Commitment and Passion

As you've heard about leadership educators' formative and crucible experiences, you've begun to get a flavor of the commitment and passion that form the core of our leadership development work. For some the commitment is to a set of values. Rick Morse cites public service and environmental stewardship. Georgia Sorenson cites "the great public values—equality, enlightenment, human potential, excellence, and fairness." The commitment to equality comes from participating in the women's movement. Enlightenment and human potential are rooted in her Buddhist practice.

> *My teacher, Reb Anderson, said there's no such thing as personal enlightenment. We all rise together, so you must go and do your work with other people.*
>
> —Georgia Sorenson

She believes people should strive for excellence—"be all they can be, like the Army says." That means that some people will certainly achieve more and have more influence than others; at the same time, everyone deserves fair treatment.

For some of us, the key values revolve around inclusion, connection, and empowerment of others. Lars Leafblad says, "My calling is to pursue avenues to connect people with each other and opportunities to develop themselves and their communities." Sonia Ospina says, "My first commitment is to the idea of participation. I seek to enhance people's capacity to participate in dimensions of their life, in their circles of influence." Similarly, Betty Robinson seeks to help people "understand their context so they can be better in dealing with it, see and seize new possibilities."

Several mention a passion for learning about leadership or how the world works. Some also emphasize their commitment to a particular institution or group (for example, in Palus's case, to the Center for Creative Leadership and his colleagues there; in Riggio's case, to the Kravis Center; or in Sorenson's case, to young people).

We have exercised leadership in many different roles: in the classroom, of course, but also within the field of leadership studies, in higher education administration, and in our communities. Several of us have founded or directed academic centers that have expanded scholarly views of leadership, fostered multifaceted research, and contributed to more integrative leadership practice. We've written books and articles that help shift traditional ways of thinking about leadership. Many have been involved in building the International Leadership Association and other networks of leadership scholars and educators.

We've also practiced leadership in our families, on the soccer field, and in institutions besides higher education. Rick Morse comments: "I'm the father of four kids. Parenting is the ultimate leadership challenge—the opportunity to nurture and develop kids day to day. It's a constant learning ground." He also has taken on leadership roles in his church, and 10 years ago became a youth soccer coach. "I stepped up when organizers asked for volunteer coaches. I've grown into it, and really enjoyed it. I've learned a lot about leadership, often the hard way." As chair of a charter school board he faced additional leadership challenges. "We had to hire a new director and cope with a fiscal crisis. This has been extremely formative for me and helps me get beyond the textbook."

Georgia Sorenson often has directed her energies to supporting people who are disenfranchised. Early on that took the form of joining the women's movement, but it also has involved speaking up in individual cases—for example, supporting a student who sued a prominent politician for sexual harassment or rallying around a friend who was threatened with disbarment.

Perspectives on Leadership

Over the years our experiences in studying, practicing, and helping others develop leadership have expanded and refined our own perspectives on leadership. Several of us began our professional careers with an interest in social change and only later came to see leadership as what we were interested in all along, or at least central to it. After training as a sociologist, Betty Robinson became a union organizer and then began teaching adult learners in the University of Southern Maine's organizational studies and management program. Along with fellow faculty member Marvin Druker, she realized that the real focus of the program was on leadership, and the two successfully advocated renaming the program Leadership and Organizational Studies. "We wanted to both inspire and support our students in their ability to embrace their potential as lead agents within their organizations and communities."

> *After being formally exposed to the leadership field, I thought very deeply and started to see the value of the concept more clearly than before. Previously, I had just been doing things that needed to be done. Now I have more intentionality about outcomes. I believe that everyone can contribute from where they are. Leadership is connected to someone intending to create spaces in which others can contribute.*
>
> —Sonia Ospina

In some cases we began by focusing on individual, often exceptional, leaders, but over time developed a view of leadership as a relational and collective phenomenon, in which leaders and followers are connected with each other in fairly fluid and overlapping roles, sometimes connected to formal positions of authority and sometimes not. Georgia Sorenson was predisposed to think of leadership as relational due to her earlier work in psychotherapy and human relations. James MacGregor Burns and others reinforced that view. Gill Hickman says her view of leadership and followership has become "more and more democratic, more inclusive." When she joined the faculty of the Jepson School, she sought to model this view in the classroom by minimizing lecturing and emphasizing active engagement by everyone in the room. "I thought students should participate in teaching. I should participate in being a student. The more I did this the more I loved it. All my classes involve students doing some of the teaching and coming up with projects and activities." Ron Riggio also has developed a more inclusive view of leadership and expanded his attention to followership over the years. "Where is the future of leadership? It's going to be dispersed, decentralized, and from the bottom up."

Rick Morse developed a collective, collaborative view of leadership early in his career, due especially to the influence of management theorist Mary Parker Follett. "I still feel very strongly about that model of leadership. I have come to appreciate, however, the role of individual agency in developing relationships, enabling others, building trust, and championing good process." He still sees leadership as a collective process, but appreciates more the contributions of individual leaders. Mary Uhl-Bien likewise began with a relational view of leadership and later embraced the view of leadership as the process of transforming organizations within complex adaptive systems. For a long time, she was engaged in debunking leadership views that seemed inadequate to her. Now, in part thanks to conversations with Chuck Palus about adult learning, she realizes that she has been on a developmental journey. "I had to debunk the old views in order to break out and develop new ones. Now I can embrace the classics."

Persistence in the Face of Failure and Evil

You've now heard a lot about the democratic values (such as inclusion, mutual respect, and fairness) that this group of educators tries to uphold and our endorsement of models of relational, distributed, and collaborative leadership. Yet we also acknowledge our own failures to live up to our values and certainly know that countervailing models of leadership continue to operate. We remember low points in our classrooms and unwelcome feedback from participants in our leadership development programs. Not everybody appreciates the interactive teaching style that research has shown to be most effective. Our jokes may fall flat or offend. We may be discounted because of our ethnicity, our gender, our age, or other characteristics. We may encounter obstacles in the way a program, workshop, or the university itself is structured. A once-supportive departmental environment may turn toxic.

Sonia Ospina once agreed to convene a workshop using Open Space Technology for a group within the United Nations Development Program (UNDP). The UNDP sponsors reluctantly agreed to the workshop design. "The big cheese basically told people to attend if they didn't have anything better to do. She was dismissive. Only five people attended. We had a good conversation, but it was a complete fiasco in terms of what we wanted to do. The woman in charge denied an opportunity to a lot of people. I was feeling a bit embarrassed." Ospina also feels keenly the limitations of teaching leadership to large cohorts of people on a rigid schedule. "Usually, because of cost and efficiency issues, you have more class members than you want for exercises and discussion. You have less opportunity to connect to each person, and provide everyone an opportunity to talk."

Georgia Sorenson can empathize with Ospina's UNDP experience. "I was invited by a government agency to talk about leadership. They were paying me lots of money. I tested the lecture with graduate students and they loved it, had plenty of questions. A week later I went to the government agency and the group was incredibly hostile. I found out they were required to go. I slipped a little about emotional intelligence into the talk even though I didn't really know the science. The group ripped me to shreds."

> *We had a good conversation, but it was a complete fiasco in terms of what we wanted to do.*
>
> —Sonia Ospina

The group ripped me to shreds.

—Georgia Sorenson

I got terrible evaluations that term.

—Rick Morse

Rick Morse welcomed the opportunity to create a course on collaborative government. "I thought I would go by the principle of collaborative work in the class itself. So I made the whole class about generating collaborative knowledge on a wiki. About a third embraced the idea and the majority hated it. This cut against all they were used to. I got terrible evaluations that term."

In his leadership development work, Lars Leafblad encounters a lot of people who have a transactional, rather than transformational orientation—that is, they are mainly interested in what they can get out of interactions with others rather than seeking to achieve mutual gains and advance the common good. "There's arrogance, dismissiveness. A series of these moments can chip away at the belief that paying it forward is worth it." At times, we ourselves have been dismissive. Dick Couto remembers a class in which he made the classic "There are no dumb questions" statement at the beginning of class. Then when a student did ask a question about the origins of driving on the left and right hand side of the road, he too quickly suggested that maybe there were some questions that didn't merit asking. He remembers that exchange and regrets his response. He recalls, "It caused laughter at a student's expense and embarrassed her. She has not forgotten the exchange either, as our encounters at alumni reunions make clear. Fortunately, she pushed back and pointed out substantial merit to the question. Fortunately for me, I learned the limits of my own curiosity and not to be so quick to pull in its boundaries."

How do leadership educators accept the limitations of our models and our own shortcomings? How do we cope with continued reverence for the individual leader, regardless of whether he or she upholds inclusive, democratic values? Or the pervasive failure to see leadership in many distributed and often humble acts of individuals and groups? Terrible injustices occur daily around the world, even at times perpetrated by democratic governments.

For one thing, we try to learn from our failures and revamp our practice accordingly. Mary Uhl-Bien says, "I've had a lot of failure on a personal level. It's always hard. I'm a perfectionist, and I like things to go well. I have embraced failure and frame it as learning. I vent, I emote, I process, and then learn." She also has learned to move on when an environment becomes too toxic. Georgia Sorenson expresses a similar view: "I take so-called failure as a learning experience. I spend lots of time talking to friends and reflecting. Forgiveness is hard. I have found the ability to forgive myself; forgiving others can be harder." Lars

Leafblad comments, "One of the best indicators of empathy and humility is the ability to face failure. I've experienced personal and moral failure. For example, I was in a job for three months, and realized I had failed to assess the fit properly. Failure can be about not living up to your own or others' expectation. What follows is the real question—do you have the resilience to say this is a setback, an unexpected twist?" When things go awry, Leafblad has learned to fight the impulse to immediately try to correct the situation. "It's a learned behavior for me to say I don't know, I'll get back to you. We might need some other perspectives."

The leadership educators featured in this book tend toward an optimistic stance. Rick Morse says, "I tend to have faith in humanity. In the long run there is more good than evil. Human nature, though it has trouble spots, is much more good than bad. Great leaders pull the good out of people. I'm reading *Positivity* by Barbara Frederickson, and this orientation [positivity] has powerful consequences." Sonia Ospina, agrees: "We all have capacity to do harm. All of us are capable of doing bad, evil stuff. I also believe all of us are capable of rising above, of choosing the good. At the core of our humanity is the capacity to do good, to seek solidarity with others. This keeps me thinking leadership development is a good thing. Leadership development is about helping people draw on their capacity for good and working from there." Chuck Palus adds, "I feel bad about what some of my fellow human beings do. You have to block out a certain amount, and hope our work can do some good."

> *Commitment to stay the course and move forward in the face of evil is leadership. Think about society's orientation to share stories of things going wrong—murder, loss, tragedy. You can say, thank heaven, it's not my family or community, but part of leadership at the individual and system level is to invest in creating stories about an act of goodness. "Woe is us" sells newspapers. When we talk to leaders and ask what do we do in the face of evil, some will say their response is rooted in a faith construct. For another it's a moral platform. The person says, "I will make the right decision. I am going to be ethical." Those leaders I want to work with want to recognize evil and change it.*
>
> —Lars Leafblad

Gill Hickman said that growing up in a strong African American community in the segregated South helped her deal with failure and the persistence of evil in the world. "The one thing that did get lost in integration was an environment where teachers and parents and others reinforced that there was evil in the world and there were barriers, but your job was to go forward. I learned not to internalize negativity." She got the message that whites' unjust and discriminatory behavior had nothing to do with her own merit. "Lots of women and minorities don't have that now. I see so many students, particularly students of color, who have low self-esteem. It's difficult now to know whether when you don't do well, it's because of discrimination or a lack of competence. Feeling discrimination is not easy but it's easier to know it's not you."

This awareness plus a sense of humor has helped Hickman resist mistreatment. She recalls an interaction with the supervisor who had treated her dismissively. "He had to come to a training I was leading. He walked in and said, 'Where's the coffee?' I said, 'Instant coffee and creamer are over there.' He said, 'Why didn't you make coffee?' I said, 'I don't know how.' He responded, 'If I were your husband I'd put you over my knee.' I said, 'And that's why you're not my husband.' I didn't take it personally. I could joke with him about it." After that the two had a much better relationship.

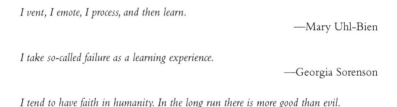

> *I vent, I emote, I process, and then learn.*
>
> —Mary Uhl-Bien

> *I take so-called failure as a learning experience.*
>
> —Georgia Sorenson

> *I tend to have faith in humanity. In the long run there is more good than evil.*
>
> —Rick Morse

Quite a few of us find joy in doing research about leadership practice, building the field, and helping others apply research findings to their own work. We've been sustained especially by those moments when students or program participants experience ah-ha moments, produce an outstanding project, exercise leadership in new ways, join in leading our classes, or become scholars themselves. Lars Leafblad receives emails and phone calls that let him know his work is appreciated. Georgia Sorenson revels in the knowledge that she has helped people see the world around them differently. She mentions her work with students in a class at the University of Maryland Law School in Baltimore.

> *A park in front of the school attracts homeless people, old people, often in wheelchairs. Almost at the beginning of my class, students were talking about robberies that had taken place near the park. Most of the students came to law school because they were attracted to public interest law. I said the park is why we're here. I want you to go out to the park and talk to one person. They didn't want to. I said, just sit down on a bench beside someone and ask, 'Are you from Baltimore?' Some didn't do it. The ones that did came back with a wonderful experience.*

Dick Couto recalls the satisfaction of helping students at the Jepson School reflect deeply on Hermann Hesse's *Journey to the East*. "I asked them [in light of Hesse's story] to consider whether the University of Richmond has been a place to get in touch with the creative, artistic person within each of us. There was silence for what seemed like eternity. It was the first time when everyone was thinking so seriously." Chuck Palus mentions the pleasure of working with Leadership Beyond Boundaries, an initiative of the Center for Creative Leadership. "In the last four years we have had an office for this program in Ethiopia. I spent a month in Addis Ababa and met people who are using my materials. It's gratifying."

What About You?

In this chapter you have met a diverse group of leadership educators, as we shared parts of our personal narrative with you. You have heard about early experiences that had lasting effect. You've heard about challenges and crucible experiences that shaped us further. You've gained insights into our commitment to developing leaders, pursuing research into leadership dynamics, and integrating research and practice. We have explained the evolution of our thinking about leaders and leadership. We've described some of the low points in our professional and personal lives and what has sustained us as we persisted in our work despite our own shortcomings and other obstacles. Essentially, this chapter is a story about a group of leadership educators who come from diverse backgrounds and disciplines, who have pursued various career paths based on their distinctive passions and opportunities, but who also converge around a relational view of leadership. The chapter touches on the elements of personal narrative that reveal what shapes us as leaders and followers, what resources (including our views of leadership) we have to work with, what our learning trajectory has been, and what we hope to achieve.

Crafting the story of one's leadership journey contributes fundamentally to the self-awareness and reflective practice that are essential to helping others become integrative leaders. The next chapter will explore the theories and research behind this conclusion. Before we go there, however, I invite you to respond to the questions considered throughout this chapter.

Developing Your Leadership Narrative

- In what ways have you been called to lead in your family, organizations, or communities at various stages of your life?
- How did your early formative experiences shape your interest in leadership and leadership development?
- What crucible experiences, critical moments, or key challenges have affected your leadership development?
- What commitments inspire you in your leadership work?
- What distinctive resources do you bring to leadership development?

- What is your own view of leadership and how is it evolving?
- What sustains you in the face of failure and evil?

You may want to record your responses in a leadership learning journal and return to them as you experiment with suggested exercises in Chapter 3.

References

Bryson, J. M., & Crosby, B. C. (1992). *Leadership for the common good: Tackling public problems in a shared-power world.* San Francisco: Jossey-Bass.

Thomas, R. J., & Bennis, W. G. (2002). *Geeks and geezers: How eras, values, and defining moments shape leaders.* Boston, MA: Harvard Business School Press.

2

USING PERSONAL NARRATIVE AND THE HEAD

Various strands of theorizing and research link personal narrative to leadership development. In this chapter I will highlight the work of scholars who explore how personal narrative helps develop one's leader identity, moral commitment, and self-efficacy. Also considered will be the empowering effects of crafting and relating a personal narrative and the role of traits, values, and socialization in forming leadership identity and style. You will encounter scholars who focus on the ways that narrative is embedded and conveyed by our physical bodies. Throughout, you will hear about the insight to be gained from reflection on past experience and on other's personal stories.

Narrative and Leader Identity, Commitment, and Self-Efficacy

As human beings, to narrate our life stories is to relate—that is, we connect in some way to the facts and memories of our lives, relate them to each other and consider where this places us in society and our own life trajectories. We relate our stories to others as well, thus building a connection with them. We may compare our stories to those of peers, of people we admire, or people we dislike. Of course, memories may be faulty, and we may tell others a different story than we tell ourselves. In my youth, "telling a story" meant telling a lie. It was something made up. To some extent, a personal narrative *is* "made up." Some portion will be verifiable, but the process of selection, sequencing, explanation, and pattern identification will always be subjective. A story's authenticity rests ultimately with its coherence and whether the teller's behavior matches the story. (If I claim to be a leader and have no discernible followers, observers will conclude that I'm delusional!)

Boas Shamir and Galit Eilam (2005) help us think about the life stories of *authentic leaders*, those whose "talk and actions are consistent with their beliefs and values" (397). They argue that life stories, continually constructed and reconstructed, provide a meaning system that helps these leaders interpret reality and choose and justify their actions. They add that applying reflective thinking to an experience involves "returning to the experience (replaying it in the mind and/or recounting it to others), attending to the feelings accompanying the experience and its memory, re-evaluating the experience and drawing lessons from it" (410).

To fit the authors' definition of authentic leader, a person should develop a leader identity as a core self-concept, develop self-knowledge (especially concerning values and commitments), develop goals consistent with self-concept, and behave consistently with self-concept (399). (The authors see *authentic leadership* as consisting of both authentic leaders and authentic followers—that is, followers who share the leader's beliefs and values. Note that the authors do not consider the morality of the leader's values; they are concerned mainly with leaders' effectiveness in bringing about changes they and their followers desire.)

Shamir and Eilam's (2005) article reports on previous research by Shamir and two other researchers focusing on autobiographies of "recognized leaders" in several spheres and interviews with high-performing organizational managers. That research found that these leaders' life stories were organized around the following themes:

- Leadership development as a natural process—that is, the sense that one was naturally inclined to be a leader and either moved into leadership roles early in life or responded to an opportunity later on
- Leadership development out of struggle—that is, the sense that a person develops leadership qualities by enduring a crucible experience or by overcoming challenges
- Leadership development as finding a cause—often through relating one's own challenges to wider social needs or injustice
- Leadership development as learning from experience—for example, learning from failures or role models

Shamir and Eilam also note that some researchers have highlighted an additional possible theme of leadership development as responding to "unique experiences of success or appreciation" (411), or "positive jolts" (Spreitzer and Grant, 2004). Finally, Shamir and Eilam report that some people in leadership positions do not have a coherent story to tell about their leadership and find leading difficult.

Other researchers have delved further into how one develops a leader identity and integrates it with other core identities. David Day, Michelle Harrison, and Stanley Halpin (2009) argue, "An individual's overall identity develops as sub-identities are expanded, defined, and integrated through experience, self-reflection, and discourse" (60). These researchers are especially interested in how individuals develop a moral identity, or purpose, and how that is integrated with an understanding of oneself as a leader and follower. They cite James Rest's model of moral development to suggest that a well-developed moral identity would consist of a high degree of moral sensitivity, moral motivation, and implementation of moral decisions.

Many models of moral development essentially progress from a central concern with satisfying one's own basic needs, to meeting social expectations, to caring for others and the well-being of larger entities, stretching most grandly to the planetary ecosystem (Maslow, 1943; Heller, 1990; Kheel, 1991; Western, 2013). Developing a leader identity of necessity requires moving beyond simple attention to one's own needs; ultimately, that identity may grow to include devotion to the well-being of others, of communities, and even larger entities. Note how many of the stories in Chapter 1 involved service to others via scouting, social movements, teaching, and other activities.

Day, Harrison, and Halpin (2009) suggest that as one's cognitive capacity grows, one is better able to develop stronger moral reasoning and behavior, and thus a stronger moral identity that is integrated with one's leader identity.

These authors argue that the ongoing development of leader identity over a lifetime may best be thought of as a spiral, in which an individual works from an initial foundation that he or she acquires early in life. This foundation serves as a platform that he or she builds on with the help of mentors, instructors, skill practice, feedback, and reflection. In this constructivist view, once the individual develops new competence and understandings, that new level of achievement and sense of self provides a platform for the next stage of development.

Bandura (1997) provides key insights about the role that self-efficacy (basically, the conviction that our efforts will have desired impact) plays in the development of a strong leader identity. A person's sense of self-efficacy as a leader in a particular context grows as s/he builds competency and receives positive feedback from the environment. As a journalist, I got a jolt of self-efficacy when I saw my by-line in the newspaper, when my editor gave me a compliment, when I was able to draw attention to a neglected issue, or when I won an award. As leadership educators, we develop increased self-efficacy as we see engaged students in our classrooms, as a team project we assigned succeeds, as a former student returns to say that he is using something he learned in our classes every day. When we publish path-breaking articles in leadership journals, or start new leadership programs, or win recognition for leadership studies as a field, our self-efficacy is enhanced, our identity as a field leader grows, and we want to keep doing this, perhaps aspiring to take on even greater challenges (Day and Sin, 2011). The implication of what I have said so far is that one's store of self-efficacy is constantly increasing as one keeps practicing and learning from successes and failures. Clearly that is not always the case, especially in the short term. When I attempted to introduce a new multimedia project in a recent class, I felt much less smart and efficacious than I had the previous time I taught the class. As leadership educators attempt to learn new behaviors, we often have to unlearn old ones; ironically, we have to accept feelings of incompetence before we can achieve new levels of efficacy. Thus our leader development spirals may head downward for a time before they head upward.

A spiral is not the only image that can capture one's continual crafting of a life story in which a leader identity is central. For many of us, the image of weaving a tapestry may be more appealing. It's a tapestry that has richer patterns as time goes on. Threads may end and others appear. Some people may prefer the image of life cycle, or circle of the seasons. We begin as little chicks, develop into spring chickens or cocky adolescents, become mature fowl, and then enter a ripe old age before fading from the scene and making way for new generations.

Narrative and Empowerment

Telling one's story, especially to an appreciative audience, is an expression of personal power. I remember the first time I wrote a personal essay and received favorable feedback in elementary school. Wow! I thought. This is a way I can insert myself into the world and make something of myself. Usually, when I assign exercises that require learners to reflect on their values and experiences, I ask them to share the results in dyads or small groups. Often, those who listen to another's story see things in the story that the writer didn't; they enrich the tale, so to speak.

Howard Gardner in his book *Leading Minds* (1995) notes that the most effective leaders tell stories that open up opportunities for others to tell their story. When you, as a leadership educator tell your story—highlighting the challenges you have faced, the values you live by, the joys you have experienced—to people in your classes or other audiences, you offer a model that they can relate to and adapt for themselves. This may be an especially important leadership act when you are telling a story that is somehow unacceptable or does not fit the society's dominant assumptions.

Think of the effect that Barack Obama's stories of growing up as a biracial young man in the U.S. have had on people who share his heritage. In *Dreams of My Father* and his public speeches he has recounted his own struggles to come to terms with his identity and to realize his ambitions to improve conditions in poor communities. His stories can help any of us whose identity doesn't match received models of leadership realize that our stories could have a similar trajectory.

Exposing ourselves and those we teach to a diverse array of life stories, of the famous and not-so-famous, makes sense. As a child I consumed the biographies in my school library. They were hardly diverse—I remember mainly men who were presidents, soldiers, and inventors—but at least Amelia Earhart was there. I didn't aspire to fly airplanes, but I did see that women might accomplish the same things men could. In her book, *Salsa, Soul, and Spirit* (2012), Juana Bordas tells the story of her family's immigration to the U.S. from Nicaragua when she was a child. In telling her own story and stories of other people of color she presents leaders and leadership models ignored or neglected in most leadership texts. The authors in *Authentic Leadership: An Engaged Discussion of LGBTQ Work as Culturally Relevant* (Watson and Johnson, 2013) tell their stories of leading as LGBTQ persons within higher education. Notes one of the authors,

> I live at the cross-roads of my identities. As a South Asian/Desi, Queer man from a working class, orthodox Hindu-Brahmin family and being the first in my family to complete undergraduate and graduate degrees, I often find myself in spaces where I do not quite fit in.
>
> *(29) (Desi refers to the Indian subcontinent.)*

Genetic Blueprints, Other Foundations, and the Air We Breathe

So far I have focused on crafting one's life story, or as Catherine Bateson (2007, 2010) would say, composing a life. Now I want to shift attention to the raw materials we have to work with and how we develop our early foundations. Recent research has revealed that humans' genetic blueprints affect much more of our values and behavior—from political views, to morality, to leadership styles—than we might like to think (Riggio and Mumford, 2011; Haidt, 2012). Equally important for leadership development, however, are early influences, such as treatment by parents and exposure to learning experiences that help a child self-regulate and practice leadership skills (Murphy and Johnson, 2011). To some extent, this research has settled the hoary debate over whether leadership is born or made— clearly, it is both. Just as clear is that one's genetic blueprint and early foundation are not the end of development, but rather a base on which we continue to build.

A longstanding strain of leadership research has been the quest to discover which personality traits seem to predict "leader emergence," generally defined as moving into leader roles—for example, senior manager or elected representative. Personality traits, shaped by genes and early development, are stable ways in which a person approaches the world. Psychological theorists often rely on a five-factor categorization, called the Big Five, to conduct research on how personality traits affect behavior, and some of this research has focused on leader emergence. The Big Five categories are extraversion, agreeableness, openness (to experience), conscientiousness, and neuroticism. Of these, extraversion is the best predictor of leader emergence, while openness and conscientiousness also have significant positive correlations with leader emergence; neuroticism has a significant negative correlation with leadership emergence (Judge, Bono, Ilies, and Gerhard, 2002). Other researchers have identified additional traits that increase the likelihood that a person will acquire a leadership role. Of these, intelligence has often emerged as crucial (Reichard et al., 2011). Traditionally, researchers defined intelligence as scores on IQ tests; then came researchers like Daniel Goleman, Richard

Boyatzis, and Annie McKee (2002) who found strong evidence that cognitive intelligence—that is, ability to solve problems that appear on IQ tests—was less important than "emotional intelligence" in building successful careers. Emotional intelligence refers to the ability to understand and regulate one's own emotions and to understand others' emotional responses. Clearly, when we view leadership as a relationship between leaders and followers, emotional intelligence assumes prime importance.

Howard Gardner (2011) has widened consideration of intelligence even further. In addition to the linguistic and logical intelligence prized by IQ tests and the intrapersonal and interpersonal awareness of emotional intelligence, he identified spatial, musical, kinesthetic, naturalist, and existentialist intelligences. Every human being, he asserts, has access to all of these intelligences, though each of us will develop strengths in some more than others, given our developmental paths.

Because leadership scholars adopt different leadership models and leader definitions, we differ quite a bit in the lists of traits and related characteristics that we deem vital to leadership (and engaged followership). To the extent that we are concerned with human flourishing and fostering the common good, we are likely to turn to inventories of classic and modern virtues (these might be considered the traits associated with higher levels of moral development). Martin Seligman and his colleagues, for example, have put together a list of 24 character strengths that are "widely recognized across cultures" (Park, Peterson, and Seligman, 2004, 605). They are hope, zest, gratitude, curiosity, love, perspective/wisdom, persistence, self-regulation, spirituality, forgiveness, social intelligence, humor, leadership, bravery, citizenship, integrity, kindness, fairness, prudence, love of learning, judgment, appreciation of beauty, creativity, and modesty/humility. (Leadership, in this case, is defined as "encouraging a group of which one is a member to get things done and at the same time maintaining good relations within the group; organizing group activities and seeing that they happen" [606].) Seligman is a central figure in the relatively new field of positive psychology, which fosters a strengths-based view of personality and leadership development; in his view, the most fulfilled adults develop signature strengths (their own distinctive subset of the 24) that allow them to nurture both self and others (Seligman, 2002).

Personality assessments can be useful in helping you better understand your own life story, identify leadership successes and shortcomings, and choose future directions. A caveat is in order: Just because a trait like extraversion is generally an asset for leaders, does not mean that introverted people can't lead! An introverted person certainly can learn to engage with small and large groups of people, establish credibility with them, and win their hearts and minds. Meanwhile, an extravert may fail badly at listening carefully to others' ideas. Particular traits, intelligences, or strengths may be more valuable than others in specific contexts, but we can learn new behaviors, we can find more favorable contexts, and we can recruit others who complement our own strengths. You may also realize that what you previously perceived as negative qualities are actually strengths. In my own case, I had a reputation in my family for being "hard-headed" and stubborn. Reassessing this characterization in light of desirable leadership traits, I have concluded that what my parents saw as stubbornness might just as easily be labeled persistence, which has been a leadership/followership strength for me.

Another approach to assessment is to reflect on the socialization that strengthened or dampened our genetic predispositions. Researchers have found that experiences that promote "self-management and emotional control, social skill development, and team skills," along with opportunities to lead, help children and adolescents develop a leader identity (Riggio and Mumford, 2011, 454). Susan Murphy and Stephanie Johnson (2011) add that children who have secure attachment to their parents and experience authoritative parenting are best prepared to be leaders. Psychoanalytic theory points more generally to the importance of early authority figures (experienced firsthand or from afar) in shaping our ideal selves (Islam, 2014).

Another component of socialization that affects leader development is prevailing cultural assumptions about what type of person can lead and what leadership might consist of. In this regard, I am thinking of culture as the air we humans breathe, meaning the pervasive societal environment in which we exist. Like the air, we tend to take it for granted. We are hardly ever aware of the molecular structure of the air, just as we are usually not conscious of the deep cultural assumptions that affect how we view and behave in the world. The very idea of authoring one's own life and developing a distinctive leader identity resonates with the individualistic U.S. culture of which I am a part. The view that almost everyone has leadership potential and is likely to be called on to lead in some facet of his or her life is most in sync with the egalitarian, democratic ethos of this society. A more collectivist society is likely to emphasize more than mine the obligation to be a responsible group member and fulfill age- and gender-appropriate roles. Psychology professor Qi Wang reminds us that people from Asian countries may be reluctant to expound on their life stories. "Asians," he says, "believe that a person is largely defined by his or her social status and relationships, leaving little reason to broadcast detailed and revealing personal stories to establish a unique self" (http://tinyurl.com/ofxnpr7). His comments suggest that when leadership educators ask people from more collectivist cultures to write a personal narrative, they may focus more on "external facts than personal details." Additionally, even relatively egalitarian societies may associate "male" behaviors with leadership, or downplay the leadership potential of those who are too young, too old, too "different" (Eagly, 2005). Robin Ely, Herminia Ibarra, and Deborah Kolb (2011) cite numerous studies that show women, and especially women of color, tend to be viewed as less leaderly than men:

> [W]omen are thought to be communal—friendly, unselfish, caretaking—and thus lacking in the qualities required for success in leadership roles (Fletcher, 2004; Heilman, Block, Martell, and Simon, 1989; and Schein,

2001). Women of Asian descent are particularly likely to be stereotyped as passive, reserved, and lacking in ambition, and Latinas are often seen as overemotional (for a review see Giscombe and Mattis, 2001), characteristics that would appear to disqualify these women for leadership. . . . Women in positions of authority are thought too aggressive or not aggressive enough, and what appears assertive, self-confident, or entrepreneurial in a man often looks abrasive, arrogant, or self-promoting in a woman (for a review, see Heilman and Parks-Stamm, 2007). African American women are especially vulnerable to such stereotypes and risk being seen as overly aggressive and confrontational (Bell and Nkomo, 2001).

(477)

Those of us who do not fit mainstream images of leadership may benefit from considering ways that we have defied (and perhaps altered) expectations. Gill Hickman had a head start when her mother named her. Gill was derived from her father's middle name, but her mother chose it because it wouldn't alert those who didn't know her that she was female.

The Rest of the Story

After adolescence, one's readiness for leadership development has a lot to do with predictable phases of life. In young adulthood people are completing vocational or professional training, beginning careers, looking for mates, starting families; in middle age they may be reassessing their paths and seeking renewal, coping with parenting one generation and caring for aging parents; in their 60s they may be contemplating retirement, retooling, coping with empty nests; in old age they may be focused on solidifying their legacy and handing over leadership to younger generations. Of course, crucible experiences, critical moments, positive jolts may come at any time and aren't necessarily linked to particular phases of life.

Herminia Ibarra, Scott Snook, and Laura Ramo (2010) are especially interested in the ways in which people reshape their identities as they undergo role transitions, especially the transition to roles with greater leadership responsibility. Though their work focuses on people who identify as professionals, their argument makes sense for anyone who is called upon to make a major shift in her/his identity as a leader and follower. Building on the work of numerous other researchers, Ibarra, Snook, and Ramo describe personal identity as including historical constructions and social negotiation of current roles, but also ideas of what one might become—that is, possible selves. These possible selves might be attractive or fear-inducing to a person. Stretching into a new leadership role or becoming a more engaged follower may feel scary and inauthentic, if the person has not yet mastered all the competencies needed for the role.

To develop a new story of oneself as a leader at times like these—according to Ibarra, Snook, and Ramo—one essentially must pass through a rite of passage that incorporates three key phases: separation, transition, and incorporation. In the separation phase, a person leaves familiar environments and modes of operating (as, for example, Chuck Palus did when he moved from a focus on engineering to work with human systems). "By doing new things and interacting in different networks, people make new meaning of who they are and who they want to become" (665). Meanwhile, they decrease some previous activities and become less central in older networks. In the transition phase, they are likely to feel conflict about their identity, as they see themselves as not fully who they have been and not yet who they might be. An example from my own leadership journey would be the years I spent during the 1980s helping develop the Reflective Leadership Program at the Humphrey School, when I wasn't certain that I wanted to abandon my previous, more journalistic career for a life as a leadership scholar and educator. In the incorporation phase, people assess the internal and external feedback they have received in the course of practicing new activities. They learn from what works and what doesn't and judge whether the new behaviors seem authentic and congruent with their sense of who they are and want to be; they look for evidence that others are validating them in their role. For someone becoming a leadership educator, important validation would be good course evaluations or published articles.

Ibarra, Snook, and Ramo suggest three methods of helping oneself and others successfully navigate the transition to new leader roles. The first is finding or providing a safe transitional environment, where participants are allowed to play, imagine possibilities, and experiment. This could take the form of participating in simulations, retreats, experimental courses, design charrettes, or studio exercises. Or, you could take a time-out, such as "sabbaticals, educational programs, vacations," and volunteer work (20). (See also Ronit Kark's [2011] exposition of the contributions of "play" to leadership development.) The second method is obtaining guidance from mentors, coaches, and peer groups who are vested in your well-being. The third is ensuring that once you have committed to a new role that you have ongoing support.

Of course, sometimes you and I are thrown into challenging environments (such as Thomas and Bennis's crucibles) that are far more dangerous. Safety is not always guaranteed. Still, we can seek out mentors, coaches, and supportive peers for advice and cheer. We also can develop what Bob Terry calls "exit cards," strategies for getting out of the threatening job or assignment if we can't thrive there. He recommends always having three of these cards. Examples would be starting a degree program that offers a way out, saving money, or developing a consulting practice.

As we reflect on our life stories, we may see that some obstacles to carrying out our commitments are of our own making. Perhaps our egos, our need for approval, our shame, or desire to control has harmed our relationships, tarnished our reputation, and prompted us to take on the wrong or too many assignments. Ron Heifetz and Marty Linsky (2002) urge us to take care of our ego-based "hungers" outside of our leadership practice. Therapy or spiritual practice may be helpful.

Honing courage—the willingness to confront dangers, to consider our own untapped potential, to risk rejection and failure, to reveal our flaws, to seek forgiveness—is an important part of this process. Margaret Wheatley (2002) notes that the root of courage is the French word for heart. "We develop courage for those things that speak to our heart" (25). Reviewing our life stories to discern when we have acted courageously on behalf of the people (including ourselves) and causes we care about may help us see that we are more courageous than we think we are.

The Embodied Self

Our bodies tell our stories in multiple ways. So far I've emphasized writing and speaking. We also communicate our stories and our leaderly stance via the clothes we wear, the adornments we choose, the way we move, our physical features (Ladkin and Taylor, 2010). Erving Goffman's *Presentation of Self in Everyday Life* (1959) reminds us that clothes and body language create social meaning. They help humans know what role a person is playing, what to expect, whether the person is one of the group, and what degree of authority he or she carries. Our bodies connect us to categories and narratives about gender, ethnicity, sexual orientation, and physical ability.

As leadership educators in the classroom or other learning spaces, we want our bodies to tell something of our personal story, but also respect our audience's expectations. We want to receive the audience's respect in turn even while stirring them up. Perhaps we teach in a setting that attaches authority and credibility to "dressing up," so we wear the required suit and well-shined shoes, but we alter the usual formal outfit, by adding a signature adornment or letting that tattoo show a bit. Maybe we don't dress up, and make it clear as we go that we think there are more important ways to show respect. As an elementary school student, I squirmed with boredom as I watched many of my teachers appear before us hour after hour, day after day, in the same drab, unimaginative attire. I vowed that if I ever found myself in their role, I would at least wear an outfit that was pleasing to look at. Thus today, my clothing in the classroom or workshop setting might convey that I'm a visual artist in my spare time and—because I want to engage with everyone—that I am ready to move around our shared space.

Obviously, we can never control the way that others see us and the meaning they make of our physical presence. For example, I'd like for the people I work with to see my wrinkles as a sign of experience and wisdom, but I can't help it if their first reaction is to think, oh, she's probably behind the times. The best we can do is to consciously connect the stories we tell through our bodily presence to the stories we tell in other ways.

Donna Ladkin and Steven Taylor (2010) explain further how we might "create authentic performances" as embodied leaders. Drawing on the acting system articulated by Constantin Stanislavski, they suggest that audiences are likely to see our performances as believable if they express emotions that we truly feel. They note,

> Stanislavski works to overcome the tendency we have in the West to sever the externally active physical body from its interior life of thinking and feeling. His system highlights the inseparability of inner and outer bodily being, and the critical nature of that relationship in authentic enactment.
>
> *(68–69)*

Thus, if we are truly excited about leadership development and committed to students, we show that through our energetic movements, through our animated faces, through our commiseration when a student isn't getting it. Ladkin and Taylor go on to suggest that one activates his/her emotional response to the work by "recalling and articulating the narrative of one's life and particular key incidents in the generation of one's leadership identity" (69). In expressing that response, we take cues from those around us, we are in "communion" with them, "authentically connecting and being influenced by and influencing others on a moment by moment basis" (69). We may also rehearse and experiment with varying ways of expressing the complexities of our emotions. We make choices, for example, about just how vulnerable to be. At the same time, Ladkin and Taylor suggest that a certain amount of discomfort may be necessary to keep experimenting and developing. They argue that "equating authenticity with a felt sense of comfort or familiarity limits the potential for developing a dynamic and robust enactment of the 'true self,' which necessarily needs to grow in response to changing circumstances and situational demands" (71). Finally, Ladkin and Taylor suggest that effective leaders shape their performances in keeping with a story about the group's identity. They cite Keith Grint's view that leadership

> involves the art of articulating a group's identity, framing a narrative of who they are and how they have come to be, as well as where they are going. This identification in some way also prescribes the actions which a leader can embody and still be accepted as a leader of a group.
>
> *(72)*

For example, as leadership educators we may foster a group identity as a leadership learning community and choose at times to move our bodies out of the way and turn the floor over to class members.

★★★

Scholars link the telling of life stories to leadership development in several ways. From a psychological and moral perspective, life stories provide a meaning system that can help leaders and engaged followers articulate and honor their commitments. Telling these stories can empower the teller, but hearing diverse leadership stories also has an empowering effect on others. Because these stories are an expression of one's identity as a leader (or engaged follower), this chapter has explored the effect of genetic blueprints, early experiences, and culture on identity development. I also suggested paying attention to personality traits, multiple intelligences, and signature strengths, and noted the possibility of reshaping one's identity in the course of role transitions and other challenging experiences. Finally, I've drawn attention to the stories that our bodies tell as we engage in leadership and followership work. The next chapter will describe several practical methods for helping participants in leadership programs develop and reflect on their personal narratives.

References

Bandura, A. (1997). *Self-efficacy: The exercise of control.* New York: Freeman.

Bateson, M. C. (2007). *Composing a life.* New York: Grove.

Bateson, M. C. (2010). *Composing a further life.* New York: Knopf.

Bell, E., & Nkomo, S. (2001). *Our separate ways.* Cambridge, MA: Harvard Business School Press.

Bordas, J. (2012). *Salsa, soul, and spirit: Leadership for a multicultural age.* San Francisco: Berrett-Koehler Publishers, Inc.

Day, D. V., Harrison, M. M., & Halpin, S. M. (2009). *An integrative approach to leader development: Connecting adult development, identity, and expertise.* New York: Routledge.

Day, D. V., & Sin, H. (2011). Longitudinal tests of an integrative model of leader development: From childhood through adulthood. *Leadership Quarterly, 22*(3), 545–560.

Eagly, A. H. (2005). Achieving relational authenticity in leadership: Does gender matter? *Leadership Quarterly, 16*(3), 459–474.

Ely, R. J., Ibarra, H., & Kolb, D. M. (2011). Taking gender into account: Theory and design for women's leadership development programs. *Academy of Management Learning & Education, 10*(3), 474–493.

Fletcher, J. K. (2004). The paradox of post heroic leadership: An essay on gender, power, and transformational change. *Leadership Quarterly, 15*, 647–661.

Gardner, H. (1995). *Leading minds.* New York: Basic Books.

Gardner, H. (2011). *Frames of mind: The theory of multiple intelligences.* New York: Basic Books.

Giscombe, K., & Mattis, M. C. (2001). Leveling the playing field for women of color in corporate management: Is the business case enough? *Journal of Business Ethics, 37*, 103–119.

Goffman, F. (1959). *The presentation of self in everyday life.* New York. Anchor/Doubleday.

Goleman, D., Boyatzis, R., & McKee, A. (2002). *Primal leadership: Realizing the power of emotional intelligence.* Boston, MA: Harvard Business School Press.

Haidt, J. (2012). *The righteous mind: Why good people are divided by politics and religion.* New York: Pantheon.

Heifetz, R. A., & Linsky, M. (2002). *Leadership on the line: Staying alive through the dangers of leading.* Boston, MA: Harvard Business School Press.

Heilman, M. E., Block, C. J., Martell, R. F., & Simon, M. (1989). Has anything changed? Current characterizations of men, women and managers. *Journal of Applied Psychology, 74*, 935–942.

Heilman, M. E., & Parks-Stamm, E. J. (2007). Gender stereotypes in the workplace: Obstacles to women's career progress. In S. J. Correll (Ed.), *Social psychology of gender: Advances in group processes* (pp. 47–77). Greenwich, CT: JAI Press.

Heller, C. (n.d.). "Notes on an ecology of everyday life," retrieved April 14, 2016 from http://social-ecology.org/wp/1999/01/notes-on-an-ecology-of-everyday-life/

Ibarra, H., Snook, S., & Ramo, L. G. (2010). Identity-based leader development. In N. Nohria & R. Khurana (Eds.), *Handbook of leadership theory and practice* (p. 22). Boston, MA: Harvard Business Press.

Islam, G. (2014). Identities and ideals: Psychoanalytic dialogues of self and leadership. *Leadership, 10*(3), 344–360.

Judge, T. A., Bono, J., Ilies, R., & Gerhard, M. (2002). Personality and leadership: A qualitative and quantitative review. *Journal of Applied Psychology, 87*, 765–780.

Kark, R. (2011). Games managers play: Play as a form of leadership development. *Academy of Management Learning & Education, 10*(3), 507–527.

Kheel, M. (1991). Ecofeminism and deep ecology: Reflections on identity and difference. *The Trumpeter Journal of Ecosophy, 8*(2), 62–71.

Ladkin, D., & Taylor, S. S. (2010). Enacting the 'true self': Towards a theory of embodied authentic leadership. *Leadership Quarterly, 21*(1), 64–74.

Maslow, A. H. (1943). A theory of human motivation. *Psychological Review, 50*, 370–396.

Murphy, S. E., & Johnson, S. K. (2011). The benefits of a long-lens approach to leader development: Understanding the seeds of leadership. *Leadership Quarterly, 22*, 459–470.

Obama, B. (2007). *Dreams from my father: A story of race and inheritance*. New York: Crown.

Park, N., Peterson, C., & Seligman, M. E. P. (2004). Strengths of character and well-being. *Journal of Social and Clinical Psychology, 23*, 603–619.

Reichard, R. J., Riggio, R. E., Guerin, D. W., Oliver, P. H., Gottfried, A. W., & Gottfried, A. E. (2011). A longitudinal analysis of relationships between adolescent personality and intelligence with adult leader emergence and transformational leadership. *Leadership Quarterly, 22*(3), 471–481.

Riggio, R. E., & Mumford, M. D. (2011). Introduction to the special issue: Longitudinal studies of leadership development. *Leadership Quarterly, 22*(3), 453–456.

Schein, V. E. (2001). A global look at the psychological barriers to women's progress in management. *Journal of Social Issues, 57*, 675–688.

Seligman, M. E. P. (2002). *Authentic happiness: Using the new positive psychology to realize your potential for lasting fulfillment*. New York: Free Press.

Shamir, B., & Eilam, G. (2005). "What's your story?": A life-stories approach to authentic leadership development. *Leadership Quarterly, 16*(3), 395–418.

Spreitzer, G. M., & Grant, A. M. (2004). *Leading to grow and growing to lead: Some lessons from positive organizational scholarship*. Paper presented at the Leadership: Bridging Theory-Practice Divide Conference, INSEAD, France, May 10.

Watson, L. W., & Johnson, J. M. (Eds.). (2013). *Authentic leadership: An engaged discussion of LGBTQ work as culturally relevant*. Charlotte, NC: Information Age.

Western, S. (2013). *Leadership: A critical analysis*. London: SAGE.

Wheatley, M. J. (2002). *Turning to one another: Simple conversations to restore hope to the future*. San Francisco: Berrett-Koehler.

3

USING PERSONAL NARRATIVE AND THE HANDS

Leadership arises at the intersection of personal passions and public needs.
Barbara Crosby and John Bryson (2005)

As leadership educators we will encounter learners with varying degrees of training in human psychology, spirituality, and so on. They will have different learning styles and personality types. All, however, will be meaning makers, and telling their stories can help them make sense of their (and others') lives. These narratives help their creators integrate past, present, and future selves; shadow and light; successes and failures. They help them show up as authentic human beings—and that's what leadership is all about. You—your embodied self—are the prime instrument you have to work with in leadership. As Bob Denhardt asserts, "Leadership development is the same as personal development."

Creating narratives of leadership and engaged followership, sharing them with others, and revisiting them constitute a key reflective practice for those who aspire to be better leaders. The aim of the practice is deepened self-awareness of the following kinds:

- Identifying strengths (in order to build on them), acknowledging weaknesses, and knowing where you get in trouble
- Developing lessons or guidance for the future
- Telling your own story as an opening for others to tell theirs
- Understanding your dual identities as leader and follower
- Understanding what has shaped you, and what is likely to shape you
- Identifying core concerns or commitments that are your basis for leadership

This chapter focuses on the nitty-gritty of guiding participants in our classes and workshops through creating personal narratives (of many forms) as a foundation for their effort to gain more knowledge and skill in their leadership work. The first section covers some general considerations for planning and introducing exercises involving reflection on personal values, experiences, and aspirations. The next offers several written and oral exercises that have been especially successful in my own practice; and in addition, I suggest some exercises that other leadership educators find to be highly valuable. The chapter concludes with attention to visual narratives and consideration of how learning about ourselves better prepares us to work with diverse groups.

Getting Started

Leadership educators who are sharing their ideas in this book variously see the classroom or workshop setting as a learning laboratory, a studio, or place of play and reflection—much like Ron Heifetz's (1994) "holding environment." In this environment, participants ideally will be shifted out of habitual responses yet feel safe enough to talk about the emotional discomfort that reflection on their lives may induce (Petriglieri, Wood, and Petriglieri, 2011). In my own classes and workshops, I usually begin with low-risk exercises designed to help participants reveal something of their life stories and start to develop a picture of the multiple leadership and followership definitions that they hold. One of my favorite icebreakers is the "grandparent exercise," because it moves participants away from the usual identification with titles and roles, prompts reflection on early influences, and reveals something about their leadership perspectives. The directions are simple: "Take two minutes to describe one of your grandparents and how that person has affected your leadership development." I might put the directions on a flip chart sheet or projector screen before the class begins so that everyone, especially the introverts, has time to get a response in mind. After everyone has had a chance to talk about a grandparent for two minutes, I ask participants to comment on what themes they heard in the comments. They are likely to note themes like the following: grandparents who insisted on (or served as a role model for) the value of hard work or education, grandparents who were community leaders, or grandparents who cared for others.

Often in these settings, the participants are a mix of international and U.S. people. This exercise often reveals that many of the U.S. people have ties to countries around the world, and that family experiences and influences aren't entirely different from one culture to another. The exercise is a start for both the self-awareness and understanding of others that will be developed throughout the course or workshop.

I may follow this exercise with one more directly aimed at surfacing the definitions of leadership and followership that people bring with them to the classroom. An example is Pictures of Leadership and Followership. I first invite everyone to quickly draw a picture of leadership. When the sketches are done I may ask the group to tape them to the walls or I may simply ask participants to take turns holding up their sketches and talking about them. After participants have explained their sketches, I ask them to look for themes across the pictures, and I may begin connecting those themes to major leadership perspectives that we will review later.

I then ask everyone to quickly draw a picture of followership and repeat the process of sharing the pictures and talking about them. As the group mentions themes across the pictures, I link those themes to scholars' different views on followership. Two key takeaways emerge from this exercise: first, that the group represents a wide range of views about leadership and followership and, second, that leadership and followership may have similarities.

How much attention I give to exploring major theories of leadership will vary depending on the length of a course or the purpose of a workshop. I do explain, as Wilfred Drath (2000) has pointed out, that different individuals and groups can be expected to have their own leadership theories, and it's helpful both to clarify your own and to know some of the main perspectives you are likely to encounter.

Tracey Manning notes that many participants in our courses and workshops will have to unlearn their implicit theories about leadership if they are to see themselves as leaders. Kevin Gerdes asks participants to reflect on how they are constrained by their definitions of leadership. Once a midcareer student in my Leadership for the Common Good course noted after a few sessions: "Now I get it. All along I've focused on 'Big L leaders,' like the President of the country or the CEO of a company. Now I see there can be 'little l leaders,' like the rest of us."

I emphasize that the two starting places for leadership are what you bring to the work, and the context (including prevailing leadership theories) in which you are working. The next three parts of this book will give more attention to the context for leadership. For now let's proceed to additional exercises that can help course or workshop participants tell their life stories effectively.

Deepening the Work

Clearly, working with personal narrative is sensitive territory, and leadership educators must introduce exercises involving deep personal reflection accordingly. To allay fears and build enthusiasm for exploring the territory, we can emphasize the valuable outcomes of the exercises, the virtues of reflective engagement with one's life story, and our commitment to providing a safe environment for these explorations. We should acknowledge that creating and reflecting on our life stories will summon a variety of emotions—for example, pride, regret, anger, sadness, joy, and hope. We may explain that taking time to attend to these emotions helps us better understand what our experiences mean for us and allow us to craft self-guidance for the future. (The article by Shamir and Eilam and the chapter by Ibarra, Snook, and Ramo—both described in the previous chapter—may be helpful assigned readings.) When I introduce many of the exercises that will be described in this chapter, I encourage participants to be as honest as possible, but also assure them that they will decide how much of their writing to share with others. My colleague Kevin Gerdes notes, "We should recognize that not everyone is ready to deeply explore emotions and thoughts. We should help, rather than push."

In some group learning environments, trust may be too low to allow much openness among participants. Perhaps people in the room are from competing organizations or groups. Several years ago, I led a leadership development workshop for top managers from heavy industry in Poland. These men were not about to reveal much about their deepest hopes and fears in a large group, though some spoke to me afterward about their desire to be more self-aware.

Personal narrative exercises also offer opportunities for us to model the authenticity we encourage in our students. When Gary DeCramer introduced the Narrative of Commitment into the leadership course he and I taught together for several years, he offered his own narrative as a model. The personal story I offered at the beginning of Chapter 1 is my version of this exercise. Carol Pearson notes that leadership educators have a responsibility to convey research findings in our classes, but theories and data help only up to a point. Providing insights from our personal experiences can help participants make sense of the theories and data. "Then my truth," says Pearson, "can help you find your truth."

By revealing our aspirations and failures, by making clear what we care deeply about, we model the vulnerability we believe is essential to learning. Still, crafting a personal narrative for leadership development is not mainly confessional; many details of our personal struggles are best reserved for the therapist's couch, conversations with closest friends, or private contemplation.

We have additional ways to make our learning environments safe for participants' deep reflection and experimentation. At the outset of a workshop or course, we can set appropriate ground rules and give participants a chance to discuss and alter them. If the group will be together for some time, I engage participants in a norm-setting exercise (see Inset 3.1)

INSET 3.1   USING SNOW CARDS TO IDENTIFY AND AGREE ON NORMS

1.   Ask the group the question: What norms or standards would be good for us to establish to help us accomplish our work together? Think of "the unwritten rules" that might improve performance, inspire commitment, or enhance satisfaction.

2.   Have individuals in the group brainstorm as many ideas as possible and record each idea on a separate "snow card," such as a:

Post-It note
5" x 7" cards
oval
square of paper

3. Have individuals share their ideas in round-robin fashion.
4. Tape the ideas to the wall. As a group, remove duplication and cluster similar ideas in categories. Establish subcategories as needed. The resulting clusters of cards may resemble a "blizzard" of ideas—hence the term "snow cards."
3. Clarify ideas.
4. Once all the ideas are on the wall and included in a category, rearrange and tinker with the categories until they make the most sense. Place a card with the category name above each cluster.
5. If needed, help the group decide which clusters or individual norms have strong group support (for example, by giving each person a certain number of sticky dots to apply to the norms he or she deems most important).
6. As a group, decide how to monitor and reinforce the norms.

After the exercise, distribute a copy of the norms listed by categories to all members of the group.

The exercise never fails to elicit participants' desire to respect each other's ideas, to listen to each other, and to be heard. After the snow cards have been organized on the wall, you may ask participants to talk about what the norms mean to them and offer ideas for monitoring and reinforcing them. The conversation may reveal norms that should be altered or set aside. The final collection of cards can then be typed up and distributed to the group and perhaps posted on the wall in future meetings. Naturally, the norms will be observed unevenly as the group works together, but they provide a touchstone that can be called on as needed.

Organizing ongoing small groups, or "Action Learning Circles," also can support learning. Action Learning Circles focus on members' leadership practice and allow each person to share his/her own leadership actions and aspirations with the group. The groups can be a setting for sharing the Narrative of Commitment or the Leadership Highs and Lows exercise described below. In describing the circles, I explain that the aim is not to solve each other's problems, but to listen deeply to each other, and respond with inquiry and insights. Everyone should try to maintain the practice of not fixing or advising. (The use of Action Learning Circles will be described further in Chapter 15.)

Working with leadership narratives in safe learning environments can be highly therapeutic. At times, though, participants may be grappling with psychologically stressful issues that require the aid of psychotherapists. Gianpiero Petriglieri, Jack Wood, and Jennifer Petriglieri (2011) actually include consultation with a psychotherapist in their leadership curriculum for M.B.A. students and report on the benefits of doing so. Most leadership educators might not be able to have a psychotherapist on our teaching staff, but we can stay attuned to learner needs and be prepared to refer participants to appropriate counseling and care if they need it.

Leadership Highs and Lows

Exploring Personal Highs and Lows (see Inset 3.2) is an exercise I have used in many settings in the U.S. and Europe. It asks participants to construct a personal timeline that helps them identify connections between their personal lives and leadership work, and identify themes that link their successes and failures. It prompts them to articulate lessons for their future work.

INSET 3.2   EXPLORING PERSONAL HIGHS AND LOWS

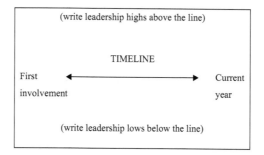

Create a personal timeline

- Take out a sheet of paper, turn it sideways, and draw a line from left to right that divides the paper into top and bottom halves of equal size.
- At the right-hand end of the line, write in the current year. At the left-hand end of the line, write in the date of your first involvement in dealing with organizational or societal problems.

Identify leadership highs and lows

- Think about the organizational or societal problems you have worked on over the time-span you have marked out.
- Leadership highs: In the appropriate place above the timeline, mark, date, and label times when your involvement helped remedy these problems.

The distance of each mark above the timeline should represent just how successful the experience was.

- Leadership lows: In the appropriate place below the timeline, mark, date, and label times when you were unable to help remedy these problems. The distance of each mark below the timeline should represent just how unsuccessful the experience was.

Add other personal events

- At the appropriate points on the timeline, fill in as highs or lows any important events that have occurred in your personal life, such as weddings, births, divorces, deaths of relatives or friends, the establishment or breakup of important relationships, graduations, layoffs, and so forth.

Identify themes

- Write down themes that are common to the "highs."
- Write down themes that are common to the "lows."

Discover lessons

- What lessons do you learn from this analysis? What guidance would you give yourself for the future? Write some notes about the lessons and guidance.

Share results

- Share these results with someone who knows you well and whose friendship, support, and insights you value. Ask for observations and feedback.

Typically, I lead participants through the exercise, which takes at least an hour and a half for completion and debriefing. I encourage them to include as many key experiences and events as possible. Note that the exercise asks the participant to begin plotting events on the timeline by identifying "organizational or societal problems you have worked on." The language is intentional. First of all, it fits with the understanding that leadership is about tackling the shared problems that a group confronts. Second, it may help expand the participants' thinking about leadership. The exercise does not ask about filling leader roles or positions but rather about involvement in problem solving. You could strip the word leadership out of the exercise in order to help participants think about when they have had or not had desired impacts as leaders and committed followers.

Once participants have completed developing their timelines, I ask them to choose one other person with whom to share the results. You should set aside at least 10 minutes for this part of the exercise, so that each participant has five minutes to report on his/her timeline and receive some feedback from the partner. Once everyone is paired with a partner, the room usually erupts with intense conversation; if there's time, you might extend the time for this part of the exercise.

After 10 minutes, I call the group together once again and ask for ah-has, or surprising insights that people had or heard from partners. Typical responses might be: "I realized that my professional highs were accompanied by personal lows and vice versa" or "A terrible low became the starting place for my climb toward a high." A participant might realize that all his leadership highs occurred when he was part of a strong team or when he was able to exercise more control over a group's process. I wind up the exercise by encouraging participants to continue adding to and reflecting on the exercise following the session.

If you want to add to this exercise, you might do something that Carol Pearson recommends: Ask participants to review their timelines and think about times they held back from leading. Perhaps they will see that was a wise decision, but they might also see a missed opportunity for having needed impact; from this reflection, they might formulate guidance for their future leadership.

Cares and Concerns

Other exercises help clarify the values that are core to participants' identity as leaders. Discovering Cares and Concerns (see Inset 3.3) directly reveals core values by helping us think about what we profess to care about and how that matches with our behavior. "Concern," here carries a double meaning—both what I pay attention to or feel connected to and what I worry about. The exercise could be a homework assignment or done in a class session. The results could be shared in person or online in order to encourage feedback and reveal similarities and differences among participants. Completing the exercise only requires a few minutes, but it helps people think about what fuels (or might fuel) their leadership work.

INSET 3.3 DISCOVERING CARES AND CONCERNS

1. What do I deeply care about in my family, occupational, and community (or public) life? What are my main concerns connected to my family, occupational, and community (or public) life? In other words, what truly matters to me?

2. What is the extent of my commitment to acting on these cares and concerns? Is there a gap between what I really care about and how I spend my time?

3. How do or might my cares and concerns summon me to leadership?

Numerous other values clarification exercises could replace or supplement these. Ronnie Brooks asks participants in her leadership development sessions to focus on two or three core values. Other colleagues have used a "Personal Credo" or "This I Believe" exercise, which asks participants to state quite succinctly the key beliefs that guide their lives. The result might be a written or videotaped statement. (An option is to invite participants to contribute their essays or recordings to the This I Believe Project [http://thisibelieve.org/], which was inspired by Edward R. Murrow's radio series in the 1950s.) Another, visual version of the exercise is construction of a personal shield or crest that bears various symbols of one's key values or beliefs.

Narrative of Commitment, Crucible Experiences, Critical Decisions

The Narrative of Commitment (see Inset 3.4) is an extended essay about how a person enacts his/her values. The directions ask the narrator to identify a moral commitment that is central to his or her life and proceeds to ask about the roots of the commitment, what difficulties the narrator has encountered in trying to live out the commitment, and what helps him or her stay committed despite the obstacles. This works best as a homework assignment that is brought to a face-to-face session for sharing with a partner and engaging in a large group discussion about the experience of completing the essay. In extended courses, I assign the essay for an early session and ask participants to refine it toward the end of the course in light of additional insights they have gained as the course progressed.

INSET 3.4   COMPOSING A NARRATIVE OF COMMITMENT

This is an exercise that serves as a means of examining the values that shape and support your ethical practice. Be prepared to discuss *with one other person in class* what you have learned about the connection between the story of your own leadership and your commitment to ethical practice. This assignment is collected by the instructors but it is not graded.

This Narrative of Commitment was created by Dr. Stephen Brookfield, a professor at the University of St. Thomas in St. Paul, MN. Professor Brookfield sees narrative as a way of knowing, a way of reflecting on our moral commitments and exploring how we have lived those commitments in light of the critical incidents in our lives. This exercise is a way of telling the story of how we have come to live our own values.

The final version of the narrative should be three to four double-spaced pages. Here is guidance for composing it.

1) Choose one commitment. State this succinctly.
2) Describe the process by which you came to develop this commitment. Did an event, a person, your faith, or some other source inspire you?
3) Describe the barriers, frustrations, and failures you have experienced in your struggle to live out this commitment.
4) What sustains you in the practice of this commitment? Say what moments of joy, affirmations of faith, and/or peak emotional experiences and satisfactions sustain you, keep you moving forward on your quest to live out this commitment.

In a certain way, the Narrative of Commitment follows the arc of a hero's journey. It begins with a commitment to act on one's moral calling and with recognition that the calling is connected to the people and places that have shaped us. It then proceeds through trials and concludes with a sense of achievement and momentum (Pearson, 1991). Of course, not all will feel that they have accomplished what they sought to do; the exercise might be a prompt to seek more support and find more joy in the effort.

Note that the exercise emphasizes the importance of critical incidents (which might include crucible experiences). In assigning the exercise, you may explore the nature of such incidents. These are the times when our values are tested, when we have to summon the courage to persist despite our own self-doubts, pushback from the authorities, and no guarantee of success. In my own narrative I hint at several critical incidents, but give most attention to a prolonged effort to become an adept public speaker. That effort included a string of critical incidents and decisions; it also taught me the value of seeking help from others—my spouse, who was a supportive coach; speech pros; and therapists.

To foster learning specifically about crucible experiences, you might ask participants in your course to do the following:

1. Think about an especially challenging time in your life, a time that might be labeled a "trial by fire."
2. What feelings did that evoke? How did you respond?
3. How has that experience shaped you since?

You could construct a similar exercise around decisions that have affected participants' leadership trajectory. To help participants recall critical decisions, you might evoke the metaphor of a crossroad: When were they at a crossroads in their lives? How did the choice of path affect their subsequent work and identities?

A useful additional exercise prompts participants to consider the experiences within their families, schools, and communities that helped them develop their strengths, other-regarding values, and sense of self-efficacy. The exercise is likely to reveal ways in which they deviate from the "best" preparation for leadership. Their parents or parent may have taken a laissez-faire or even punitive approach to child-raising. Perhaps another relative, a teacher, or a coach provided that adult support that is so vital to a child's well-being and development. Perhaps they identify ways in which early experiences are still hampering their ability to lead effectively. As part of the debriefing of the exercise, an instructor or coach can help participants consider reframing those experiences, possibly with the aid of psychotherapy, and seeking retraining in particular skill areas.

Other Assets and Liabilities

Leadership educators can choose from a wide array of instruments that help participants identify the traits and other characteristics that may strengthen or undermine their leadership and followership work. Among the most popular is the Myers-Briggs Type Indicator (MBTI), which I have used extensively. I also will describe several other personality and intelligence assessments. Two exercises I find helpful are Analyzing Social Group Membership and Assessing Additional Strengths and Weaknesses (Crosby and Bryson, 2005).

Myers-Briggs

The MBTI, based on a psychological theory developed by Katherine Cook and Isabel Briggs Myers, is an instrument with decades of use around the world. According to Myers-Briggs theory, everyone has a personality type based on his/her orientation to the world (extraversion vs. introversion), preferred way of taking in information (sensing vs. intuiting), preferred way of evaluating that information (feeling vs. thinking), and preferred approach to experiences (judging vs. perceiving). When I include the MBTI in my courses and workshops, I explain that it was originally conceived as a tool to reduce violent conflict by fostering interpersonal understanding. (Isabel Briggs Myers believed that if human beings could communicate more perceptively with people who were different from them, violence would become less likely.) I note that the publishers of the MBTI can cite lots of evidence that the instrument is reliable and valid across cultures. Although I describe MBTI as a valuable tool for personal and group development, I emphasize that it is often misused to "typecast" people and prejudge their capabilities.

I emphasize that the Myers-Briggs is designed to reveal preferred ways of behaving; it can be thought of as revealing one's default mode. To demonstrate this, I ask participants to cross their arms, while doing so myself. Then I ask them to try the opposite way. If we are physically able to do this, we all have a default for how we cross our arms. At the same time, we can cross our arms in the opposite direction. Similarly, the MBTI indicates preferences and how clear one is about those preferences, while recognizing that people can engage in a wider range of behaviors.

My aim in leadership development is not to explore type theory deeply, but to encourage participants to reflect on whether the four-letter type that emerges from completing the instrument seems to fit for them. I arrange for participants to take the MBTI online, and distribute their reports when we meet face-to-face. After giving them time to read the descriptions of their type, I engage them in several exercises designed to help them understand their own preferences and opposing preferences. (See Figure 3.1 for a list of the four Myers-Briggs dichotomies.)

To focus on the extraversion-introversion distinction, I ask all the people with extraversion preference to stand on one side of the room and those with introversion to stand on the other. I ask each group to come up with a list of questions they would like to ask the other group. Usually the extraverted group immediately launches into spirited conversation, while the introverted group begins more tentatively. (Later, I can draw attention to this as further evidence of different tendencies for the two groups.) After each group has developed a list of at least

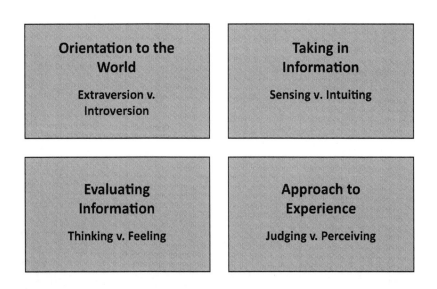

FIGURE 3.1 Myers-Briggs Dichotomies

five questions, I ask the introverts to begin the questioning. The groups then take turns answering and asking questions. Often, the extraverts interrupt each other and even the introverts. Once the questions and answers are complete, I ask for observations and offer some of my own.

To illuminate the sensing-intuiting distinction, I may ask participants individually to look at an object or a picture and describe it. I then ask a participant with sensing preference to give his or her description and then someone with intuiting preference to do the same; I do this for a few rounds until I have generated several entries on a two-column flip chart sheet. The sensing column is likely to include very concrete descriptors and the intuiting column far more abstract and imaginative descriptors, making the point that people with sensing preference attend to data that can be apprehended by the senses, whereas people with intuiting preference attend to patterns, symbols, and possibility. I ask participants to comment on the contrasts between the two columns and ask them to think about the strengths and weaknesses of their own preferences.

To foster insight into the thinking-feeling dichotomy, I divide the participants into small groups of like preference. I then give them an assignment that is likely to elicit contrasting responses from people who rely on an impersonal, or thinking, logic and people who rely on a personal, or feeling, logic. For example, the groups might be in charge of a soccer team that has a chance to go to a state tournament. In order to play, however, the coaches must cut their roster by three players. The group's assignment is to decide on a process for doing this. Typically, the groups with thinking preference will establish a list of "fair," skill-based criteria for choosing the players to drop. They seek to win as the primary goal. The groups with feeling preference will offer creative ways to involve all the players in the tournament even if they don't play. Their list of criteria is likely to include more than simply a player's soccer skill. Goals other than winning are likely to be significant. After hearing each group's ideas, I again ask participants to think about what the exercise might reveal about the strengths and weaknesses of their preferences and about implications for working with people who have the opposite preference.

For the judging-perceiving dichotomy, I may give participants some examples that contrast the more spontaneous lifestyle associated with perceiving preference with the more ordered lifestyle associated with judging preference. I might describe what it's like for a "mixed" couple to go on a vacation together. The person acting on a perceiving preference advocates going with the flow. "Let's just get our plane tickets and find a hotel once we're there," she proclaims. Her partner, the one with judging preference, reacts with horror. She needs to know where she'll be staying and what will be on each day's agenda. Clearly, some negotiation is required! I then turn participants' attention to working in teams and note that the judging versus perceiving differences often affect how people respond to timelines and due dates. I may ask the large group for comments on how this preference affects them in seeking to lead and follow effectively.

If I have time, I may ask participants as a whole or in small groups to comment on the following:

- surprises they have had about themselves and others as a result of our work with the MBTI
- ideas for working with the same and opposite types
- ideas for working effectively in environments that are not supportive of one's preferred ways of learning and working

Along the way or in conclusion, I highlight the potential for misusing the MBTI. People may be tempted to stereotype or pigeonhole each other. They may falsely assume that Myers-Briggs type has something to do with a person's ability to perform a particular job. The level of clarity connected to one's preferences also can be misinterpreted. For example, a low clarity score for a person with feeling preference does not mean that he or she is a "weak" feeling type, but rather has low certainty about the preference.

A drawback to using MBTI is that you should either be certified yourself in administering it, or work with a colleague who is certified. Training is available through the Myers & Briggs Foundation (https://mbtitraininginstitute.myers-briggs.org/) or CPP, publishers of the MBTI.

Additional Personality and Intelligence Assessments

An example of a Big Five assessment is the International Personality Item Pool (http://www.personal.psu.edu/~j5j/IPIP/ipipneo120.htm). About.com offers a multiple intelligences quiz based on Howard Gardner's work, though Gardner himself warns that self-report is probably not the most accurate way to assess one's intelligences. He does endorse a reflective exercise that helps people understand the different intelligences (go to http://multipleintelligencesoasis.org/what-mi-am-i/). Gardner has noted that spiritual intelligence is a candidate for inclusion in his list. A means of exploring this intelligence is to invite participants to compose a spiritual autobiography that highlights sources of deep meaning in their lives and how their understanding has evolved over time. In the emotional intelligence realm, the Hay Group offers An Emotional and Social Competencies Inventory developed with Daniel Goleman and Richard Boyatzis (http://tinyurl.com/nsypu4a).

Martin Seligman offers an assessment, based on his strengths taxonomy, that indicates which strengths are prominent for each of us. (See https://www.authentic happiness.sas.upenn.edu/). The popular StrengthsFinder assessments (Rath and Conchie, 2008) are based on a similar view of adult development.

Analyzing Social Group Membership

The first part of this exercise (see Inset 3.5) is designed to help participants reflect on how their important social identities affect their leadership practice. Ideally, the exercise will be a homework assignment so the participant can take adequate time to comment on how his or her gender, race/ethnicity, sexual orientation, nationality, religion, class, age, and physical ability both strengthen his/her leadership and make it more difficult. When participants come to class with the completed exercise, I may ask them to meet in small groups to share ah-has from the exercise. After 15 minutes, I may open a large group conversation lasting 20–40 minutes about insights that came up in the small groups. I am likely to take each identity dimension in turn. During that conversation, I want to be sure that participants or I cover the following:

- The influence of context on whether one's identity as a woman, say, is a strength or a liability. A female participant, for example, may note that her gender has been an asset in her work on aging issues. A man may concede that his gender seems to be an asset no matter the context, or he may note that his gender stands in the way of relating effectively to a predominantly female group.
- The likelihood that we take some aspects of our identity for granted and seldom question their impact on our leadership work, especially when that identity is dominant in the community in which we work. For example, the effects of our nationality may be fairly invisible if we have lived all our lives in the same country; it may make working with multinational groups more difficult, however. In the U.S., we typically downplay class identification distinctions, but being from a low-income background, for example, may mean that a person is uncomfortable working with people from wealthier backgrounds.
- The connection of social identity and power. When our identities match that of dominant groups in a particular context, we may have easier paths to leadership in that context. If I am an atheist, for example, I may have difficulty getting elected President in the U.S., because of the dominance of Christian religious identification in the country.
- The inseparability of our social identities. I am a white, over-60, temporarily able-bodied, relatively affluent, U.S. woman, now affiliated with a progressive Congregational church. In my past, some of these descriptors would have been quite different, and I remain influenced by that past.

INSET 3.5 ANALYZING SOCIAL GROUP MEMBERSHIP

Part 1

How do these personal characteristics affect your leadership?

	Strengthens my leadership	*Makes my leadership more difficult*
Gender		
Race/ethnicity		
Sexual Orientation		
Nationality		
Religion		
Class		
Age		
Physical Ability		

Part 2

Bridging differences

1. What are the causes of negative stereotypes about members of a group other than one's own?
2. What methods can be used to overcome prejudice and discrimination?
3. What strategies have you found effective for understanding and connecting with people who are different from you?

Reprinted with permission from *Leadership for the Common Good*, by Barbara C. Crosby and John M. Bryson, published by Jossey-Bass. Copyright © 2005 by John Wiley & Sons, Inc. All rights reserved.

Assessing Additional Strengths and Weaknesses

This exercise (see Inset 3.6) draws on insights from the other exercises described so far, but also can stand alone. It does presume that participants have already begun to clarify their "leadership passion," the essential asset for personal leadership. (The Discovering Cares and Concerns exercise is a means of suggesting where this passion lies.) The questions highlight qualities and resources that researchers have identified as valuable personal assets for leadership (Crosby and Bryson, 2005).

INSET 3.6 ASSESSING ADDITIONAL STRENGTHS AND WEAKNESSES

Integrity and Sense of Humor

What are my guiding principles? How well does my behavior match them? Am I honest with myself and others? Can I laugh at my own and others' foibles?

Ways of Learning and Interacting

What are my preferred or habitual ways of learning? What are my preferred or habitual ways of interacting with people? What are the strengths and weaknesses of these approaches?

Self-Efficacy, Optimism, and Courage

How confident am I that my efforts to promote beneficial change can be successful? Do I have and convey a generally positive outlook and a realistic optimism about the possibility of people working successfully together on their common concerns? How willing am I to venture into the unknown, go against the prevailing wisdom, be vulnerable, be radically innovative, keep on in the face of adversity?

Cognitive and Emotional Complexity

Do I take a systems view? Can I see connections among ideas, people, and organizations? Can I synthesize multiple strands of information? Can I envision new ways of doing things? Am I comfortable with ambiguity and paradox? Do I accept the validity of different perspectives? How good am I at identifying my own feelings? How do I practice self-discipline? How well am I able to understand and respond to the feelings of others? How well do I manage my negative perceptions of other people?

Continual Learning

How does my formal and informal training (especially in cross-cultural communication) help or hinder me in exercising leadership around the organizational or community issues I care about? Do I seek and accept frank feedback from others?

Authority, Skills, Connections

What sources and amounts of personal authority can I apply to my leadership work?

- Authority based on family position, craft, profession, position in organization or community
- Moral authority rooted in demonstrated integrity or trustworthiness

What general skills and social connections can I apply to my leadership work?

Supportive Spouses, Other Family Members, Friends, Colleagues, and Mentors

Who among my family, friends, and colleagues can be counted on to support or oppose me in this work? Who can mentor me? Are there people whose example I can follow even if I can't work with them directly?

Balance

What engagements and attachments do I have to balance my involvement with public work? How do they help and hinder my leadership?

Once participants have completed the exercise, you might prompt them to identity their key assets and, if they have completed the Signature Strengths or StrengthsFinder questionnaires or the Multiple Intelligences Quiz, how those assets relate to the strengths highlighted by those exercises. You can also ask that they identify liabilities that they want to remedy and note some strategies for doing so. For example, a participant who realizes that he or she lacks a supportive network may decide to seek a new mentor. Or, the person who lacks optimism may decide to explore "learned optimism" (Seligman, 2006) or simply be sure to consult people who are more optimistic about the prospects of a desired change. Again, participants can benefit from the chance to share results of the exercise in small and large groups. They get a sense of how they are similar to and different from others and may gain further insights about their assets and liabilities.

Those who would like to explore further aspects of their personality that may hamper their leadership could attend to what Parker Palmer in the book *Leading*

From Within (2007) calls our "shadows," those deep assumptions that human beings often would rather not acknowledge. In particular, he invites us to consider the following five assumptions:

- Who you are depends on your title
- Life is a battleground, hostile to human interests
- The ultimate responsibility for everything rests with me
- Life is chaos
- Because I am mortal my work ends with my death

As an instructor, I might introduce Palmer's conception and invite participants to reflect on the following questions: When have these assumptions been evident in your leadership practice? Are some of the assumptions more likely than others to interfere with accomplishment of your goals? After they have made notes about their answers, I might ask them to share them with a partner or in small groups. Since sharing reflections about "shadows" may be both threatening and liberating, the exercise is likely to work best when participants have gotten to know each other and developed trust over the course of several sessions.

Biographies of the Famous and Not-So-Famous

As noted in the previous chapters, learning about the lives of others who are commonly thought of as leaders can give us role models, help us understand diverse paths to leadership, and help us realize that great figures from history or current affairs are a mixture of attractive and unattractive qualities, just like we are. For example, I often assign all or part of Nelson Mandela's *Long Walk to Freedom* (1995) in my leadership classes. I ask students to consider his personal assets and liabilities, the effects of his crucible experiences and critical decisions. How were his decisions enabled and constrained by the social and political context in which he lived? How did his identity as a leader evolve within a group of antiapartheid leaders? A film like *Invictus* also could be used to explore how life stories of both Mandela and François Pienaar, the captain of the South African national rugby team, influenced their leadership.

Assigning biographies of great figures can obscure the less visible, but important work of everyday leadership. Brad Jackson assigns students to read a biography that can't be found in airport bookstores. Then he and his co-instructor interview each student for 15 minutes about what s/he learned from the biography. The assignment has the dual purpose of highlighting aspects of personal leadership and revealing students' ability to engage in dialogue.

A variation on these exercises is to ask participants to write reflective essays on the biographies or autobiographies that have shaped their lives. The biographies may be conveyed in various media, not just books.

Written, Oral, and Visual Storytelling

Many of the exercises described in this chapter call for reflective writing, which is an important skill for personal development. Writing clearly and compellingly is a key general leadership skill, so I often offer guidance and even special sessions on how to compose sentences, paragraphs, and essays that draw readers in, inform them, and persuade them to act. At the beginning of my classes, I advise participants that they can expect to receive comments from me about the quality of their writing (see Inset 3.7, Why I Scribble on Your Papers). In the case of personal reflections like those described in this chapter, I don't attend as much to grammatical correctness as I do in other assignments, but I still expect clarity and language that reveals thoughtful probing and assessment. Some of us require or encourage participants in our courses or workshops to blog about what emerges in the small- and large-group debriefing of exercises. I also expect blog posts to be clear and thoughtful.

INSET 3.7   WHY I SCRIBBLE ON YOUR PAPERS

Oral and written communication is a prime leadership skill. I will try to help you improve this skill via comments and suggestions on your written and oral work. I hope to help you make your messages clearer and more compelling. I'll suggest pruning, more apt or vivid word choice, and precise punctuation and grammar.

Some guidelines:

1. Be clear and concise.
2. Gear your message to your audience. Speak to your classmates as well as the instructor. You may have other audiences in mind, as well.
3. Help the reader; don't make him or her work too hard.
4. Engage the reader through vivid language, story lines, and road maps.
5. Think of punctuation as a sheepdog herding words into sentences, phrases, clauses, and quotes.
6. Think of grammar as the master's commands that help keep meaning and timing straight, help us convey what fits with what, and where the action is.

Oral communication is also a vital leadership skill, so ideally participants in our workshops and courses will have the chance to present at least part of their life stories orally. One method is to use the VoiceThread program (voicethread. com), which allows participants to use webcams to record and share their comments on a topic. One of my courses includes two VoiceThread assignments that focus on personal narrative. In the first, participants take two minutes to introduce themselves and describe their family, professional, and community commitments. The second, assigned in week four, asks participants to talk briefly about the following: "What's the biggest change that has happened to you as an adult? Describe it and talk about how you've responded to it." I ask that the comments be shared online a day or so before the class meets, so that everyone has a chance to listen to all the comments. Then in class we can talk about similarities and differences in these changes. In addition to giving participants the chance to tell an important part of their life story, the exercise gives everyone experience using a webcam and it fosters richer understandings of the people who constitute our learning community. Besides focusing on the content of the participants' remarks, feedback can include attention to nonverbal communication, such as looking at the camera, having an animated expression, and varying tone.

An example of a visual narrative is the collage produced as part of the Outlining and Constructing Personal Visions exercise (see Inset 3.8). This exercise weaves together aspects of participants' past, present, and future life stories. The first step is to answer several questions that can stimulate ideas for what to include in the collage. Participants complete this part of the exercise as homework and bring their answers (the vision outline) to class along with materials such as photographs, quotations, banners, magazine pictures, or logos that convey key ideas in the outline. Typically, I provide flip chart sheets, markers, magazines for clipping, scissors, glue sticks, and other art materials. I encourage everyone to fill a large flip chart sheet with images and other materials, and minimize reliance on words. I assure the group that no artistic ratings will be given. Usually, constructing the visions takes about an hour.

INSET 3.8 OUTLINING AND CONSTRUCTING PERSONAL VISIONS

Part I: Group members outline and construct individual visions

Outline

1. When you try to picture success in an area you care about   such as your life, family, work, or your case—what does it look like?
2. What important outcomes does the picture include?
3. What values, cultural traditions, and experiences from your past will you draw on to achieve these outcomes?
4. What barriers will you have to overcome to achieve these outcomes?
5. How might you make your picture of success a reality? What are the primary strategies and actions you might undertake? Who will support you in this effort?

Read the directions for constructing your vision and assemble appropriate materials.

Construction

Materials Needed: Flip Chart Sheets, Bright Markers, Magazine Pictures, Stickers, Fabric, Etc.

1. Using a flip chart sheet, markers, and other materials, create an imaginative representation of the answers you gave to the above questions. Show how your desired future is linked to values, traditions, and experiences and to planned strategies and actions. You might include photographs, mission statements, objects (edible or inedible), fabric, poems, strategy documents. Use images rather than words as much as possible. Fill the whole sheet.
2. You might accompany this representation with recordings and aromas.
3. Try to convey how things would look, feel, sound, taste, and smell if you were successful in achieving your goal or dreams.
4. The results will not be subjected to artistic judgments.
5. Please sign the sheet and place it on the wall for the group presentation.

Part II: Visions are presented to the group

Directions for group presentation

1. The group assembles in front of each vision. The creator remains quiet while the others say what they think the vision is about.
2. After group members comment, the creator responds.
3. After all visions are presented, the facilitator asks the group to identify any themes in the visions. He or she explains that a common vision might be constructed based on such themes and suggests how a team or organizational vision might be created using a similar exercise.
4. The facilitator asks why it is important to use visual imagery. (The exercise taps left and right brain; visual images may be more real, more memorable; a lot can be communicated with a picture.)
5. Everyone takes his or her vision home to serve as a reminder.

Presentation of the visions as outlined in the exercise takes a couple of minutes for each vision and about 10 minutes for conversation about themes. When I work with a large group and a co-instructor is present, we may divide the group in half, and each of us may facilitate this part of the exercise for half the group. Another approach is the Gallery Walk: Once participants have placed their completed visions on the wall, everyone simply strolls around the room and notes striking or common themes in the visions. Once the walk is complete, the instructor can invite comments and questions about the exercise from the large group.

★★★

The amount of attention that leadership educators can give to personal narrative in our courses and workshops will depend on how many other topics we seek to cover over what period of time. Regardless, as leaders in these settings we can make them safe havens for exploring influences on participants' identity as leaders and followers, examining their achievements and core commitments, acknowledging setbacks and failures, and proclaiming their hopes for the future. We can model authenticity by sharing aspects of our own life stories with participants. The exercises described in this chapter offer opportunities not only to craft one's own narrative of leadership and followership but also to understand others' narratives that are often quite different. Attention to diverse narratives sets the stage for the next part of this book, which focuses on the leadership work of hosting and hospitality.

Further Reflection on Your Leadership Narrative

I encourage you to use the exercises and prompts in Chapters 1–3 to create written, oral, or visual representations of your values, commitments, formative experiences, critical challenges, sustaining forces, and other key aspects of your identity as a leader or engaged follower. Of necessity, this will involve extensive reflection—sifting through memories and other evidence about the past and present, imagining possible selves that could play out in the future. You may share these representations with others and they, in turn, may reflect them back to you and add to your understanding as they interpret what they see and hear. This process of shared reflection also is a way of making your commitments public and increasing the likelihood that you will continue to follow through on them.

Finally, I invite you to reflect on your story as a whole. If you have adopted the architectural metaphor, you might consider what kind of dwelling you have built. Does it have numerous verandas for welcoming strangers, does it provide sanctuary, and does it blend into the natural environment? Does it have studio spaces?

If you prefer the tapestry metaphor, you could consider the patterns that have developed over time. You might look for the bright threads that run throughout and note the places where those threads are knotted, tangled, or lost all together. If I apply this metaphor, I see that writing, inquiry, persistence, and a quest for harmony have been bright threads in my leadership story. They have their knots and tangles, though. I've tried too hard at times to bring harmony to conflictual situations; I've persisted in assignments that weren't nurturing me.

Perhaps you want to consider your story as a hero's journey in the vein that Carol Pearson (1991) suggests. The hero's journey, she explains, is

> first taking a journey to find the treasure of your true self, and then about returning home to give your gift to help transform the kingdom— and in the process, your own life. The quest itself is replete with dangers and pitfalls, but it offers great rewards: the capacity to be successful in the world, knowledge of the mysteries of the human soul, the opportunity to find and express your unique gifts in the world, and to live in loving community with other people. (54, Kindle ed.)

Taking an approach related to mythology and Jungian psychology, she invites us to connect with 12 archetypal inner guides: the Innocent, the Orphan, the Warrior, the Caregiver, the Seeker, the Destroyer, the Lover, the Creator, the Ruler, the Magician, the Sage, and the Fool, as we undertake the journey and reflect on it.

References

Crosby, B. C., & Bryson, J. M. (2005). *Leadership for the common good: Tackling public problems in a shared-power world.* San Francisco: Jossey-Bass.

Drath, W. H. (2000). *The deep blue sea: Rethinking the source of leadership.* San Francisco: Jossey-Bass.

Heifetz, R. A. (1994). *Leadership without easy answers.* Boston, MA: Belknap.

Mandela, N. (1995). *Long walk to freedom.* New York: Crown.

Palmer, P. J. (2007). *Leading from within.* San Francisco: Jossey-Bass.

Pearson, C. S. (1991). *Awakening the heroes within: Twelve archetypes to help us find ourselves and transform the world.* San Francisco: Harper.

Petriglieri, G., Wood, J. D., & Petriglieri, J. L. (2011). Up close and personal: Building foundations for leaders' development through the personalization of management learning. *Academy of Management Learning & Education, 10*(3), 430–450.

Rath, T., & Conchie, B. (2008). *Strengths based leadership: Great leaders, teams, and why people follow.* New York: Gallup Press.

Seligman, M. E. P. (2006). *Learned optimism: How to change your mind and your life.* New York: Vintage.

PART II

Hosting and Hospitality

This section shifts the focus from self-understanding to working with others, in particular creating a safe yet challenging environment for experimentation and learning. As teachers of leadership we must be versed in welcoming diverse groups of people (often strangers to each other) and able help these people build productive relationships among themselves. As hosts we show up as physical beings with our own sense of identity and authority; the people we welcome will have their own interpretations of our identity and authority.

In working with others as a host or in other leadership roles, we are the instruments of leadership—our embodied words and deeds. This section will focus a lot on face-to-face interaction, in which embodiment is taken for granted; still, we'll consider how embodied words and deeds count, even at a distance.

In Chapter 4, you will hear leadership educators' stories about what separates and connects us to other people. How have we developed our gender, racial/ethnic, class, national, sexual, religious identities? How have our families and friendships affected our skills and attitudes toward hosting? When have we struggled to welcome the stranger, to provide hospitality for people not like us? What lessons have we taken to heart?

Chapter 5 presents some of the most helpful hosting methods with special attention to the Art of Hosting developed by a group of practitioners in Denmark and widely used at the University of Minnesota. Chapter 6 describes more fully how to put these methods into practice and keep them from going awry.

4

HOSTING AND THE HEART

Imagine walking into a classroom on the first day of your leadership course before the participants arrive. You see several rows of tables and chairs, all facing toward a podium and whiteboard. What does this setup communicate about the expected interaction in the classroom? Clearly, the idea is that you as the instructor will stand at the podium and show slides or scribble on the whiteboard as you impart knowledge to your rapt audience. Participants might have a chance to interact with you, but interacting with each other is not so likely, since they mainly see the back of fellow participants' heads.

Now imagine a different scene. The classroom has several groupings of tables and chairs with space for about six participants around each table. A separate table is covered with a bright cloth and displays some of the artifacts that will be used in the course: books, markers, a carved turtle, snow cards. Perhaps some snacks are on the table. Jazz is playing in the background. What does this setup communicate? It prompts participants to assume that they will be interacting with each other as well as the instructor and that the classroom will be a welcoming, visually stimulating, and nourishing environment.

The first scene, sadly, is still all too common in classrooms, though it is based on the old, discredited notion that education is mainly about opening up student brains and pouring in the instructor's expert knowledge. Every kindergarten teacher knows better. Think of the colorful rooms, student photos, and work spaces designed to stimulate the senses of five-year-olds and let them know they are valued as individuals and part of a group.

I learned about the value of making classrooms welcoming and hospitable (what I refer to as hosting) through my involvement with the months-long evening seminars offered by the Reflective Leadership Program at the Humphrey School in the mid-1980s. Most of the participants were coming to the seminar from their day jobs; we wanted them to have time to recover from work and commuting pressures, so we made food and beverages available before the seminar began. We arranged comfortable chairs in a circle to facilitate participant interaction and emphasize our expectation that everyone had an equal place in the seminar. In those pre-PowerPoint days, we didn't worry much about projectors and screens. For these seminars, we also organized opening retreats so that participants could get away from normal responsibilities, start reflecting on their own experiences as leaders, and get to know their fellow learners.

Valerie Shangreaux's leadership development program at the Blandin Foundation brings community leaders from rural Minnesota together in a retreat setting. She notes, "Way back when this program was born—about 30 years ago—a team of people from the Blandin Foundation went through the program at the Center for Creative Leadership for high-powered CEOs. The team came away saying rural community leaders deserve to be treated with the same level of respect." As a result, participants in the Blandin Community Leadership program are treated "like the important people they are! We honor their experience and we thank them for caring and getting involved."

Jodi Sandfort describes a similar approach:

In our midcareer programs at the Humphrey School we seek to receive students in a generous way, welcoming them into a learning community which will push them to probe their own backgrounds, consider their own practice, and engage others to build democratic sensibilities. Rather than seeing our value as educators merely as people who communicate content, hosting refocuses our attention to the process expertise we bring to shaping students' experience and creating the learning community.

Of course, the physical space is not the only consideration in establishing a welcoming environment. The personal attention that we pay to participants also matters. Kathy Quick comments, "When teaching at my best, I know most students personally. I know a little about what they are struggling with. I help make connections or really listen to why they are here." Adds June Nobbe, "I explain to anyone who wants to teach that you have to be willing to walk into the classroom and develop a relationship with everyone in the class." Some insights about the distinctive concerns and qualities of a participant will emerge from the structured class or workshop activities (such as those described in Part I). Additional insights can be gained through informal interactions before a class or workshop begins, during breaks, or after a session ends. To learn about participants and convey our interest in them, leadership educators can ask simple questions about their interests and activities. We can follow up on topics they have mentioned in their assignments.

For many of us, providing food is a prominent part of hosting. Mary Uhl-Bien was teaching a group of executives when she noticed that the food that was provided was "terribly unhealthy." Desiring healthier food options, she brought her own food to replace what was there. Many of us invite participants in our long-term classes to a dinner or potluck at our homes. When I do this, I usually welcome family members so they can feel connected to the learning community that is developing within the class.

Gill Hickman describes her approach to hosting:

I bring food in the classroom and set it up so people will be comfortable. I put people in groups. Hosting is important to Jepson and to me personally. I encourage students to eat together, go out and do things as a group together.

One of my favorite courses was Leadership and Film. We would view the whole film. I would bring popcorn and people's favorite candy. Then at the next class we would debrief [in light of leadership theory]. I start my classes with interviews. Students interview each other and then the whole class interviews me.

To foster optimal learning, leadership educators also seek to facilitate relationship building among participants in our classes and workshops. Sharing the personal narrative exercises with each other and having time for informal interaction, help. In longer-term classes we may organize Action Learning Circles (see Chapter 15) or other small groups that work on a project or that simply support participants' learning over the course of several weeks or months. Participants are likely to develop stronger bonds with people in these groups, compared with class members outside their group. Of course, conflict between participants may also increase when they are required to work with each other in their small groups. As instructors we are able to set the tone for reacting to conflict in the classroom or workshop setting. We can make clear that we welcome different perspectives and competing ideas as part of the mutual learning process. We can highlight the benefits of depersonalizing conflicts as much as possible—for example, when class members make clear that they respect each other even as they disagree, they are more likely to be able to learn from each other and work together productively. We also can use a number of what Sonia Ospina calls "creative technologies"—such as World Café and Open Space—that can help participants bridge their differences. These will be described in some detail in Chapter 6.

In the next section of this chapter, you will hear how several leadership educators developed our approach to hosting. The section after that focuses on the way that our social identities play out as we attempt to welcome diverse participants into our classrooms. Then we reveal frustrations we have encountered in working with people different from ourselves and how we handle the frustrations. We explore the hosting habits that help us welcome diverse participants into leadership development programs. Finally, we reflect on team teaching as a way of working more effectively with diverse participants.

How We Learn to Host

For many of us, family members taught us a lot about welcoming others. Gill Hickman says, "I am a Southern woman raised by a Southern mother who is the best hostess in the world. When I was at my mother's house I would have to get dressed right away in the morning because you wouldn't know who would drop by. I learned very young how food and a comfortable environment help people feel comfortable and relaxed." Lars Leafblad remembers the value his grandparents placed on what they called fellowship. They hosted holiday celebrations where family members and friends were welcome. "I would see my grandparents at church engaging with others. I saw the way my parents welcomed people into our home." Sonia Ospina's extended family, as well as her education at a Jesuit university, gave her experience in reaching out to people from different social classes. Georgia Sorenson noted that her parents "hosted a lot" while living in different places. Her father was in the Army and then the U.S. diplomatic corps. "My parents' attitude was very welcoming."

Several of us learned a lot about hosting from our involvement with executive, midcareer, or community leadership programs. Rick Morse gained insight from the chapter entitled "Invisible Walls" in Linda Stout's *Bridging Class Divides: And Other Lessons for Grassroots Organizing* (1996).

> *When you are seeking engagement in the community, you need to pay attention to the language you use, the physical makeup of space, times you can meet. If not, you can set up invisible walls that exclude people. I led strategic visioning processes in three states and learned that how, when, and where matter very much. The teams I worked with did natural, innovative things going well beyond norms. For example, we met in churches and workplaces. We offered lunch and had an extended lunch break in some workplaces. You need to meet people where they are at rather than expecting them to follow your agenda.*
>
> —Rick Morse

Welcoming the Stranger

Often the people in our workshops and courses are quite different from us, in terms of beliefs and social identities. We are challenged to be adept in welcoming people who are, in effect, strangers to us. This is another opportunity for deepening our self-awareness as leaders as we ask ourselves how our beliefs and identities help us connect easily to some people and separate us from others.

Lars Leafblad describes this inquiry as an "ongoing journey." He continually asks, "How does being a white male of Scandinavian origin, upper-middle-class background, and advanced education affect perceptions when I walk into a room of others not like me?" He recognizes that what seems like hosting to him may not seem so to others.

Georgia Sorenson says, "I've done a lot to overcome the separation between self and others." For example, because of her brother's illness, she has served on mental health boards and mentored people with autism. "This keeps me fresh and connected with people I wouldn't otherwise be connected to."

Gill Hickman emphasizes the positive side of her intersecting identities, but notes they also can prompt some people to downplay her abilities. "I'm an African American female married to a Presbyterian minister who also was in higher education till he retired. So the religious piece is also there. Primarily these aspects of who I am have been a huge asset."

> *I told a class where I had African American students that they have something I never had. In all my years as an undergraduate and graduate student I had no African American professors and one female professor. My background helps me understand people in many walks of life. Experience in the segregated South, city government, state government, and higher education—so many experiences wrapped up in being African American and female—helps me relate to all kinds of people. At boarding school I experienced no discrimination of any kind. This freed me to think about who you are as a person, your essence. No labels. Once you've had that experience, you are free. Being African American and female helped shape me but it can't confine me. The only liability has been in the way that other people perceive that. When I began studying for my Ph.D., I had a big natural hairdo like Angela Davis and rimless glasses. I had two professors in my first class. They wouldn't even look at me. When I turned in a paper, they said this doesn't meet our expectations of who I was going to be. They tried to put me in a box—I encountered a lot of that.*
>
> —Gill Hickman

Sonia Ospina has had similar experiences.

> *I come from a social class in Colombia that has provided me with the privilege of having education. Still, people expect me to be a stereotype of a Latino woman in the U.S. They may see me as one of them but in this different shell. I used to get the comment, 'You're so articulate.' Because of my education I have had an easier time disrupting stereotypes than some people have.*
>
> *I do ask in moments of insecurity: Who are people seeing when they look at me? Are they seeing a generalized other? When I'm grounded, I say it doesn't matter. In moments of vulnerability my ethnicity is a hindrance; when I'm grounded, it's an asset. Having a perspective that's not necessarily mainstream, I have a contribution to make. When I am working with diverse groups of people, people can see me as a role model.*

Generally, Mary Uhl-Bien has found her gender to be an advantage. "Being as strong as I was made me a role model for a lot of people." Still, being female, blond, and relational, she found that men sometimes misinterpreted her actions. "Earlier in my career I realized I had to put up an ice guard around men."

Rick Morse highlights the role of his faith-based perspective in helping him empathize with diverse students and directing attention to the importance of values in leadership. "I'm pretty mainstream—middle class, white, but I'm also a minority being LDS [Latter Day Saints]. On top of that I'm a rather liberal Mormon, which is a minority within a minority. I see this two ways. As an asset, it has really given me empathy for other, more marginalized groups. I have ancestors on my father's side who immigrated to Utah; they experienced violence and oppression." At the same time, his emphasis on personal values and public service values can seem too "religious" to some students, even though he does not bring up his own religious background in courses and workshops. He has learned that not every student is eager to talk about personal values if they see a connection with religious belief.

Chuck Palus draws attention to three different aspects of identity—given, chosen, and core—in his classes. "I can talk about where I'm from, who I am, talk about my given identity [white, male, blue collar, Catholic]." He goes on to note aspects of his identity that he has chosen and which ones he considers core. "My favorite part of the mix is researcher and loyal skeptic. This allows me to be skeptical in the classroom, disarming. Questioning assumptions helps me be a boundary-spanner."

Georgia Sorenson finds that her nationality becomes salient when she works in other countries. Being American can have "a lot of baggage." Some people may see Americans as glamorous; others may disparage them. "In formerly colonial countries, there's a complex mix of both. I always say I'm coming to learn from them, especially when I work with women's groups. I say the U.S. is 48th in terms of representation of women."

When I've worked in other countries or with international students in the U.S., I often have found that my approach (inclusive, egalitarian, and interactive) to leadership education appears to be very American and countercultural. When I began leading workshops and classes in Poland in the mid-1990s, participants clearly expected the open-brains-insert-knowledge brand of instruction. As I asked them to rearrange the furniture to facilitate interaction, they began to alter their expectations. I explained my approach and the benefits of interaction. Initially, not everyone was comfortable with expressing ideas or asking questions, but soon I had trouble getting them to quit!

Some participants will pose greater challenges than others to our hosting abilities, because they disagree with our approach or resist our invitations to connect with the other participants or engage in deep reflection. For example, I frequently have some class members, regardless of where I teach, who are still firmly attached to the idea that teaching means giving lectures.

Rick Morse concedes, "The people I have the most trouble being hospitable to are people from a hard-core right-wing perspective. I have family members who are part of the Tea Party Express, so I've learned to be hospitable to them. It's hard in the classroom when this pops up. I've learned to be patient. I try to practice what I preach about open-mindedness. But some people are closed off to broadening their perspective and that's a struggle for me." He reminds himself, "No matter how open-minded I think I am, if I'm not willing to have a conversation with someone who thinks very differently from me, I'm on a high horse and not practicing what I preach."

Georgia Sorenson was invited to teach at a school of public affairs in China and did not want to go because she disagreed with China's policies on Tibet. A friend said that was exactly why she should go. She accepted the invitation. "At the end they gave us a golden statue of Tiananmen Square. They were proud of the resistance the army put up [against the Tiananmen protesters in 1989]. I thought, 'My God,' but I was able to hold the complexity." Sonia Ospina acknowledges that she too can struggle to welcome people who have a very different ideological position than her own. "It's important to see the rest of them beyond our disagreement and to stay open."

Questioning assumptions helps me be a boundary-spanner.
—Chuck Palus

[I]f I'm not willing to have a conversation with someone who thinks very differently from me, I'm on a high horse and not practicing what I preach.
—Rick Morse

It's important to see the rest of them beyond our disagreement and to stay open.
—Georgia Sorenson

My own strongest urges to become defensive in the classroom occur when a student adopts a confrontational stance toward me or other participants. Here I'm referring to the person who moves beyond respectful disagreement to continually asserting the superiority of his or her own knowledge or questioning the validity of my or other participants' statements. Certainly, the student's confrontational style triggers my own need to promote harmony. More importantly, the person's behavior can become a barrier to other class members' sense of safety and reduce our chances of learning from each other. As leadership educators, we have multiple tools to minimize dominating and confrontational behavior—for example, by giving everyone a minute or two to share an insight in a large-group discussion. Through the years, I also have learned that the confrontational student frequently is hungering for acknowledgement of his or her intelligence or worth. Thus, I take pains to recognize useful information and reminders that the person is contributing, while maintaining my own authority in the class or workshop. I also seek to talk with the person outside of class in order to find out more about him or her and demonstrate my appreciation of his or her strengths. Often the most "challenging" students in my classes become the most avid champions of the class experience—quite possibly because I took them seriously.

Carol Pearson suggests that when we see people as very alien to ourselves, we are probably projecting our own fears or needs onto them. We may label them as hostile or lazy, say, and judge them accordingly. "The whole history of racism and sexism," she argues, "is about projection. I found myself recently judging somebody for being rich." She finds it's helpful at times like that to remember the admonition, "Judge not, that you be not judged."

Participants in our courses and workshops may also be projecting their own fears and needs onto us, and this may be reinforced by what psychoanalysts call transference—the application of feelings about an authority figure, such as a parent, to us as authorities in the classroom. This possibility simply reinforces the importance of making learning environments a place of safety and shared authority—for example, through student-led exercises.

Adapting to Diverse Audiences

At times, the sheer diversity among and within groups poses challenges to hosting. If we provide food, we may need to accommodate vegetarian, Hindu, Muslim, Jewish, and other preferences or requirements. We may have to rethink exercises that are geared to the physically abled; we may be called on to respect certain religious practices.

We find various ways to signal our programs are cross-cultural and value the cultural backgrounds and social identities of participants. Juana Bordas suggests setting up a family altar in the meeting room. She invites participants to bring family photographs and other mementos to place on the altar. When she facilitates sessions of the African American Leadership Forum, Yvonne Cheek makes sure that music and other elements of the setting convey African American culture. Georgia Sorenson puts "gay-friendly" stickers on her office door. Charles Palus discovered the value of using pictures to build cross-cultural bridges (see Inset 4.1).

INSET 4.1 CREATING VISUAL EXPLORER

Chuck Palus was part of a Center for Creative Leadership team leading a session on creativity for senior executives. "We wanted to make the point that leadership was about art and making things, about engaging the visual world. In organizations, the visual world is really dialed back. I felt I might not have a lot to offer, so I said let's use a postcard exercise. I brought a box of postcards and we invited participants to have conversations using them as props. [Each participant chose a card that symbolized something significant for him/her and proceeded to talk about that thing.] It was a big hit. Very cool. We realized, we can do this. It worked the first time! This was the exact same thing as stumbling into group of reggae musicians. I was driven by fear and need.

"The client really liked the exercise and asked for copies. We didn't know if this would work, but we put the postcards on a copier, hit the enlarge button and it worked. It was almost like the copier was magic. Thus was born Visual Explorer [a card pack and process available through the Center for Creative Leadership].

"In Africa I've found that Visual Explorer is a perfect entry point for people from all walks of life. Our card pack may have a Western bias, but people are still thrilled with it. People discover common ground in aesthetics, art, meaning making."

The concept of using pictures or objects to stimulate dialogue works regardless of whether a leadership educator uses Visual Explorer or assembles her own collection. The exercise puts something in the middle of the group that participants can focus on. As Chuck Palus notes, "I can point to a picture to tell my story. You don't have to have eye-to-eye contact [which works well for shyer participants and in cultures that dislike the direct gaze]. It's all about art making a bridge that even enemies can cross, as somebody said."

Often, we have to accommodate different levels of experience, at once or sequentially. Rick Morse describes his experience: "I go back and forth between teaching pre-career and seasoned veterans. I just finished working with the Public Executive Leadership Academy. It's a two-week program spanning one week in July and one in August. We work with executive-level government folks. With this group, I draw out their experiences and teach more inductively. For the pre-career people, I try to create experiences. We do a lot of activities to try out and play with ideas they are reading about." Gill Hickman takes a similar approach to developing the leadership of young undergraduates. She has them interview people in local organizations as well as planning new organizations.

We may also have to accommodate class and confidence differences. Georgia Sorenson recalls the ways that she and her colleagues at the University of Maryland welcomed poor people to a residency program. "They were afraid of the ivory tower. We had to create a welcoming stance. We'd meet their buses, carry their luggage. We provided sofas and catered food. I was the child care person— we had our own little leadership school in our child care center." She has found teaching people at Harvard and Williams College different from teaching people at a state school like the University of Maryland. "At state schools, people may be the first in their family to be in college. . . . I think of students as hot air balloons— some you need to let loose and fly and some need to be pulled back closer to the ground. Sometimes [for a leadership course] you have to go find them. The white male student government types may show up and it's good they are there, but you may have to find those who don't think of themselves as leaders."

We also have learned to be attuned to the differing demands on our students outside our courses and other leadership development experiences. This may affect class or workshop scheduling, the organization of team projects, and participants' availability to meet with us. I've also realized that many years spent in academia can make me think that esoteric language is normal. I have to banish highfalutin words from my explanations if I want to connect with nonacademic audiences especially.

Carol Pearson notes the need to accommodate diverse learning styles, especially those different from our own. She says, "I'm a very high intuitive. I often taught very large classes and realized I was missing a certain subset of students. I thought they weren't so smart. They were sensing types. I learned I make huge leaps in lots of ways from one idea to another. Some students get it and others don't. It's easier when I'm writing because I have to put in the missing pieces." Now when Pearson sees students' eyes glazing over, she stops her remarks and invites them to raise questions and offer comments.

Habits for Hosting

In this work of adapting to diverse audiences, several habits are useful. One, already discussed, is an ongoing effort to understand how our own life stories and identities help and hamper us in connecting to the people we teach. Others include paying intense attention to the people we are hosting, regulating our own energies, and disclosing our own experiences.

Attention to the people who participate in our courses and workshops begins well before we meet them, and requires ongoing mindfulness. When Georgia Sorenson is invited to work with a group she doesn't know well—such as generals, transplant surgeons, and law students—she gathers information about them, sometimes by consulting the sponsor of the work and sometimes by asking participants to fill out a questionnaire. "I try to get into their world, end the separation between myself and others. I try to understand the world of a general, though I am a pacifist. I try to understand a transplant surgeon, though I'm not a doctor." Charles Palus echoes her comments, "You should be aware of the assumptions and mind-set of the people you're working with. For instance, when I am working with people in Ethiopia, I am mindful that they know more about their context than I do."

> *I try to learn about people who are going to be in the group—individually and as a group. In preparation for a class, I ask students about their motivation to be in the class, their characteristics. I use this to learn about the group and tell the group who they are. When I'm ready to enter a group I think is different from others I've worked with I try to heighten my listening skills. Who are they? How are they coming to be here? People can see you as open to understanding them if you do this.*
>
> —Sonia Ospina

I often ask participants at the outset to share some aspect of their life stories, their reason for participating, and what they hope to get out of a course or workshop. Additionally, I may gather information by chatting informally with participants when they are waiting for the formal session to begin. For a multisession course, a teaching journal may be helpful in keeping track of how well different participants are responding to course activities (see Inset 4.2 for an entry in my teaching journal).

INSET 4.2   ENTRY FROM BARBARA CROSBY'S TEACHING JOURNAL

I recorded this entry around the fourth week of a course that involved midcareer students from the U.S. and several other countries.

> *The focus on personal development and student control has paid off. The international students say it's unusual for them to focus so much on personal analysis and revelation. One says it fits with what she was told about Americans: 'They will tell you about everything except their money. In my country, we'll tell you about our money and nothing else.' One U.S. student, somewhat older than the norm, resists personal introspection or admitting that she has anything to learn from the emphasis on inclusion and multiculturalism. She wants non-Western models to be emphasized.*

As leadership educators we face the challenge of regulating our own energies as we strive to respond to diverse participants' needs and group dynamics. Mary Uhl-Bien varies the rhythm of her sessions in tune with her own and participants' energies. She is likely to check in with the group to ask whether the pace of a session is right for them. She may recruit a co-teacher or tee up a TED talk to supplement her own lectures. Team teaching offers other advantages as well. When Gill Hickman began teaching a course called Leadership in a Diverse Society, she recruited a white male to teach with her. "This keeps people from feeling left out. Students can feel this is really authentic, having more than one perspective. Lots of white males are nervous about this so I haven't always been able to have a white male co-teacher. I invited another African American woman to bring her students to my class. People could see that two African American females were very different from each other."

For Mary Uhl-Bien, who describes herself as "more on the introverted side," the challenge is to avoid depleting her energy as a session progresses. For Yvonne Cheek, who is decidedly extraverted, the challenge is the opposite. She has found that her consistently high-level energy can wear some participants out.

> *A decade ago, I got feedback that I was a big energy person. Then I was doing some work that had me in a room with another big energy person and I saw what it was like. Experiencing her, I thought, "That's too much." She didn't know how to regulate. It's*

important to understand how to modulate. I can use this now in an intentional way. That was learning I really enjoyed. I realized I've been pinning a few people against the wall with my energy.

I've learned I like working at intersections of things, levels, and cultures. For some people, this drains their energy or they get lost. Because working there is a threat for most people, I try to infuse joy into the work as we go to intersected places. I like helping people address sticky issues that keep occurring. Usually it's the issue under the issue.

I like taking people to that place—using a velvet hammer—putting people on the spot and helping them like it.

—Yvonne Cheek

Disclosing aspects of our own experience at the intersection of various identities may be helpful. Some of these identities may be more obvious than others (see Inset 4.3 containing my reflections on being a Euro-American woman).

INSET 4.3 REFLECTIONS ON BEING A EURO-AMERICAN WOMAN

For a long time I didn't know I had a gender. I recognized myself as a girl, as female from my earliest years. My parents, of course, encouraged this perception; I remember gifts of dolls and majorette boots. At the same time, I was drawn to the image of the "tomboy." I loved wearing a wonderful tooled leather gun belt with metal fake six-guns on either side, which my parents must have given me as well. I liked spending time in the woods and always thought of myself as the equal of any boy. Yet, the older I got I could see that schools, businesses, churches, the government seemed to be run by men and that women tended to play supporting roles. I vaguely understood that part of my mother's depression stemmed from being an attractive, smart woman worn down by lack of opportunities to use her talents. When I entered Vanderbilt University I was part of a freshman class that included about 300 women and 700 men; only later would I learn that Vanderbilt had a quota that allowed no more than about a third of an entering class to be women. The beginnings of the 1960s cultural and feminist revolution affected Vanderbilt and I joined in the battle to bring civil rights firebrands like Stokely Carmichael to campus, to remove dorm hour restrictions on women, and to allow coed dorms. As I looked beyond college several paths seemed possible for me as a college-educated woman. There was the traditional and still dominant path of becoming a teacher, secretary, or nurse, and probably a wife who had a paid job until children came. Another career path—jobs in math and science—was starting to open for women. Neither path appealed to me. I briefly considered law school, where most of my male friends were headed, but I had no taste for being one of two or three women law students. (I had a pretty good idea of what that battle would be like.) Instead, I decided on newspaper reporting—a woman with my skills and experience might have a decent chance at that and it wouldn't mean being tied down to a desk.

So the summer after college I married the man I'd dated since high school, was hired at the Augusta, Georgia, afternoon daily newspaper, and worked mainly as a journalist, press secretary, speechwriter, or editor until the early 1980s. In that time, I would face the limitations that men and sometimes women would place on me because of my gender. After a divorce and remarriage, I grappled with the challenges of being the person in my marriage who had the primary responsibility for raising two children, while trying to do the professional work I sought to do, trying to care for others, and being a citizen activist. With the help of husband, friends, and therapists I crafted my own response to those challenges; I also benefited from the writers and activists of second wave feminism who gave me deeper insights into the potential of women's leadership as well as the barriers we faced and continue to face.

In the South of my childhood, race and racial lines were a given. Only later would I understand that race is a social construct with little basis in biology. Yet it is a social construct with great, often brutal power. My family, coming from Anglo-Irish and Swiss-German roots, counted as white in that system. We practiced what might be called polite racism—we children were instructed to speak politely of black folks, but no one questioned the prevailing assumption that white folks were in some innate way superior to and in danger of contamination from the black citizens of our city. Still there were contradictions—in the Baptist sermons about everyone being equal in God's sight, and in the classroom instruction in the founding principles of the United States of America.

I entered Vanderbilt University in Nashville, Tennessee, the same year that the first black students were admitted there—six in a freshman class of about 1,000. As an undergraduate, I had the good fortune to encounter visiting speakers, peers, administrators, and faculty who suggested ways to break out of the bonds of segregation. I became convinced that establishing a society where character, not skin color, determined life chances was both possible and a moral imperative.

The lasting effect is that I am acutely aware of the privilege that fair skin provides in the U.S. I am committed to racial justice. I am aware, to the extent I can be, of blinders constructed of my "whiteness."

Given where I came from, my becoming part of a biracial family is nothing short of astonishing. In 1982, my husband and I adopted our son from South Korea, and in 1984, we adopted our daughter from there as well. We chose South Korea once we had decided to adopt internationally, because a Minnesota adoption agency, Children's Home, had a very solid track record of working with partner agencies in South Korea. We have always acknowledged the problematic side of transnational adoption—certainly in an ideal world, all children would be raised in families in their own countries. Our own decision, however, was ultimately very basic. Two children needed parents and we wanted to parent them. Our family always feels entirely normal to me. For one thing, we've usually lived in a city with numerous other adoptive families like ours, and many of our friends have multiracial families. Occasionally, though, we're in places where we stand out and people are clearly puzzled about what our connection to each other is. Being the mother of two Asian American children has brought me the usual gifts and challenges of parenting, but it also has given me a strong connection to a non-U.S. culture. It has given me deeper insight into the stereotypes visited on Asian Americans, and it has brought home to me in a visceral way that strong families can be built in a variety of ways.

In Charles Palus's terms, we are a distinctive mix of given, chosen, and core identities, and we will connect with others as we inhabit that mix. Sonia Ospina comments, "I spend some time alone to ground myself so I have good sense of who I am and what I'm bringing [to a course or workshop] so I'm there and can connect." Carol Pearson reminds those of us in the sixth or seventh decades of life that we don't have to pretend to be all-knowing and technologically up-to-date. "I tended initially not to reveal my own examples and show my decrepitude. When I did it actually was really helpful. I would say, 'You all take tweeting for granted. In the future you are going to have to learn things you can't imagine now. So have compassion.'"

Preparing for Team Teaching

Although team teaching has the advantages noted previously and can demonstrate aspects of team leadership, it can also go badly unless we do considerable work ahead of time to ensure that co-instructors actually are working as a team in and outside the classroom or workshop space. Ideally, you and your co-instructor will develop the course syllabus or workshop outline together. You will negotiate workload and division of labor. If grading is involved, you will agree on ways to ensure that you are treating students fairly—for example, one of you might grade half the class on one assignment and the other half on the next.

Especially important is planning to handle disagreements between the two of you. Participants usually appreciate hearing different perspectives, and you can demonstrate the key conflict-management skill of listening appreciatively to the other person's view and respectfully acknowledging it even as you explain why you have a different perspective. Some of my worst times in the classroom have occurred when a fellow instructor dismissed my view, and asserted the correctness of her own. In cases like these, if I felt comfortable enough with my co-instructor to do so, I could turn the interaction into a teachable moment. Class members might be invited to think about the effects of handling a disagreement in this way and reflect on when they have experienced similar approaches to disagreements and how they might handle them more effectively.

Especially, if you haven't worked with a co-instructor previously, the two of you are likely to benefit from regular debriefings and ongoing attention to whether workload is in balance. These debriefings can give you the chance to note your positive and negative feelings about the way you've been working together and commit to improvements.

Not every co-instructor is willing to work in concert. Once, when I was leading a weeklong leadership program in another country, I was assigned two co-instructors. One of the two men joined me in thinking through the plans for our sessions; the other wasn't interested in talking to us, and indicated he would simply take responsibility for certain time slots. As the week proceeded he alienated participants by flying into our sessions with scarce knowledge of what had already occurred. He clearly had little respect for me as the lead instructor. Finally, the participants revolted, and when the man appeared for one of his sessions, a spokesperson stood up and denounced his lack of respect for both the participants and me. I love to see leadership develop before my eyes!

★★★

As leadership educators we must strive to create learning environments that help a diverse array of participants feel welcome and encouraged to work together. We do that by staying attuned to our own and participants' identities and needs; we attend to physical space, food, music, cultural symbols. We seek to establish relationships with and among participants. As Gill Hickman notes, "The more we get to know about each other, the less alien we are." We establish habits of paying attention to the people we are hosting, managing our own energies, and disclosing our experiences. We can also benefit from working with co-instructors who can complement our styles and experiences, as long as we develop mutual agreement about course design, workload sharing, and respectful handling of disagreements.

The next chapter explores theories and research findings about the role of hosting in leadership development. It delves further into leadership as a "socio-material" practice—that is, involving interaction of people and their physical and virtual environments—and it examines methods for enabling diverse groups to work together.

Reference

Stout, L. (1996). *Bridging class divides: And other lessons for grassroots organizing.* Boston, MA: Beacon.

5

HOSTING AND THE HEAD

Part I of *Teaching Leadership* focused on leadership mainly as a relationship between leaders and followers (or among a group of people who move in and out of leader and follower roles). In Part II, as leadership educators consider hosting as a leadership practice, we begin to view the socio-material aspects of leadership. From this perspective, leadership emerges in the interactions of embodied humans with each other and with their physical, virtual, and symbolic environments. As these interactions become stabilized they "collectively exert power and generate knowledge" (Fenwick, Nerland, and Jensen, 2012, 6). They also have the potential to generate trust and distrust, the former a powerful contributor to group cohesiveness and productivity and the latter an equally powerful deterrent to group success. Hosting also requires attention to time, prompting our understanding of leadership as not only a socio-material, but temporal practice. Further, as Tara Fenwick, Monica Nerland, and Karen Jensen (2012) point out, a socio-material, temporal perspective directs attention to systems, and one of the prime concerns of leaders becomes staying attuned to system dynamics, timing, and managing the boundaries of the system. A prime leadership skill in hosting is understanding and orchestrating the communication—verbal and nonverbal—emanating from our human bodies and from the media and settings in which we interact.

This chapter will delve further into the theories and research supporting the leadership practice of hosting for leadership development. The first section focuses on the art of hosting, specifically the image of leader as host and on the Art of Hosting approach. The second section turns to the aesthetics of leadership. Next, I consider the importance of gendered bodies and diverse identities in learning communities. Finally, I explore in more depth several means of bridging differences among participants in our workshops and courses.

The Art of Hosting

Mark McKergow and Helen Bailey (2014) offer the metaphor of leader as host, and leadership as hosting, as a counterpoint to both the heroic and servant models of leadership. They argue that the leader as host may be called upon to act heroically and take charge at times, as well as being continually attentive to guests' needs (as a servant would be); more often, though, he or she will be a co-participant in the activity at hand. An attraction of this image of leader and leadership is that it has cross-cultural relevance; it also recognizes a leader's special responsibility for successful process and outcomes while acknowledging the importance of forces beyond his or her control. McKergow and Bailey describe several roles for host leaders: initiator, inviter, space creator, gatekeeper, connector, and co-participator. Host leaders operate behind the scenes, in the spotlight, and in the gallery. Being in the gallery is similar to Ron Heifetz's (1994) term for removing oneself from the action (say, while participants are engaged in a small-group activity) and observing what is going on. Behind the scenes can refer both to the preparations we do before participants begin interacting in a face-to-face or online session, or the work we do on our own development.

The Art of Hosting (AOH) approach, developed originally in Denmark, offers additional insights and tools for bringing diverse participants together to learn and work on shared concerns. (The full name of the approach is Art of Hosting and Harvesting Conversations that Matter.) The profoundly democratic approach is "based on the assumption that we humans have enormous untapped wisdom and resilience; and that sustainable solutions can be created when we share that wisdom with each other" (Sandfort, Stuber, and Quick, 2012, 2). At the heart of the approach is the Four-Fold Practice, consisting of being present, practicing (or participating in) conversations, hosting conversations, and engaging in the community of practice (viewed as potentially a complex adaptive system).

Jodi Sandfort describes the Four-Fold Practice that is the foundational framework for Art of Hosting:

In this practice, the first element of being a good host is cultivating the ability to be present, clear about the need for convening people, and focused on what one can individually contribute to the project. To do so, a host must take care of her own mind, body, and spirit and engage in self-reflection. She must know how she learned to host and recognize barriers that might inhibit her from doing so. Even after practicing the method for a time and exhibiting competence in it, she must retain a novice mind-set that acknowledges the uniqueness of each group.

The second element is participating actively in the work of the group rather than seeing a facilitator's role as a neutral presence, somewhat divorced from the group. The third element is the actual hosting of conversations, which includes techniques such as World Café, Open Space, and 'harvesting conversations that matter.' The final element is participating in a larger community of hosting practitioners.

At the University of Minnesota, under the sponsorship of the Center for Integrative Leadership, we now use the Art of Hosting in a variety of courses, workshops, and design sessions. It is a way of reducing a phenomenon every teacher has experienced: those who feel most comfortable speaking out in a classroom or seminar setting dominate the conversation and others remain silent. Even worse, a few people may engage in unproductive competition and argument about whose ideas and experiences are most valid or worthy. The methods of Art of Hosting are inclusive, offer several modes of expression, and diminish verbal battles aimed at winning rather than developing shared insight.

Art of Hosting workshops are based on and teach "holistic design processes" that consider participant needs, purposes and principles, invitation, and support for implementation. Key engagement tools are Peer Circle Process, Appreciative Inquiry, Open Space Technology, World Café, ProAction Café, and Harvesting. The first four processes were initially developed outside the Art of Hosting community.

The Peer Circle Process derives from long-standing traditions that invite participants to sit together in a circle and take turns speaking, possibly using a talking stick or other object (the person who has the object is the one who speaks) (Baldwin and Linnea, 2010). Appreciative Inquiry, or AI (Cooperrider and Whitney, 2005), is a strengths-based approach to investigating organizational or societal issues. AI is a multiphase process of defining the focus of inquiry, evoking stories of success and fulfillment related to the focus, building on those stories to describe a desired future, and designing and creating that future (http://www.centerforappreciativeinquiry.net/). Open Space Technology (Owen, 1997) helps groups shape their own agendas. The World Café (Brown and Isaacs, 2005) consists of multiple rounds of table conversations on one or more focal questions. Table hosts stay at their assigned tables and participants circulate to different tables as the rounds proceed. Hosts pose a question to participants, facilitate the conversation, and collect participant ideas in a form that can be shared with other participants in the next round. ProAction Café blends Open Space and World Café processes to provide a space for action-oriented conversation (Sandfort, Stuber, and Quick, 2012). Harvesting refers to multimedia methods of collecting stories, ideas, and themes of a conversation. Several of these processes revolve around the formulation of "powerful questions" (http://www.scribd.com/doc/18675626/Art-of-Powerful-Questions).

More about the Art of Hosting approach and the international community of practice that develops and sustains it can be found at http://www.artofhosting. org/home/. Probably the best way to understand the Art of Hosting philosophy and processes is to participate in the workshops listed on the website.

Jodi Sandfort and Kathryn Quick are skilled in facilitating Art of Hosting workshops and also have conducted valuable research on workshop outcomes. They have found that seasoned facilitators (compared to those with less experience) more readily grasp the adaptive design thinking underlying the workshops (Quick and Sandfort, 2014; Sandfort and Quick, 2015). Seasoned practitioners especially appreciate Art of Hosting as a way of tying various process tools together. While some participants in the workshops Sandfort and Quick studied were able to use hosting to enable a group to examine power relations and inequities, others "critiqued the training for not doing enough both to enact an awareness of identity, power and privilege in deliberation, the hosting role or the training workshop itself" (Quick and Sandfort, 2014, 308). Some participants were turned off by what they identified as specialized, new age-y language. Sandfort and Quick have concluded that the power of the Art of Hosting approach is greatest when hosts fundamentally understand and accept AOH's "techniques, patterns, and iterative nature of design" (12). Also vital is careful thinking about how the knowledge harvested in Art of Hosting sessions will be used (Sandfort and Quick, 2015).

Aesthetics of Leadership

Arja Ropo, Jaana Parvlalnan, and Nlina Koivunen (2002) assert that actual human bodies are largely absent from much traditional and modern leadership theory. In arguing for redirecting attention to embodied leaders and followers, they turn to aesthetics, that is, a concern with sensory knowledge and judgments of beauty. They say,

> In relation to leadership, social bodily presence means to us the recognition of the value of human experience, reflection, and recognition of what is going on in the workplace, instead of a priori knowing based on hierarchical or professional status. It also means that the social, bodily reality in the workplace involves roughness, dislikes, and arguments with enduring tension in leadership processes.
>
> *(23)*

Their observations about workplace dynamics apply equally to our learning communities and remind us that tensions and disagreements are to be expected.

Dominant leadership theories, these scholars argue, take a particular aesthetic stance that finds beauty in hierarchical structure, standardization, and harmony.

> Common to different leadership style suggestions (coaching, human relations, autocratic, transformational, visionary, transactional exchange, and

servant leadership style) is the inherent assumption that the leader, even after follower consultation and frequent interaction, has the superior wisdom of what needs to be done. The followers are seen in this leadership paradigm as passive objects that are observed, evaluated, trained, and provided counseling services without being capable of developing anything new themselves. This view of leadership emphasizes the overarching dominance of hierarchical dominance and top-down rationality. To us, this represents one kind of aesthetics in leadership: the beauty of geometry.

(27)

Ropo, Parvlalnan, and Koivunen invite us to apply a second type of aesthetics to leadership by considering the embodied relational processes prominent among musicians, dancers, and research scientists. This type of aesthetics focuses on the beauty of living human bodies. From this perspective, leaders and followers share tacit knowledge with each other through bodily presence and intense listening to each other. A person in a leader role, say an orchestra conductor, uses his or her deep knowledge of and feel for the work that's underway along with the information emanating from followers to summon the group to high levels of embodied performance.

A relational view of leadership, they argue, recognizes both individual and collective bodies. They add, "The bodily and social entities are inseparable in practice even if they are distinguishable theoretically. Social relations are based on the mutuality of gaze and touch, speech and listening, resonance of feelings and emotions" (35). Collective leadership emerges through negotiation among the participants.

> Nobody has the right and complete knowledge, only different pieces of information and skills. In the negotiating process these are discussed and shared with others in order to make a synthesis. In this process, listening is of crucial importance, the ability to receive instead of only sending out information. Openness and sensitivity to the moment are required in order to reach unity. The outcome of these negotiations is always unique, like an art performance or a lecture based on the same transparencies.
>
> *(35)*

If we adopt Ropo, Parvlalnan, and Koivunen's preferred aesthetic stance, we should attempt to make teaching environments ones that appeal to participants' senses and invite them to be active, rather than passively occupying seats. Ideally, our PowerPoints will be livelier, walls will be covered with colorful flip chart sheets, chairs will be more comfortable, and everyone will move around the space. Of course, as Ropo, Parvlalnan, and Koivunen concede, this approach becomes more difficult as leadership educators rely a great deal on virtual classrooms, even when we use online forums and video conferencing. In order to preserve the advantages of face-to-face interaction in actual physical spaces while gaining advantages of online instruction, several of us have developed hybrid courses that blend the two modes.

Diverse Bodies, Diverse Communities

Attention to the role of social identities and positions in leadership has come fairly late to leadership studies. I recall the frustration in the 1980s of trying to find readings that connected leadership to the experience of women and people of color. The team at the Reflective Leadership Center could find troves of research and stories about leaders and leadership in organizations and politics, but the protagonists were almost all white men (or the groups being discussed were undifferentiated "bosses" and "subordinates"). We had to wander well outside leadership studies to find models of female leaders or of leadership by Native Americans or poor people, for example. By the 1990s, the general invisibility of women and people of color in leadership studies began to change for a number of reasons. The late-20th-century women's movement and various civil rights movements in the U.S. and other parts of the world had brought many more women and people of color into visible leadership roles and raised expectations that these groups would have the same chances as white men to advance in organizations and political life. Those movements also brought policy changes that opened doors to women and people of color. Another important driver of leadership studies' realization that gender and race/ethnicity mattered was organizations' growing awareness that they needed to recruit and retain women and people of color in greater numbers. Thus, "managing diversity" became an important requirement for organizational leaders, and scholars offered their findings about the barriers to diversifying workforces and establishing diverse leadership cadres in organizations (see, for example, Morrison, 1992).

By the second decade of this century, considerable research has accumulated on women in leader roles, perceptions of women as leaders, barriers to women's advancement in organizations and politics, and the distinctive contributions of women as leaders. Attention to the leadership effects of race/ethnicity and other social identities and positions has increased, but not nearly as much. With some exceptions, much of the "mainstream" leadership literature continues to consider gender, race/ethnicity, and other important social identities as add-ons. Part III of this book will suggest several helpful overviews of leadership theory as it has evolved over the last 100 years. In adopting a chronological approach, these books reserve any in-depth attention to diverse leaders and followers till later chapters. Even such a fine recent overview as Doris Schedlitzki and Gareth Edwards's *Studying Leadership: Traditional and Critical Approaches* (2014) has a single chapter on gender and diversity in the book's final section, though the authors have critiqued the exclusionary nature of many leadership theories throughout.

In practice, our social identities and positions are never add-ons as we engage in leadership and followership. The remainder of this section highlights key studies that investigate how race/ethnicity affects the enactment of leadership, followed by attention to scholarship on women and leadership. The section concludes with a focus on the connection of leadership with other social identities and positions, such as sexual identity, religion, class, age, and physical ability.

Race and Ethnicity

In 2009 Sonia Ospina and Erica Foldy published "A Critical Review of Race and Ethnicity in the Leadership Literature" in the annual year-end review issue of *Leadership Quarterly*. They found that few leadership scholars had published work directly on their topic but unearthed plenty of rich material in other fields, chiefly education. (The two women excluded studies on "managing diversity," because they generally take a very broad brush to diversity, rather than focusing specifically on race and ethnicity.) In making their case for investigating the links between leadership and race/ethnicity, Ospina and Foldy note the importance of understanding how individuals and groups can forge connections with each other "without suppressing difference" (877). They note that paying attention to race/ethnicity highlights the importance of context and power dynamics in leadership work. This focus, they argue, fosters an "understanding of power not only as a resource for individuals, but also as a web of institutionalized inequities that systematically, and at the expense of others, provides privilege to some communities and some perspectives" (Ospina and Foldy, 2009, 877).

Focusing mainly on organizational leadership, Ospina and Foldy found important insights about how race/ethnicity of leaders and followers affects perceptions of leadership, how race/ethnicity affects enactment of leadership, and how leaders and followers cope with "the social reality of race-ethnicity" (878). They note that much of the research into the effects of race/ethnicity on perceptions of leadership has been done in U.S. and British contexts, where "whiteness" is dominant. The findings generally, but not always, highlight disadvantages or constraints associated with being a person of color. Ospina and Foldy cite this finding from a typical study (Chung-Herrera and Lankau, 2005):

> when participants compared profiles of a successful manager to stereotypical profiles of managers of different races, they tended to see a greater correspondence between ratings of white and Asian American managers and the successful manager prototype, compared with black and Hispanic managers.
> *(Ospina and Foldy, 2009, 879)*

Numerous studies have recounted the isolation, discounting, racism, and other obstacles that African American, Latino, and Native American managers have experienced in the workplace due to stereotypes as well as systemic inequities.

Ospina and Foldy cite research that shows race/ethnicity can be a key resource for individuals as they lead within organizations and communities. It may shape their sense of purpose and offer communal ties, and it can certainly offer strength as they turn to cultural traditions of resilience and mutual support. This research also highlights the skill of bicultural fluency that enables non-white managers to "lead in ways that resonate with members of their own racial-ethnic group but also connect with the dominant ways of working in their white-majority contexts" (882).

Research focusing on race/ethnicity as a pervasive aspect of social reality emphasizes individual as well as collective aspects of racial identity and considers how leaders and followers "grapple with race-ethnicity as a reality that infuses specific meanings in concrete social contexts" (884). Such research, for example, investigates the ways that a leader like Barack Obama manages his identity as a biracial man in relation to diverse constituencies or the ways that civil rights leaders activate racial solidarity. Some researchers in this category use critical race theory to highlight the role of institutions in maintaining the power and privilege of the white population, but also opportunities for (and necessity of) altering those institutions in order to remedy inequities.

Ospina and Foldy identify possible reasons that the "mainstream" leadership literature has paid so little attention to diverse leaders and followers. They note that studies of leadership by women and people of color have often relied on narrative and phenomenological methods that are not the norm in leadership studies. Additionally, they finger the underlying assumption in most of the leadership literature that the standard identity of people in leader roles is white and male. They join Collinson (2005), DiTomaso and Hooijberg (1996), and others in highlighting the inadequacy of the "color-blind and gender-blind assumptions" of traditional leadership theory. The result, they say, is loss of "a full recognition of the leadership experience of both non-white leaders who tend to be dismissed and white leaders whose race is unseen" (888).

The article ultimately builds a case not just for fully incorporating attention to race/ethnicity into leadership studies, but for fully exploring how the intersection of multiple social identities (gender, race, profession, physical ability, profession, etc.) constrains and enables an individual's leadership and followership.

Sonia Ospina, Erica Foldy, and their colleagues at New York University (NYU) have done outstanding work examining leadership by and within ethnically diverse social change organizations. They have advanced the use of narrative methodology in leadership studies, while illuminating the ways that these organizations build bridges between different groups while confronting social inequities. For example, Ospina and Foldy's article for the *Leadership Quarterly* special issue on integrative leadership (2010) identifies five bridge-building practices: prompting cognitive shifts, naming and shaping identity, engaging in dialogue about difference, creating equitable governance mechanisms, and weaving "multiple worlds together through interpersonal relationships" (297). They also identify two assumptions that underlie these practices: "the importance of minimizing power inequities, and recognition of the strategic value of 'difference'" (Ospina and Foldy, 2010). The practice of prompting cognitive shifts is evident when people in organizations find ways to frame their concerns in a way that can include diverse constituencies. To name and shape identity, organizations celebrate and redefine particular social identities—for example, being a Oaxacan immigrant woman in the U.S. Engaging in dialogue around difference often requires multiple rounds of often difficult conversation and dedicated effort to include diverse voices and ideas. To achieve equitable governance mechanisms, organizations set up both inclusive structures (boards and committees) as well as inclusive processes. Establishing personal relationships takes the form of one-to-one meetings between two people from different geographic or ethnic communities, or ongoing staff efforts to welcome constituents. Though the focus of the NYU research has been on social change organizations, Ospina and Foldy make a convincing case that their findings have much broader applicability, as scholars and practitioners develop collaborative models of leadership that can overcome the limitations of command-and-control models.

The article might prompt us as leadership educators to consider how to incorporate the bridge-building practices it identifies more intentionally into our learning communities. For example, we can foster cognitive shifts such as reframing leadership as an inclusive, relational practice. We might encourage participants to engage in co-designing at least some portion of our workshops and courses. We might ensure examples of effective leadership in our courses show how racial/ethnic identities that are often marginalized can be assets. (Such examples may enhance participants' collective racial esteem, which Dugan, Kodama, and Gebhardt [2012] found builds undergraduate students' capacity for socially responsible leadership.)

In *Diversity and Leadership* (2015) Jean Lau Chin and Joseph Trimble add to the case for understanding diverse cultural influences on leadership styles. They note, especially, the forces of globalization that foster increased population flows across national borders and require so many people these days to work with people from a variety of countries. In my own classes, for example, I am likely to have participants from 10 or more countries. These authors also point to the growth of various minority American communities and the prediction that by 2050 the main ethnic minority groups will constitute over half of the U.S population. They discuss and critique findings from the ambitious GLOBE study that surveyed managers in 62 countries to discern preferred leadership styles associated with national cultures (see House et al., 2004, and numerous follow-up reports). They highlight the diversity of cultures within countries and also recognize key distinctions among Eastern versus Western parts of the world (for example, the Western emphasis on individual achievement and the Eastern emphasis on collective achievement). They suggest research methods that are helpful for investigating diverse leadership and offer extensive guidance on developing culturally competent leaders and organizations. Their chapter on leader training (written with Roger Husbands and Beauregard Stubblefield-Tave) highlights the ASK (for awareness, skills, and knowledge) approach developed by Josepha Campinha-Bacote (2003); the approach emphasizes awareness of one's own and others' cultural backgrounds, cross-cultural skills (especially communication) and knowledge about cultural differences.

Ideally, the training helps participants become what Stubblefield-Tave calls "culturally fluent," that is, able to work effectively as leaders and followers both in home cultures and cultures represented in their organizations (211). This chapter also notes the value of training programs designed specifically for racial/ethnic groups or women and provides three examples of such programs.

In *Salsa, Soul, and Spirit* (2007), Juana Bordas explores the distinctive strengths that infuse Latino, African American, and Native American leadership. Salsa is the metaphor she chooses for Latino leadership: "Salsa is the spice of life—the energy, vitality, and *gusto*! . . . Latino leadership reflects a social and celebratory nature, a community-oriented centered approach, and a people-centered process" (12). The essence of African American leadership is captured in soul, which "reflects a deep well of resilient hope, a spiritual family bonded by common hardship, and an emotional connection that forges community consciousness" (13). Spirit typifies Native American leadership: "Like the Great Spirit—which is pervasive, life-generating, and timeless—American Indian leadership brings a spiritual foundation, which respects and benefits all life and ensures the continuity of future generations" (17).

Bordas lists and elaborates eight principles of multicultural leadership based on core values of Latino, African American, and American Indian cultures. They are:

- Learning from the past
- Moving from individualism to collective identity
- Developing a spirit of generosity
- Recognizing community-conferred leadership
- Building on a tradition of activism
- Working for the common good
- Developing a sense of kinship with other people and the planet
- Adopting an attitude of gratitude, hope, and forgiveness

Throughout the book, Bordas offers examples of how Latinos, African Americans, and Native Americans have enacted these principles. She concludes with a call for adopting a multicultural approach to leadership in U.S. society. The approach would require acculturation by white people as well as by people of color (the people who are often expected to acculturate). "On a societal level, to achieve cultural equity and reciprocity, White Americans must acculturate to other cultures' norms and ways of thinking and acting" (188). Bordas calls for dismantling "hierarchical pluralism" (the dominant U.S. view of inclusion, in which multiple cultural values are acceptable, but Euro-American cultural norms are at the top of the hierarchy) and establishing "egalitarian pluralism." Ultimately, her hope is that adopting the leadership principles that are celebrated in communities of color can foster a regeneration of American democracy and provide inspiration for people in other countries.

Another important book that emphasizes the connections between race/ethnicity and leadership is the second edition of Glenn Singleton's *Courageous Conversations About Race* (2015). He explores six conditions for practicing "racial equity leadership":

- Getting personal right here and right now
- Keeping the focus on race
- Engaging multiple perspectives about race
- Keeping us all at the table
- Exploring the meaning of race
- Talking about whiteness

Although the book focuses specifically on eliminating racial disparities in K-12 education, the approach is useful for leaders seeking to level the playing field for racial/ethnic groups in other contexts. In addition to offering guidance for hosting courageous conversations, the book includes a number of racial autobiographies and prompts to readers to reflect on their own racial experience.

Gender

Most of the leadership research and theorizing about gender has focused on the achievements of women leaders and the obstacles they encounter as they seek formal leadership positions. Recently, as the concept of gender has become more fluid, often overlapping with sexual identity, the focus is shifting a bit to leadership by and of people who identify as transgender (usually grouped with gay, lesbian, bisexual, and queer leadership).

Using gender rather than the designators male and female was a means for feminist theorists a few decades ago to emphasize that biological sex is less important in most of our social interactions than the socialized roles that are assigned to the different sexes. Accordingly, many studies have shown that women who aspire to political office or executive positions are expected to employ the more assertive behaviors associated with masculine gender roles, yet when they do they will be criticized for not conforming to feminine gender roles. The work of Alice Eagly, in particular, offers an overview of research and theorizing about women and leadership in recent decades (see Eagly, 2005). Books like Alice Eagly's and Linda Carli's *Through the Labyrinth* (2007), and the recent *Women as Global Leaders* (2015), edited by Faith Ngunjiri and Susan Madsen, chronicle the considerable advances that women have made in the world of politics, as well as business and nonprofit leadership. They also highlight the slow pace of change. For example, in chapter 2 of *Women as Global Leaders*, Nancy Adler reports a very substantial increase in female heads of state starting in the 1990s, but emphasizes that while "the increase is impressive, the total is not" (25). In the U.S. business world, by early 2014 only 23 of the Fortune 500 companies had women CEOs, and extending the report to the Fortune 1000 only added another 23 with women CEOs. The U.S. Congress presents a somewhat more positive picture: as of 2015, 84 women were serving as representatives and 20 were senators, constituting 19.4% of the membership; this percentage has steadily, though slowly, increased in recent decades (http://www.cawp.rutgers.edu/current-numbers).

Research has tended to focus on perceptions of women in leader roles and on women's aspirations, with some attention to women's disproportionate responsibility for child-rearing and household management. The research reveals positive trends—for example, more and more people profess willingness to accept women in leader roles, and increasingly girls around the world aspire to match boys in their achievements. Increasingly, management and leadership experts argue in favor of the collaborative, participatory leadership style that women are more likely to adopt than men (Eagly, 2005). Even so, Eagly notes, women in leader roles also may have to project authority and "gravitas," which may not only be counter to expected gender roles but require considerable "emotional labor" and feel like a violation of their authentic selves. She adds, "Finding relational authenticity by knowing and being oneself is a luxury enjoyed by people from groups that have traditionally inhabited high-level leadership roles—in most contexts, white men from relatively privileged backgrounds" (471). She urges those of us who offer leadership training to acknowledge this bind for women leaders.

In chapter 3 of *Women as Global Leaders*, Roya Ayman and Karen Korabik report on the positive outcomes associated with leaders who adopt an androgynous style—that is, behaving both communally (the social norm for women) and agentically (the social norm for men). They note that in theory "men and women should be equally likely to possess the qualities that make them androgynous leaders" and suggest an androgynous style may be especially advantageous for women since it "allows them to have characteristics that correspond to the ideal of the masculine leader" yet also incorporate feminine qualities (63). Ayman and Korabik also offer helpful descriptions of gender as both intrapsychic and social interaction processes, which are embedded in power hierarchies.

Most research focusing on women and leadership deals with the realms of the psyche and social interactions rather than on the power hierarchies that pose structural or institutional barriers to women's advancement. Scholars interested in women's access to leadership positions have at times focused on eliminating structural barriers within organizations (see chapter 6 in *Women as Global Leaders*), but little work has been done on the barriers to women's leadership caused by the high incidence of violence against women (Sengupta, 2015) or their lack of political representation. A teaching resource that helps fill this gap is an e-case entitled "Safe Harbor," published on the Hubert Project website (http://tinyurl.com/

pwl3bch). The case traces the efforts of several women leaders and some male leaders to end sex trafficking of girls in Minnesota by passing statewide legislation.

Gender identity, of course, includes masculine and transgender identities. Interaction of masculine identity with leadership mainly has been studied obliquely via investigations of women and leadership. (An exception is an experimental study by Samuel Bendahan, Christian Zehnder, François Pralong, and John Antonakis [2014] linking leader power, testosterone levels, and corruption.) As for studies on transgender leadership, Lemuel Watson and Lemuel Johnson (2013) note, "Scholarship on and investigations conducted by leaders who are 'openly' LGBTQ are virtually nonexistent" (viii).

Intersections

So far I have mainly considered the impact of racial/ethnic and gender identities on leadership separately, and I could have devoted sections to other identities—for example, those linked to physical ability, sexual orientation, class, and religion. In practice, however, each of us is influenced by a mesh of past, present, and future identities; moreover, multiple group identities are usually salient in a given leadership context.

For example, I have often assigned one or more chapters from Joseph Shapiro's *No Pity* (1994), about the U.S. disability rights movement. Leaders in the movement had multiple identities—for example, representing a group with a particular disability as well as being Republican—that strengthened their influence. The authors in Lemuel Watson and Joshua Johnson's *Authentic Leadership* (2013) examine the ways that LGBTQ identities intersect with being a professional in higher education.

Another Hubert Project e-case, "The African American Leadership Forum" (http://www.hubertproject.org/hubert-material/257) describes the efforts of African American leaders in several northwestern U.S. cities to build on the advances of the civil rights era to tackle racial disparities that persist today. These leaders have realized they must be aware of how African American identity overlaps with generational, class, and professional identities if they are to develop an agenda to end disparities. They have intentionally designed their meetings and other events to build bridges among different generations, between professionals and grassroots community leaders, and among leaders from different sectors.

Often very diverse groups find common ground in at least one shared identity. For example, women from different ethnic backgrounds find commonality in resisting gender-based stereotypes. For many years I worked with a group of midcareer fellows who came from many different nations; in some cases, their countries had a history of conflict with each other. Relations in the group weren't necessarily smooth, but the common experience of being part of their countries' professional elite, plus being a part of a shared fellows' community helped bind them.

Bridging Differences

This chapter already has explored several means of connecting people in their diversity. I want to present additional ideas for fostering mutual understanding in diverse groups. In my classes I often begin this work by exploring David Bohm's distinction between dialogue and discussion. Dialogue, says Bohm (Bohm and Nicol,1996), is a process of presenting one's ideas and attentively listening to those of others, without evaluating others' ideas. In contrast, discussion emphasizes evaluation: I pose an idea and others pounce on its strengths and weaknesses. Such an approach can dampen participants' desire to offer ideas at all; in problem-solving sessions, the likely result is killing off proffered ideas before they are properly explored. Dialogue requires "suspension of judgment," an active effort on the part of the listener to postpone evaluation until ideas have been fully developed.

"Crucial conversations" is a well-developed dialogic approach that fosters effective communication among people with different perspectives and backgrounds. These methods can be practiced within our learning communities and in participants' own workplaces and communities. Kerry Patterson, Joseph Grenny, Ron McMillan, and Al Switzler (2002) describe crucial conversations as those in which stakes are high, opinions vary, and strong emotions are involved. They note that the built-in default response for human beings when they engage in conflictual situations like this is to flee or fight, resulting in "silence" or "violence." We avoid true conversation by being polite or walking away (forms of silence) or we become defensive, determined to defend our own views and reputation at all costs (forms of violence).

The authors developed their guidance for effectively holding crucial conversations by researching the practices of the most influential people in workplace settings. The key talent, they found, was dialogue, which they describe as the "free flow of meaning between two or more people" (20). Patterson and colleagues offer a set of tools for fostering productive dialogue. They advise us to "start with the heart"—that is, at the outset of conversation, have good intentions, stay focused on your overall goals for the conversation, and avoid either/or thinking. They advise searching for the "ever-elusive *and*" (40) by:

1.   Clarifying what you *really* want
2.   Clarifying what you really *don't* want
3.   Combining the first two into an *and* question "that forces you to search for more creative and productive options than silence or violence" (40)

In a recent class I taught, some students endorsed campus protests against the use of "Redskins" as the name of a professional football team. One student was uncertain that the protests were warranted, but he knew the issue was sensitive, especially since another class member was Native American. Following

Patterson and colleagues' advice, he would have asked himself a question like this: "How can I find out more about this issue, while not seeming insensitive to the concerns of Native Americans?" In reality, he opened the conversation in keeping with the spirit of this question. He didn't remain quiet or jump in with a comment that belittled people who are offended by some team mascots, but simply said that he didn't understand the issue very well and hoped that his classmates could explain why the name was offensive. Class members (who may well have been thinking, "Why doesn't he get it?") responded in a dialogical spirit with information about the impact of stereotypes.

Patterson and colleagues underscore the importance of safety for fostering productive conversations. When a leadership educator observes herself (or participants) avoiding conversation, being defensive, or going on the attack, that's a sign she (or they) feel threatened. Safety, Patterson et al. emphasize, is established when the educator makes clear to participants that she cares about their interests as well as her own, when she shows respect. In order to do this, she may have to apologize for something she said that was self-serving or disrespectful and she may have to directly address a participant's mistrust by confirming good intentions or respect for the person.

For a conversation to produce good results for everyone involved, the partners must find a mutual overarching purpose, say Patterson and colleagues. Sometimes, that occurs easily, but when it doesn't, they suggest using a CRIB approach: Commit to seek mutual purpose, recognize *real* purposes behind an initial stance, invent a mutual purpose when necessary, and brainstorm strategies based on the purpose. If strong emotions are keeping you from moving ahead, they suggest telling yourself a different story about what is going on; they urge you to consider multiple explanations for a partner's behavior, avoid stories that cast yourself as victim or villain, and focus on facts. As a model for dialogue, Patterson et al. suggest that the initiator first share facts (such as what he/she has observed or feels), then move to a tentative interpretation or story about what could be going on or might happen, and then encourage the other person to tell his/her story. Means of encouragement include asking questions, mirroring (reflecting back to the other person what his/her tone and body language are conveying), and paraphrasing (in which the initiator summarizes what he/she is hearing). Sometimes, when the other person still seems reluctant to talk, an initiator may also have to prime the conversation by offering his/her guesses about how the other person views the situation. The result of using all of the "crucial conversation" tools effectively is what the authors call a "pool of shared meaning" that can be the basis for deciding on joint strategies and actions.

Other approaches have similarities to courageous conversations. Marshall B. Rosenberg's nonviolent communication (Rosenberg, 2015) and Tom Rusk's ethical persuasion (Rusk and Miller, 1993) are two that I also have included in my practice. They suggest an important shift in the crucial conversations process, and that is inviting the other person to tell his/her story before you tell yours.

   In his analysis of undergraduate leadership development programs, John Dugan (2011) notes that participants' opportunities to interact across cultural differences (including race, religion, sexual orientation, and political perspective) has especially high impact on increasing their leadership capacity. He argues that the "importance of teaching students how to engage in meaningful dialogue about and across differences and then purposefully creating opportunities to do so in the context of leadership education cannot be overstated" (72).

★★★

Several scholars deepen understanding of hosting as a leadership practice that brings diverse human beings together in physical and virtual spaces at particular times to tackle shared tasks. This chapter has considered elements of what McKergow calls "host leadership" and explored in some depth the Art of Hosting approach. Then I used the lens of aesthetic leadership to consider the importance of attending to embodied learners and the sensory environment within leadership courses and workshops. From there, I moved to theories and research about gendered and diverse bodies in the enactment of leadership. Clearly, actual leaders and followers have multiple, intersecting identities, which tie them to various communities. Finally, the chapter explored dialogue and the crucial conversations approach as a means of connecting people, while honoring their diversity. The next chapter will focus on practical details of how leadership educators make our courses and workshops welcoming and productive environments for diverse learners.

References

Baldwin, C., & Linnea, A. (2010). *The circle way: A leader in every chair*. San Francisco: Berrett-Koehler.

Bendahan, S., Zehnder, C., Pralong, F. P., & Antonakis, J. (2014). Leader corruption depends on power and testosterone. *Leadership Quarterly, 26*(2), 101–122.

Bohm, D., & Nicol, L. (1996). *On dialogue*. London: Routledge.

Bordas, J. (2007). *Salsa, soul, and spirit: Leadership for a multicultural age*. San Francisco: Berrett-Koehler Publishers, Inc.

Brown, J., & Isaacs, D. (2005). *The world café: Shaping our futures through conversations that matter*. San Francisco: Berrett-Koehler.

Campinha-Bacote, J. (2003). *The process of cultural competence in the delivery of healthcare services: A culturally competent model of care*. Cincinnati, OH: Transcultural C.A.R.E. Associates.

Chin, J. L., & Trimble, J. (2015). *Diversity and leadership*. Thousand Oaks, CA: SAGE.

Chung-Herrera, B. G., & Lankau, M. J. (2005). "Are we here yet?": An assessment of fit between stereotypes of minority managers and the successful-manager prototype. *Journal of Applied Psychology, 35*(10), 2029–2056.

Collinson, D. (2005). Dialectics of leadership. *Human Relations, 58*(11), 1419–1492.

Cooperrider, D. L., & Whitney, D. D. (2005). *Appreciative inquiry: A positive revolution in change*. San Francisco: Berrett-Koehler.

DiTomaso, N., & Hooijberg, R. (1996). Diversity and the demands of leadership. *Leadership Quarterly, 7*(2), 163–187.

Dugan, J. P. (2011). Research on college student leadership development. In S. R. Komives, J. P. Dugan, J. E. Owen, C. Slack, & W. Wagner (Eds.), *The handbook for student leadership development* (2nd ed., pp. 59–84). San Francisco: Jossey-Bass.

Dugan, J. P., Kodama, C. M., & Gebhardt, M. C. (2012). Race and leadership development among college students: The additive value of collective racial esteem. *Journal of Diversity in Higher Education, 5*(3), 174–189.

Eagly, A. H. (2005). Achieving relational authenticity in leadership: Does gender matter? *Leadership Quarterly, 16*(3), 459–474.

Eagly, A. H., & Carli, L. L. (2007). *Through the labyrinth: The truth about how women become leaders*. Boston, MA: Harvard Business School.

Fenwick, T., Nerland, M., & Jensen, K. (2012). Sociomaterial approaches to conceptualising professional learning, knowledge, and practice. *Journal of Education and Work, 25*(1), 1–13.

Heifetz, R. A. (1994). *Leadership without easy answers*. Boston: Belknap.

House, R. J., Hanges, P. J., Javidan, M., Dorfman, P. W., & Gupta, V. (2004). *Culture, leadership and organizations: GLOBE study of 62 societies*. Thousand Oaks, CA: SAGE.

McKergow, M., & Bailey, H. (2014). *Host: Six new roles of engagement*. London: SolutionsBooks.

Morrison, A. M. (1992). *The new leaders: Guidelines on leadership diversity in America*. San Francisco: Jossey-Bass Publishers.

Ngunjiri, F., & Madsen, S. (Eds.). (2015). *Women as global leaders*. Charlotte, NC: IAP.

Ospina, S., & Foldy, E. (2009). A critical review of race and ethnicity in the leadership literature: Surfacing context, power and the collective dimensions of leadership. *Leadership Quarterly, 20*(6), 876–896.

Ospina, S., & Foldy, E. G. (2010). Building bridges from the margins: The work of leadership in social change organizations. *Leadership Quarterly, 21*(2), 292–307.

Owen, H. (1997). *Open space technology: A user's guide* (2nd ed.). San Francisco: Berrett-Koehler.

Patterson, K., Grenny, J., McMillan, R., & Switzler, A. (2002). *Crucial conversations: Tools for talking when stakes are high*. New York: McGraw-Hill.

Quick, K. S., & Sandfort, J. R. (2014). Learning to facilitate deliberation: Practicing the art of hosting. *Critical Policy Studies, 8*(3), 300–322.

Ropo, A., Parvlalnan, J., & Koivunen, N. (2002). Aesthetics in leadership: From absent bodies to social bodily presence. In K. W. Parry, & J. R. Meindl (Eds.), *Grounding leadership: Theory and research* (pp. 21–38). Greenwich, CT: IAP.

Rosenberg, M. (2015). *Nonviolent communication—A language of life* (3rd ed.). Encinitis, CA: PuddleDancer.

Rusk, T., & Miller, P. (1993). *The power of ethical persuasion*. New York: Viking.

Sandfort, J. R., & Quick, K. S. (2015). Building deliberative capacity to create public value: The practices and artifacts of the art of hosting. In J. M. Bryson, B. C. Crosby, & L. Bloomberg (Eds.), *Public value and public administration* (pp. 39–52). Washington, DC: Georgetown Press.

Sandfort, J. R., Stuber, N., & Quick, K. S. (2012). *Practicing the art of hosting: Exploring what art of hosting and harvesting workshop participants understand and do*. Minneapolis: Center for Integrative Leadership, University of Minnesota.

Schedlitzki, D., & Edwards, G. (2014). *Studying leadership: Traditional and critical approaches.* London: SAGE.

Shapiro, J. (1994). *No pity: People with disabilities forging a new civil rights movement.* New York: New York Times Books.

Sengupta, S. (2015, March 10). U.N. reveals "alarmingly high" levels of violence against women. *New York Times*, p. A4.

Singleton, G. (2015). *Courageous conversations about race: A field guide for achieving equity in schools* (2nd ed.). Thousand Oaks, CA: Corwin.

Watson, L. W., & Johnson, J. M. (Eds.). (2013). *Authentic leadership: An engaged discussion of LGBTQ work as culturally relevant.* Charlotte, NC: Information Age.

6

HOSTING AND THE HANDS

The work of hosting in leadership courses and workshops begins well before participants assemble. As leadership educators, we may be involved in recruiting participants, but even when we aren't we can get to know our audience before they arrive. To the extent we can, we acquaint ourselves with the physical space where we will convene and arrange it appropriately. We help participants feel welcomed into a learning experience, and we introduce processes that will help them communicate effectively with each other and bridge differences. As Ron Riggio emphasizes, "Leadership begins when you teach people to communicate." We seek to model the communication skills we are teaching and we help participants prepare to be attentive hosts. Throughout we stay focused on the chief aim of this practice: to create stimulating learning environments and build relationships—between ourselves and each participant, and among the participants. Time after time, I have heard from participants in my classes that it is the connections they have made with other participants, many quite different from them, that have been the most valuable aspect of the course.

Knowing the Audience

Getting involved in the recruitment process, directly or indirectly, helps us ensure that the people who show up for a course or workshop are the right people (or, conversely, that we design the course or workshop for the people who are going to show up). Ideally, we will be able to recruit participants who represent the diversity of the organizations or communities in which they live and work. We may have to think about the best time for offering a workshop or course and whether some people will require transportation or childcare.

Valerie Shangreaux describes the recruitment process for the Blandin Community Leadership Program:

> *We are place-based; typically each program has 24–26 people from one community. We bring a broad representation of the community together, not just administrators and CEOs. It's established and emerging leaders. We recruit around nine common dimensions of healthy community—spirituality and wellness, economic opportunity, community leadership, life-long learning, inclusion, recreational and artistic opportunity, safety and security, infrastructure and services, and environmental stewardship. We try to have equal representation of men and women, and a distribution of ages. Our only real requirements are they're engaged in community or want to be, willing to take risks, and are open-minded.*

Even if we are not involved in the recruitment process, we can ask participants to provide biographical information and a photo before the class begins so we can know more about them. We should find out if participants have a physical disability or particular needs, such as dietary restrictions, that we should factor into our plans. Sometimes the best we can do is learn more about the participants as a group—perhaps they all come from the same organization, social group, or profession. To start building relationships with them, we try to understand their context. To take an example from my own practice, I agreed in the late 1990s to provide leadership training in Poland for people who were trying to acquire new professional skills following the breakup of the Soviet Union. I knew very little about the Polish context, and had little time to learn. My solution may not have been the most academically respectable, but it did help me relate to participants in my classes. I acquired a copy of James Mitchener's very fat novel *Poland* (2015) and read it all the way across the Atlantic.

Welcoming Participants

In order to welcome participants to a mutual learning experience, we pay attention to the physical space in which we meet and to the need to engage participants' senses. Ideally, we will be able to do some reconnaissance on the physical space where we convene our courses and workshops. We want to be sure that technical systems are functioning and that tables and chairs are set up to facilitate planned learning activities. As participants enter the room, we may play music—possibly lively, possibly relaxing—that lifts spirits and prompts the expectation that learning will be enjoyable. A table might hold food and flowers; a screen might show an eye-catching PowerPoint image. In keeping with

Juana Bordas's idea of setting up a family altar, we could spread a bright cloth on a table where participants can display family photographs. We might also display other objects that communicate something about the work that will be under way in the course or workshop. Providing name tags or name "tents" makes sense as a way of helping both instructor and participants make personal connections with people present. An abbreviated agenda can be posted or distributed as a handout so that people know when breaks occur and what topics will be covered.

When we are unable to organize a space ahead of time we always can enlist participants in rearranging tables and chairs. (It's never too early to communicate the message that leadership involves heavy lifting.) At times, we may be assigned a space that can't be rearranged as we would like. Even in a setting as rigid as a large auditorium, however, we can design activities involving audience participation. We can greet people as they enter, and during a presentation provide prompts for talking with seatmates. We may even channel our inner Oprah and move into the aisles to elicit audience reaction if microphones permit.

A number of the educators contributing to this book open face-to-face gatherings with a circle in order to emphasize the inclusive nature of the class or workshop. In welcoming everyone into the circle, we explain briefly the benefits of assembling in this way. We invite everyone to respond briefly to the question or topic we pose, and take turns going around the circle so that anyone who wishes to speak can. (A sample question might be: Mention a hope you have for this course.) Usually we return to someone who has passed up his/her turn in case the person is ready to speak after others have had their chance. In order to keep responses brief when time is limited, we may model a short comment or perhaps ask for a two-word response. When she needs to conserve time, Sonia Ospina sets a one-minute timer on her smartphone and passes it around as an automatic prompt to limit comments.

Many of the things I've talked about so far in this section may seem trivial, but far from being trivial they are absolutely vital to whether learners will feel included and stimulated to think and express themselves deeply (Huxham, 1990). What is astounding is how often we simply take for granted how classrooms are set up and the limitations they place on learning. At some point in my classes, I emphasize the power of settings to affect our leadership work and ask participants to reflect on how a typical classroom setting allocates power, a central component of leadership.

When our classroom extends to online work, we still must consider the "trivialities." How user-friendly are our websites, how accessible is the VoiceThread assignment? When I ask participants to use an unfamiliar technology, I often provide tutorials and explain the value of using it.

Peter Shea, Chun Li, and Alexandra Pickett (2006) emphasize the special importance of "teacher presence" in online or hybrid courses. Teacher presence encompasses course design, facilitating effective discourse, and instructing.

Especially relevant to hosting is facilitation of effective discourse, which the authors (drawing on Anderson, Rourke, Garrison, and Archer, 2001) describe as identifying "areas of agreement and disagreement, seeking to reach consensus and understanding; encouraging, acknowledging, and reinforcing student contributions; setting the climate for learning, drawing in participants, prompting discussion, and assessing the efficacy of the process" (177).

No matter how much we prepare for face-to-face or online courses, our plans may go awry. The computerized projector system may fail, the people who set up the room may not have followed our instructions, two people show up in wheelchairs without warning, the course website may have glitches. We may have little control over the timing of face-to-face sessions. What matters, however, is our ability to greet these challenges with good humor and pursue learning within the constraints. Even setbacks and glitches offer teaching potential, since leadership also involves improvisation.

At times, we may learn that a person who has joined a workshop or class really isn't ready for it—or it may simply not be a good fit. Our task at that point is to help the person make a graceful exit and perhaps direct him/her to additional resources.

> *What makes for better leadership educators? I find that the most important factor for me is in knowing who the audience is in front of me and adjusting my emphasis for what is most likely to be helpful for them, rather than focusing on what I like to teach. While my textbooks have enough for everyone and then some, the teaching challenge is to gear the tenor of the class to those who I am teaching. Sometimes I am teaching executives with significant policy-making responsibilities. When that is the case, I focus more on organizational competencies and theories that push outward like transforming leadership, attribution theories (e.g., culture and gender), complexity leadership, social change leadership, etc. I often have audiences who will start at the bottom of the pyramid and will be proud to be supervisors or first-rung managers someday—very honorable managerial leaders. Many of my students are the first in their families to have gone to college. So there I focus leadership a bit more on good management practices— the proverbial task and people competencies; the theories I particularly emphasize are transactional and shared leadership. I personally find that an important theory set for everyone is distributed leadership, which ensures that the leadership process is not so leader-centric. Everyone is reminded that sometimes less leadership is more leadership in the operational world.*
>
> —Monty Van Wart

Acquiring Group Process Skills

I already have described several group process skills—chiefly engaging in dialogue, convening a circle, and establishing group norms in Chapters 3 and 5. Early in my course, I identify these and related skills as part of leading in small groups (team leadership), but they can also be useful in large groups. (Crucially, many large-group interaction processes, such as World Café and Open Space, are essentially a means of breaking down large groups into smaller ones.)

I also introduce team development frameworks that help participants understand that building a cohesive and productive group takes time and that leadership tasks vary throughout a team's development. Many people are already familiar with the "forming, storming, norming, and performing" framework (Tuckman, 1965) that depicts team members as moving through an initial stage of coming together, running into conflict as they try to decide what to do and how to do it, then setting some rules for making decisions and working together, and finally getting assigned or chosen tasks done. I might ask class members who know about this framework to explain it to others. I emphasize that the strength of the framework is that it reminds us that conflict in groups is normal, and unless some conflict of views occurs, a group is unlikely to be very creative. A limitation of the framework is that it implies that groups move through the stages in an orderly way. As noted, I invite groups to set norms very soon after they come together. The norms may only be solidified (and sometimes modified) after the group experiences conflict, but along with instructor ground rules, they describe aspirations for how people will work together. At times, norms will be violated—for example, when a participant takes up more air time than allotted when the group has agreed to honor time limitations. Ideally, another participant respectfully will remind everyone of the norm. If not, as instructors we may do the reminding and also ask the group if the norm should be altered—for example, by allocating more time to an exercise or allowing participants to surrender their own time so the speaker can continue.

I may also assign Susan Wheelan's *Creating Effective Teams* (2016), now in its fifth edition. Wheelan also identifies stages of team development, somewhat different from Tuckman's, and provides guidance about matching leadership style to development stage.

I often introduce Joyce Fletcher and Katrin Kaüfer's (2003) relational framework that describes groups' moving from talking nice to talking tough, to reflective dialogue, and finally to generative dialogue. The first two stages of this developmental framework are analogous to the forming and storming stages in the previous framework. In order to move to the third stage, Fletcher and Kaüfer say, leaders help group members adopt a relational stance by promoting empathy, listening, relational inquiry, vulnerability, and tolerance for uncertainty. In this stage, participants reflect on their own perspectives and realize they can learn from other group members. In the final stage, group members co-create ideas and strategies. After explaining this framework to a class, I usually ask small groups to discuss the following:

- What are my best skills for relating to others in a group?
- How did I learn those skills?
- Which skills would I like to develop further?

FIGURE 6.1   Fletcher and Kaüfer's Relational Dialog Process

Patterson et al.'s crucial conversations process, described in Chapter 5, offers helpful guidance for engaging in reflective and generative dialogue. One caveat about Patterson et al.'s advice: Silence is not always a bad thing in our classroom conversations. Certainly, we want to encourage speaking out, but allowing moments of silence may foster reflection and help people speak who need time to get their thoughts together.

"Maybe because I was raised Quaker, I find that being comfortable with silence is helpful," says Kathy Quick. When no one immediately responds to a question she poses, she does not fill the silence. "It's useful to wait, to call for a few minutes of reflection time."

In her book *Turning to One Another* (2002), Margaret Wheatley offers six principles that foster productive conversations about shared concerns:

1.   Acknowledge one another as equals ("a gesture of love" [140]).
2.   Try to stay curious about each other (remember that everyone has something to teach you).
3.   Recognize that we need each other's help to become better listeners.
4.   Slow down so we have time to think and reflect.
5.   Remember that conversation is the natural way humans think together.
6.   Expect it to be messy at times.

Yvonne Cheek underscores the importance of being a better listener: "Listening and innovation go hand in hand. Listen to yourself to access your creative mind. Listen to others to access theirs. Listen to the environment. I love putting together these two things."

Additionally, I emphasize the importance of not making assumptions about others' intentions or motivations. Usually, erring on the side of assuming positive intention makes sense. Certainly, the kinds of conversation I introduced in Chapter 5 can help reveal participants' motivations.

To supplement the group process tools already mentioned, I often introduce the Thomas-Kilmann model of conflict management (http://www.kilmanndiagnostics.com/overview-thomas-kilmann-conflict-mode-instrument-tki). The model identifies five different modes of handling conflict, depending on the emphasis one places on assertiveness versus cooperativeness. The five modes are:

- Avoiding, involving low assertiveness and low cooperation
- Accommodating; using this mode, one mainly cooperates with another's aims
- Competing; using this "win–lose" mode, one mainly asserts or defends one's own aims
- Compromising; using this "lose some–win some" mode, one makes trade-offs between one's own and another's aims
- Collaborating; using this "win–win" mode, one tries to accomplish one's own and another's aims

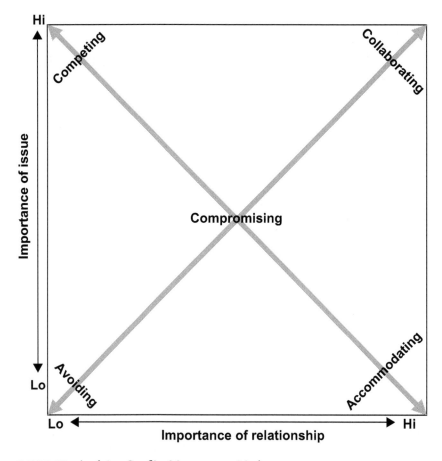

FIGURE 6.2   Applying Conflict Management Modes

Based on *Thomas-Kilmann Conflict Mode Instrument* (Kilmann, 2012) http://www.kilmanndiagnostics.com/catalog/thomas-kilmann-conflict-mode-instrument

An individual is likely to have a preferred mode among these five, but ideally s/he will learn to vary his/her approach depending on characteristics of the conflict situation. Two key characteristics are the importance of the issue and the importance of the relationship with the other party or parties (see Figure 6.2). If neither the issue nor the relationship is important, avoiding the conflict likely makes sense. If the relationship is much more important than the issue, accommodating is likely to be the best strategy. When the issue's importance significantly outweighs the relationship, competing is best, and when both the issue and the relationship are highly important, partners should strive for collaboration (win-win). Compromise is often presented as a way to preserve relationships and at least partially achieve each party's goals, but in this model it is very often the least desirable option, since both sides get less than they want. I also remind participants to be especially wary of the competing mode, since the relationship they devalue may be a relationship they need in the future. Ralph Kilmann, the co-creator of the model and the accompanying Thomas-Kilmann Conflict Mode Indicator, makes the case for developing the entire repertoire of modes and using them in the appropriate situations with sensitivity and respect (https://www.cpp.com/Pdfs/conflict_whitepaper.pdf).

Exploring Social Identities

Attending to social identities in our courses and workshops heightens respect for the rich diversity among participants and helps participants practice relating to people unlike themselves. We can choose from an array of tools for doing this. The Social Group Membership exercise presented in Chapter 3 is a means both of exploring different social identities and their effects on leadership efficacy (Part 1) and gathering group wisdom about how to build connections across these differences (Part 2). As noted previously, the exercise highlights the leadership advantages and disadvantages associated with social identities. It helps participants consider the greater power and privilege associated with particular social identities. The relational stance that characterizes Fletcher and Kaüfer's third stage is especially useful when participants join in small and large group conversations after completing this exercise individually.

Gill Hickman offers an entire course on Leadership in a Diverse Society. She begins with a focus on participants' national diversity, and assigns Ronald Takaki's *Different Mirror: A History of Multicultural America* (2008). She organizes immersion experiences to help students experience how it feels to be different from majority identities. Charles Palus asks participants in his programs to reflect on their given, chosen, and core identities.

Other leadership educators help participants recognize the ways that identities intersect within themselves. In a modification of an exercise she learned from Phyllis Braxton, Kathy Quick asks participants in her classes to jot down the five most important aspects of their identity, however they define that. Often they make notes relating to gender, family role, race, ethnicity, nationality, sexual orientation, religion, class, and physical ability. Then she asks them to pare the list to three and then to one. She asks them to describe their feelings about having to discard important parts of their identity, and thus drives home the importance of treating people as multifaceted rather than single-dimension persons.

One of my students introduced me to another method of demonstrating an intersectional approach to identity. In a face-to-face session, the exercise leader would draw a flower with several petals on the whiteboard and ask everyone to draw a flower on a sheet of paper. S/he then would invite participants to fill in the petals with descriptors for several aspects of their identity. To demonstrate, s/he might begin with gender and write cis male (meaning a man whose biological sex matches his social identity), trans, female, or something else. For the next petal s/ he might proceed to ethnicity and write the relevant descriptor and so on for the remaining petals. Once the petals are full, s/he might ask participants to identify the petals they think about most often, or the ones that are more important to them.

Several other tools are aimed specifically at appreciating and bridging cultural differences. The widely used and well-validated Intercultural Development Inventory (https://idiinventory.com/) is one, though instructors must take a two-and-a-half-day seminar to qualify for administering it. The IDI and accompanying training are intended to help individuals identify their current cultural mind-set and move along a continuum of five core mind-sets ranging from a monocultural to intercultural orientation. Proceeding from the monocultural end, the mind-sets are denial, polarization, minimization, acceptance, and adaptation (see Figure 6.3). If I operate from a denial mind-set, I simply don't see cultural difference. In the polarizing mind-set I notice difference but make negative judgments about people and practices different from my own. The minimization mind-set is transitional between a monocultural and intercultural orientation. I may notice differences but I emphasize commonalities. In the acceptance mind-set I appreciate cultural diversity, and in the adaptive mind-set I respond and adapt to difference.

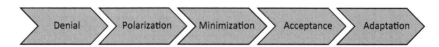

FIGURE 6.3 Intercultural Development Inventory Continuum

Modeling Communication Skills

An important part of introducing and reinforcing the skills of hosting is to practice dialogue and inclusive storytelling ourselves. For example, I begin my Leadership for the Common Good course by telling brief stories of leadership by people like the participants. From the outset, I minimize lectures in favor of asking questions. I draw out multiple views and promote comfort with complexity. I greet conflict with happiness (despite my innate desire to squash it).

I say directly just how fascinating I find the study and practice of leadership and I intend for my body language and stance to convey how energized I am by the beginning of another class or workshop. I move around the learning space as appropriate so that I am not always up front (when using slide presentations, a remote clicker can help).

To emphasize bodily communication and keep everyone's energy high I often use exercises that require people to vote with their feet or demonstrate a concept without words. In the beginning of a workshop I may divide participants into groups and ask them to develop a wordless skit that shows their view of leadership. Or, to show participants' reaction to an assigned reading, I might ask them to envision an imaginary continuum across the front of the room. At one end might be thorough disagreement with the author's view of leadership and at the other end, thorough agreement. Then I would ask participants to stand and arrange themselves along the continuum in sync with how much they agree or disagree with the author's arguments.

Modeling potent visual communication also includes the use of compelling PowerPoints, Prezi shows, and flip charts. In his book *Zen Design* (2014), Garr Reynolds offers excellent suggestions for improving slide presentations. He advises us to rely on three principles: restraint in preparation, simplicity in design, and naturalness in delivery. Among his pointers for preparing slide decks are: minimizing the use of text, avoiding clutter, and choosing images that convey messages effectively. He advises us to embed short videos in the presentations whenever appropriate:

> In my experience, a video clip is great for showing a problem or a paradox or highlighting salient points of a controversial issue. The video stimulates greater involvement and encourages people to discuss an issue or ask questions. . . . The type of things we can show in a video to engage, illustrate, and make things clear and more memorable to the audience are limited only by our imaginations and the time we need to find or create the video content (no small thing).
>
> *(134)*

Garr also offers advice for preparing accompanying handouts. He notes that handouts can include additional slides—showing, for example, supportive statistics or references that will clutter up the presentation. He advises providing handouts following a presentation, so people will not be distracted by them. An objection to handouts is that they can consume a lot of paper. A remedy for that is to post slide presentations to an accessible website. In my courses, I post slides to the course website before face-to-face sessions so that participants can print them if they wish. Another helpful resource is Nancy Duarte's *slide:ology: The Art and Science of Creating Great Presentations* (2008).

Using flip charts and markers to capture highlights of a large or small group conversation is by now commonplace in workshops and classrooms. Often I will ask small groups to produce flip chart sheets showing the ideas they have generated in response to some topic. Typically, a group member then stands by his/her group's flip chart sheet and explains the jottings. After all the groups' ideas have been presented I might ask participants to look at the flip chart sheets and identify similarities and differences among the groups or to point out an especially striking idea. This use of markers and flip charts is certainly useful for capturing and comparing participant ideas.

More visually stimulating, however, are flip chart sheets that are filled with symbols and images in bright colors along with key words. Figure 6.4 shows Avril Orloff's illustration of the World Café process. You can see that Orloff uses several types of simplified human figures, including what I call star figures (see Figure 6.5).

FIGURE 6.4   World Café Etiquette Graphic Illustration

By Avril Orloff, available in color at http://www.theworldcafe.com/ibank_guidelines.html

FIGURE 6.5   Example of a Star Person

silverlily/Shutterstock.com

Drawing images on flip chart sheets probably doesn't come naturally to most of us and we may need considerable practice to produce something as polished as Orloff's creation. The important thing is to try the technique and drop concerns about artistic polish. I have found that people are delighted when their ideas are recorded on flip charts via visual imagery rather than word lists, even when the artistry is rough. Helpful resources for assembling a kit bag of images and techniques are Dan Roam's *Back of the Napkin* (2009) and Tony and Barry Buzan's *The Mind Map Book* (1993).

Besides helping participants create visually stimulating representations of small-group conversations, I often use exercises emphasizing visual communication. Examples are Pictures of Leadership and Followership, and Outlining and Constructing Personal Visions described in Chapter 3.

In addition to paying attention to visual media, we may also use music to stimulate learning. As noted, I play music to create a welcoming, upbeat atmosphere at the beginning of classes and workshops. We may choose particular songs or type of music to help participants relate to a class topic or case. For example, I play sitar music in the class session focusing on Katherine Boo's *Behind the Beautiful Forevers* (2012), which is set in a Mumbai slum. We can also feature music that has been a vital part of a change initiative or social movement; we can even urge class members to sing along and consider how music invigorates and connects leaders and followers in common cause. Ron Heifetz often asks people in his classes to perform "music without words" in order to help them overcome their conviction that they can't sing and to help class members to tune in to each other (Parks, 2005).

> *Whether in a dialogue, retreat, workshop, or meeting with one or more people, I usually design something infused with the arts, like choreography or musical composition, so that it touches the head and heart simultaneously.*
>
> —Yvonne Cheek

Preparing Attentive Hosts

Early on in my classes I draw attention to our physical learning environment, ask class members to reflect on the expectations (about learning and power) conveyed by traditional auditorium seating as well as alternatives. I explain the advantages of using circle check-ins and small groups. I remind everyone that the most important resource in the course is likely to be each other, and I invite suggestions for making any aspect of the face-to-face and virtual learning environment more welcoming. Depending on the timing of the course, I may ask class members to take turns providing snacks for the group. Numerous group process skills will be woven through the course.

As instructors we may also assign readings that underscore the centrality of hosting to leadership and the importance of a socio-material and embodied view of leadership. We might assign Mark McKergow and Helen Bailey's 2014 book and ask for responses in an online forum. To heighten attention to leadership and embodiment, we might highlight the example of U.S. First Lady Michelle Obama. A possible reading assignment is "Michelle Obama's Embodied Authentic Leadership: Leading by Lifestyle" by Elizabeth Wilhoit (2013), and show or provide a link to her exuberant dance routine at the White House celebrating the fifth anniversary of her Let's Move campaign (http://tinyurl.com/pty8wtt).

The Wilhoit chapter is in *The Embodiment of Leadership* (2013) edited by Lois Melina, Lena Falkman, and Antonio Marturano. "The Anatomy of Leadership," and "Shall I Lead Now? Learner Experiences of Leader-Follower Relationships through Engagement with the Dance" are two other chapters that reinforce attention to leaders and followers as physical beings with an array of senses that help them relate to each other, interact with their environments, and interpret their experiences.

Robert and Janet Denhardt's *Dance of Leadership: The Art of Leading in Business, Government and Society* (2006) is another possible reading. Their extensive research on outstanding dance troupes allows them to draw parallels between effective leading and beautiful dancing. Like skilled dancers, they say, effective leaders sense what is around them, they improvise, and are attuned to space, rhythms, and energy. Finally, these leaders have focus, passion, and discipline.

Arja Ropo, Jaana Parvlalnan, and Nlina Koivunen's chapter "Aesthetics in Leadership: From Absent Bodies to Social Bodily Presence" (2002) is mainly theoretical and may be most appropriate for a graduate leadership course. If we use the reading, we can always ask participants to draw out its implications for their leadership practice.

Several books noted in Chapter 5 are especially helpful for comprehending the effects of social identity on leadership. I recommend *Salsa, Soul and Spirit* (2007) by Juana Bordas, *Diversity and Leadership* by Jean Chin and Joseph Trimble (2015), *Women as Global Leaders*, edited by Faith Ngunjiri and Susan Madsen (2015), and *Authentic Leadership*, Lemuel Watson and Joshua Johnson (2013).

★★★

Hosting in leadership classes and workshops is about helping participants feel welcome and prepared for learning, but it also is about preparing them to tend relationships and recognize the physicality of the people engaged in leadership practice. This work begins with recruiting diverse participants and learning about their backgrounds. Hosting also includes creating a learning environment (in physical and virtual spaces) that fosters engagement of participants' senses and connection with each other. As hosts, we educators also model improvisation in the face of glitches and setbacks.

In our workshops and courses we introduce team development frameworks and group process skills—such as relational dialogue and conflict management— that foster group creativity and productivity. We explore social identities and means of connecting across diverse identities. We help participants hone skills of dialogue and storytelling through our speech, movement exercises, visual presentations, and music.

The practice of hosting, along with the practice of using personal narrative, prepares the way for a third essential leadership practice: tackling organizational and societal problems. This practice is featured in the next part of this book.

References

Anderson, T., Rourke, L., Garrison, D. R., & Archer, W. (2001). Assessing teaching presence in a computer conferencing context. *Journal of Asynchronous Learning Networks, 5*(2), 1–17.

Boo, K. (2012). *Behind the beautiful forevers*. New York: Random House.

Bordas, J. (2007). *Salsa, soul, and spirit: Leadership for a multicultural age*. San Francisco: Berrett-Koehler Publishers, Inc.

Buzan, T., & Buzan, B. (1993). *The mind map book: Radiant thinking: The major evolution in human thought*. New York: Penguin.

Chin, J. L., & Trimble, J. (2015). *Diversity and leadership*. Thousand Oaks, CA: SAGE.

Denhardt, R. B., & Denhardt, J. V. (2006). *The dance of leadership: The art of leading in business, government and society*. Armonk, NY: M.E. Sharpe.

Duarte, N. (2008). *Slide:ology: The art and science of creating great presentations.* Sebastopol, CA: O'Reilly Media.

Huxham, C. (1990). On trivialities in process. In C. Eden & J. Radford (Eds.), *Tackling strategic problems: The role of group decision support* (pp. 162—168). London: SAGE.

Fletcher, J. K., & Kaüfer, K. (2003). Shared leadership: Paradox and possibility. In C. L. Pearce, & J. A. Conger (Eds.), *Shared leadership: Reframing the hows and whys of leadership* (pp. 21–47). Thousand Oaks, CA: SAGE.

Kilmann, R. (2012). *Ralph Kilmann's overview of the TKI.* Retrieved January 8, 2016 from http://www.kilmanndiagnostics.com/catalog/thomas-kilmann-conflict-mode-instrument

McKergow, M., & Bailey, H. (2014). *Host: Six new roles of engagement.* London: SolutionsBooks.

Melina, L. R., Burgess, G. J., Falkman, L. L., & Marturano, A. (Eds.). (2013). *The embodiment of leadership* (1st ed.). San Francisco, CA: Jossey-Bass.

Michener, J. (2015). *Poland.* New York: Dial.

Ngunjiri, F., & Madsen, S. (Eds.). (2015). *Women as global leaders.* Charlotte, NC: IAP.

Parks, S. D. (2005). *Leadership can be taught.* Boston, MA: Harvard Business School Press.

Reynolds, G. (2014). *Presentation Zen design.* San Francisco: New Riders.

Roam, D. (2009). *Back of the napkin.* New York: Penguin.

Ropo, A., Parvlalnan, J., & Koivunen, N. (2002). Aesthetics in leadership: From absent bodies to social bodily presence. In K. W. Parry, & J. R. Meindl (Eds.), *Grounding leadership: Theory and research* (pp. 21–38). Greenwich, CT: IAP.

Shea, P., Li, C. S., & Pickett, A. (2006). A study of teaching present and student sense of learning community in fully online and web-enhanced college courses. *Internet and Higher Education, 9,* 175–190.

Takaki, R. (2008). *Different mirror: A history of multicultural America.* New York: Back Bay Books.

Tuckman, B. (1965). Developmental sequence in small groups. *Psychological Bulletin, 63*(6), 384–399.

Watson, L. W., & Johnson, J. M. (Eds.). (2013). *Authentic leadership: An engaged discussion of LGBTQ work as culturally relevant.* Charlotte, NC: Information Age.

Wheatley, M. J. (2002). *Turning to one another: Simple conversations to restore hope to the future.* San Francisco: Berrett-Koehler.

Wheelan, S. A. (2016). *Creating effective teams: A guide for members and leaders* (5th ed.). Thousand Oaks, CA: SAGE.

Wilhoit, E. (2013). Michelle Obama's embodied authentic leadership: Leading by lifestyle. In L. Melina, L. Falkman, & A. Marturano (Eds.), *The embodiment of leadership* (pp. 149–170). San Francisco: Jossey-Bass.

PART III

Tackling Organizational and Societal Problems
Leadership Praxis

As leadership educators, we seek to enable learners to apply the best of leadership theory and research to the challenges they face in their organizations and communities. We also prepare learners to scrutinize the leadership of others in order to learn from good and bad examples and to be more engaged followers. In Chapter 7, educators tell our personal stories of tackling organizational and societal challenges. You will hear about what habits of mind, frameworks, and skills have guided and helped us lead and teach effectively. We will also note which of these students say have been most useful to them in the years after they have completed a leadership course or training.

Chapter 8 will dive more deeply into leadership theories and frameworks introduced in Chapter 7. It will give special attention to the habits of mind and skills involved in developing humane and effective teams, organizations, and communities. Chapter 9 will offer guidance for teaching and learning some of the key habits of mind, frameworks, and skills that leadership educators have identified.

7

LEADERSHIP PRAXIS AND THE HEART

So far in this book leadership educators have focused on the people (ourselves and others) in our leadership courses and workshops. We have considered the environments we create or access for learning. We now expand our attention to how leaders and committed followers tackle organizational and societal challenges. This requires that not only do we school ourselves in leadership theory and research, but also recognize that participants in our workshops and courses have already been engaged in leadership and followership and are interested in how they can become more effective practitioners in specific contexts. They must become judges of what works in their own practice. As Ron Riggio notes, leadership development must provide opportunities to master the behaviors we are supporting: "How dare we talk about teaching and not practice!" We are in the business of helping people constantly interweave theory with practice in a way that improves both. I refer to this as a praxis approach to leadership development.

In this chapter you will learn more about the leadership challenges that the people featured in this book have tackled. We will present learning from our leadership practice. We describe the frameworks, habits of mind, and skills that have helped us lead effectively and note which frameworks and methods are most highly valued by course and workshop participants.

Creating Programs, Centers, and the Field of Leadership Studies

When I first engaged with the Reflective Leadership Center at the Humphrey School of Public Affairs in the mid-1980s, the study of leadership was a long way from being a well-developed field and many academics considered leadership a fuzzy topic that didn't merit serious attention. Both popular and scholarly studies of leaders had existed for centuries, but they tended to focus on very visible figures, usually men, who had been heads of state, prominent politicians, or corporate executives. Some scholars, interested in organizational dynamics, conducted extensive studies of boss-subordinate relationships, seeking to find out what bosses (leaders) should do to increase employee and organizational performance. Since the 1980s, thanks to the work of many people (including very prominently those featured in this book), leadership has become a multi-faceted, trans-disciplinary, global academic field that is still developing. The educators in this book have launched and directed centers (for example, the Kravis Leadership Institute at Claremont McKenna College, the Burns Academy at the University of Maryland, the Reflective Leadership Center and Integrative Leadership Center at the University of Minnesota, the Research Center for Leadership in Action at New York University, and the Institute for Innovative Leadership at the University of Nebraska). We have initiated academic and community programs that give leadership a central role (for example, the University of Minnesota's undergraduate leadership minor, the African American Leadership Forum, the Shannon Leadership Institute). In 1999, several people in the group helped launch the International Leadership Association, now a global network of approximately 2,400 academics, students, and practitioners from diverse organizations and communities (see www.ila-net.org). Educators featured in this book have been major contributors to the expansion of leadership theory and research by publishing numerous influential books and articles and assisting with important new academic journals, such as *Leadership Quarterly* and *Leadership*.

Linking Leadership Theory and Practice

For many leadership educators, theory and practice are inseparable. Gill Hickman says, "Linking theory and practice is absolutely my favorite thing to do because they inform each other. I appreciated this the most in my Ph.D. program because I was working in the field of public administration while a doctoral student. I was integrating all the time. I'd go to work and theories would kick in. I'd read theories and think how they could be improved to use in practice. I've been able to use both so well in administrative and academic work." For example, Hickman cited her experience with merging three schools at her California university. She was asked to be dean of a school of health and oversee the merger, which would bring together the large nursing program with health administration and a medical technology program. "I protested that I knew nothing about these medical fields, but the president of the university said you are the only person who can do this. He said, 'You've worked at every level in the Cal State system.' Most important was my ability to bring together a disparate group. It was a matter of setting context so other people can thrive and building relationships so people would cooperate to make things happen. I couldn't fall back on expertise." This experience taught her the value of being able to draw on a preexisting network of relationships and ensuring that everyone had the resources and tools to work productively. Thus, she can draw on her own experiences to illustrate relational leadership theory.

Sonia Ospina likewise highlights interconnections between theory and practice. "Particularly for leadership the best knowledge we can develop is very grounded in practice. Theory doesn't have to be difficult or complicated. We have to convince practitioners of the value of theory. The importance of not dividing the world into theory and practice is reflected in my own journey." For example, as director of the Research Center for Leadership in Action, she engaged grassroots leaders in research and theory building about collective leadership in community organizations.

> *I'd go to work and theories would kick in. I'd read theories and think how they could be improved to use in practice. I've been able to use both so well in administrative and academic work.*
>
> —Gill Hickman

> *Particularly for leadership the best knowledge we can develop is very grounded in practice. Theory doesn't have to be difficult or complicated.*
>
> —Sonia Ospina

Rick Morse emphasizes the effect of leadership theory on practice. Since his undergraduate years, he has embraced the ideas of Mary Parker Follett and others who have developed the "fundamental idea that democracy is integration of difference. When we understand it in that way, we celebrate and appreciate difference and understand leadership is not a leader-follower dichotomy. Leadership is about helping integration to happen so a community can develop common understanding. This is really different from the traditional view that leaders set the vision and persuade followers to follow it."

Along with colleagues at the Humphrey School, John Bryson and I have considered what theories of power have to say about how leaders can inspire and mobilize others to tackle shared problems that typically spill beyond organizational boundaries. John and I developed the Leadership for the Common Good framework based on a multidimensional understanding of power and have drawn on that framework as we have consulted with community and government groups and secured support for leadership centers and programs at the University of Minnesota. Our research, case studies, and consulting experiences have helped us enrich the framework.

The remainder of this section introduces the main theories and frameworks that have inspired and served the leadership educators featured in this book;

several of the theories and frameworks will be discussed in more depth in Chapter 8. Whether due to personal inclinations, participant needs, or changing times, we have gravitated toward views of leadership as a pervasive human activity. We are less interested in the traits of effective leaders and more interested in leadership practices at the interpersonal, organizational, interorganizational, and societal levels.

Transformational Leadership

For several of us, James MacGregor Burns's description of transforming and transactional leadership is foundational. My own copy of his 1978 book *Leadership* is battered from long use. Georgia Sorenson, Carol Pearson, and Tracey Manning all worked closely with Burns in establishing or sustaining the Burns Academy of Leadership at the University of Maryland. When asked what leadership theories and frameworks have been most useful in her courses, Pearson cited transformational (used synonymously with transforming) leadership first of all. "It's really about managing and inspiring human beings and being an agent for retaining the best of the past and moving towards what's needed for the future." Manning said, "Jim Burns was my inspiration from my earliest days of teaching leadership; his transforming leadership work brought me to the Academy of Leadership, where we all appreciated his regular visits from Massachusetts. It was a wonderfully stimulating time and changed the course of my life." She noted the centrality in Burns's view of leaders' building an authentic relationship with followers. "I've seen a number of gurus act as if transformational leadership is a way to manipulate people to go along with the leader's vision. I like Burns's idea of mutually developing the leader-follower relationship. People have missed the radical soul of Burns's work. They sorted through transformational leadership and made it fit a preconceived view."

Burns's leadership theory was both compelling and controversial. Although he used prominent *leaders* of social movements and heads of state as his main examples, he firmly identified *leadership* as a relationship between leaders and followers, and zeroed in on the connection of power and leadership. Moreover—and here's the controversial part—he argued that leadership is inherently moral—in other words, genuine leaders use their power on behalf of followers and broader social good. People may occupy leader positions and affect events, but if they fail to foster the well-being of others they are merely wielding power, not leading, in Burns's view.

Servant Leadership, Adaptive Leadership, and More

Since Burns's seminal work, other thinkers have developed frameworks and theories that put ethics and follower well-being at the heart of leadership. Some educators interviewed for this book refer to the leadership model introduced in Robert Greenleaf's (1977) book *Servant Leadership*. Greenleaf and his numerous disciples argue that the best leaders in business, government, or nonprofits serve their constituents, not the other way around.

The focus on the relationship between leaders and followers continues in other theories that are frequently used by my colleagues. Several cited Ronald Heifetz's adaptive leadership model elaborated in *Leadership Without Easy Answers* (1994), *Leadership on the Line* (with Marty Linsky, 2002), and *The Practice of Adaptive* Leadership (with Marty Linsky and Alexander Grashow, 2009). Heifetz and his co-authors describe practices, such as providing a holding environment and moving between the dance floor and the balcony, by which leaders engage followers in solving their own problems. Several of us incorporate the leadership practices described by James Kouzes and Barry Posner in their book *The Leadership Challenge* (2012), now in its fifth edition. The practices are modeling the way, inspiring a shared vision, challenging the process, enabling others to act, and encouraging the heart. Kouzes and Posner offer guidance for how organizational leaders carry out the practices through specific commitments (see Figure 7.1).

Sharon Turnbull draws on Richard Barrett's *New Leadership Paradigm* (2012), which describes leadership as sourced from different levels of consciousness, each of which is associated with a set of values. The levels are survival, relationships, self-esteem, transformation, internal cohesion, making a difference, and service. He and his colleagues have concluded that the most effective leaders draw on all seven levels of consciousness. In her teaching, Turnbull also draws on the managerial mind-sets described by Jonathan Gosling and Henry Mintzberg (2003):

- Managing self: the reflective mind-set
- Managing organizations: the analytic mind-set
- Managing context: the worldly mind-set
- Managing relationships: the collaborative mind-set
- Managing change: the action mind-set

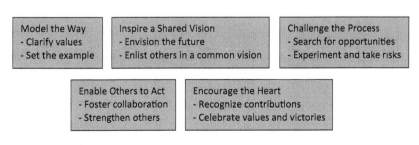

FIGURE 7.1 James Kouzes and Barry Posner's Five Practices and Ten Commitments

Collective Leadership

Several colleagues have been drawn to or helped create theories that highlight collective as well as individual leadership and that view organizations and communities as systems, in which stability and change result from human activity as it interacts with preexisting structures and environmental forces. Chuck Palus relies on the DAC (Direction, Alignment, and Commitment) model developed by Cindy McCauley, his colleague at the Center for Creative Leadership. Her review of the leadership literature led her to identify three essential outcomes of leadership work—whether at the team, organizational, or community level—and they are direction, alignment, and commitment (McCauley, 2014) resulting from exchanges among the people involved. Direction refers to agreement on what the group is trying to achieve; alignment to "effective coordination and integration of different aspects of the work so it serves the shared direction" (1); and commitment to participants' commitment to the success of the group. Palus refers to the model as "simplicity on the other side of complexity." In his workshops and courses he helps participants apply the model at four levels—society, organization, group, and individual (or SOGI).

Sonia Ospina has worked with colleagues at the Research Center for Leadership in Action (RCLA) to develop an understanding of the practices that contribute to collective leadership, especially leadership within and by grassroots, social change organizations. This work was partially supported by a substantial Ford Foundation grant that allowed the RCLA scholars to involve people in these organizations as co-researchers. The practices are reframing discourse, bridging differences, and unleashing human energies (Ospina et al., 2012).

Mary Uhl-Bien has been at the forefront of investigating leadership within complex adaptive systems, whether they are organizations or inter-organizational networks. This approach extends the insights presented by Margaret Wheatley in the 1990s in editions of *Leadership and the New Science* (1999)—the view that organizations and networks are "living systems" and that effective leaders within these systems will be responsive to system dynamics such as feedback effects and growth mechanisms. With co-author Russ Marion (for example, Marion and Uhl-Bien, 2001) Uhl-Bien approaches leadership as a relational and collective phenomenon that includes nurturing interdependencies and developing resilient organizational structures (including dispersing the power to adapt and innovate).

Leadership for the Common Good

Like many of the theories and frameworks described so far, the Leadership for the Common Good framework which I developed with John Bryson (Bryson and Crosby, 1992; Crosby and Bryson, 2005) views leadership as a relationship that operates at multiple levels, from interpersonal to societal. The impetus behind developing the framework was twofold: to understand how leaders and committed followers remedy complex public problems, and to provide a practical guide for midcareer people who wanted to become more effective leaders in their organizations and communities.

The framework emphasizes eight interconnected leadership capabilities that build on each other:

- *Leadership in context*—understanding the social, political, economic, technological, and ecological "givens" as well as potentialities
- *Personal leadership*—understanding and deploying personal assets on behalf of beneficial change in particular contexts
- *Team leadership*—building productive work groups
- *Organizational leadership*—nurturing humane and effective organizations
- *Visionary leadership*—creating and communicating shared meaning in formal and informal forums
- *Political leadership*—making and implementing decisions in formal and informal arenas
- *Ethical leadership*—sanctioning conduct and adjudicating disputes in formal and informal courts
- *Policy entrepreneurship*—coordinating leadership tasks over the course of policy change cycles

Leadership for the common good is a foundation for the integrative leadership framework (Crosby and Bryson, 2010, 2012) that focuses on leadership in cross-sector collaborations.

Social Change Model

The undergraduate leadership minor program at the University of Minnesota, as well as similar programs around the country, has drawn on the social change model developed by an ensemble led by Helen and Alexander Astin at the University of California, Los Angeles, in the mid-1990s. This model emphasizes the interconnection of individual, group, and community development (Komives et al., 2011).

Followership

Increasingly, leadership educators are giving attention to followership, which can be viewed as the flip side of leadership, or the leader-follower relationship from the follower perspective. Like leadership, it can be viewed as a social construction involving social identities, performances, and interpretations of behavior. Robert Kelley's book *The Power of Followership* (1992), Barbara Kellerman's *Followership* (2008), and Ira Chaleff's *The Courageous Follower* (2009) are all helpful sources.

Adult Learning

Additional keys to linking theory and practice in our work can be found in adult learning theories that emphasize the need to make instruction relevant to the challenges that adults are facing in their own lives and to give them opportunities to learn through practical application. I have been especially drawn to Donald Schön's idea of the reflective practitioner (1983). Since I began my academic work on leadership at the Humphrey School's Reflective Leadership Center, my attraction to this idea is hardly surprising. From the standpoint of reflective practice, we adults come to the study of leadership with some experience already in place. We then use the theories and tools we encounter in a course or workshop to make sense of that experience and consider new ways of leading and following. We return to our field of practice and try out those new methods and reflect on the results. We go on to acquire additional theoretical insights or tools, return to the field of practice, reflect, and continue to repeat the process.

Chuck Palus is drawn to William Torbert's action inquiry model of transformational learning (Torbert and Associates, 2004). In this model, people and organizations can progress through developmental stages by becoming increasingly adept at "listening to the present moment from which the future emerges," being alert to dangers and opportunities, and performing in more "effective, transformative and sustainable ways" (1). To lead through action inquiry, a person attends to his or her own intention and checks in the moment how well actions are accomplishing that intention and adjusts actions accordingly.

June Nobbe and other instructors in the University of Minnesota's undergraduate leadership minor program are advocates of Ron Heifetz's case-in-point teaching method. Interactions within class sessions or in class teams become grist for understanding acts of leadership and followership, as well as the role of authority.

Developing Habits of Mind to Guide Practice

In creating and applying leadership theories and frameworks inside and outside the classroom or workshop, leadership educators featured in this book are guided by some basic assumptions, orientations, and operating rules. These include the stance they take as educators and their understandings of the purpose of leadership development.

To begin with, we are persuaded that leaders come in a variety of sizes, shapes, ages, genders, and ethnic backgrounds. Clearly, this view conflicts with the notion that leadership development should focus exclusively on those who stand out from their fellows as high performers or as charismatic opinion leaders. At the same time, we recognize that people have different abilities to master particular leadership skills and very different opportunities to exercise leadership.

> *Virtually anyone can provide leadership if one thinks of it as taking action on something cared about.*
>
> —Ronnie Brooks

We see our own roles in leadership development as being a facilitator, or as Valerie Shangreaux puts it, "a guide on the side," who makes our expertise available as needed. Sharon Turnbull views herself as a "co-creator of learning." Yvonne Cheek emphasizes the importance of valuing the personal and community knowledge that participants contribute to the learning experience. June Nobbe adds, "You have to let go of being the subject expert, but rather be a facilitator. That's a struggle when you come into classroom. You realize, oh my gosh, this is about helping the students decide what leadership means to them and helping them become expert in their own leadership issue areas."

> *[W]e developers of leaders have defined ourselves as visible (and perhaps risible) actors who take center stage with propositions and acronyms, runes, and rituals, an assessment or insight that inspires those in our vicinity to break an habitual pattern and look at the world with new eyes. In that way we are identical to those we teach: what more or less is leadership than a fresh and compelling look at a problem? We are the slap on the newborn's bottom: we do not teach the baby to breathe, we jump start the innate apparatus that, once begun, continues to work on its own.*
>
> —Janet Rechtman (2008, 16), Fanning Leadership Institute at the University of Georgia

Seeing ourselves as co-creators of learning rather than founts of expert knowledge requires, as Bob Denhardt notes, minimizing our own egos. Brad Jackson admonishes us to remember, "It's not about affirming you. It's about what students end up doing differently, what they are doing in five years." Jonathan Gosling strives to remember that at some point in his courses, "I'll know I'm incompetent, failed to say the right thing. I'm impotent and incompetent. It's sort of a necessity. I can't learn if I'm already full." We have to squelch the desire to be the learned professor or consultant with answers to every question.

Being mentally healthy is part of this, says Janet Denhardt, and leadership educators should work out their personal issues via therapy or other means, not allow them, as she says, "to interfere with the space I'm trying to create for students."

Lars Leafblad relies on "recovery" principles. "I use the Serenity Prayer [https://en.wikipedia.org/wiki/Serenity_Prayer] daily as a leadership framework to ask for humility and peace. It balances my desire to create and begin. I also believe in paying forward because so many others have done this for me."

At the same time that we strive to minimize our egos, we recognize the importance of modeling the behaviors that we deem essential in leadership practice. Paradoxically, being courageous and bold, while conveying humility—which I often call combining hubris and humility— is something many of us strive for. Yvonne Cheek emphasizes the importance of "having good energy that attracts people like a magnet." While I associate "good energy" with boldness, a quiet energy can emanate from admitting my limitations or acknowledging my failures as I work with leadership learners. Georgia Sorenson emphasizes the value of being open and honest about what matters to us. "In almost every class I find a way to say I have a mentally ill brother," she notes.

> *Really effective leaders make people feel good to be around them and to feel better about themselves.*
>
> —Yvonne Cheek

Being compassionate is a habit of mind I seek to cultivate. I have a passion for being an excellent leadership educator, just as people in my courses might have a passion for saving small farms, cleaning up the atmosphere, or educating girls in India. Personal passion alone, however, may blind us to the downsides of single-minded pursuit of a vision; compassion, on the other hand, makes us concerned first and foremost with the well-being of ourselves and others.

Compassion for myself means acknowledging the invisible scars that cover childhood wounds, or the ways I've fallen short of the standards I set for myself. It also means giving myself credit for my accomplishments. Compassion for others means reveling in their achievements, grieving at their setbacks, while avoiding pity and accepting them as quite different from myself.

Why not give primacy to love? After all, Kouzes and Posner (2012) say love is the secret ingredient of leadership. We've probably all heard the phrase "Love 'em and lead 'em." I choose compassion because it goes beyond love to embrace the suffering that inevitably befalls leaders and followers.

Being adaptive is another key behavior that we are called on to model. As already noted, we are at our best in classes and workshops when we have prepared extensively but then improvise as needed in response to what happens once a session is under way. Being adaptive in the moment requires paying intense, but relaxed attention to what is going on around and within us and being open-minded about how the session might develop.

> *Realize that rules are a point of departure. Be willing to create a new playbook when the situation needs it.*
>
> —Yvonne Cheek

> *Part of wisdom is knowing what rules you can break and which ones you can't until you arrive at a position of power and can change them.*
>
> —Kim Boal

We recognize the need to keep up with developments in leadership studies by reading and attending conferences. Most of us publish our own research to help advance the field (and abide by academic norms). We remain curious about big questions such as, "How do groups construct leadership?" "How do we assess the impact of individual leaders' actions or of collective efforts to tackle a shared problem?" "How can leaders help their constituents build more humane societies?" We seek to continually refresh the design of our courses and workshops. We look for material in unlikely places, such as plays, movies, and novels.

The value of reflection for improving practice is a fundamental guiding assumption for most of us. We take time to review, interpret, and assess our own behavior and other aspects of our courses and workshops, and we build plenty of reflective activities into our teaching. Georgia Sorenson likes to do her reflecting in the woods, or along the Chesapeake Bay. She often takes her dogs along. "I feel like an alien if I don't do this. Nature is a great teacher and healer."

> Janet Denhardt distinguishes between self-reflection and self-absorption. "There is danger in being self-absorbed and narcissistic. There is great potential in being self-reflective."

Another important habit of mind is tolerance for paradox, uncertainty, tension, and adversity. In leadership studies we find tensions among theories—for example, between those that focus on individual agency and those that emphasize system dynamics. Ron Heifetz and his colleagues (Heifetz and Linsky, 2002; Heifetz, Grashow, and Linsky, 2009) also emphasize the important leadership work of regulating tension, so that it is enough to motivate people to tackle their shared problems but not so much as to overwhelm them. Brad Jackson says he is constantly monitoring the class to discern: "Is there enough tension, too much? 'I say to the class, if you are feeling really content, have it all sorted out, I've done a lousy job.'"

Earlier I highlighted the paradoxical pairing of humility and hubris. In leadership courses, I am also likely to emphasize the fun to be found in tackling serious problems and cite approvingly E.F. Schumacher's assertion, "Our problems are so serious that the only way to talk about them is lightheartedly." I may seek to help every participant acquire some charismatic qualities, even while developing healthy skepticism about overreliance on charismatic leaders.

I often find that students, even midcareer ones, enter my courses expecting they will find clear answers and directions for leadership challenges. Especially those who have been trained in rational and logical disciplines may be dismayed when this expectation is dashed. Sandhya Gupta, a midcareer engineer who came to my course with a desire to establish an institute for social change in her native India, had exactly this reaction. She went on, however, to embrace the value of listening to multiple perspectives and accepting the lack of correct answers. She returned to India, began her institute, and applied what she learned in her leadership course. When I asked her recently about what aspect of being in my leadership course had affected her the most, she said, "Listening to my peers and instructors, I realized there is no single truth or ultimate defining boundary, unlike my engineering work where the boundary is set and I just have to find the solution. So now I feel at my institute compelled sometimes to take an alternate view. I have to argue for the benefits of globalization when others are focused strictly on the value of local development. I have taken this lesson to here," she said touching her chest.

As for the purpose of leadership development, the leadership educators featured in this book assume that it extends beyond improving participants' career prospects. Yvonne Cheek seeks to help participants "connect to their higher selves." For most of us that means helping participants identify their core values, their responsibilities for others' well-being, and their potential for making unique contributions to their organizations and communities. Janet Denhardt emphasizes to students, "Leadership is not about them, their preferred style, needs, vision. It's about the people they serve—the followers—and the larger public good."

Defining Problems, Crafting Solutions, and Achieving Sustainable Change

Essential skills for developing self-awareness and hosting diverse participants have been introduced in the first two parts of this book. As leadership educators we use and teach many additional skills that are needed for the leadership work of tackling organizational and societal problems.

Skills for Diagnosing Context (The System You're In)

As we or our students seek to build new programs, invigorate organizations, or strengthen our communities, we are likely to go astray unless we understand the context in which we are working. I advise participants in my workshops and courses to look for the relevant social, political, economic, technological, and ecological "givens" and consider how changes in those conditions are opening up opportunities for leadership.

Within the social realm, my colleagues and I place particular importance on culture, the way that things are typically done in the organization or community. Culture includes deep assumptions about authority, roles of men and women, time, the sacred, human nature, and spatial relationships. Also in the social realm is demographic information about the people in the relevant organization or community.

Focusing on the political realm, we consider how formal and informal authority is exercised and how policy decisions are made. If voting is involved, we might track voting trends and note election cycles. Turning to economics, we consider internal financial conditions and external economic forces that may be threatening internal financial stability or opening up opportunities for improvement. In the technological realm, today the focus frequently is on the challenges and opportunities embedded in the burgeoning power of Internet communication and multiple other digital technologies. Depending on the context, however, more basic technologies may be at the fore. The person who is trying to combat malaria, for example, we will want to know about the supply of mosquito nets.

Ecological aspects of context would include climate and other aspects of the natural environment. What's the weather like? Do we have enough water or too much? How are the plants and animals around us faring? Perhaps because I live in Minnesota I am aware that any time I want to attract people from elsewhere to a program in my state, I must acknowledge the state's reputation for fierce winters and reframe that as an asset (cross-country skiing, anyone?), offer coping mechanisms, or schedule activities in warmer months.

Analyzing the key continuities and shifts within the context can help us decide if the situation is ripe for the initiative we are considering. Also vital is stakeholder analysis. I will describe a repertoire of stakeholder analyses in Chapter 9, but for now I will explain why John Bryson and I have long asserted that stakeholder analysis and involvement are essential in the leadership work of tackling organizational and societal challenges.

We define stakeholders as individuals, groups, or organizations that are affected by an organizational or societal problem, have partial responsibility to act on it, or control important resources. The techniques presented in Chapter 9 are designed to help leaders and followers identify the stakeholders and their interconnections; assess their interests, power, and opportunities for convergence; and decide how to involve stakeholders in a change process. Two types of stakeholders—sponsors and champions—are especially important at the beginning of an effort to launch a new project or reinvigorate an existing program or system. Sponsors are people who have formal authority and control over key resources (such as staff and money). They can use their positions to give legitimacy and visibility, as well as more tangible resources, to an initiative. Champions are people who lead mainly through informal authority. They tirelessly use their relational skills and zeal for the initiative to build networks of support and oversee the process of developing and implementing change.

Skills Associated With Team and Organizational Leadership

The hosting chapters described many methods for fostering productive dialogue within a group, and skill in using those methods is essential for building strong teams. The Leadership for the Common Good framework also highlights the importance of helping team members agree on the team's mission, goals, decision-making procedures, rules, norms, work plan, and evaluation methods. There are numerous leadership roles to be filled in a team, from planning meetings to reinforcing norms, and sharing those roles contributes to team cohesion and greater leadership capacity of the group. (Such a shared leadership approach is likely to work best in egalitarian organizational or societal cultures.) Finally, team leaders should hone the skills of trust building and sustaining team spirit.

Skills of organizational leadership are aimed at carrying out the following tasks:

- Attending to organizational purpose and design
- Dealing adeptly with internal and external change
- Building inclusive community inside and outside organizations

Key skills are strategic planning; constructing an inspiring organizational vision; aligning organizational design and culture with purpose; and being entrepreneurial, collaborative, and politically astute.

Skills for Tackling Problems That Spill Beyond Organizational Boundaries

As leaders move into the realm of issues that involve many organizations and groups, sometimes entire societies, nations, and even the world, the Leadership for the Common Good framework prompts them to exercise skills involved in designing and using an array of forums, arenas, and courts that can produce a sustainable new policy regime. (By policy regime, I mean the system of policies, programs, laws, rules, and norms for handling a particular public issue.) Formal and informal forums are the settings in which stakeholders develop shared understanding of a public problem or challenge, evaluate potential solutions or responses, and craft proposals for specific policy changes, programs, and projects. Formal and informal arenas are the settings in which policy makers debate and decide on competing policy proposals and oversee implementation of adopted policies. Formal and informal courts are the settings in which leaders and followers rely on ethical principles, laws, and norms to sanction conduct and adjudicate competing claims related to the policies adopted in arenas.

In designing and using forums effectively, leaders require, in addition to the hosting or convening skills discussed in the previous chapter, skills that help their groups develop and communicate a strong guiding vision for change efforts. These skills include interpreting the situation and giving direction; keeping the common good in mind; developing inclusive, action-oriented problem frames; and crafting compelling visions that preserve the best of the past, are grounded in current realities, and illuminate a path toward a better future. Also important is the ability to make core messages credible and "sticky," to use Dan and Chip Heath's term (Heath and Heath, 2007). To work effectively in arenas, leaders must engage in political analysis—for example, they must understand which arenas are likely to treat their group's proposals favorably, or they may seek to reform an arena that is unfavorable toward a proposed reform. Once their groups focus on a particular arena, these leaders ensure that formal proposals emerging from multistakeholder forums will appeal to the arena's powerful decision makers. Additionally, leaders must be adept at assembling and sustaining coalitions that can pressure the decision makers. To achieve desired outcomes in formal and informal courts, leaders must be skilled in analyzing means of enforcing the policies that are adopted and implemented in executive, legislative, and administrative arenas. They will promote awareness of how ethical principles, laws, and norms apply to particular cases and develop ways of resolving conflicts among principles, laws, and norms.

In carrying out any major policy change effort, long-range strategizing is also important. This includes the ability to think of policy change as a multiphase process occurring in a series of interconnected forums, arenas, and courts over an extended period of time. Part of the strategizing is building in the flexibility to accommodate changing conditions and loss of initial champions and sponsors. Research skills are vital throughout. Possibly guided by research philosophies like appreciative inquiry or action inquiry, leaders help their groups craft probing questions, gather evidence from a variety of sources (including personal observation and experience), analyze the evidence, and develop conclusions about optimal policies and strategies.

My colleagues and I frequently help participants in our courses develop the skills of case analysis. Chuck Palus might introduce the DAC framework and then ask participants to read a written description of a successful or failed effort to start a new school. Individually or in small groups the participants then might describe what seemed to hamper or contribute to the development of direction, alignment, and commitment in the case and what the actors might have done differently to achieve better leadership outcomes. Cases also can be presented in video clips or online modules. Participants are often working on their own cases and, and as noted above, some of us also treat interactions in our classes or workshops as cases-in-point. We can describe our own live leadership cases and ask for participants' insights. Jonathan Gosling trains students in ethnographic techniques and has student pairs engage in a leadership exchange, in which the pair visits the workplace of first one and then the other student, usually in two different countries. The visits last three days and the student who is not part of the workplace carefully observes "how leading is accomplished here." After each visit, the two students together reflect on what the observer saw and the experience of the person who was actually working there. Gosling says that students report that the exchange is the "most amazing experience I've had." He learned a great deal from doing the leadership exchange himself.

★★★

Leadership educators weave together theory and practice as they undertake change efforts themselves and guide participants in their courses and workshops. I've introduced several of the theories and frameworks that are prominent in our work. These include James MacGregor Burns's foundational work on transformational and transactional leadership, Ron Heifetz's formulation of adaptive leadership, the DAC model developed by Cindy McCauley, and Mary Uhl-Bien's work on leadership in complex adaptive systems. I also described the Leadership for the Common Good framework, which John Bryson and I developed.

In this chapter leadership educators also have elaborated several habits of mind that guide our practice. They include seeing leadership potential in everyone and seeing our own role as a facilitator, or co-creator of learning. We balance self-confidence with humility, and have compassion for ourselves and participants in our courses and workshops. We are adaptive, curious, innovative, and reflective. We cultivate tolerance for paradox, uncertainty, tension, and adversity. We keep in mind our mission of helping individuals and groups develop their leadership capacity in order to benefit their organizations and communities.

We tie together skills of self-awareness and hosting, with numerous other skills of team, organizational, and societal leadership. Stakeholder analysis, long-range strategizing, and research skills are especially important skills in tackling complex problems that spill beyond organizational boundaries.

The next chapter will explore in more depth several of the theories and frameworks that we leadership educators find most helpful for helping participants in our courses and workshops deal productively with organizational and societal challenges. The chapter also will consider research that describes the need for leaders to develop cognitive, social, and behavioral complexity in themselves and their groups in order to apply the theories adeptly.

References

Barrett, R. (2012). *New leadership paradigm*. Bury, UK: Barrett Values Center.

Bryson, J. M., & Crosby, B. (1992). *Leadership for the common good*. San Francisco: Jossey-Bass.

Burns, J. M. (1978). *Leadership*. New York: Harper Collins.

Chaleff, I. (2009). *The courageous follower: Standing up to and for our leaders* (3rd ed.). San Francisco: Berrett-Koehler.

Crosby, B. C., & Bryson, J. M. (2005). *Leadership for the common good: Tackling public problems in a shared-power world*. San Francisco: Wiley.

Crosby, B. C. & Bryson, J. M. (2010). Integrative leadership and the creation and maintenance of cross-sector collaboration. *Leadership Quarterly, 21*(2): 211–230.

Crosby, B. C., & Bryson, J. M. (2012). Integrative leadership and policy change: A hybrid relational view. In M. Uhl-Bien & S. Ospina (Eds.), *Advancing relational leadership research: A dialogue among perspectives* (pp. 303–334). Charlotte, NC: Information Age.

Greenleaf, R. K. (1977). *Servant leadership: A journey into the nature of legitimate power and greatness*. New York: Paulist Press.

Heath, C., & Heath, D. (2007). *Made to stick*. New York: Random House.

Heifetz, R. A. (1994). *Leadership without easy answers*. Boston: Belknap.

Heifetz, R. A., Grashow, A., & Linsky, M. (2009). *The practice of adaptive leadership: Tools and tactics for changing your organization and the world*. Boston, MA: Harvard Business Press.

Heifetz, R. A., & Linsky, M. (2002). *Leadership on the line: Staying alive through the dangers of leading*. Boston: Harvard Business School Press.

Kellerman, B. (2008). *Followership: How followers are creating change and changing leaders*. Boston: Harvard Business Press.

Kelley, R. (1992). *The power of followership*. New York: Doubleday Currency.

Komives, S., Dugan, J. P., Owen, J. E., Slack, C., Wagner, W., & Associates. (2011). *Handbook for student leadership development* (2nd ed.). San Francisco: Jossey-Bass.

Kouzes, J. M., & Posner, B. Z. (2012). *The leadership challenge: How to make extraordinary things happen in organizations* (5th ed.). San Francisco: Jossey-Bass.

Marion, R., & Uhl-Bien, M. (2001). Leadership in complex organizations. *Leadership Quarterly, 12*(4), 389–418.

McCauley, C. D. (2014). *Making leadership happen*. Greensboro, NC: Center for Creative Leadership.

Mintzberg, H., & Gosling, J. (2003). Five minds of a manager. *Harvard Business Review, 81*(11), 54–63.

Ospina, S., Foldy, E. G., El Hadidy, W., Dodge, J., Hofmann-Pinilla, A., & Su, C. (2012). Social change leadership as relational leadership. In M. Uhl-Bien & S. M. Ospina (Eds.), *Advancing relational leadership research: A dialogue among perspectives* (pp. 255–302). Charlotte, NC: Information Age.

Rechtman, J. (2008). Towards an ideal of global leadership. *Integral Leadership Review, 12*, 10–18.

Schön, D. A. (1983). *The reflective practitioner: How professionals think in action*. New York: Basic Books.

Torbert, W., & Associates. (2004). *Action inquiry: The secret of timely and transforming leadership*. San Francisco: Berrett-Koehler.

Wheatley, M. J. (1999). *Leadership and the new science: Learning about organization from an orderly universe*. San Francisco: Berrett-Koehler.

8

LEADERSHIP PRAXIS AND THE HEAD

There's an easy answer to the question, "What is leadership?" It's what leaders do. From this perspective, scholars who want to develop theories that both describe the phenomenon and offer guidance for being more effective as a leader should simply study both effective and ineffective leaders. What characteristics and behaviors seem to distinguish the good from the bad? This approach permeates much of traditional scholarship about leadership in organizations and societies, and indeed it is still potent. This is especially true of studies that focus on people (CEOs, senior managers, bosses, team leaders) who occupy positions of formal authority in organizations. It also is evident in studies of political leaders. Think of the countless studies of Abraham Lincoln that identify his leadership qualities (vision, moral strength, humor and humility, political astuteness, and so forth).

Shortcomings of this approach have attracted scholarly attention for some time now, and considerable energy has developed around the view that leadership is a relational phenomenon, in which individuals and groups interact with each other and their environment to achieve desired goals. In this view, someone who is considered a leader by others may or may not occupy a position of formal authority. In any given situation, many people can be acting in leaderly ways—by inspiring the group to persevere, by offering a good idea for a new direction, by pointing out political realities. The relational approach also accepts that groups, organizations, and possibly societies can lead. For many scholars who adopt this approach, labels like leader and follower have very little meaning on their own, but acquire meaning only as groups work together on particular tasks over time.

This chapter first will focus on theories and research investigating leadership from a relational perspective. We begin with James MacGregor Burns, then turn to the recent work of several scholars featured in this book. Following attention to relational leadership, I will recommend several books that offer an overview of leadership approaches and theories. The final section will describe more fully habits of mind and skills that can foster the cognitive, socio-emotional, and behavioral complexity that leaders and their groups need to effectively tackle organizational and societal problems. This section will include attention to learning as a prime function of leadership development.

Viewing Leadership Through a Relational Lens

When he published his influential book *Leadership* in 1978, James MacGregor Burns still had a fairly traditional view of who leaders were. His exemplars were people who had outsized reputations as presidents, fomenters of revolution, or intellectuals. His crucial shift was to probe into the connection of leaders with followers. In an oft-quoted early passage in his book *Leadership*, he proclaimed, "Leadership is one of the most observed and least understood phenomena on earth" (2). He concluded that it could only be understood by focusing on the psychological dynamics and the flow of power within the leader-follower relationship. He recognized that followers influenced leaders, not only the other way round. As a political historian, Burns was used to studying how men acquired and exercised power. To understand psychological dynamics, he turned to the work of developmental psychologist Abraham Maslow, who posited a hierarchy of human needs ranging from physiological to transcendence. Burns's study led him to the conclusion that people who deserved the label leader were mainly of two types: *transforming* (helping followers move up the human needs hierarchy) and *transactional* (working with followers at the level where they were). Both types of leaders paid attention to follower needs as well as their own, and thus leadership could be viewed as a relationship of mutual influence. Transforming leaders, Burns contended, were the ones who could orchestrate conflict creatively to help their organizations and societies be more humane and committed to the common good. In his view, a person who used power for self-aggrandizement and non-humane ends was not a true leader, but merely a tyrant. In his 2003 book *Transforming Leadership*, he declared,

> Summoned forth by human wants, the task of leadership is to accomplish some change in the world that responds to those wants. Its actions and achievements are measured by the supreme public values that themselves are the profoundest expressions of human wants: liberty and equality, justice and opportunity, the pursuit of happiness.
>
> *(2)*

Burns's typology of transactional and transforming leadership provided the foundation for a huge stream of empirical studies once Bernard Bass and Bruce Avolio (Bass and Avolio, 1994; Avolio, 1999) incorporated it into their "full-range model" of leader behaviors in three categories (transformational, transactional, and passive-avoidant). The behaviors related to transformational leadership are individualized consideration, intellectual stimulation, inspirational motivation, and idealized influence. The behaviors related to transactional leadership are contingent reward (making expectations clear and recognizing goal achievement), and active management-by-exception (focusing on mistakes and taking corrective action). Bass and Avolio added a category they called passive/avoidant leadership, which includes passive management-by-exception (failing to interfere until problems occur) and laissez-faire behavior. On the whole, empirical studies have shown that the transformational behaviors plus contingent reward are associated with measures of effectiveness such as follower satisfaction and organizational performance.

Relational views of leadership have taken off in many other directions in the last few decades. Mary Uhl-Bien and Sonia Ospina's edited book *Advancing Relational Leadership Research: A Dialogue Among Perspectives* (2012) presents a diverse set of scholars focusing on relational leadership at the interpersonal, organizational, and societal levels. It is an attempt to elucidate and interrelate what the editors call two opposing paradigms—on the one hand, the view that gives primacy to the characteristics and behaviors of individuals and groups and, on the other hand, the view that seeks mainly to understand "processes of social construction and emergent practices . . . through which leadership gains legitimacy and produces outcomes" (xxii).

The DAC framework, described by Chuck Palus in Chapter 7, is an example of the second, constructionist view. In this framework leadership practices are those aimed at producing collective direction, alignment, and commitment to an agreed-upon course of action. The practices in turn are influenced by individual and collective beliefs about how to obtain direction, alignment, and commitment. As Bill Drath and his colleagues explain, the practices are "beliefs put into action. . . . The efficacy of leadership beliefs and practices in producing DAC provides feedback that may cause changes in practices or, more developmentally, changes in beliefs" (Drath et al., 2008, 642). Also important are aspects of the context that help constitute leadership beliefs. Drath et al. apply "the term *leadership* to ways of producing DAC that may not have been traditionally thought of as leadership or to which the term is not applied in a given context or culture: This includes, for example, teamwork, organizational learning, the operation of some systems in a collective, dialogue, and even intentional culture change" (643).

In his book *The Deep Blue Sea* (2001), Drath suggested that groups tend to adopt one of three leadership models as they strive to accomplish the leadership tasks of achieving direction, alignment, and commitment. The first and most basic is based on the "personal dominance" principle: that is, leadership resides in an exceptional individual and followers receive direction from him or her. The second model is based on the principle of "interpersonal influence": that is, leadership emerges from negotiations among group members and the most influential person becomes the leader. The third model is based on the "relational dialogue" principle and assumes that leadership happens via shared dialogue and collaborative learning. In this model, leadership is the property of a social system and provides the greatest capacity (compared to the other two models) for coping with adaptive challenges.

Mary Uhl-Bien, Russ Marion, and Bill McKelvey have been prime developers of complexity leadership theory, which focuses on leadership in organizations and interorganizational networks viewed as complex adaptive systems. They are interested in emergent practices within these systems, but also in leader behaviors that can help these systems thrive; thus they bridge the two main paradigms in relational leadership theory. Complex adaptive systems are "neural-like networks of interacting, interdependent agents who are bonded in a collective dynamic by common need" (Uhl-Bien and Marion, 2009, 631). Within traditional hierarchical organizations, complex adaptive systems operate in the mesh of informal relational ties and information flows within the organization. These informal systems interact with the organization's formal structures and processes to produce various outcomes. Within complex adaptive systems at the organizational or interorganizational levels, leaders do not obtain desired results by setting goals or issuing directives. Instead adaptive leaders "engage the potential of emergent complexity dynamics to produce adaptive change" (638). Uhl-Bien and Marion propose that they do this by actions such as fostering a "rich flow of information (in the form of ideas, innovations, changes, technologies, etc.)" within the system (639); by reading patterns of interactions; and by "engaging in dialogue that helps connect past, present, and future" (639). Further, they argue that if hierarchical organizations are to reap the benefits of the creative energy generated by the complex adaptive systems within them, formal ("administrative") leaders should ensure that formal structures are flexible enough to allow information to flow easily and foster interaction among diverse people and resources. Additional functions of these leaders include nurturing the visions that emerge from local networks and ensuring that people in the organization are experiencing appropriate levels of adaptive tension, that is, "pressure on a system to elaborate and adjust" (645). In addition to adaptive and administrative leadership, Uhl-Bien and Marion suggest that a third type of leadership—enabling—may be needed to help the adaptive system and formal hierarchy work well together. Enabling leaders

> can protect the adaptive dynamic from suppressive rules, overly specific missions, micro-managing, personnel reassignments, unsupportive policy changes, oppressive pressure, and over-planning—all of which compromise the effectiveness of adaptive processes. Enabling leaders can also help manage the innovation-to-organization interface by helping champion ideas produced by the adaptive function and bringing them to the attention of administrative leaders who can recognize and validate their potential.
>
> *(645)*

Other theorists espousing a systems view of leadership are Kathleen Allen and Cynthia Cherry (2000) and Rian Satterwhite (2010).

The frameworks that I have developed with Humphrey School colleagues—Leadership for the Common Good and integrative leadership—focus on tackling public problems that affect multiple organizations, groups, and individuals. The frameworks also bridge the two paradigms in relational leadership theory. As John Bryson and I note in chapter 10 of the 2012 Uhl-Bien and Ospina book,

> Leadership aimed at tackling complex public challenges is necessarily a shared and collective phenomenon. At the same time, we have found that the characteristics, strengths, and weaknesses of particular individuals who act as formal and informal leaders significantly affect the outcome of this leadership.
>
> *(304)*

The integrative leadership framework brings together elements of leadership for the common good with recent theorizing and research on cross-sector collaboration for public purposes. As John and I note in chapter 10, we are convinced that all major sectors (government, business, nonprofits, media, and community) are implicated in complex public challenges and therefore must be involved in tackling the challenges. For the last 10 years we, along with our colleague Melissa Stone, have conducted research on cross-sector collaborations focused on complex public challenges (Bryson, Crosby, and Stone, 2006; Crosby and Bryson, 2010; Bryson, Crosby, and Stone, 2015). We created a framework and a set of propositions that highlight the importance of five elements: initial conditions, inclusive processes, structure and governance, constraints and contingencies, and outcomes and accountabilities. Integrative leadership essentially is a long-term process of building and sustaining cross-sector collaborations through basic practices attached to these elements. As a shorthand, we define integrative leadership as the work of linking and integrating diverse constituencies—along with resources, processes, and structures—in sustainable arrangements for remedying a complex public problem or responding to a "grand challenge."

The large numbers of empirical studies that have contributed to or tested relational leadership theories include both quantitative and qualitative research. The use of variable-driven quantitative methods is most appropriate within the paradigm that focuses mainly on the attributes and behaviors of leaders and followers. An example would be the extensive research testing leader-member exchange theory. A typical study would collect data about independent variables (say, a leader's delegation behaviors) and about dependent variables (such as follower satisfaction or productivity), use statistical methods to analyze the data, and draw conclusions about the effectiveness of leader or follower behavior or characteristics (Graen and Uhl-Bien, 1995).

The use of qualitative methods such as discourse or narrative analysis is more appropriate as the focus shifts to collective leadership within dynamic systems. Mary Uhl-Bien and Russ Marion (2009) emphasize that variable-based research aimed at prediction is "more suitable for exploration of relationships among constructs rather than dynamic relationships among *actors* and *events*" (636). Researchers can use qualitative methods as well as quantitative network analysis to reveal the patterns of interaction that seem to foster system innovation or stagnation.

Interpretive narrative analysis has been the prime methodology of the research conducted by Sonia Ospina and colleagues into leadership in U.S.-based community organizations. To begin, the research team interviewed people who were chosen to represent their organizations in a multiyear program aimed at celebrating and understanding effective leadership for social change. These initial interviews elicited information about the work of these organizations, and follow-up interviews (with the original interviewees plus other stakeholders) prompted people to tell stories about how the work was accomplished. Here is a detailed description of how the resulting data were analyzed:

> There were multiple rounds of data analysis, beginning with largely descriptive summaries of each organization's leadership practices and ending with higher-order analyses that required interpretation and synthesis across the dataset. In the first round, two members of the research team—including the person who had conducted the interviews—developed and wrote an "analytical memo" for each organization, based on their analysis of interview transcripts as well as additional program documentation. (This analytical memo is roughly comparable to a case description.)
>
> In the second round of analysis, the research team read all the analytical memos systematically to identify cross-patterns of themes associated with the work of leadership. At this point particular practices became salient and, ultimately, the focus of analysis, as the team generated a list of practices engaged in by multiple organizations within the dataset. For example, we noted that many of the organizations attempted to influence how external audiences saw key elements of the organization's work, while a large subset of organizations drew on cultural identity as a source of strength and connection.
>
> Then, in the third round of analysis, subsets of the research team undertook methodical investigations of individual practices by going back to the original transcripts, systematically coding the interviews for examples of those practices, as well as for antecedents and consequences. This resulted in a number of finished and working papers on how particular practices worked in multiple organizations.
>
> *(Ospina et al., 2012, 296)*

Joe Raelin (2011) advocates comprehensive observation of leadership practice "in the making," which would include attention to "material artifacts, the language, the emotions, the technologies, the stories, the physical arrangements of work, the rituals" (201). He seeks to gauge the extent to which teams or organizations are "leaderful"—that is, everyone can lead, many members are serving simultaneously as leaders, members are "co-creating their enterprise," and members are committed to "preserving the dignity of every single member of the entity regardless of background, status, or point of view" (204).

The research that John Bryson, Melissa Stone, and I (along with several research associates) have conducted on cross-sector collaboration and leadership has relied on similar qualitative methods. Using a protocol designed to elicit information about the key elements of cross-sector collaboration, we interviewed key actors in several collaborations. We frequently used NVivo content analysis software to help us organize and interpret the interview data. In addition we collected archival information (news coverage, reports, meeting minutes). In one of our cases, a major federal transportation program, we collected data on collaborations in different cities and at different stages of the collaborations' development. John Bryson's and my chapter in the Uhl-Bien and Ospina book and our *Leadership Quarterly* article (Crosby and Bryson, 2010) outline the integrative leadership practices that we have identified in cases of cross-sector collaboration that we have studied.

Reviewing the Leadership Field

Several well-regarded scholars have published books that provide an overview of the development of leadership theory and research over the last century. One of the most popular is Peter Northouse's *Leadership: Theory and Practice* (2012), now in its sixth edition. The book has chapters on major leadership approaches (trait, skills, style, situational, and psychodynamic) and theories (contingency, path-goal, leader-member exchange, transformational, servant, and authentic). Chapters also cover team leadership, women and leadership, and culture and leadership. Leadership case studies, mainly focusing on the small group or organizational level, and assessment tools are sprinkled throughout.

Recently Doris Schedlitzki and Gareth Edwards have published *Studying Leadership: Traditional and Critical Approaches* (2014). The special value of this book is clear in its sub-title: the incorporation of critical perspectives. In their introduction the authors highlight their intention "to give voice to different methodologies, epistemological and geographical approaches to the study of leadership that have formed leadership studies into the complex and exciting field it is today" (1). In Part I they cover many of the same theories that are featured in the Northouse text, and in Part II they delve into "Current Issues in Leadership," such as leadership and power, distributed leadership, leadership and culture, and leadership learning and development. Part III covers "Critical Issues in Leadership," such as gender and diversity, ethics and sustainability, language and identity, and arts and aesthetics. The authors weave the views of critical theorists throughout, though they are most prominent in Part IV. They also offer prompts for critical thinking and reflection, and they include six extended case studies of leadership in organizations.

The attention to critical approaches is not surprising since, as European leadership scholars, Schedlitzki and Edwards likely have had more exposure to critical leadership scholars than most U.S. scholars have had. These critical scholars (for example, Mats Alvesson and Simon Western) sharply challenge "the still heavily individualistic, white, male dominated and western assumptions embedded within mainstream leadership studies" (5). The chapter on leadership and culture offers an especially insightful analysis of the ambitious GLOBE study that focused on the interaction of "national" cultures and leadership. The analysis includes an explanation of the GLOBE methodology and key findings and then turns to the chief criticisms of the study. Critics have objected to what they see as simplistic conceptualizations (and even misrepresentations) of cultures, as well as raised methodological concerns—e.g., the oversampling of managers. In her own research Schedlitzki has taken an alternative approach which "stresses the active, dynamic element in culture and leadership and stresses that individual leaders and followers actively draw on different value sets in different contexts over time" (184).

Now that leadership scholars have increasingly focused on the role of followers in leadership, they are also producing texts on followership. Barbara Kellerman in *Followership* (2008) and Ira Chaleff in *The Courageous Follower* (2009) offer somewhat different typologies of follower behaviors. Kellerman sorts followers into five categories: isolates, bystanders, participants, activists, and diehards. Chaleff distinguishes among the following followership styles:

- Resources, those who only do what they have to do (they offer low support and seldom challenge their leaders)
- Individualists, who are independent and entrepreneurial (they offer low support but are not afraid to challenge leaders)
- Implementers, who focus on carrying out assigned tasks (they tend not to challenge leaders, but offer high levels of support)
- Partners, who assume responsibility for their own and leaders' behavior (they offer both high support and frequent challenges)

Courageous followership in Chaleff's view includes the courage to support and challenge leaders. In his followership development work, he aims to help participants understand their own default style and how they may choose to reinforce or change it (Chaleff, 2009).

Several excellent leadership textbooks focus on the range of leadership theories that are relevant for managers of organizations. Gary Yukl's *Leadership in Organizations* (2012) is now in its eighth edition and highlights mainly business cases. Montgomery Van Wart's *Dynamics of Leadership in Public Service* (2011) is directed mainly at managers at various levels of government. The importance and means of building productive relationships within and across U.S. government bodies is examined in a text used by Rick Morse: *The Trusted Leader: Building the Relationships That Make Government Work* (2011), edited by Terry Newell, Grant

Reeher, and Peter Ronayne. Paul 't Hart's *Understanding Public Leadership* (2014) explores leadership mainly in parliamentary/ministerial government settings. The book is especially astute in its attention to institutional, social, and temporal context. 't Hart also offers tools for assessing "leadership capital" and approaches to evaluating public leadership. Two helpful books focusing on leading nonprofits are Leslie Crutchfield and Heather Grant's *Forces for Good: The Six Practices of High-Impact Nonprofits* (2012) and Howard Berman's *Making a Difference: The Management and Governance of Nonprofit Enterprises* (2015). Neither book dwells on leadership theory, and both draw mainly on U.S. examples, but they consider the specific challenges of leading organizations committed to educational, charitable, and social causes. The six practices highlighted by Crutchfield and Grant are:

- Advocate and serve (by working on policy change as well as offering programs)
- Make markets work (for example, by starting income-producing ventures)
- Inspire evangelists (by helping donors, volunteers, and advisers be passionate supporters)
- Nurture nonprofit networks (by sharing information and other resources)
- Master the art of adaptation (by innovating in response to environmental shifts)
- Share leadership (by CEOs' encouraging leadership in the organization and its networks as well as working with highly engaged boards)

Berman is more concerned with putting nonprofits into a societal context and considering the nitty-gritty of governing and operating these organizations.

Participants in my classes have often responded very favorably to James Kouzes and Barry Posner's *The Leadership Challenge* (2012) because it describes the five practices and associated commitments (see Figure 7.1) via accessible stories and offers practical guidance for carrying out the commitments. Sharon Turnbull endorses Steve Kempster's *How Managers Have Learnt to Lead* (2009).

Leadership that spans national boundaries has also received specialized attention, and now "global leadership" is a recognized subfield within leadership studies. In *Global Leadership: Research, Practice and Development*, Mark Mendenhall and his colleagues (2008) define global leaders as

> individuals who effect significant positive change in organizations by building communities through the development of trust and the arrangement of organizational structures and processes in a context involving multiple cross-boundary stakeholders, multiple sources of external cross-boundary authority, and multiple cultures under conditions of temporal, geographical and cultural complexity.
>
> *(17)*

Global Leadership: Research, Practice and Development is intended mainly for business audiences, but it has considerable application to cross-border nonprofit and government operations. The chapter on assessing global leadership competencies is useful for people in any of the sectors. My book *Leadership for Global Citizenship* (1999) analyzes leadership in transnational citizen organizations (e.g., Amnesty International), using the Leadership for the Common Good framework.

Anyone preparing to teach leadership also should dive into *The Quest for a General Theory of Leadership* (Sorenson and Goethals, 2006), which grew out of the efforts of several scholars (including some of those featured in this book) to pursue a challenge that Jim Burns first laid out in *Leadership*—namely to develop a theory that would integrate multiple disciplinary views of leadership. Burns, along with George Goethals and Georgia Sorenson, launched the project in 2001 at a meeting of leadership scholars at the Jepson School. Over time, the intellectual energy of the initial group attracted others; many papers were generated and debating sessions organized at annual conferences of the International Leadership Association, the Jepson School, and elsewhere.

Participants engaged in heated cross-disciplinary debates over whether a grand theory of leadership was possible and even desirable. Ultimately, the group agreed to focus on three essential questions:

1. What about the human condition makes leadership necessary?
2. What makes it possible?
3. What processes or conditions characterize the emergence, maintenance, or transformation of leadership? (*Sorenson and Goethals, 2006*, 22)

The results of their thinking together about these questions are presented in *The Quest for a General Theory of Leadership*, which does not offer a general theory, but rather ways of organizing key debates about the nature of leadership. Chapter 2 by Mark Walker presents several of the participating scholars' ideas for mapping the main schools of thought about leadership. Other chapters focus on the central role of power in leadership, leader-follower relations, leadership ethics (dealing especially with inequality among groups and between leaders and followers), and leadership and social change. In chapter 8, Sonia Ospina and Georgia Sorenson present a constructionist view of leadership and its implications for research. "A constructionist lens," they say, "suggests that leadership happens when a community develops and uses, over time, shared agreements to create results that have collective value" (188). In chapter 10, leadership ethics scholar Joanne Ciulla sums up the project. She notes:

> [T]he real problem with leadership studies is not that it is too lightweight, but that it is too heavy. It takes more than one scholar, discipline, or theoretical approach to understand leadership. The study of leadership forces us to tackle the universal questions about human nature and destiny.
>
> *(233)*

The link between leadership and destiny is especially explicit in *Leaders Make the Future* (2012) by futurist Bob Johansen, who puts contemporary leadership into the context of what he calls the VUCA World, referring to the complex, interconnected, and uncertain environment that affects human societies around the world now and into the foreseeable future. (VUCA stands for volatile, uncertain, complex, and ambiguous.) He describes specific leadership skills that can help groups, organizations, and communities deal with trends such as the growing rich-poor gap, immense refugee flows, the rise of "digital natives and cloud-served supercomputing" (10). The skills are:

- Deploying one's maker instinct, "the inner drive to build and grow things," in concert with other people (27)
- Developing clarity about a desirable possible future
- Dilemma flipping—that is, discerning opportunities in intractable problems
- Immersive learning—that is, engaging directly with unfamiliar environments
- Practicing bio-empathy—that is, adopting nature's point of view in order to "understand, respect and learn from its patterns" (95)
- Constructive depolarizing—that is, redirecting the energy generated by conflict toward dialogue and reimagining possibilities
- Practicing quiet transparency, or open and authentic without over self-promotion
- Rapid prototyping—that is, creating early, failure-prone versions of innovation
- Smart-mob organizing, and
- Commons creating, or "seeding, nurturing, and growing shared assets" (165)

Johansen makes a persuasive case that leaders who care about their organizations, communities, and the planet must "immerse themselves in the future" (3), not because it can be predicted, but because understanding trends and likely outcomes can help leaders and constituents choose the best ways to respond to and shape those trends. One of my favorite quotes from the book is, "Leaders must listen for the future, but make decisions in the present" (xxii). I have used this text in a course called Leadership and Change in an Innovation Society and students have responded well to it, because it relates so closely to the major challenges they see in their lives or just over the horizon.

Fostering Leaders' Cognitive, Socio-Emotional, and Behavioral Complexity

Several scholars provide understanding of the cognitive, socio-emotional, and behavioral complexity that aids leaders in helping constituents handle organizational and societal challenges. Cognitive power has long been associated with leader effectiveness. Certainly, when I began my work in leadership education, we believed in the importance of helping program participants thoroughly analyze problems or challenges, think through alternative solutions and their likely consequences, and choose sound courses of action. Then along came the researchers (e.g., John Salovey and Peter Mayer, 1990) focusing on emotional intelligence, or EQ. Daniel Goleman (1995) popularized the concept and the finding that the most successful people in organizations might not be those with the highest IQ but those who had finely tuned emotional sensitivity. As noted in Chapter 2, these people are especially good at discerning their own and others' emotional responses and regulating their own reactions. Clearly, those of us taking a relational view of leadership see emotional intelligence as a prime leader asset. This does not mean that people seeking to lead well no longer need the ability to conceptualize and analyze problems, strategies, and systems. To be effective and humane, they need both cognitive and emotional intelligence and the ability to deploy them appropriately in particular contexts at particular times. Robert Hooijberg, Jerry Hunt, and George Dodge captured this notion in their Leaderplex model (1997). Their model presents cognitive and social complexity as precursors to behavioral complexity, which in turn is a precursor of leader and organizational effectiveness (377).

What might this model imply for those of us seeking to develop our own and others' leadership? As Hooijberg, Hunt, and Dodge describe it, cognitive complexity consists of differentiation and integration—that is, cognitively complex individuals are able to see the world through a rich array of dimensions or lenses and identify commonalities or relationships across dimensions. They are avid gatherers of evidence (for example, through appreciative inquiry), seek to understand system dynamics, and imagine possibilities (Martin, 2009). They have what Barbara Kellerman (2015) calls contextual expertise, attention to historical influences and contemporary trends in areas as diverse as religion, class and culture, politics, media, and money. Cognitively complex leaders also value different types of knowledge: tacit as well as formally documented knowledge embedded in community traditions, as well as universal principles. They engage in critical thinking—that is, questioning their own assumptions and received wisdom and seeking to understand how institutions and the status quo support privileges of certain groups and the oppression of others (Western, 2013). They see human systems as intimately connected to ecosystems (Hawken, 2007). Lee Bolman and Terrance Deal (2013) suggest that cognitively complex leaders are able to frame and reframe organizational challenges using four main metaphors: organization as factory, as family, as jungle, and as theater (see Figure 8.1).

For Hooijberg, Hunt, and Dodge, social complexity includes interpersonal skills as well as sensitivity to social context, including culture and status hierarchies such as those based on gender and race. I prefer the term socio-emotional complexity since these skills include emotional intelligence. Increasingly, scholars highlight emotions' power, not just in fostering empathetic relationships with oneself and others, but also in cognitive processing. As Megan Boler (1999) has pointed out, emotions direct our attention to aspects of our environment and cue our responses. Clearly, they affect our sense of spirituality and aesthetic judgments. Jonathan Haidt in *The Righteous Mind* (2012) emphasizes the role of emotions in

Structural Frame

Focus: Organization as *factory*. Formal organization, rules, roles, and authority relationships

Assumptions:

Organizations have established goals and are rational systems

Vertical and horizontal integration are as important as differentiation and control

Problems = faulty structures and systems

Human Resources Frame

Focus: Organization as *family*. Individuals have feelings and needs

Assumptions:

Organizations exist to serve human needs

Organizations and people need each other (talent and energy & careers and salary)

Problems = misfit between organization and individual

Political Frame

Focus: Organizations as *jungles*, contested terrains

Assumptions:

Organizations are coalitions with differing interests competing for scarce resources

Conflict management, bargaining, negotiation, coercion are part of everyday organizational life

Problems = power is too concentrated or dispersed

Symbolic Frame

Focus: Organizations as *theater*, as cultures rather than rational systems

Assumptions:

Events are more important for what they mean than for what actually happened

Many interpretations of meaning are possible

Symbols, rituals, stories as sense-making tools

Problems = when symbols no longer work

FIGURE 8.1 Bolman and Deal's Organizational Frames

moral reasoning, and Marshall Ganz says, human beings "experience our values through our emotions," which "provide us with vital information about how to live our lives, not in contrast to reasoned deliberation but more as a precondition for it" (3). Hooijberg, Hunt, and Dodge list a number of other ways that emotions affect cognition.

Behavioral complexity involves drawing on one's cognitive and socio-emotional skills in order to respond appropriately to multiple stakeholders and suit actions to the demands of the situation. Stuart Albert in his book *When: The Art of Perfect Timing* (2013) emphasizes the importance of knowing the right time for making a particular intervention (as well as taking time into consideration as people plan some activity). He offers guidance for attending to beginnings and endings, sequencing, intervals, rates of change, and rhythms.

As I have noted elsewhere, behavioral flexibility should not be confused with opportunism and lack of morality. "Leaders who hope to sustain integrity (and effectiveness) must adopt behavior that clearly reflects their core values" (Crosby and Bryson, 2005, 57). Let's consider an example. Stakeholder analysis is a skill that I emphasize in my leadership courses and workshops. It draws certainly on cognitive skills of categorization, identification of linkages among groups, and power analysis. It also involves the socio-emotional ability to see the world from the perspective of diverse individuals and groups, and it offers guidance for how to frame an issue in different ways in order to appeal to different stakeholder groups and to craft a vision that will have wide support, but also improve the world in some way. Many of the habits of mind noted in Chapter 7 relate to socio-emotional complexity—for example, the recognition of learners as unique individuals with potential for leadership in particular situations, sensitivity to one's own ego needs and mental health, a compassionate stance toward self and others, an optimistic outlook. Habitual curiosity and exploration of big leadership questions help increase our cognitive complexity. Behavioral complexity shows up in our call for astute balancing of various tensions—between being a facilitator and a source of expert knowledge, between boldness and humility, between openness and restraint, between planning and spontaneity, between unity and diversity. Leadership educator Gerard Seijts (2014) identifies judgment as the necessary virtue in this balancing work: it is what enables a leader to balance and integrate other virtues of humility, integrity, collaboration, courage, temperance, accountability, humanity, avoidance of expedience, long-term focus, and drive. Additionally, reflection is essential to judgment. Chris Argyris (1982) and Donald Schön (1983) and have highlighted the importance of people's reflecting on the adequacy of the theories that guide our actions. Reflecting on our emotional reactions both in the moment and afterward can help us engage in behaviors that stimulate rather than shut down learning. As you will see in the next chapter, we leadership educators have many ways of building reflection into our courses and workshops.

> *Without judgment, all the other virtues aren't enough to guide good actions. Every leader must learn to make decisions and take actions in complex, multi-stakeholder, and often paradoxical situations that depend on sound judgment.*
> —Gerard Seijts (2014, 12)

Developing and drawing on cognitive and socio-emotional complexity in order to achieve behavioral complexity is essentially a learning process; thus leadership educators have reason both as teachers and leaders to examine theories of learning. As noted, I have often turned to Donald Schön's ideas about learning through reflection on and in practice. In his 1983 book, *The Reflective Practitioner*, he describes reflection in action as a process in which

> inquirers encounter a problematic situation whose reality they must construct. As they frame the problem of the situation they determine the features to which they will attend, the order they will attempt to impose on the situation, the directions in which they will try to change it. In this process, they identify both the ends to be sought and the means to be employed. In

the ensuing inquiry, action on the situation is integral with deciding, and problem solving is part of the larger experiment in problem setting.

(165)

Reflection on practice, then, allows the inquirers to step back from the interventions they undertook, consider the effects, and plan for improving the interventions, which can subsequently be undertaken and reflected upon. (This sequence echoes Torbert's action inquiry process, described in Chapter 7.) This infinitely repeatable process is similar to Kolb's learning cycle, consisting of concrete experience, reflective observation, formulation of hypotheses based on observation, and testing the hypotheses. In a 2005 article, Alice and David Kolb explain experiential learning theory, which incorporates the Kolb cycle and provides a foundation for the action learning approach espoused by many of the leadership educators featured in this book. Though the focus is on individual learning styles, the authors also consider the socio-material spaces, including classrooms, in which learning occurs. They draw on situated learning theory that views learning as a "process of becoming a member of a community of practice." In this view,

> learning spaces extend beyond the teacher and the classroom. They include socialization into a wider community of practice that involves membership, identity formation, transitioning from novice to expert through mentorship, and experience in the activities of the practice, as well as the reproduction and development of the community of practice itself as newcomers replace old-timers.

(200)

As leadership educators, we do not seek simply to assist individuals in learning how to ever more adeptly tackle organizational and societal problems: we want them to be able to help their teams, organizations, and networks do the same. To foster such learning, leaders set up systems that foster information sharing, after-action reviews, and institutional memory. Mary Crossan, Henry Lane, and Roderick White (1999) offer a helpful framework that links individual, group, and organizational learning via four social and psychological processes: intuiting, interpreting, integrating, and institutionalizing. They also emphasize that leaders should shake up institutionalized processes from time to time; if procedures are hampering organizational learning they should be set aside in order "to enact variations that allow intuition, insights, and action to surface and be pursued" (533). John Bryson and I highlight additional ideas for establishing a culture of learning in organizations in *Leadership for the Common Good* (92–95).

★★★

As leadership educators prepare ourselves and others to tackle leadership challenges in organizations and communities, we have a wealth of theories and related guidance to draw on. We may fruitfully begin our exploration of these theories with James MacGregor Burns's (1978) formulation of transforming and transactional leadership. We may derive insights from subsequent frameworks like Direction-Alignment-Commitment, advanced by the Center for Creative Leadership, or theories, such as complexity leadership, that deepen understanding of collective leadership. The integrative leadership framework (Crosby and Bryson, 2012) directs attention to individual and collective leadership practices required to tackle complex public problems. This chapter has examined these and other key investigations of relational leadership at the organizational and societal levels, and described the use of qualitative methods, especially interpretive narrative analysis, to illuminate relational leadership.

To put relational leadership in context, I also have recommended several excellent overview books that trace the development of leadership theory and research over the last decade, and I have suggested a number of leadership books that focus on particular realms of organizational and societal life—for example, leadership in government organizations and global leadership. Additionally, I have introduced Bob Johansen's list of leadership skills attuned to the particular challenges of the early decades of the 21st century.

This chapter also has explored the cognitive, socio-emotional, and behavioral complexity needed to help groups tackle complex organizational and societal challenges. I have argued that drawing on cognitive and socio-emotional complexity in order to achieve behavioral complexity is a learning process, and I have explored key theories of learning that inspire many of the educators featured in this book.

The next chapter describes in some detail experiential and reflective exercises that can help participants in leadership courses and workshops connect leadership theories and research to the challenges they confront in their organizations and communities. Taken together, these exercises link the self-awareness and interpersonal skill development described in Chapters 3 and 6 to the skills needed to lead at the organizational and interorganizational levels.

References

Albert, S. (2013). *When: The art of perfect timing*. San Francisco: Jossey-Bass.

Allen, K. E., & Cherrey, C. (2000). *Systemic leadership: Enriching the meaning of our work*. Lanham, MD: University Press of America.

Argyris, C. (1982). The executive mind and double-loop learning. *Organizational Dynamics*, (Autumn), 5–22.

Avolio, B. J. (1999). *Full leadership development: Building the vital forces in organizations*. Thousand Oaks, CA: SAGE.

Bass, B. M., & Avolio, B. J. (1994). *Improving organizational effectiveness through transformational leadership*. Newbury Park, CA: SAGE.

Berman, H. (2015). *Making a difference: The management and governance of nonprofit enterprises*. Rochester, NY: CCE Publications.

Boler, M. (1999). *Feeling power: Emotions and education*. New York: Routledge.

Bolman, L. G., & Deal, T. E. (2013). *Reframing organizations: Artistry, choice, and leadership* (5th ed.). San Francisco: Jossey-Bass.

Bryson, J. M., Crosby, B. C., & Stone, M. M. (2006). The design and implementation of cross-sector collaborations: Propositions from the literature. *Public Administration Review, 66*(s1), 44–55.

Bryson, J. M., Crosby, B. C., & Stone, M. M. (2015). Designing and implementing cross-sector collaborations: Needed and challenging. *Public Administration Review, 75*(5), 647–663.

Burns, J. M. (1978). *Leadership.* New York: Harper Collins.

Burns, J. M. (2003). *Transforming leadership: The pursuit of happiness.* New York: Atlantic Monthly Press.

Chaleff, I. (2009). *The courageous follower: Standing up to and for our leaders* (3rd ed.). San Francisco: Berrett-Koehler.

Crosby, B. C. (1999). *Leadership for global citizenship: Building transnational community.* Thousand Oaks, CA: SAGE.

Crosby, B. C., & Bryson, J. M. (2005). *Leadership for the common good: Tackling public problems in a shared-power world.* San Francisco: Wiley.

Crosby, B. C., & Bryson, J. M. (2010). Integrative leadership and the creation and maintenance of cross-sector collaborations. *Leadership Quarterly, 21*(2), 211–230.

Crosby, B. C., & Bryson, J. M. (2012). Integrative leadership and policy change: A hybrid relational view. In M. Uhl-Bien & S. Ospina (Eds.), *Advancing relational leadership research: A dialogue among perspectives* (pp. 303–334). Charlotte, NC: Information Age.

Crossan, M. M., Lane, H. W., & White, R. E. (1999). An organizational learning framework: From intuition to institution. *Academy of Management Review, 24*(3), 522–537.

Crutchfield, L. R., & Grant, H. M. (2012). *Forces for good: The six practices of high-impact nonprofits.* San Francisco: Jossey-Bass.

Drath, W. H. (2001). *The deep blue sea: Rethinking the source of leadership.* San Francisco: Jossey-Bass.

Drath, W. H., McCauley, C. D., Palus, C. J., Van Velsor, E., O'Connor, P. M. G., & McGuire, J. B. (2008). Direction, alignment, commitment: Toward a more integrative ontology of leadership. *Leadership Quarterly, 19*(6), 635–653.

Goethals, G. R., & Sorenson, G. L. J. (Eds.). (2006). *The quest for a general theory of leadership.* Cheltenham, UK: Edward Elgar.

Goleman, D. (1995). *Emotional intelligence.* New York: Bantam.

Graen, G., & Uhl-Bien, M. (1995). Relationship-based approach to leadership: Development of leader-member exchange (LMX) theory of leadership more than 25 years: Applying a multi-level, multi-domain perspective. *Leadership Quarterly, 6,* 219–247.

Haidt, J. (2012). *The righteous mind: Why good people are divided by politics and religion.* New York: Pantheon.

Hawken, P. (2007). *Blessed unrest: How the largest social movement in history is restoring grace, justice, and beauty to the world.* New York: Penguin.

Hooijberg, R., Hunt, J. G., & Dodge, G. E. (1997). Leadership complexity and development of the Leaderplex model. *Journal of Management, 23*(3), 37–408.

Johansen, B. (2012). *Leaders make the future.* San Francisco: Berett-Koehler.

Kellerman, B. (2008). *Followership: How followers are creating change and changing leaders.* Boston, MA: Harvard Business Press.

Kellerman, B. (2015). *Hard times: Leadership in America.* Stanford, CA: Stanford University Press.

Kempster, S. (2009). *How managers have learnt to lead.* New York: Palgrave Macmillan.

Kolb, A., & Kolb, D. (2005). Learning styles and learning spaces: Enhancing experiential learning in higher education. *Academy of Management Learning & Education, 4*(2), 193–212.

Kouzes, J. M., & Posner, B. Z. (2012). *The leadership challenge: How to make extraordinary things happen in organizations* (5th ed.). San Francisco: Jossey-Bass.

Martin, R. (2009). *The opposable mind: Winning through integrative thinking.* Boston, MA: Harvard Business.

Mendenhall, M. E., Osland, J. S., Bird, A., Oddou, G. R., & Maznevski, M. L. (Eds.). (2008). *Global leadership: Research, practice and development.* New York: Routledge.

Newell, T., Reeher, G., & Ronayne, P. (Eds.). (2011). *The trusted leader: Building relationships that make government work* (2nd ed.). Washington, DC: CQ Press.

Northouse, P. G. (2012). *Leadership: Theory and practice* (6th ed.). Thousand Oaks, CA: SAGE.

Ospina, S., Foldy, E. G., El Hadidy, W., Dodge, J., Hofmann-Pinilla, A., & Su, C. (2012). Social change leadership as relational leadership. In M. Uhl-Bien & S. M. Ospina (Eds.), *Advancing relational leadership research: A dialogue among perspectives* (pp. 255–302). Charlotte, NC: Information Age.

Raelin, J. A. (2011). From leadership as practice to leaderful practice. *Leadership, 7*(2), 195–211.

Salovey, P., & Mayer, J. D. (1990). Emotional intelligence. *Imagination, Cognition and Personality, 9*(3), 185–211.

Satterwhite, R. (2010). Deep systems leadership: A model for the 21st century. In B. W. Redekop (Ed.), *Leadership for environmental sustainability* (pp. 230–242). New York: Routledge.

Schedlitzki, D., & Edwards, G. (2014). *Studying leadership: Traditional and critical approaches.* London: SAGE.

Schön, D. A. (1983). *The reflective practitioner: How professionals think in action.* New York: Basic Books.

Seijts, G. (2014). *Good leaders learn: Lessons from lifetimes of leadership.* New York: Taylor & Francis.

't Hart, P. (2014). *Understanding public leadership.* New York: Palgrave Macmillan.

Uhl-Bien, M., & Marion, R. (2009). Complexity leadership in bureaucratic forms of organizing: A meso model. *Leadership Quarterly, 20*, 631–650.

Van Wart, M. (2011). *Dynamics of leadership in public service: Theory and practice* (2nd ed.). Armonk, NY: M.E. Sharpe.

Western, S. (2013). *Leadership: A critical analysis.* London: SAGE.

Yukl, G. (2012). *Leadership in organizations* (8th ed.). Upper Saddle River, NJ: Pearson.

9

LEADERSHIP PRAXIS AND THE HANDS

This chapter will consider effective methods for helping participants grasp a range of leadership theories and know about the evolution of leadership theory so they can make sense of disparate views of leadership and of their own experience. Additionally, this chapter will describe the action learning methods that I and others have found to be effective in helping participants strengthen their ability to help their organizations and communities tackle the challenges they face. (An overarching aim is to heighten participants' cognitive, socio-emotional, and behavioral complexity.)

Teaching Leadership Theory

In keeping with Ken Bain's (2004) finding that the best teachers help students engage with the compelling questions in their fields, I introduce participants in my courses to the major debates in leadership studies and connect the different views to specific theories. Indeed, the debates are the central organizing themes for the modules in a semester-long, partly online, partly face-to-face version of Leadership for the Common Good, a graduate course at the Humphrey School. Via the course website, I introduce each module with an exercise or video clip that raises one or more Big Questions about leadership. Then participants are directed to readings and exercises that prepare them for the module's face-to-face session. They use online forums to post analyses of readings and reflections on the face-to-face sessions, and in some modules, participants also are assigned to use their webcams to film and post their responses to a VoiceThread assignment. Attention to leadership skills or habits of mind is woven into the course fabric. Every module helps participants hone their capacity for reflection and self-awareness, relationship building, and written and oral communication. Additionally, I identify particular skills—e.g., persuasive communication or appreciative inquiry—that I want to emphasize in the face-to-face sessions. Table 9.1 lists the learning outcomes and assigned readings for each module.

TABLE 9.1 Leadership for the Common Good Course Design

Module	Takeaways	Assigned Readings
What Is Leadership? Leadership in Context	Leadership is multifaceted, context dependent, and consequential. Leadership may be exercised by prominent individuals, ordinary people, and groups.	*Leadership for the Common Good* (LCG), Preface, Ch. 1
Leadership in Context & Personal Leadership	Personal leadership assets are our commitments plus what we're born with and what we've acquired—in relation to the context. Also important is acknowledging personal liabilities and blind spots.	LCG, Ch. 2 Murphy, Susan E., & Johnson, Stephanie K. (2011). Benefits of a long-lens approach to leadership development: Understanding the seeds of leadership, *Leadership Quarterly, 22*(11), 459–470. Haidt, Jonathan. (2012). *The righteous mind; why good people are divided by politics and religion*, Ch. 6 Goleman, Daniel, Boyatzis, Richard, & McKee, Annie. (2002). *Primal leadership*, Ch. 4
Personal & Team Leadership	Self-knowledge is a basis for welcoming others. Strangers can become familiar through structured processes.	Humphrey, Hubert. (1976). *Education of a public man*, introduction Mandela, Nelson. (1995) *Long walk to freedom*, Chs. 13 & 14 Ibarra, Herminia, Snook, Scott, & Ramo, Laura. (2010). Identity-based leader development Bordas, Juana. (2007). *Salsa, soul and spirit*, introduction
Conflict Management & Organizational Leadership	Conflict and leadership are intertwined. Effective leaders draw on a repertoire of approaches to orchestrate conflict productively.	LCG, Ch. 3 Sessa, Valerie. (1994). Can conflict improve team effectiveness? Gerzon, Mark. (2006). *Leading through conflict*, introduction Kellerman, Barbara. (2009). *Followership*, Ch. 4 Optional: Jerry Harvey: The Abilene paradox (http://www.crmlearning.com/abilene-paradox)

(Continued)

TABLE 9.1 (Continued)

Module	Takeaways	Assigned Readings
Adaptive Leadership	Formal and informal authority are leadership assets. Use them to help people distinguish between technical and adaptive problems, confront and work on adaptive problems. Use framing and reframing to assist in this work.	Bolman, Lee, & Deal, Terrance. (2013). *Reframing organizations*, Ch. 1 Mandela, Nelson. (1995). *Long walk to freedom*, Ch. 20 Heifetz, Ronald, Grashow, Alexander, & Linksy, Marty. (2009). *The practice of adaptive leadership*, Ch. 2
Visionary, Political, & Ethical Leadership	Visionary, political, and ethical leadership are linked together in fostering democratic practice, policies, and institutions.	LCG, Ch. 4 & Resource D Bryson. (2004). What to do when stakeholders matter. *Public Management Review, 6*(1), 21–53. Shapiro, Joseph. (1994). *No pity*, Ch. 4
Integrative Leadership	Integration at personal, group, organizational, and societal levels can add up to beneficial outcomes.	Boyte, Harry. (2005). Reframing democracy. *Public Administration Review, 65*(5), 536–546. Crosby, Barbara, & Bryson, John. (2010). Integrative leadership and the creation and maintenance of cross-sector collaborations. *Leadership Quarterly, 21*(2), 211–230.
Putting It All Together	As leaders and followers engage in shaping and reshaping policy systems, they debate and shape the common good in overlapping forums, arenas, and courts over the course of a policy change cycle.	LCG, Ch. 5 Gerencser, Mark, Van Lee, Reginald, Napolitano, Fernando, & Kelly, Christopher. (2008). *Megacommunities*, Preface & Ch. 6

In the video clip for the first module, I pose two questions:

• What is leadership and why does it matter?
• How is leadership linked to context?

The chief takeaways, or learning outcomes, that I intend participants to have at the end of the module are: Leadership is multifaceted, context dependent, and consequential. Leadership may be exercised by prominent individuals, ordinary people, and groups of people.

Script for Module 1 video

What is leadership?

One of the difficulties in answering this question is that almost everyone uses the term without thinking much about it.

Is leadership simply something we expect people in positions of authority to do?

Is it something that emerges in any human group, from a kindergarten class to an orchestra?

Is it a relationship, a process, a practice?

Are leaders and leadership the same thing?

And what about followers and followership? Many wise people have pointed out that leaders would be nowhere without followers. Yet most leadership development programs hardly pay attention to followers.

Meanwhile, how does leadership vary depending on whether one is leading oneself, a small group, an organization, a community, or a country?

And surely context matters. In what ways is leading in India different from leading in the U.S.?

In the early pages of *Leadership for the Common Good* (2005), John Bryson and I explain how we think about some of these questions. That doesn't mean that our thinking is firmly gelled, however. One of the reasons I stay excited about the study of leadership is that these questions are not settled, and yet striving for more humane and effective leadership is of the utmost importance.

Researchers have long tried to discover whether leaders really do make much of a difference. They conclude that we humans tend to attribute more impact to leaders than we should, given the effects of natural and man-made systems. Yet, the actions of people in organizational leadership roles have been shown to affect organizational performance. All of us can probably offer an example when a leader's actions affected a situation for better or worse.

What I take away from this is that leaders and leadership matter. Yet, our preoccupation with individual leaders—say, President Obama or Rep. Rubio, or Aung Sun Suu Kyi, or an outstanding soccer player—certainly obscures the leadership work being done by countless other individuals and groups. Meanwhile, leaders operate within numerous systems—and their impact is determined in large part by how adept they are in using leverage points for changing the system.

I look forward to further exploring the questions I've raised with you in our upcoming class. I'm eager to hear what you think leadership is and what your experience has taught you about leading and following.

I ask participants to prepare for the first face-to-face session by watching a movie about Hubert Humphrey's life. Then in class I note that Humphrey is someone we might call a "big L" leader, with accompanying strengths and weaknesses. I say that I will introduce them to some people we might call "small l" leaders. I then quickly tell the stories of four people (including two former students) who have taken on formidable challenges (racial disparities in Minneapolis and St. Paul, homelessness in the local county, and poverty in New Delhi) and helped organize coalitions to make improvements. I then ask participants in small groups to talk about: How did these people exhibit leadership? Is their leadership different from Hubert Humphrey's? In what way?

After debriefing the small group exercise, I ask everyone to draw a quick picture of leadership. We post the images on the wall and consider the views of leadership they convey.

By highlighting the stories of a very prominent statesman along with people who are like the participants in the class and following this up with the small group conversation and drawing exercise, I hope participants will generate insights about the diversity of leaders, identify with others who have successfully practiced leadership, and consider what counts as leadership and how it might differ depending on contextual pressures, level of responsibility, and so forth.

I organize the second module around the hoary old question, Is leadership born or is it made? The takeaway I intend for the module is: Personal leadership assets are our commitments (passions) plus what we're born with and what we've acquired—in relation to the context. Also important is acknowledging personal liabilities and blind spots.

Script for Module 2 video

A perennial debate in leadership studies and even popular conversation is whether leaders are born or made.

Are leaders a breed apart who have certain genes, predispositions, or other early advantages that prepare them for leadership roles?

Or can just about anyone learn and exercise leadership skills effectively?

Perhaps you have seen the film *The King's Speech*. The focus is on the second son of King George V of Britain, just prior to World War II.

Bertie, as the prince was known to his family, was a consummate follower, reluctant to be in the limelight, but determined to be a good adviser and supporter for his older brother, who was in line for the throne.

Circumstances changed, however, when his father died, and his brother abdicated the throne. Bertie became King George VI!

Certainly, this man had an innate advantage from the beginning—he was a prince! He also had a marked disadvantage—a pronounced stutter that made him an extremely awkward public speaker.

Enter his spouse, who believes that her husband could overcome his speech impediment. She in turn is aided and abetted by a determined speech therapist, Lionel Logue.

The two men clash at first—they are from different classes, to be sure, but the therapist's methods are also unconventional. In time, though, the therapist manages to lead the king through his fears. The king tries a series of new behaviors that ultimately allow him to speak clearly. In the end, he becomes a beloved war-time monarch.

In this story, who is the leader? Several candidates are possible: the king, his wife, the therapist.

What role did genes, predispositions, and early advantages play?

As part of this module you will be considering how your own predispositions and acquired skills affect your leadership. For example, the Myers-Briggs Type Indicator is a tool for understanding your preferred ways of learning and working in the world.

Knowing those preferences may help you understand what type of leadership comes naturally to you and how you prefer to follow. The MBTI may also be a jumping-off point for practicing leadership in ways that don't come naturally to you.

A second enduring question about personal leadership is related to the born versus made debate. Is good character required for good leadership and, if so, how does one acquire good character? Research by well-known leadership gurus James Kouzes and Barry Posner tells us that people around the world want to follow leaders who have integrity (plus some other qualities like competence and vision).

While good character is commonly thought to include many virtues, usually integrity is high on the list, so for now let's focus on integrity. The word has a strong moral flavor, and refers to people who both espouse moral values and act on them.

So where do our moral values come from? Are we born with them, learn them at our parents' knees, in school, in a religious institution? Does integrity come naturally for some of us, or is it built through determined practice and rebounds from failings?

The work of Jonathan Haidt (2012) suggests that variations in our moral intuitions have a stronger genetic foundation than we usually recognize. Yet he also acknowledges the effects of upbringing and other experiences.

Haidt encourages us to consider the validity of different constellations of moral values. Taking this perspective, liberals might think better of conservatives and vice versa. In general, people of different religious and political persuasions might attribute good character to a wider array of leaders.

> Still, that doesn't entirely solve the question of the link between good character and effective leadership. People who are morally good aren't always effective as leaders, and we may know of examples in which people who are fairly immoral seem to be effective leaders. What do you think?

The third module highlights the debate between the view that leadership is mainly about the special skills and qualities of individuals versus the view that leadership is mainly about the work of groups. The big question for the module is "How do we welcome the other, the stranger, in order to develop diverse, productive groups or teams?" The takeaways are:

- Self-knowledge is a basis for welcoming others
- Strangers can become familiar through structured processes

Script for Module 3 video

Some argue that charismatic or well-trained individual leaders are the people who have the greatest impact. We should study and learn from those people, so that we might follow in their footsteps or at least join their initiatives. (I certainly hope this course can help participants increase their charisma factor!)

Nowadays, though, the focus is frequently on teams as the real engine of sustainable change. Great teams are able to draw on complementary skills and resources of all their members and together get things done. Sure, one or more people will take on leader roles in the team, but the point is that it's the group that really gets things done.

A first step is learning how to bring diverse people together and help them build working relationships.

How do we do this?

One way is to differentiate "us" from "them." Thus, a leader may draw lines between those with professional training and those without, or between castes, or between political persuasions. Then he or she might build group cohesiveness around a shared identity of "us" on one side of the line, emphasizing separation or even competition with "them" on the other side. Sometimes the competition is quite benign, but sometimes it becomes highly destructive if leaders reinforce group members' fears or disdain toward "them." These are the leaders whom Mark Gerzon (2006) in a reading for the next module calls "demagogues."

At times, a group may have authentic reasons for fearing another group. The group may need to focus on building its own strength and recruiting allies before negotiating with that group.

Ironically, whether leaders are attempting to build commonality within or across groups, they would be wise to honor differences and their implications for power dynamics.

Do some differences matter more than others? That will depend on the context, of course. The Social Group Membership exercise lists some differences that matter in many contexts.

Leaders seeking to be authentically inclusive must recognize that some people have been marginalized, excluded, even killed on the basis of these differences. Inclusive leaders now have many resources—such as Juana Bordas's *Salsa, Soul, and Spirit* (2007)—that can heighten respect for the leadership and followership contributions from many cultures, genders, nationalities, religious groups, and so on. They have many methods such as Art of Hosting that can be used, often with adaptations, to include all kinds of people on an equal footing.

Commonality in well-functioning teams revolves around the team's mission, and a shared commitment to the mission. The shared commitment, in turn, is inextricably linked to the relationships among people on the team—so the work of building relationships across difference is hardly unproductive.

The fourth module focuses on the question: How can leaders and followers deal effectively with conflict in teams (and beyond)? The takeaway is that conflict and leadership are intertwined. Effective leaders draw on a repertoire of approaches to orchestrate conflict productively.

Script for Module 4 video

Whenever you set out to inspire and mobilize a group to accomplish something new, you are bound to encounter conflict.

Change can be threatening—and the universal human response to threat is deep-seated and emotional. We want to fight or flee.

So as a leader you have to keep some folks from fleeing and others from engaging in attacks. For the first group, establishing a sense of safety is important. The second group, especially, wants opportunities to have their ideas and needs taken seriously.

Both groups may be reassured by a leader's reminder that conflict in groups is normal and even healthy. Many of us have come across the four-stage model of team development:

Forming, storming, norming, and performing

Not every group follows those stages precisely, but knowing the stages helps remind people that conflict is normal and that groups can move beyond storming. (Of course, when Minnesota Nice prevails, moving beyond forming can be tough.)

Fortunately, you can take advantage of many time-tested processes to ensure that conflict in groups is productive rather than destructive, task-oriented rather than people-oriented.

Setting ground rules at the outset can be helpful.

One extremely helpful process is dialogue—similar to the process that Judy, the manager in the Sessa (1994) article, implemented once she realized that her own methods weren't working. As we describe it in chapter 3 of *Leadership for the Common Good*, dialogue involves listening to everyone's ideas without evaluating them. This approach allows many different ideas to emerge and to be explained fully.

It is very different from common practice in groups, which is to jump on an idea that is offered and proclaim it terrific or the worst thing possible. The result, often, is that groups end up with a solution that hardly anyone really supports or a bunch of dead ideas. (Listen, sometime, to Jerry Harvey talk about "The Road to Abilene," http://www.abileneparadox.com/).

Once lots of well-developed ideas are on the table, we still have the challenge of deciding which one or which combination to pursue. In the Sessa article, team members agree to divide into smaller study groups to gather more information and develop recommendations.

Deciding among recommendations may require negotiation skills. For example, Harvard's Negotiation Project has developed guidance that helps negotiating partners identify their real interests rather than their hardened positions.

Often, partners find out that they can build agreements more easily on interests than a position. For example, I or my group may come into a community meeting convinced we need to build a wall around our living space—that's a position. Perhaps others object because the wall will interfere with their access to sunlight. If we shift the focus to the interest behind the position—that is, security or privacy—we are likely to be able to consider other ways of getting our needs met.

The *Leadership for the Common Good* book also offers methods for evaluating different solutions—for example the multicriteria assessment grid described in chapter 8.

I want to be sure that I haven't made this sound too rational or "heady." Usually people will also need a chance to express how they feel about the issue at hand or recommended solutions.

Finally, I urge each of you to consider your default way of responding to conflict. Some time ago Kenneth Thomas and Ralph Kilmann identified five main ways that people respond to conflict:

We may avoid the conflict
We may accommodate another person's demand
We may compete
We may compromise, or
We may co-promote, that is, figure out ways to achieve both parties' goals

Kilmann suggests that we choose an approach based on importance of relationships versus the issue at hand. If I don't care much about the issue or about the relationship with the person I'm in conflict with, my best approach is to avoid the conflict.

If I don't care much about the issue but really care about the relationship, I will accommodate.

Conversely, if I care about the issue but not the relationship, I will compete.

If I care about both the issue and the relationship, I will either compromise (in which each party gives up something) or co-promote.

Ideally, we can become more adept at using all of these, depending on what we want to achieve in a conflict situation.

In the fifth module, the big question is whether leadership is a technical or adaptive practice. Assigned videos, readings, and exercises are intended to help participants distinguish between technical and adaptive problems (based on Ron Heifetz's work), consider the uses of formal and informal authority in helping groups work on problems, and apply the four organizational leadership frames that Lee Bolman and Terrance Deal (2013, 2014) have elaborated in their books (see Chapter 8). The takeaways from this module are: Formal and informal authority are leadership assets. Use them to help people distinguish between technical and adaptive problems, confront and work on adaptive problems. Use framing and reframing to assist in this work.

Instead of introducing the module myself, I ask participants to view an interview with Tom Vellenga, who served as an adviser in the Clinton White House. He first discusses the adaptive challenges faced by Mac McLarty as he attempted to organize the White House staff; he then describes the reframing that occurred when Leon Panetta took over as chief of staff. He also explains how he has used Bolman and Deal's four frames to organize and sustain Heartland Democracy, a nonprofit organization that promotes citizen engagement.

Module 6 marks the transition from an organizational to an interorganizational and societal focus. To begin, participants view two online video lectures on stakeholder analysis and strategic thinking and read "What to Do When Stakeholders Matter" (Bryson, 2004). A reading and in-class presentations focus on the disability rights movement in the U.S. and how a variety of movement leaders exercised visionary, political, and ethical leadership to achieve enactment of the Americans with Disabilities Act. The Big Questions are: Is leadership based on universal ethical principles? What happens when ethical principles conflict with each other or political requirements? The takeaway is: Visionary, political, and ethical leadership are linked together in fostering democratic practice, policies, and institutions.

Module 7 focuses on integrative leadership, which as noted earlier is the work of bringing diverse groups and organizations together across sectoral, geographic, and cultural boundaries to tackle complex public problems and advance the common good. I begin the module with an online mini-lecture on integrative leadership and Rotary International's highly successful campaign to eliminate polio worldwide. The Big Question for the module is: How do we cross boundaries without getting lost? The takeaway is: Integration at personal, group, organizational, and societal levels can add up to beneficial outcomes.

"Putting It All Together" is the title of Module 8, the last. The Big Question is: How do leaders and followers enact the common good over the course of a policy change cycle? The takeaway is that as leaders and followers engage in shaping and reshaping policy systems, they debate and shape the common good in overlapping forums, arenas, and courts over the course of a policy change cycle.

Script for Module 8 video

The Policy Change Cycle, described in chapter 5 of *Leadership for the Common Good*, is a systems view that can help you and your groups think about and navigate through a policy change effort in its complex, sometimes loopy, entirety. The remainder of the book describes key dynamics and leadership challenges for each phase in the cycle.

All of the previous chapters have been designed to help you improve the leadership skills that can help you move through the cycle in ways that enact the common good.

The chapter raises the thorny question: What is the common good? Can there be a common good in such a diverse and contentious world as the one in which we live?

Are there some basic tenets such as the Universal Declaration of Human Rights that everyone can use in assessing whether a society's institutions, policies, and practices achieve the common good?

Is the common good achievable in a nondemocratic environment? Or can it emerge only through democratic practices?

These are questions that I doubt can be fully settled, but are vital to consider as we strive for policies, programs, laws, rules, and norms that yield widespread benefits at reasonable cost and tap people's deepest interest in their own well-being and that of others.

A concept that seems very helpful in this process is "public value." Several scholars, especially Mark Moore and Barry Bozeman, have elaborated the idea of public value and public values as a way of countering what they feel is a tendency to devalue and erode the benefits of governments and public endeavors in favor of a market-based approach to meeting society's needs. In 2012, the Center for Integrative Leadership (CIL) sponsored a conference that brought diverse public value scholars together and resulted in a special issue for *Public Administration Review* and two books (Bryson, Crosby, and Bloomberg, 2015a, 2015b).

My hope is that this CIL project can provide some systematic ways of considering whether the common good is resulting or likely to result from particular policy regimes, programs, or projects. Beyond these publications, everyone involved in the project hopes that focusing on public value might also be a way to improve politics and political discourse in this country and others. This is definitely part of our current leadership work!

When leadership educators teach workshops or shorter courses, we must condense our consideration of the big debates or questions in leadership theory. In those cases, the exercise called Clarifying Your Leadership Perspective (see Inset 9.1) can be helpful. I have used the exercise in conjunction with a role play in which 16 participants are assigned one of the views described in the exercise. I give each of these participants a more detailed description of the assigned role and instruct him/her to prepare to explain to the class, with as much conviction as possible, why this view of leadership makes more sense than the one with which it is paired. When the role play begins, the participant assigned "leadership is inborn" is given two minutes to make his/her case. Then the participant assigned "leadership is learned" responds in kind. I then ask class members to mark their position along the first continuum in the exercise. I ask for a show of hands to indicate the level of support for each side of the debate, then speak briefly about the competing schools of thought in the born versus made debate. We continue the process through the other seven paired views. The atmosphere is often very energetic and very humorous, as people find themselves arguing for perspectives they may not really support. Passions are aroused as the group listens to one student argue, for example, that leading is an inherently ethical process followed by another who claims it is no such thing, but rather that leading is about gaining followers and carrying out actions effectively, regardless of ethical considerations. Often participants find some truth in both sides of the continuum.

INSET 9.1 CLARIFYING YOUR LEADERSHIP PERSPECTIVE (BASED ON THE WORK OF ROBERT TERRY, THE TERRY GROUP)

Eight dualities are evident among prominent views of leadership:

- **Born v. made**—the view that leadership qualities and potential are mainly inborn versus the view that leadership qualities are mainly learned
- **Individual v. relational**—the view that leadership is about the activities of heroic, powerful, exemplary individuals versus the view that leadership is a relationship among leaders and followers (or constituents, members, etc.)
- **Positional v. everywhere**—the view that leaders are people in top positions of authority versus the view that people can lead no matter what their positions
- **Engagement v. results**—the view that leadership is about undertaking versus the view that leadership is about achieving high performance
- **Coercion included v. coercion excluded**—the view that leadership can include the use of force versus the view that leadership relies only on noncoercive methods of influence
- **Realistic v. idealistic**—the view that leadership focuses on what is really going on and framing that reality versus the view that leadership focuses on a vision of what can be
- **Unethical means and ends included v. only ethical means and ends included**—the view that leadership includes ethical and unethical behavior versus the view that leadership includes only ethical behavior
- **Secular v. spiritual**—the view that leadership is of this world and mainly outside the spiritual realm versus the view that leadership connects to the deepest human connections and highest aspirations

Exercise

1. These dualities are presented on the next page at either end of a continuum. Place an **X** on each continuum to indicate to which end you gravitate and how strongly. Avoid the neutral midpoint.
2. Focus on the continua on which you easily located your view. What merit might there be in the contrasting view?
3. The next time you hear a conversation or read about leadership, consider which of the views of leadership is implicit in what you hear or read. Note those views here.
4. How do the views you heard or read relate to your own?
5. How do competing views of leadership affect your leadership case?

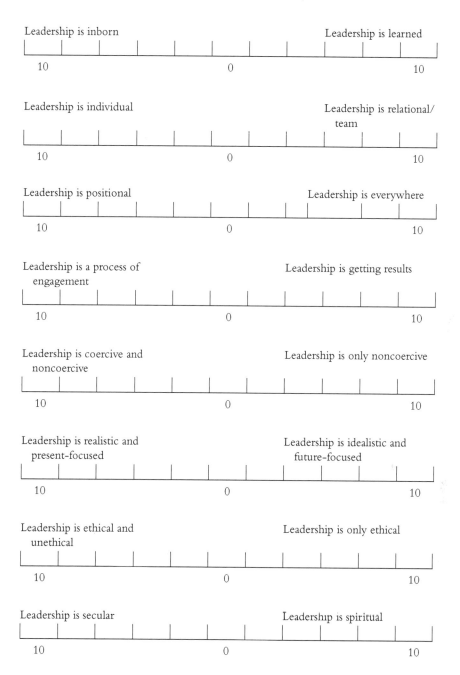

The exercise can be accompanied by a list of theories and research that exemplify each perspective. You may wish to substitute other contrasting perspectives in leadership studies—for example, the view that leadership is mainly about exercising formal authority versus the view that leadership is mainly constituted by informal authority, or the view that leadership varies widely across cultures versus the view that many leadership principles are universal.

To help participants understand and apply relational leadership theory, I designed an exercise with two parts, the first focusing on the participant and the second focusing on the ways in which groups, organizations, and communities lead (or not). The directions for Part 1 are: Reflect on your efforts to lead in your family, schools, work and volunteer sites, and communities. Pay particular attention to the other people involved. What did they teach you? How did they help or hinder you in this work? Describe in three or more pages your efforts and learning in at least three group settings in which you have been active. The directions for Part 2 are: Now consider the leadership of the groups themselves. In what way did the group exercise leadership? My own responses to Part 1 of the assignment focus on my family, newspapers, governors' offices, and the university.

Barbara's Crosby's Relational Leadership Narrative

My first leadership practice field was my family. Only I didn't call it leadership; I thought of it as survival. As a girl, I set out to "lead" my family into something I considered normal—a household where people sat down to supper and talked to each other, where the floors were swept, and clothes were hung in closets. I'm not sure where I got this idea of normal—maybe television and other families played a role, but my parents also seemed to want this normalcy yet couldn't quite achieve it. So, I took on more and more of the household responsibilities, which included persuading my younger sister to do her share, counseling my depressed mother, and figuring out how to spark a supper-time conversation over rice, salmon cakes, and lettuce and tomato salad with Miracle Whip.

This experience taught me patience—the patience to wait for hours while my mother got organized enough to go shopping, the patience to work on the things I could or was allowed to tackle rather than striving for thorough renovation, the patience to wait an hour or more past the appointed time when my father was supposed to take me to or from some event. I learned that determination and attention to relationships could improve conditions, up to a point. Trying to lead my family also taught me dissembling: I became expert at reading while listening to my mother's troubles; I learned the pitfalls of speaking my own mind. I also learned the virtue of self-sacrifice, and only later understood just how double-edged that virtue is. I learned the trickiness of leading without formal authority. I learned about the complexity of human nature: The same parents who often let me down also had wonderful qualities. My father was adventurous, liked to dance and garden, and took pride in my accomplishments. My mother was patient and kind and came through for me at some crucial junctures.

In high school, my main leadership role was as co-editor of the *Golden Columns*, Butler High School's monthly newspaper. The *Golden Columns* was a far cry from actual journalism, but it helped me make the connection between leadership and responsibility; also clear was that my co-editor and I couldn't produce the paper on our own and needed to secure the reliable cooperation of many other students. Some "followers" were more reliable than others.

As a college student from 1964 to 1968, I preferred the second-in-command role, whether it was being an assistant editor on the *Vanderbilt Hustler*, a section editor for the yearbook, or helping my male friends run a campus group that brought prominent politicians, civil rights activists, and other leaders to campus. Although one of my professors encouraged me to run for editor of the newspaper, I declined because I knew I'd be a long shot (no woman had ever had the job) and I didn't relish the battle. A leadership lesson learned during these years was that you can have impact without being in a top position, and that relationships, persistence, and writing skill were my greatest assets for making the kind of impact I sought.

As a reporter for Augusta, Georgia's afternoon daily paper after college, I wanted my reporting to wake up Augusta to the various revolutions going on all around the South and the country. So, I covered the integration battles in the school district, I went to the neglected parts of town where newly vocal black citizens were demanding paved roads and sewer lines, I covered the ragtag antiwar marches and the first Earth Day. Officially, I had the education beat; unofficially, I developed a poverty beat. I had some successes, but was also often at loggerheads with my city editor, John Barnes, who came to work every day wearing a crisp, white, long-sleeved shirt and tie, dark thinning hair slicked back, a bit slumped from a spinal problem and long years of hunching over the copy desk. He represented the South that was courtly and thoroughly unprepared for racial equality. Later I would recognize him as a partial mentor, a man who taught me some rock-bottom basics of reporting and schooled me in resisting authority (his). A searing experience during these years was the eruption of a riot in Augusta's black neighborhoods brought on by simmering hostility between the local police and the black community and triggered by the death of a young black man in the county jail. I wanted to join the paper's male reporters in covering the riot, which went on for several days, but the editors said no way. The governor called out the National Guard and the riot was quelled, but not before six black men were shot and killed. Finally, my newspaper and her sister paper, the morning daily, decided that they needed to understand better what was going on in the black community. Editors agreed that the papers would produce a special joint Sunday section, and I was one of those summoned to plan and write the section, because I had been covering events in the black community for some time. This period taught me about the possibilities and limitations of trying to lead through reporting, and it reinforced my sense that persistence is a valuable leadership practice.

After Augusta, I moved to Baltimore, where among other things, I was co-editor of a struggling inner-city weekly and later editor of a suburban weekly. In 1975 I moved to the other side when I took a job in the press office of Gov. Pat Lucey of Wisconsin. I learned new lessons there about fighting back against a male-dominated, and in many ways dysfunctional, organizational culture. By painfully overcoming my own fears (of being incompetent and discounted), I proved my abilities as a press officer and speechwriter, and was able to offer alternatives to the way the office worked. By the time I became press secretary myself near the end of Lucey's term, I could see the impact of my efforts. Here again, relationships were crucial for my being effective. Jeff Smoller, a brusque former reporter, taught me how to be a respected press secretary. John Bryson, my husband, coached me on facing the trial by fire that I faced many a day in that office.

Fast-forward to the early 1980s, when my writing projects and interest in social change and public affairs took me to the Reflective Leadership Center (RLC) at the Humphrey Institute of Public Affairs. The center had been created by the institute's first dean, Harlan Cleveland, who felt that a public affairs school should have a program to build the confidence and thinking skills of Minnesota's emerging leaders. The first director of the RLC was Robert Terry, a larger-than-life advocate of free-flowing conversation, bending of boundaries, and social justice. He engaged me and others in organizing the center's seminars, and together we set out to understand what public affairs leadership was all about. We searched the leadership literature, we invited leading leadership scholars (including James MacGregor Burns, Barbara Kellerman, Ron Heifetz, and Harold Prince) to meet with us and with seminar participants, and we hashed out our own leadership framework that could guide reflective practitioners. I worked with Bob until 1990, when he left the university to establish a consulting practice. Certainly he was my most influential leadership mentor. Not only did he invite me into the highly stimulating search for suitable public affairs leadership frameworks and tools, but he also gave me the chance to lead seminars myself and didn't hesitate to tell me where he thought I could improve. He had his flaws, and I learned new lessons about how hard it is to hold an extremely charismatic individual accountable.

After Bob left the Humphrey Institute, I would experience the joys of co-leadership. Sharon Anderson had long been the Reflective Leadership Center's assistant director. For the next decade, she, John Bryson, and I would work to keep the center alive and, at different times, each of us served as center director. We also took on the daunting task of launching the institute's new midcareer degree program in 1999. Working as a team with shifting responsibilities we often achieved the kind of "flow" described by Mihalyi Csikszentmihalyi (1990). We knew each other's skills to the core, we shared a common purpose, and we had an amazing level of trust built on past experience, trials endured, and friendship. When one of us said, here's a project that needs doing, the others said, fine, just tell me what I'm responsible for. We had disagreements, to be sure, and we had lengthy conversations at times among ourselves and with others about how we should proceed. During my stint as center director, I learned again the close ties between responsibility and leadership, and how the thrill of having authority to make certain decisions is offset by the knowledge that you are accountable for those decisions.

In 2002, the RLC merged with another Humphrey program to become the Public and Nonprofit Leadership Center, and I became one of several faculty members who joined in building that center. A few years later, some of us answered an invitation to develop an additional leadership center, but this one—the Center for Integrative Leadership (CIL)—would be an all-university center, that is, encompassing the entire University of Minnesota. I liked the scary notion of building a new center that required a lot of intellectual work and program design (although I knew that we could build on many preexisting relationships among university faculty interested in leadership). The main leadership task I assigned myself was illuminating the intellectual foundations of integrative leadership (which we founders described as leading across sector, geographic, and cultural boundaries to advance the common good). Later I would become one of the center's academic co-directors, responsible to two deans. This was a tough role, because the center was trying to do what it was studying—that is, leading across boundaries (in this case the boundary between a school of public affairs and a school of business management). I learned new lessons about negotiating with and between powerful people, about sensitivity to culture and timing, about shaping conversations and debates, and about taking painful but necessary actions. Again, I benefited from a reliable partner, the other co-director.

In 2009, I left the co-director role to go on sabbatical and was perfectly happy to return to an informal leadership role with the CIL. I was clear that my energies were flowing away from administrative leadership and toward further refinement of my research and teaching about integrative leadership. That provided another lesson for me: the value of moving in and out of formal leadership roles.

I've had leadership roles in volunteer activities. In Minneapolis, I've edited a neighborhood newspaper, been an officer of peace and communication groups, and served on numerous church committees, some of which I chaired. Some lessons: Pay attention to budgets, work with co-chairs, remember you don't have to do it all.

Forming a biracial family and parenting have taught me plenty of leadership lessons. John and I went through quite a process of deciding whether we would be suitable parents, then after we decided to go ahead, we found it wasn't so easy. In the midst of a long string of tests and treatments, we agreed to explore adoption. The day came when we'd had enough of the medical intervention route and decided to adopt. We chose the Korean program through Children's Home Society for two main reasons: At that time adopting a baby domestically was truly difficult, and the Korean program was well-established, aboveboard, and reliable. We realized that we were making a decision that would ever after mark us as an unusual family and that represented a crossing of racial and cultural lines that was almost unprecedented among our relatives. The various orientation programs and home studies also brought home to us that parenting is not for the faint-hearted or lily-livered. We sometimes joked that putting all adults through the rigors of something like the adoption process before they could have children would be a great form of birth control!

We also recognized that our children would come to us because their mothers were living in a society that would not accept them as full citizens, nor would it support their mothers in raising them. So our family in a way would be formed out of painful injustice. We also knew that we were bringing our children into a U.S. society that all too often devalues, discriminates against, or exoticizes non-Anglo people. Ultimately, however, we were motivated by a rock simple conclusion: two children needed parents and we wanted to parent.

In the years since, our family has been both thoroughly normal and fairly unusual. We experienced common ups and downs, endless trips to soccer games, family trips, school challenges and successes. We consciously chose to live in Minneapolis, where many other people have adopted internationally or assembled families in unconventional ways. Still, we've all had those moments when someone reveals that he considers adoptive families different from "real" families. Our children have had to sort out exactly what their identity is when they have been completely separated from their biological parents and native culture. (Yes, we have sent our children to Korean Culture Camp and celebrated their Korean origins, but our family certainly hasn't truly been bicultural.)

How has being a mother and an adoptive parent affected my leadership practice? It taught me about limits—I realized I couldn't do everything I thought I should; I couldn't continue to assume so much psychic responsibility for my family of origin. I concluded there is no such thing as work-family balance. During many of the years when I was in the thick of child-raising, first one, then the other side of the work-family pair would be out of whack. Yet, the effort to give proper attention to multiple aspects of my life gave me connection with the struggles of other midcareer people who like me were trying to practice leadership while raising children and caring for aging parents. It also prompted me to ask young people in my undergrad classes to think about their future lives as parents.

Being a parent has taught me humility. When our children were teenagers, our family went through severe emotional stress. Even as John and I pulled out all stops to cope, we often felt powerless and overwhelmed. It sometimes felt that the only thing that stood between us and complete chaos was our regular Saturday morning excursions to Java Jack's coffeehouse. So the learning was that sometimes you do what you can in the midst of great uncertainty, you admit powerlessness, you stay present and connected to the people you care about, and you draw on the support of community. I will forever be grateful to Sara Evans, who said, Barbara, some other moms of Korean-born children are getting together to support each other and you should come. This group is one of those precious circles where commiseration is absolute, where one can rejoice at small steps forward, cry over setbacks, and howl with laughter at the absurdities of human struggles and humiliations.

Using Action Learning Methods

Many of us assign various versions of case studies in order to help participants apply theories and advance their own change initiatives in organizations and communities. Additionally, we offer internships and community projects.

Using Case Studies

Two main types of case studies are useful in our classes and workshops. One type focuses on how other people have succeeded or fallen short in their efforts to lead their organizations and communities. The other type is constructed from the participant's experience.

Cases about *other people's leadership experiences* abound and they are often offered as written narratives that feature a protagonist—say, a new mayor, government department head, senior executive, or nonprofit CEO—who works to place the organization on a sustainable path or seeks to help the organization or community make significant progress in resolving a major issue or responding to a promising opportunity. Studies can have multiple protagonists, and those probably reflect actual practice best.

Traditionally, cases have been written presentations in two or three parts. The stage is set in part 1, and the protagonist reaches a decision point. Students are asked to apply theories, research findings, and their own experiences in analyzing the situation and recommending a course of action. In part 2, the actual decision is revealed and possibly a new challenge presented. Occasionally, case writers will include a part 3, featuring yet a subsequent challenge. In the integrative leadership course that I have taught with other University of Minnesota colleagues, we have invited to class the actual protagonists in cases involving leadership across sectoral, geographic, and cultural boundaries. Students can then acquire additional knowledge that was not part of the written case.

In choosing cases, leadership educators not only should seek those that illuminate leadership theories, but also that feature diverse leaders in contexts both familiar and novel for participants. A good source of leadership cases related to public policy and public administration is The Electronic Hallway, hosted by the Evans School of Public Affairs (http://hallway.evans.washington.edu/). Harvard Business Review (https://hbr.org/store/) is a good source for business cases. Schedlitzki and Edwards include several case studies in *Studying Leadership* (2014). I have used several multimedia case studies available through the Hubert Project (http://www.hubertproject.org) to help students apply the integrative leadership framework. These cases are: "The African American Leadership Forum," "Heading Home Hennepin" (focusing on the effort to end homelessness in the county that includes Minneapolis), "Ending Sex Trafficking in the U.S. and Minnesota," and "Mission Convergence" (focusing on the efforts of Rashmi Singh and others to build a government-nonprofit collaboration to support New Delhi's most impoverished people). Each of the four cases feature multiple leaders.

Kevin Gerdes and Jodi Sandfort also assign book-length treatments of organizational and societal challenges. For example, they use Isabel Wilkerson's *The Warmth of Other Suns: The Epic Story of America's Great Migration* (2010) to help participants develop insights about how African American families have resisted racial injustices. After reading a book, participants write an analysis that identifies key leadership concepts that emerge in their reading and relate these concepts to their own experience or to other leadership concepts they've previously read about. They post their analysis to an online forum, so they can respond to each other's posts. In the subsequent face-to-face class, Kevin and Jodi often organize a World Café to draw out the key leadership concepts that the group has identified.

Leadership educators often encourage participants in our workshops and courses to construct their own "live" leadership cases. Cases about *participant experiences* are constructed in a variety of ways. We may ask each participant to develop a case statement about a challenge s/he faces in an organization or community and then analyze the challenge, decide on actions, and then assess the outcome. In leadership courses at the Humphrey School, my colleagues and I often have set up Action Learning Circles, small groups of students with the assignment of supporting each other in clarifying the cases, taking action, and learning from the experience.

Participant teams may work jointly on a case that interests or affects them all. For many years, I taught a course called Transforming Public Policy, in which participant teams worked on public problems—such as U.S. drug sentencing laws, transportation in a poor neighborhood, or neglected tropical diseases—that affected many groups and organizations. Over the course of a semester, the teams worked through a sequence of assignments in which they framed the problem, considered a wide range of solutions, and developed policy proposals that would have a good chance of being adopted by relevant policy makers. Guidance for the process can be found in Appendix C, Guidance for Transforming Public Policy Teams.

Leadership educators can help participants think comprehensively and creatively about organizational and societal challenges by encouraging them to use structured brainstorming (for example, a snow card exercise), an array of stakeholder analysis techniques (Bryson, 2004; Crosby and Bryson, 2005), and action-oriented strategy mapping (Bryson, Ackermann, and Eden, 2014). Kathy Quick provides toys—Legos, craft supplies, recycled packaging materials, and the like—that participants can use to develop visual representations of a problem and potential solutions. In a similar vein, Brad Jackson assigns student teams the task of creating a visual representation of the leadership needed to tackle an organizational or societal problem. "It could be mime, dance, movies. I am really trying to get teams to think and solve problems visually." Additional ideas may be found on the Liberating Structures website (http://www.liberatingstructures.com/).

In my course Leadership and Change in an Innovation Society, I invite participants to share their own live cases with the class in order to hear class members' analyses of the case and perhaps learn about additional resources. For example, one participant asked class members to help her sort through the effort to reconfigure a successful web-based nonprofit. The reconfiguring required layoffs of dedicated staff, but also offered the participant a chance to play a stronger leadership role. Class members helped her explore her own ambivalences, fears, and hopes in this situation. In another example, a participant reported on the searing experience of helping people in his academic unit heal after a strike by unionized staff and a breach of trust by managers. He shared the case in order to better understand how he and another manager could have led more effectively. He drafted a version of the case (changing participant names) that I have used in subsequent classes.

Janet Denhardt sees her leadership course as a studio space in which students can examine their own behavior in a particular situation and rehearse different responses. Often, she notes that students have a notion of what they should do in the situation, but "then they do something else. I say who's that for, why did you do that? They say, this is where I'm comfortable." Or perhaps, the student chooses an action to serve his or her ego. By revealing the barriers that ego and the desire for security pose for effective leadership, she helps students make conscious efforts to minimize ego and take needed risks. Denhardt and co-author Kelly Campbell (2005) describe the studio approach as

> real-time practice, with the teacher and students sharing responsibility for course discussion and direction. Students can be responsible for leading class discussions and creating activities and assignments. The instructor provides opportunities for feedback and student self-reflection and awareness and engages students in dialogue. Moreover, through the collaboration and facilitation of process, the instructor ultimately models and practices this shared and value-based leadership approach.
>
> *(176)*

Along with his mentor, Henry Mintzberg, Jonathan Gosling designed an intensive six-day roundtable experience for executive M.B.A. students that focuses on students' leadership and management "predicaments." Each student has a chance to present the challenges he or she faces at work and is asked to consider: How am I framing this challenge? Is my way of framing blinding me to options? Says Gosling, "Using psychotherapy-derived techniques we get people into a witness position. People witness the phenomenon in which they are engaged and they witness on behalf of each other. We call this the slow fix." Gosling and his colleagues adopted the term "slow fix" in response to an American student who thought the course was proceeding too slowly. "We're not engaged in the quick fix," Gosling emphasizes. "It's helpful to signal to a group that the pace will be slow. It is okay to have silence to reflect."

On the first day of the roundtable, participants talk in small groups about the challenges they face and make 3-D collages of the key features of their predicaments, and common elements. On the second day, participants get to know each other better as individuals—for example, by finding a partner and sharing life stories during a walk with each other. On the third day of the course, participants divide into four groups and each group visits a small business in order to discern how leadership is accomplished there. Afterward, each student group reports to one other group as the remaining two groups watch (thus reinforcing the witness stance). Ultimately, the entire group develops conclusions about the experience—for example, what generalizable leadership lessons it revealed. On the final day every participant has a chance to receive "friendly consulting" about his/her leadership predicament, which by now s/he is likely to see quite differently compared to day one of the course. (A more detailed description of the roundtable program is in Gosling and Case, 2013.)

Jonathan Gosling describes "friendly consulting" as a process in which each participant has 15 minutes to present his/her leadership challenge to one other participant (the chairperson), while the remaining participants sit in a circle around them. Then the presenter responds to questions that the other participants have formulated while listening and given to the chairperson. The presenter then sits outside the circle with his/her back turned. The group talks for 15 minutes while the presenter listens. Says Gosling, "People find this exercise hugely affirming. Often the presenters learn what they knew already, but until now they were just living with and defending their situation."

Leadership development based within an organization can focus productively on cases involving previous or ongoing challenges in that organization. For example, for a number of years, I organized a leadership foundations program for the Minnesota Department of Transportation and used a case tracking the drawn-out controversy over building a new bridge over the river separating Minnesota and Wisconsin. In their book *Experience-Driven Leadership Development* (2013), Cynthia McCauley and co-authors offer extensive ideas for using on-the-job experiences to develop "leadership talent."

Role plays—that is, a structured exercise in which participants act out assigned or chosen roles as they confront organizational and societal challenges—also can be helpful. If the case directly involves a participant, the participant could play him/herself, or possibly someone who is a "difficult" stakeholder in the case (in order to get more insight about that person's behavior). The role play might focus on a meeting, planning session, or public forum. Following the role play, those who played roles can talk about their strategies, emotions, and learning; then other participants in the course or workshop offer their observations.

Informal cases also can be ripped from the daily news headlines. Perhaps the news media are full of reports about a terrorist attack in a U.S. city. I might ask class members: Which individuals and organizations are leading in the fight against domestic terrorism and how? Or, perhaps the latest crisis within the European Union is receiving lots of coverage. I might ask: Can we see examples of visionary and political leadership in the current struggles of the E.U.?

One final note about the use of cases in leadership education: Many approaches to analyzing cases or organizational or societal change focus mainly on data gathering and strategizing; as leadership educators we must take care to highlight the socio-emotional aspects of the case. For example, when Brad Jackson asks students to write a case study in which they were the protagonist, he prompts them to talk about what angered and frustrated them in the situation. We can also use stakeholder analyses and role plays to help participants see the situation from others' perspectives; role plays, in particular, can evoke some of the emotions sparked by the challenges or proposed courses of action.

Internships and Community Projects

Georgia Sorenson requires her undergraduate students to do internships with an organization that operates on a local, state, or national level. These experiences can help students understand policy issues in a way that classroom instruction can't. Sorenson endorses the comment by a colleague who said, "It's not enough to have students understand policies about soup kitchens; they should work in soup kitchens."

Often leadership educators assign participant teams the challenge of actually seeding or achieving a desirable change in their communities. June Nobbe and her colleagues in the University of Minnesota's undergraduate leadership minor help undergraduates see themselves as reciprocal learners as they seek to lead in particular communities. Using Peter Block's *Community: The Structure of Belonging* (2008), leadership minor instructors help students see the importance of inviting people in a community to engage in conversation about possibilities for desirable change.

In his analysis of research on undergraduate leadership development, John Dugan (2011) notes that students' community service and involvement with campus organizations significantly increase their leadership capacity. He advises leadership educators to combine these learning experiences with opportunities for peer-to-peer "sociocultural conversations"—that is, dialogues across cultural and political differences.

As part of the Blandin Community Leadership Program, participants establish leadership goals they want to work on. They then form Going Forward Teams of four to six people who are tasked with meeting between the opening retreat and the first workshop to check in with each other on their progress. These same groups meet again between the first and second follow-up workshops to practice framing an issue affecting their community. Valerie Shangreaux explains, "The intent is to give participants the opportunity to work with a small team of fellow participants with a real issue that is important to the health of their community. Additionally, it is intended to help them practice and strengthen their leadership skills." Each team gathers information about a community issue with a particular focus on hearing multiple perspectives within the community. They then develop a framing statement about the issue designed to reflect multiple perspectives and allow for multiple approaches or solutions. At the second follow-up workshop each team gives a brief report on what they heard and learned and the framing statement they developed.

In my Leadership and Change class, I require students to use the web platform Storify (https://storify.com/) to explore a public issue and promote a desired future. Storify also helps participants draw content from various social media in order to develop a story about the issue and possibilities for change. Directions for the assignment are in Appendix D.

★★★

Preparing ourselves and others to apply leadership theories in tackling organizational and community problems requires, first of all, understanding the range of those theories and discerning which are more sound and useful. This chapter described methods I have used to help participants in my courses understand leadership theories. Following the focus on theory, the chapter considered how to help participants in leadership courses and workshops apply these theories to their own practice. My colleagues and I described several types of case study assignments, as well as internships and community projects that can serve this purpose. I invite you to consider which may be most appropriate for your own leadership program.

The next part of this book will explore how the work of leading in organizations and communities is tied to the leadership work of strengthening citizenship. You will hear a lot more about leadership and leadership education as democratic practice.

References

Bain, K. (2004). *What the best teachers do*. Cambridge, MA: Harvard University Press.

Block, P. (2008). *Community: The structure of belonging*. San Francisco: Berrett-Koehler.

Bolman, L. G., & Deal, T. E. (2013). *Reframing organizations: Artistry, choice, and leadership* (5th ed.). San Francisco: Jossey-Bass.

Bolman, L. G., & Deal, T. E. (2014). *How great leaders think: The art of reframing*. San Francisco: Jossey-Bass.

Bordas, J. (2007). *Salsa, soul, and spirit: Leadership for a multicultural age*. San Francisco: Berrett-Koehler Publishers, Inc.

Boyte, H. C. Reframing democracy. *Public Administration Review, 65*(5), 536–546.

Bryson, J. M. (2004). What to do when stakeholders matter: Stakeholder identification and analysis techniques. *Public Management Review, 6*(1), 21–53.

Bryson, J. M., Ackermann, F., & Eden, C. (2014). *Visual strategy mapping*. Hoboken, NJ: Wiley.

Bryson, J. M., Crosby, B. C., & Bloomberg, L. (Eds.). (2015a). *Creating public value in practice*. Boca Raton FL: Taylor & Francis.

Bryson, J. M., Crosby, B. C., & Bloomberg, L. (Eds.). (2015b). *Public value and public administration*. Washington, DC: Georgetown Press.

Crosby, B. C., & Bryson, J. M. (2005). *Leadership for the common good: Tackling public problems in a shared-power world*. San Francisco: Wiley.

Crosby, B. C., & Bryson, J. M. (2010). Integrative leadership and the creation and maintenance of cross-sector collaborations. *Leadership Quarterly, 21*(?), 211–230.

Denhardt, J. V., & Campbell, K. B. (2005). Leadership education in public administration: Finding the fit between purpose and approach. *Journal of Public Affairs Education, 11*(3), 169–179.

Dugan, J. P. (2011). Research on college student leadership development. In S. R. Komives, J. P. Dugan, J. E. Owen, C. Slack, & W. Wagner (Eds.), *The handbook for student leadership development* (2nd ed., pp. 59–84). San Francisco: Jossey-Bass.

Gerencser, M., Van Lee, R., Napolitano, F., & Kelly, C. (2008). *Megacommunities: How leaders of government, business and non-profits can tackle today's global challenges together*. New York: Palgrave Macmillan.

Gerzon, M. (2006). *Leading through conflict*. Cambridge, MA: Harvard Business Review Press.

Goleman, D., Boyatzis, R., & McKee, A. (2002). *Primal leadership: Realizing the power of emotional intelligence*. Boston, MA: Harvard Business Review Press.

Gosling, J., & Case, P. (2013). Give me the answer: The paradox of dependency in management learning. *E-Organizations & People, 20*(3), 57–64.

Haidt, J. (2012). *The righteous mind: Why good people are divided by politics and religion*. New York: Pantheon.

Heifetz, R. A., Grashow, A., & Linsky, M. (2009). *The practice of adaptive leadership: Tools and tactics for changing your organization and the world*. Boston, MA: Harvard Business Press.

Humphrey, H. H. (1976). *The education of a public man: My life and politics*. New York: Doubleday.

Ibarra, H., Snook, S., & Ramo, L. G. (2010). Identity-based leader development. In N. Nohria & R. Khurana (Eds.), *Handbook of leadership theory and practice* (p. 22). Boston, MA: Harvard Business Press.

Mandela, N. (1995). *Long walk to freedom*. New York: Crown.

McCauley, C., DeRue, D. S., Yost, P. R., & Taylor, S. (2013). *Experience-driven leadership development*. San Francisco: Wiley.

Murphy, S. E., & Johnson, S. K. (2011). The benefits of a long-lens approach to leader development: Understanding the seeds of leadership. *Leadership Quarterly, 22*, 459–470.

Schedlitzki, D., & Edwards, G. (2014). *Studying leadership: Traditional and critical approaches*. London: SAGE.

Sessa, V. (1994). Can conflict improve team effectiveness? *Issues & Observations, 14*(4), 1–5.

Shapiro, J. (1994). *No pity: People with disabilities forging a new civil rights movement*. New York: New York Times Books.

Wilkerson, I. (2010). *The warmth of other suns*. New York: Vintage.

PART IV

Strengthening Citizenship

If the purpose of leadership is to improve conditions for everyone in your organization, community, or society, then leadership development necessarily will include attention to citizenship, governance, and the common good. Democratic forms of government are most in sync with this view, though admittedly some other forms can produce public benefits.

Harlan Cleveland (2002) articulated the link between leadership and citizenship several years ago. "When nobody can be in general charge, and some self-selected subset of everybody is partly in charge, the notion of educating for leadership morphs into educating for citizenship" (209).

In Chapter 10, leadership educators describe how we see our work as education for citizenship. We also will explain how we came to view ourselves as public persons, with an emphasis on our economic and political histories. Chapter 11 presents theoretical perspectives on leadership and the common good, community organizing, and political leadership. In Chapter 12, I will describe several exercises and assignments that can help you as well as participants in leadership programs, courses, and workshops develop a fuller sense of being citizen leaders.

Reference

Cleveland, H. (2002). *Nobody in charge: Essays on the future of leadership*. San Francisco: Jossey-Bass.

10

STRENGTHENING CITIZENSHIP AND THE HEART

Everyone in our courses and workshops, even the elected officials, are (or are seeking to be) citizens—officially of a country and unofficially of various communities and organizations, even of the world. Likewise we, the "leaders" of leadership development experiences, are citizens. As I see it, being an engaged citizen oneself and promoting the engagement of others is a prime leadership practice; it is the work of strengthening democracy. Engaged citizenship is a foundation for achieving the common good.

> Valerie Shangreaux says, "You can't have democracy if you don't have engaged citizens. If any group is marginalized, it's not true democracy."

In this chapter leadership educators will describe our efforts to be engaged citizens and consider how we came to see ourselves as "public persons," that is, people with rights and responsibilities tied to our citizenship in organizations and communities. We will consider how our economic and political history has affected our engagement with the public realm. We will explain how we link leadership, citizenship, and democracy in our leadership development work. Finally, I describe the approach I use to help participants in my courses and workshops to demystify and reform the policy process.

Being Engaged Citizens

Gill Hickman plunged into active citizenship as a teenager, when she joined the civil rights movement. She acquired values of public service early in life and applied them in her government and academic work in California. Then she heard about the Jepson School. Jepson's linking leadership to citizenship was what attracted Gill Hickman. "I was in California, divorced, and wanted to be near family on the east coast. I saw an ad for the dean of a brand new school [Jepson]. The ad said part of the school's purpose was to prepare ethical leaders for service to society. That totally grabbed me. I said if I could work anywhere, it would be there." Time went on, and Hickman remarried. Her husband got a job in Richmond, so she took a leave of absence and moved with him to Virginia, where she worked at Virginia Commonwealth University. Then several positions opened up at Jepson, and she applied for one. "I said, that's it, this is my job! This is my calling." She hardly remembers her interview except that there was a lot of smiling and laughter. She was hired as part of the inaugural faculty group at Jepson.

Hickman says she tends not to think of herself as a public person, but is willing to step into the public arena when necessary. "I really like being behind the scenes; I like developing things. I'm willing to go public when I think something is really important, when I really care about it. Jepson is one of those things."

The desire to remedy inequities also brought Georgia Sorenson and Sonia Ospina into the public realm. Sorenson says "I'm basically a private person, an introvert, but I'm also the oldest daughter in my family. I couldn't keep my mouth shut about injustice." Sonia Ospina felt the need to contribute to societal change as a young woman because she was "outraged by things in the world." In her view, "being a public person is having a say in how to change something in the world. . . . It is possible to be a public person in different ways. I feel I'm a public person but several degrees removed from direct action. . . . In my role as a professor, I have influence on people who are having an impact. I'm bringing frameworks that support democracy and the value of citizenship."

Chuck Palus credits being part of the Boy Scouts as giving him a sense of being a public person. He remembers working on the citizenship merit badge, which emphasized service to God and country. "I didn't go for the God part, but country—I bought that."

Rick Morse became politically engaged as an undergraduate student, as he sought to see his ideals of social equity and due process honored in the democratic process. He recalls, "When I was a sophomore at Brigham Young, a Democratic congressman Bill Orton in Provo, a real quality person, lost his re-election campaign. It was a dirty campaign. It was the biggest turning point for me. I was so incensed. I became very much politically active." He switched his major to public policy and began to speak out at public meetings.

Now, being on the faculty at the University of North Carolina School of Government suits him well. He teaches and advises local government officials as well as teaching master's students, and provides resources and assistance to local governments that offer citizen academies. "In all my leadership teaching," he says, "I emphasize public service values: democratic responsiveness and community stewardship." Being a soccer coach and board member for a charter school is part of his engaged citizenship.

Gary DeCramer became deeply involved in public life as a result of a political opportunity and issues affecting Minnesota's family farms. Later, after serving 10 years in the Minnesota Senate, he worked in the Clinton administration before becoming director of the midcareer master's program at the Humphrey School.

From Gary DeCramer's Narrative of Commitment

In 1981, I ran for the state legislature in a special election. I was working three jobs to keep the family farm going but I suddenly had a notion that I could fill the seat of an inspiring law maker, my state senator who was made to step down from office due to a tragedy in his family. I ran in that special election. I loved the campaign. I loved the issues facing my home area, especially the issues arising from the injustice of the bankers foreclosing on my neighbors' and cousins' farms. I was convinced my opponent was a know-nothing, conservative, wealthy farmer who had no credibility. He beat me 2 to 1. Nonetheless, due to reconfiguration of districts based upon the 1980 census, a new district was created that had no incumbent. So, I announced that I would run. I did run and won by 200-plus votes. I served in the Minnesota Senate for 10 years. During that time I went through a divorce, but my love for the work of serving in the Senate and my effectiveness must have been evident. I won again in 1986, was remarried in 1988, and ran again in 1990 and won a two-year term.

During that final race, I decided that I needed to end my legislative career in 1992. My wife, Estelle, and I were parents of one daughter and dreaming of having another child. The life of a legislator was far too demanding on a marriage. I did not want another failure. Then, surprisingly, in 1991, the chancellor of the state university system, Bob Carrothers, urged the system board to appoint me president of Southwest State University. I loved that work plus the work of being in the Senate. I enjoyed the challenge of coming to work with passion on issues I cared deeply about and working in the midst of conflict with the "loyal opposition," which in my time of service was made up of conservatives who held deep convictions but were not filled with hatred of government or public service. In my work as interim president, I was inspired to go back to graduate school and join a cohort of doctoral students studying educational leadership at University of St. Thomas.

To my surprise, in my final months of serving in the Senate, I was invited to become a senior fellow at the Humphrey Institute. I served for five years in the State and Local Policy Program, and the week of my graduation with an Ed.D. from St. Thomas, Sen. Paul Wellstone called and asked me to take an appointment at the U.S. Department of Agriculture (USDA) in the Clinton administration. I did and was thrilled to be back in public service again. For four years I served as USDA rural development state director, a job that allowed me to "give back" to rural Minnesota, its tribal communities, and small towns. When that appointment concluded, I was lucky to be invited back to Humphrey to direct the midcareer Master of Public Affairs degree program. In that position, I once again enjoy teaching and more than ever, enjoy being beside smart, experienced professionals, students, staff, and instructors, who have a passion to make a difference in this world. My commitment to "know, love, and serve" is lived out every day in my family and my work as a teacher of public affairs students, especially of midcareer students who have a passion for making a difference in this world.

For Lars Leafblad, the experience, as an undergraduate, of launching an innovative project linking students with alumni solidified his commitment to work for the "benefit of the broader whole." He sees his work in leadership development and recruitment as a way of ensuring that the country's "leadership pool" is bigger, more diverse, and more committed to the common good. Leafblad also clearly sees himself as an engaged "Netizen," the popular term for citizens of the Internet. He maintains a strong social media presence in order to share information about his own work and about opportunities for networking and civic involvement. He realizes that being highly visible in social media carries risks, but also provides accountability for matching one's actions and espoused philosophy. Maintaining a zone of privacy remains important to him, but he emphasizes, "I lead my life as an open Facebook."

In her work with business students and executives, Mary Uhl-Bien promotes organizational citizenship behavior (OCB). "Almost everything we teach in management and leadership is OCB," she says. She does not typically focus on citizenship of a polity, but does emphasize businesses' social responsibility. "Organizations should not just focus on the bottom line. They are always citizens of the world."

Like Rick Morse and Lars Leafblad, I became seriously engaged with public life as an undergraduate, when I joined fellow students and some faculty in critiquing the War in Vietnam and the state of race relations in the U.S. I was very active in a student group that brought speakers to campus to offer competing views on public issues. In my role as a campus journalist, I attempted to make sense of the contemporary student experience, but also raise questions about students' responsibilities to each other and to the rest of society. Later on, I viewed my work as a journalist and community volunteer as heightening attention to and helping remedy social inequities. Throughout my professional life I have aimed to help the organizations I'm part of—whether they are businesses, nonprofits, or government offices—be forces for societal good.

As leadership educators we practice organizational citizenship by getting engaged in the nitty-gritty work of maintaining and reforming our organizations. We practice societal citizenship both through the organizations and through civic activities. We also are active in the community of educators and researchers seeking to build the field of leadership studies. For example, many of those interviewed in this book have helped establish and sustain the International Leadership Association as a place where multiple approaches to leadership can be examined, standards for leadership education can be developed, and good practices can be shared—all with the aim of fostering "the greater good of individuals and communities worldwide" (http://ila-net.org/).

Reflecting on Economic Status and Political Experience

Because economic status and political experience have such strong effects on our engagement as community citizens, I asked my colleagues to reflect on their economic and political histories. Several of us were born into families that struggled economically, and others had solidly middle-class upbringings. A few felt very privileged. Although our education and professional accomplishments have made all of us relatively well-off by now, our early experiences of socioeconomic class and observations of economic injustices have affected our understanding of the links among leadership, citizenship, and democracy.

Gill Hickman grew up "middle class, very privileged, but not wealthy." She lived in a neighborhood with considerable economic diversity and where few families had two working parents. "My mother always stressed with privilege comes responsibility." She adds, "My background was very enriched. I come from three generations of college graduates on my father's side and two on my mother's. I felt I was in a position to move forward and give back." Her family's politics were Democratic and when she went to boarding school, she considered whether she fit the family political mold and decided she did. "I care about everybody having a home and food and education. On social policies, I'm really way left."

Chuck Palus thinks that growing up in a blue-collar family has made him an outsider to this day. "I've been in a lot of venues where I see wealth and privilege and I still feel like an outsider. I still identify with the blue-collar underdog."

Rick Morse grew up "middle class, pretty privileged." His father was a professor at Virginia Tech. As noted in Chapter 1, Rick initially saw himself as a Reagan Republican, but shifted to the liberal side of the political spectrum as a result of his experiences as a missionary and an undergraduate.

Lars Leafblad's upper-middle-class family made visible to him the links among education, a strong work ethic, and financial success. His father was a physician, his stepmother a nurse-midwife, and his mother was a corporate attorney. His grandparents were small-business owners. He grew up in two households, one "more liberal and one more conservative." He describes himself as "pretty purple, independent" and has found people across the political spectrum whose views resonate with his. He adds, "I grew up seeing the importance of politics. My wife and I bring our kids to the polls. We try to make clear the sacrifices that paid for this. I went to the polls with my parents and they told me why voting is important."

Mary Uhl-Bien came from a family of nine children (she was third-youngest), where resources were tight. Her father preached self-sufficiency to his children. "He wouldn't let us take out student loans." In the first years of her marriage, Mary struggled financially, but today is well-off. She says her family of origin was not politically active. "Personally, I'm independent, fiscally conservative and socially liberal. I see problems on both sides [of the conservative-liberal divide]; being independent just fits with my personality."

Georgia Sorenson grew up in a middle-class family. Her mother was in the advertising business and her father served in the army and the U.S. diplomatic corps. His work took the family overseas, which altered the family's status. "When we lived abroad, we became rich," says Sorenson. "We had chauffeurs and laundresses." The experience gave her understanding of a broader economic spectrum. Her parents were "Roosevelt Democrats"; compared to most military families, hers was "pretty liberal." At one point, Sorenson worked for a Democratic U.S. president, but she enjoys political diversity. "I'm always threatening to change to be an independent," she says, but since Democrats are the powerful liberal force in Maryland, she has stayed in their camp. Her travels have helped her see that the U.S. democratic system isn't the only way to organize a government. "I don't think democracy is a perfect system," she emphasizes.

My own childhood household was perched perilously on the lower edge of the middle class, but over the years I've moved into relative affluence as a result of my parents' and spouses' economic support, my own hard work, some public policies, and no doubt, my "whiteness." My parents were Eisenhower Republicans, but my own social justice principles have usually aligned me with Democrats. I've included here an extended essay on my economic history; it derives from an assignment used in Humphrey School leadership seminars. That assignment, to be described more fully in Chapter 12, asks participants to write an economic autobiography that reflects on their economic and social status, family influences, and the connection of economic experiences and their worldview.

Barbara Crosby's Economic Autobiography

Like many people, my economic history is rooted in family, land, and work. I'll start with my grandparents.

My father's parents were Minnie and Barney Crosby, South Carolina sharecroppers who for much of their married life would pile their children and possessions into a wagon every year after the harvest and move on to the next farm that would hire them. Land ownership was out of the question for them, but by the time I knew them they were settled on a piece of Colleton County government property used by road crews. The weather-beaten, tin-roofed house was surrounded by piles of lumber and oyster shells and a creosote vat under the moss-hung live oaks. My grandparents raised hogs and chickens there; my grandfather planted cotton in a nearby field and provided some meat by hunting in the nearby woods. The household economy was mainly based on the labor of my grandparents and their children, though neighboring black families helped with the cotton harvest. My father was behind the plow by the time he was eight. While Barney and Minnie never learned to read or write, they valued education and encouraged their children and grandchildren to study hard.

On my mother's side were Rosa and David McGoldrick, owners of a 75-acre farm that my grandfather secured in the early years of the Depression in the bluegrass region of Kentucky. They raised tobacco, chickens, sheep, and cows and lived in a large brick, white-columned pre-Civil War house. I'm not sure how much schooling this grandfather had, but this grandmother had finished eighth grade and was an avid reader of the Bible and prolific letter writer. She, too, was a believer in education and supported my mother in her desire to follow her older brother to college.

My parents met and married when both were in the Navy during World War II. My mother was among the first Navy women officers as part of the WAVES, the Navy division set up for women enlisting in the war effort. After the war my father accompanied my mother (and me) back to Kentucky, where he attended her alma mater, the University of Kentucky, on the GI bill. Then it was back to the Deep South, when my father took a job with the new Savannah River Plant, a nuclear reactor site operated by DuPont in Aiken, South Carolina. Locally the site was called the Bomb Plant, referring to the plant's main product—plutonium to be used in nuclear weapons.

By this time, the early 1950s, I had a younger sister and we lived in a four-room house thrown up as part of the postwar construction boom in Augusta, Georgia. My parents had a mortgage on the place and paid it off slowly but surely over the years. My father worked as a health physics inspector, monitoring safety at the Savannah River Plant until his retirement in the mid-1980s, and had decent wages and benefits, supplemented by small payments for being an active Army reservist or member of the National Guard. Yet an atmosphere of economic vulnerability surrounded our family throughout my childhood and teenage years. Here's a dominant image I have of that time: my mother lying on the couch most of the day with her back to the room and my father up before dawn, going to work, coming home, and retiring to his Lazy-Boy before the television—day after day after day. On the weekends, my Dad did the grocery shopping and some of the cooking, but he also was often out drinking.

We didn't have much money for "luxuries" like dental care or paint for the house shutters that soon weathered and warped. When my shoes developed holes in the soles, I lined them with cardboard and kept on wearing them. One of our worst episodes was the purchase of a $200 vacuum cleaner—a very significant expense at the time. I still remember the machine as an ominous round, wheeled, beige and brown thing with fancy attachments that loomed over our lives for a spell. My parents were convinced by a fast-talking salesman that not only was this machine likely to clean our house on its own, but that by persuading others to purchase their own versions, my parents could get credits that would allow them to pay for the vacuum in no time. The task of persuading others was left to my depressed mother, who spent much more time worrying about it than calling the few friends she knew. I was convinced we were all going to jail for failure to make the monthly interest-accumulating payments. Finally, my mother talked one or two other families into buying a machine and somehow we paid it off.

Though money was always tight, we had enough food to eat, the mortgage got paid, and my father was able to buy a new Chevy every few years. We always managed to spend a few days in the Smoky Mountains every year on the way to visit my grandmother in Kentucky. By the time I was in my mid-teens, we were a bit better off. My father wasn't drinking so much and my mother was less depressed. I did most of the housework, with some help from my sister. Somehow, my parents did save money for my sister's and my college education. In 1964 I went off to Vanderbilt University, supported by their savings, a very substantial scholarship, and my part-time jobs. After college I married, became a newspaper reporter, and soon paid off the small college loan I had taken out. By the time I separated from my husband a few years later, I still had no savings and a meager tangible asset, a yellow Maverick.

Several years of graduate school, remarriage, more work as a journalist brought me to 1977, when my husband and I bought a house with help from his parents. From that point on, we've managed to save money, work hard at good jobs, and reap the benefits of mortgage deductions, employer-funded health care, home equity loans, and inheritance tax exemptions. That doesn't mean that we haven't pinched pennies many times along the way. We've done wild and crazy things like having two children, investing in uncertain consulting ventures, and taking salary cuts to live abroad or leave unsatisfying work. The bottom line though, is that four decades after securing my first real job as a $110-a-week reporter at the Augusta Herald, I'm firmly a part of the upper-middle class. Together with my spouse I own two mortgaged homes, a car, and probably have enough invested for retirement (though who knows how that will be affected by continued market gyrations in the global economy).

My family of origin gave me two main economic assets: support for education and impetus to work hard. I also learned about the possibilities of making something from very little and the necessity of splurging on a good outfit. Christian faith and my own experience have helped me counter attachment to material things (though my closet might cause people to question how much countering has occurred). I've also benefited from a first marriage that ended in amicable divorce and even more from a second marriage that has been an enduring personal and professional partnership. (As a young woman, I sneered at the idea of looking at marriage through an economic lens—after all, I was one of those in rebellion against the notion that we college women's primary pursuit should be a suitable husband. Later, my colleague and mentor Arvonne Fraser, along with feminist economists, would help me understand marriage as an economic—as well as romantic—arrangement.)

I've also benefited from public and nonprofit initiatives. My parents went to public universities and my dad benefited from the GI bill. In the 1950s, my high school curriculum was enriched by funding from the National Defense Education Act (designed to improve U.S. competitiveness with the Soviet Union), which prepared me to succeed at a top-notch university. One of my graduate degrees is from a public university, and I received scholarships from nonprofit organizations. As noted above, tax policies have helped.

Losses accompany some of these benefits—hard work can drive out attention to friends and family; not all the tax policies that benefit me can be justified; I may not get just how hard it is for people with less money to get by. I've also been on the privileged side of the racial divide in this country. For example, African Americans didn't have the same chance that my Scots-Irish Kentucky grandfather had to buy property. My 1,000- strong freshman class at Vanderbilt included exactly six African Americans.

Formal and informal education helped me better understand some of the economic and cultural forces that limit opportunities for so many people in this world—including my South Carolina grandparents, especially, but also my parents, and to a lesser extent, myself. My experience with economic vulnerability has convinced me of the importance of assisting people in need—especially via public policy reform. My Baptist upbringing made me a believer in tithing and charitable giving. Being female and the beneficiary of white privileges has made me a fighter against economic discrimination.

Summing up my economic history I would say it is a story about the expansion of choice. My increasing economic security has given me an ever-wider range of choices. Have I lain awake in recent years worrying about finances? Yes, but the worries are likely to be about a second home, not a vacuum cleaner.

Linking Leadership and Democracy

Leadership development, as practiced by the educators featured in this book, is itself democratic, in that we view leadership as everyone's business (as James Kouzes and Barry Posner [2012] emphasize). Furthermore, we believe that remedying public problems and upholding democratic political process is everyone's responsibility.

As Lars Leafblad scrutinizes candidates for fellowships and executive positions he looks for evidence not just about leading on the job, but also how candidates "invest their skills beyond what they are paid for. How engaged are they in school, neighborhood, and public policy issues? Are they taking action to benefit the broader whole?"

For Ronnie Brooks, leadership to benefit the broader whole is rooted in personal agency connected to public values. She says,

> I believe that everyone has the capacity to lead for something he/she truly believes in or cares about, but that morally good and effective leadership requires clarity about purpose and values—one's own and one's association, organization, or nation. Contemplation and exploration of these values helps people to put their talents and interests to work for what they care about and to recognize and support the leadership of others as well as their own. Democracy and citizenship require constructive thought and constructive participation. To me that comes from what leadership requires and what leadership education/development should nurture: understanding of self, meaningful relationships with others, and commitment to action.

My Humphrey School colleagues and I promote inclusive, democratic practice in several ways. In her teaching, Kathy Quick keeps the focus on leadership rather than leaders. "There is a democratizing effect of this. I talk about leaderly actions and the opportunity for anybody to undertake leadership actions." Kevin Gerdes says, "Using circle practice, minimizing lectures, allowing more time for small and large group discussion—basically adopting a 'flipped classroom'—allow participant voices to be heard more often." We choose readings and case examples that also prompt greater awareness of social justice, which in turn stimulates participants' desire to remedy injustices. As they build their personal leadership capacity, participants then recognize they can act on these "public desires."

Similarly, Sonia Ospina believes that separating leadership development from efforts to combat wicked public problems is misguided, and indeed contributes to the problems. She adds, "I do conflate leadership with being a good citizen. I give the message that leadership is about caring for others." Both as a researcher and teacher, she seeks to expand democratic work: "My work on leadership is about increasing participation and voice and addressing issues of exclusion. It's all about creating spaces that are more democratic, where everyone can contribute to the common cause." In her leadership research and teaching, she operates from a "little bit of a critical perspective," which involves questioning the status quo, especially the ways that institutionalized policies and practices disempower particular groups.

For Chuck Palus, the Leadership beyond Boundaries program, offered in Africa by the Center for Creative Leadership, is a prime example of leadership development focused on empowering citizens. "We say our work in Africa is about democratizing leadership at the bottom of the bottom of the pyramid [referring to the very lowest income groups]." In his work with Ravenscroft School in the U.S., he seeks to equip students to be citizens of their schools and the world.

In her work with the undergraduate leadership minor at the University of Minnesota, June Nobbe helps students realize they don't have to rely on formal government agencies to solve community problems. "We help them understand that one person's actions can have a ripple effect, whether it's voting or stepping up and using your skills." Drawing on the Social Change model of leadership development (see Chapter 8), she and her colleagues help students understand the key leadership task of helping individuals and groups see how their interests are linked to the common good.

Robert Denhardt argues that leaders, regardless of whether they are in government or nongovernmental organizations, should draw values from the public sphere. The idea is "not I believe this, but *we* believe this." In his classes, he emphasizes "there are broad issues that affect everyone in society and people from all sectors have a responsibility to address them." To drive this point home he invites guest speakers who have put corporate social responsibility into action to talk to his class about their experiences. Janet Denhardt notes that not all students readily accept that citizenship and civic engagement are important elements of leadership. "They ask, 'Is there a common good? Are citizenship and civic engagement good and, if so, how?'"

My own way of responding to questions like these is to help participants explore different ways of thinking about and enacting the common good. Exercises like Clarifying Your View of the Relation of Individual and Society, included in Chapter 12, help participants position debates about the common good within larger conversations about the relationship between the individual and society. This exercise also notes some philosophers' skepticism about common good language. They fear that the term common good can too easily be a synonym for majoritarianism that ignores the well-being of people in the minority. In my classes I emphasize that the common good is an inherently contested concept. I seek to equip participants with tools for pursuing public policies and social change that achieve widespread benefit at reasonable cost and tap key public values such as liberty or equity.

For Monty Van Wart, attention to the common good is not a hard sell, since he teaches in a public administration program. He explains his approach:

> Since my students have almost entirely self-selected themselves into the challenges of public service, their virtues and ideals are generally as good as or better than mine. Where I can try to help is in inspiring them to be as excellent as possible—in concrete terms—so that they have the time and tools to exercise their innate moral compass as situations present themselves. They say that power without accountability is a dangerous thing. Power without competence is surely a close second in my book.

Yvonne Cheek had a visceral response when I asked her, "In what ways does leadership education, as you practice it, contribute to democracy?" She answered, "This question almost alienated me. I wondered why is my stomach in turmoil, as I try to answer this question." She found the question hard to answer because the U.S. democratic system continually violates many democratic principles.

Yvonne Cheek on the connections among leadership, citizenship, and democracy: "Okay democracy—what is it to me? I looked it up—it's a form of government in which eligible citizens are able to participate equally. It's rule of the majority, a system that allows people to have direct voice in decision making.

"This is not what is happening, not consistently enough. When I see growth of people behind bars, who they are and how they got there, I think: Our democracy is for sale, being purchased every day. That bothers me.

"When I see our country trying to bring democracy to other countries around the world, I think for democracy to work normally, there needs to be a free press, people, not worrying about food and shelter. Lots of those countries don't have that. We have all these things and still our democracy is not working. It makes me suspicious and sad that leadership education might assume it's working and we need to train leaders to function well in the system.

"We might need a more controversial, bolder approach—to infuse leadership training with stuff that will get us somewhere different. Democracy and citizenship have a role in community building, and community building and leadership are connected. You need to contribute to leadership wherever you are—academic, professional, and geographic communities. People need to be willing to lead in several communities."

Demystifying and Reforming the Policy Process

I became involved in leadership education in the mid-1980s because of my efforts to understand how individuals and groups could remedy complex public problems, problems which spill over organizational boundaries and affect broad swaths of society. As a political science major, I understood that government had a key role to play in tackling public problems, but as a woman who came of age in 1960s I also understood that government was unlikely to undertake major reforms without pressure from outside groups. At the Reflective Leadership Center I was introduced to moral philosophers like Hannah Arendt, which, coupled with my undergraduate training in political philosophy, enabled me to think more expansively about public life and the connections among personal, collective, and institutional power. Joining me in the quest to better understand public problem solving, John Bryson brought his own background in planning and community organizing. As we probed our questions about mechanisms of power, he suggested we consider Anthony Giddens's (1979, 1984) structuration theory, and we subsequently adapted that theory as a foundation for our view of how leaders and engaged followers actually accomplish major change in public policies and major systems. In our adaptation of Giddens, we see the exercise of power in the public realm as consisting of three social practices:

- the creation and communication of shared meaning in formal and informal forums
- the making and implementing of policy decisions in formal and informal arenas, and
- sanctioning of conduct in formal and informal courts

Each practice, in turn, comprises three dimensions, the first being action; the second being ideas, rules, modes, and media; and the third being deep structures such as language or forms of government.

Our fundamental assertion, based on our theoretical understanding and case research, has been that leaders who seek political and social reform will be most effective if they work at what we call the second dimension of power as they focus on the wise design and use of forums, arenas, and courts, the settings in which public problems are interpreted and possibly remedied.

Whether as a journalist or leadership educator, I have tried to demystify the process of policy making and social reform. I've highlighted strategic actors and levers of power, and I've emphasized the power of unified groups insisting on more just outcomes. I've insisted that participants in my courses practice using various stakeholder analysis tools that help them identify potential members of a policy change coalition and figure out how to frame issues in ways that can appeal to a diverse set of coalition members. I've framed conflict as an unavoidable part of the policy process and helped participants learn ways of handling these conflicts constructively. I've emphasized the importance of taking a long-term view of policy change, and I've encouraged participants in my courses and workshops to run for public office themselves.

For the last 10 years, I've worked with colleagues at the Center for Integrative Leadership to understand integrative leadership, which focuses on pulling together and sustaining cross-sector collaborations that attempt to remedy particularly difficult public problems, or "grand challenges"—for example, climate change, sex trafficking, or malaria. As Kathy Quick notes, the integrative leadership work of mobilizing diverse groups to deal with shared problems is "surely a democratic style of leadership." Our work is based on the understanding that any grand challenge encompasses failures from all sectors—government, business, nonprofit, community, and media, and that effective responses must involve all of the sectors and capitalize on their strengths. Says Quick, "It's important to talk about leadership, not just in government but everywhere. Work on a public problem like sex trafficking has to happen within police departments, the hotel business, and nonprofits." The hallmark of integrative leadership is working across many types of boundaries—among organizations, sectors, cultures, and regions. Integrative leaders operate as citizens of their communities, their countries, and the world. As they seek sustainable solutions to grand challenges, they must draw on democratic processes, but of necessity will also be required to work with nondemocratic governments. The three-dimensional view of power I described earlier can help them be effective in both democratic and nondemocratic settings.

I accept Hannah Arendt's view that a crucial part of being fully human is to be active in the public realm and contribute to the tasks of governing one's community. I align with pragmatic democratic philosophers who, as Chris Ansell (2011) says, emphasize the ability of "both individuals and communities to improve their knowledge and problem-solving capacity over time through continuous inquiry, reflection, deliberation, and experimentation" (5). Like Barry Bozeman (2004), I see public aspects in every organization. To the extent that the organization relies on public investments (such as highways and education), to the extent the organization affects its community, and to the extent its practices affect the rights of its members, the organization is public. Thus organizational leaders cannot evade public responsibility and the term public leadership is redundant. I encourage participants in my courses and workshops to avoid the misguided assumption that they can ignore politics as a dirty process that doesn't have a lot to do with them. Yes, politics is messy and often corrupt, but it affects every citizen, and organized citizens can alter it.

★★★

The leadership educators featured in this book see leadership development as inseparable from democratic practice, and we seek to strengthen democracy in a number of ways. We are ourselves engaged citizens of our organizations, our communities, and the world. We use democratic processes in our classes and workshops, and we highlight everyone's responsibility to remedy public problems and sustain public life. We are constrained and enabled in this work by our economic and political experiences and endowments. We seek to equip others with insights about the policy-making process and tools for reforming it.

The next chapter will describe in more depth the contemporary theories and research that connect leadership, citizenship, and democracy. Working on grand challenges that spill across sector, cultural, and geographic boundaries will receive particular attention.

References

Ansell, C. K. (2011). *Pragmatist democracy: Evolutionary learning as public philosophy*. New York: Oxford University Press.

Bozeman, B. (2004). *All organizations are public: Comparing public and private organizations*. San Francisco: Jossey-Bass.

Giddens, A. (1979). *Central problems in social theory: Action, structure and contradiction in social analysis*. Berkeley, CA: University of California Press.

Giddens, A. (1984). *The constitution of society: Outline of a theory of structuration*. Berkeley, CA: University of California Press.

Kouzes, J. M., & Posner, B. Z. (2012). *The leadership challenge: How to make extraordinary things happen in organizations* (5th ed.). San Francisco: Jossey-Bass.

11

STRENGTHENING CITIZENSHIP AND THE HEAD

Fortunately, or unfortunately, democracy, citizenship, the common good, and public life are all contested concepts. As numerous scholars and philosophers have pointed out, competing views of the good society, desirable public policies, and the roles of elected leaders and citizens are inherent in democratic forms of government. A stable democracy must have at least three elements:

- effective means of managing competing ideologies, interests, and political parties
- means for citizens to affect the deliberations and decisions of government
- methods of carrying out the public will and protecting public values

Attention to leadership emerges in connection with each of these elements. Students of political leadership often focus on the skills and qualities that citizens' elected and appointed representatives should have in order to achieve these democratic means. Students of public administration outline the leadership responsibilities of executives and managers in government agencies. Students of social movements and civic life focus on skills and qualities of community organizers (another word for leaders), who often are critical of elected and appointed representatives and government employees for government failures.

This chapter will explore the work of several practical scholars who prescribe practices of leaders and citizens that are needed for sustaining democratic governance systems. I will include attention to scholars who focus specifically on the desired virtues and skills of elected and appointed officials and public managers, as well as leaders in other sectors. I will present the integrative leadership framework in more detail and delve into approaches to discerning the common good.

Fostering Democratic Habits of the Heart and Public Work

In his book *Healing the Heart of Democracy* (2011), Parker Palmer is reacting to several trends in contemporary U.S. politics: for example, increased partisanship and gridlock in Congress; growing distrust of government and other institutions, such as the press; and harsh public rhetoric reflecting political divides. He urges all citizens to practice five "habits of the heart" (a phrase taken from Alexis de Tocqueville) that he believes are essential to remedying adverse trends in U.S. public life. He quotes writer and environmental activist Terry Tempest Williams:

> The human heart is the first home of democracy. It is where we embrace our questions. Can we be equitable? Can we be generous? Can we listen with our whole beings, not just our minds, and offer our attention rather than our opinions? And do we have enough resolve in our hearts to act courageously, relentlessly, without giving up—ever—trusting our fellow citizens to join with us in our determined pursuit of a living democracy? (p. 49).

The five habits of the heart recommended by Palmer are:

- an understanding that we are all in this together
- an appreciation of the value of "otherness"
- an ability to hold tension in life-giving ways (referring to, for example, tension between one's aspirations and behavior, one's view and another's)
- sense of personal voice and agency
- capacity to create community

Marshall Ganz, a senior lecturer at Harvard and former United Farm Workers organizer, offers guidance for crafting public narratives that draw on these habits and link personal stories (see Part 1 of this book) to public life. Public narrative comprises "a story of self, a story of us, and a story of now" (Ganz, 2011, 282). The story of self focuses on personal values and experiences, the story of us focuses on shared values and experiences, and the story of now is what actions are important at this particular juncture in time. He explains how leaders inspire and motivate constituents via stories that evoke urgency, hope, anger, efficacy, and solidarity while challenging feelings such as fear and apathy. He recommends a "dialog of the heart," in which diverse individuals express countervailing emotions and values and make choices about which values to act on (277). Ganz gives special attention to the power of hope. Leaders who wish to help their groups tackle daunting public problems can convey hope through several types of stories—such as stories of previous victories or successes achieved by similar groups or stories from faith traditions. Furthermore, when these stories are told in public gatherings, celebrations, and other shared experiences, solidarity is created.

Howard Gardner, in his book *Leading Minds* (1995), explains that leaders who can construct compelling communal narratives open the door for each follower to tell his/her own story, to relate his/her life to some greater development. Chapter 12 will provide further guidance for constructing public narratives.

My colleague Harry Boyte has developed the concept "public work" to describe how citizens inside and outside government can reinvigorate democracy. He argues in a variety of publications (Boyte and Kari, 1996; Boyte, 2004, 2015) that the American republic was built on the notion of an engaged citizenry who participated, often through voluntary associations, in the work of producing new institutions like schools, agitating for policy reforms, and providing public services like integration of new immigrants into their communities. By the early 20th century, however, this tradition was severely eroded as government bureaucracies expanded and administrators became increasingly professionalized, partly as a result of the Progressive movement, which sought to eradicate corruption and introduce more scientific methods of management and service provision. Nearly a century later, while some of the older traditions of citizen engagement persist, all too often citizens are largely viewed as consumers, or voters to be wooed, rather than co-creators of public services and public policies. Meanwhile, the clout of moneyed interests in policy making has increased tremendously.

In order to counter these trends, Boyte and collaborating scholars draw attention to the potential of workplaces and institutions like universities for engaging diverse citizens in tackling public problems—once again elevating public work, but in ways attuned to the 21st century. Boyte would have universities help students tie their career plans to a sense of public purpose and efficacy in whatever profession they choose. His own Center for Democracy and Citizenship at Augsburg College in Minneapolis is part of a nationwide effort to give universities a stronger citizenship focus. For example, Boyte and like-minded advocates praise campus-based service learning experiences that emphasize engagement with community partners rather than one-shot volunteer activities. At his center, staff teach students organizing skills like one-on-one interviewing and community power mapping in order to prepare them to help community partners build their own capacity for public work.

Boyte argues that empowering students from elementary school onward to take on issues that matter to them is more likely to produce successful graduates than the prevailing hyper-reliance on standardized testing. In a 2016 article, he and Margaret Finders report on a project that taught organizing skills to "special needs" middle school students. "Over three years the results were dramatic. 'Problem' students, mostly low-income and minority, who in many schools would be strictly confined to their classes, became public leaders on issues like school bullying, healthy lifestyles, campaigning against animal cruelty, and creating a support network for terminally ill children" (23). From Boyte's perspective, the line between truly engaged citizens and leaders is thoroughly blurred.

Building Virtues and Skills of Elected and Appointed Officials and Public Managers

Identifying and inculcating virtues of society's governors or rulers has long preoccupied political philosophers, and modern views of exemplary officials in democratic as well as nondemocratic systems often draw on classical works by people like Aristotle, Confucius, and Niccolò Machiavelli (Kellerman, 2010). Even in a democracy, officials have powers that are not accorded to ordinary citizens and thus they share with any governor or ruler the need for virtues that constrain the abuse of their power and direct it toward the common good.

Kenneth Ruscio, president of Washington and Lee University, has examined what liberal democratic theory says about the obligations and responsibilities of political leaders (Ruscio, 1999, 2004). In the republican form of government adopted in the U.S., elected leaders have special responsibility for upholding the virtues (or values) of civility, tolerance, respect for difference, and sympathy for fellow citizens, which are vital to a democratic system. The influential men who shaped the U.S. system believed that citizens elected to public office should not merely represent their constituents' views, but seek to "refine and enlarge" public opinion in order to achieve the public interest (Ruscio, 2004, 29, quoting *The Federalist Papers*). They established a federal political system with checks and balances designed to prevent any official from violating the public trust and behaving tyrannically. They intended for their system to attract legislators like themselves who would have a sense of duty to the public and a commitment to reasoning together to discover the public interest. (Of course, the system they established also dampened direct citizen participation in government and privileged well-educated and economically advantaged men like themselves.)

Ruscio highlights three enduring themes of liberal democratic theory that undergird expectations of elected and appointed leaders even today. First is the centrality of public reason as a means of managing the conflict between differing ideologies and interests in a way that fosters societal well-being:

> We must be willing to live with others who differ from us; the end of politics is not the imposition of the good life on all but the creation of conditions that allow each to achieve his version of the good life without being unjust to others.
>
> *(Ruscio, 1999, 66)*

If laws and policies are to be accepted by the citizenry, the advocates

> must justify their reasons for a particular course of action, if that action calls upon the coercive power of the state, in terms that are understandable to others. They must reason publicly. . . . Leaders must not only do the same

(indeed their obligation is greater), but they also must create the conditions that allow for public deliberation.

(Ruscio, 1999, 66)

The second theme is the need for citizens' trust in their political system, and leaders foster this trust by reinforcing the perception that they are acting, not in their self-interest, but in pursuit of the public interest. (Ruscio does not say so, but I would add that the perception rests on evidence that leaders are upholding additional democratic values like fairness, equity, and transparency.) Third, is belief in the possibility of a common good. "A search for the common good obligates leaders to act in a manner different from if their main obligation were only to respond to and balance separate and competing interests" (Ruscio, 1999, 66).

Ruscio concludes his 2004 book, *The Leadership Dilemma in Modern Democracy*, by calling upon leaders to combine moral purpose and political pragmatism:

If the course of democratic theory in modern times, from Machiavelli to Rawls, teaches us anything, it is the need for leaders to demonstrate prudence, practicality and the acceptance of the art of the possible within a context of moral purpose, ethical reasoning, and transforming vision.

(120)

In his book *Transforming Leadership* (2003), James MacGregor Burns admonishes national democratic leaders to focus on prime public values. They must try

to mobilize people behind values that powerfully express the wants and needs, hopes and expectations of large numbers of people. It is in the interaction and likely conflict between general values and more local interests that the opportunity for mobilization appears.... In turn, as grassroots leaders already close to their constituents become more engaged with national leaders, their local interests are re-framed by the wider, deeper sphere of values. In the process, their followers are extended beyond narrow self-interests toward a broader view of the common good.

(211)

Elected and appointed officials also must be adept in the design and use of policy-making arenas such as city councils, legislatures, and cabinets. As John Bryson and I note in *Leadership for the Common Good* (2005), they should understand the importance of decision agendas and rules, committee structures, budget cycles, and the like. They must practice the fine art of hanging onto their own principles and the animating vision that brought them to office, while negotiating with other powerful decision makers who have competing visions and power bases. They often must discern how to craft an overarching narrative, or public vision, that may continue themes from the narrative they emphasized as they ran for office, but may borrow themes from elsewhere (including from opponents).

The conflicts and power struggles inherent in public life also require emotional intelligence, something which liberal democratic theory downplays. Conflict and confrontation can be expected to evoke powerful emotions in officials as well as among constituents. Thus, officials must manage their own reactions to public criticism and be able to weather the heat of even uncivil conflict. They are called on to discern when to heighten and when to dampen emotional fervor. Because they at times mobilize government's coercive powers they also must accept the psychological burden of doing harm (sometimes necessary and sometimes inadvertent) to their fellow citizens.

Like elected and appointed officials, public administrators and managers have special responsibility for upholding democratic values like transparency, fairness, civility, and equity. Also like officials, a sense of duty to the public, or a public service ethic, is paramount. Public administrators also must be well-versed in the functioning of policy-making arenas and exert influence over enactment of new laws and programs, but their main responsibility is to implement the laws and programs effectively. Monty Van Wart in his *Leadership in Public Organizations* (2012) and *Dynamics of Leadership in Public Service* (2011) covers in detail characteristics and skills of effective public administrators.

In his 2011 book *Pragmatist Democracy*, Chris Ansell encourages public managers to make their agencies "a central linchpin in building consent for public problem solving" (5). He believes that public managers should be guided by the pragmatist philosophy of civic learning (which also undergirds Harry Boyte's idea of public work). The first chapter of his book offers a lucid description of central tenets of American pragmatism, a philosophical stance that emerged following the Civil War. Hoping to keep American democracy from being torn apart again by ideological disputes, the men and women who developed the philosophy gave preeminence to an evolutionary learning process that allows people with very different perspectives to tackle their shared problems together. While pragmatism has what Ansell calls a "family relationship" with liberalism, republicanism, and communitarianism, its distinguishing characteristic is an "emphasis on the open-ended process of refining values and knowledge" (8). This learning process employs three main practices:

- Problem-driven experimentation—involving the application of "received knowledge, principles, and values" to actual challenges and seeing what works, which may require revised thinking (11)
- Reflexivity—involving critical scrutiny of common sense and habits
- Deliberation—involving "reflexive inquiry produced by the clash of different, sometimes incommensurate perspectives" and communication aimed at probing, adjudicating, and bridging differences (11–12)

Ansell is among contemporary scholars, including myself, who highlight the importance of public officials' and managers' having a collaborative mind-set in order to respond effectively to complex public problems that require sustained public work involving multiple stakeholders, all sectors (business, government, nonprofits, media, and community groups), and many government jurisdictions. A collaborative mind-set includes the belief that government needs partners from throughout society in developing an understanding of these problems and advancing an agenda for beneficial change. It includes a willingness to accept that different partners can apply their distinctive strengths to a part of the agenda and carry it out somewhat autonomously. For public servants, a collaborative mind-set includes the willingness to share power and leadership, along with resolute devotion to democratic values and common good outcomes. As Ansell notes, this involves transforming rigid government hierarchies in ways that "harness the values of decentralization and bottom-up initiative to the values of centralization and hierarchical steering" (17). A collaborative mind-set is one of the hallmarks of integrative leaders, who will be discussed more thoroughly later in this chapter.

Building Democratic Virtues and Skills of Nongovernmental Leaders

Jeffrey Luke in his book *Catalytic Leadership* (1998) identifies three main character traits for effective social reform leaders from any sector. They are a "continuous focusing on desired results, a sense of connectedness and relatedness, and exemplary personal integrity" (220). Other scholars focus on democratic virtues and skills of leaders in community groups, nonprofits, and business—chiefly community organizers and nonprofit and business executives.

The chief virtue of community organizers is their commitment to championing and empowering groups that they feel have been disadvantaged by prevailing political, legal, and economic systems. In an article for *Educational Theory* (2011) Aaron Schutz draws on the precepts of community organizing gurus like Saul Alinsky to argue that the core aim of organizing is to make one's group "a force to be reckoned with" (502). To do that, community organizers help groups articulate their interests, develop policy positions, and get the attention of policy makers. They foster the kind of problem solving that Harry Boyte describes as public work and the pragmatist philosophers call evolutionary learning, but in contrast to many other advocates of citizen engagement, community organizers give more attention to confronting powerful decision makers, whether they are in government, business, or the nonprofit sector. Schutz explains, "The public sphere, organizers argue, is a realm of conflicts over power and resources. The central aspect of public relations is not trust, but *accountability*" (497). In order to hold policy makers accountable, community organizers help their groups deploy a range of pressure tactics from informational meetings with officials to demonstrations and sit-ins. They help their groups calibrate the best mix of confrontation and negotiation (see also Ospina and Saz-Carranza, 2010). Organizers often have something of a love-hate relationship with leadership, since they play down their own leadership role, preferring to help others become the public face of a group.

Two experts on social innovation, Leslie Crutchfield and Heather Grant, published a highly influential book in 2008 that presented their findings about the practices that characterize high-impact nonprofits. One of the key practices was sharing leadership both inside and outside the organization. The nonprofits featured in the book had very gifted and committed individuals as CEOs, but a hallmark of these people was their willingness to extend leadership throughout the organization and collaborate with leaders outside their organizations. As an example, Crutchfield and Grant cite Edwin Feulner, who served as president of the Heritage Foundation for 36 years and made an intentional effort to share leadership, beginning with his appointment of a strong co-leader. The authors conclude that Heritage's "triumvirate of leadership—the shared executive leadership, a broad tier of senior managers and a strong and supportive board—has created an unstoppable organization" (155). After describing similar patterns in the other organizations they studied, they say:

> Although we can't prove a simple cause-and-effect link between collective leadership and organizational performance, we have come to believe that sharing leadership has in fact enabled these nonprofits to have more impact. Because they focus so much on influencing players outside their organizational boundaries, they need to manage hundreds of relationships and access many networks. Further, working across sector boundaries to advocate for policy change, partner with business, build a network, or engage thousands of individuals takes many different skills—not all of which can be found in one person. And the problems these groups are trying to solve are complex, requiring large-scale systemic solutions involving many stakeholders.
>
> *(156)*

For business leaders, the key democratic virtue is a sense of responsibility to community stakeholders as well as shareholders and employees and a willingness to deploy the businesses' resources to remedy public problems. In their edited book *Responsible Leadership* (2006) Thomas Maak and Nicola Pless bring together a number of authors with complementary ideas for fostering socially responsible leadership in business. In their own chapter they note that responsible business leaders face the demanding challenge of aligning corporate values with personal, interpersonal, and societal values. The ability to "build and sustain trustful relationships to all relevant stakeholders is key" to handling this challenge effectively (39).

In some cases, a socially responsible stance may mean that corporations become partners with governments and nonprofits in ameliorating problems; in other cases, as Scherer and Palazzo (2007) point out, when governments are weak or repressive, corporations can partner with nongovernmental organizations. Sandra Waddock (2007) emphasizes the need for business leaders to have an integrated view of the world. "Businesses," she argues, "are *part of society*, creatures of society, and need to be *subject to the interests of society* not function as the dominant agents of creating society" (544). She argues that business leaders should realize that "what is done in one part of the world actually does affect what happens in other parts" (546). She urges those of us who teach in business schools to use field studies, organizational consulting, and service learning to help students develop relational skills and cross-cultural understanding, as well as the ability to think through the consequences of business decisions. She seeks to expose students to critiques of modern business methods and to alternative modes of capitalism (such as increased employee ownership). She hopes to develop in her students the courage "needed to tell the truth, to be willing to change the system, to share power with those who currently do not have it, and to redirect the world's resources" (555).

The most obvious democratic virtue for leaders in the news media is devotion to freedom of expression, accompanied by determination to hold powerful people and organizations accountable for their actions affecting citizens. We see examples in accounts like Bob Woodward and Carl Bernstein's *All the President's Men* (1974) or coverage of the actions of the journalists who released the classified documents obtained by Eric Snowden. Clearly, leaders in the media require skills of investigative reporting and balancing of freedom of expression with other public values like national security and personal privacy.

Media leaders also have crucial roles to play in media's presentation of public problems—their stories make problems visible or invisible to large numbers of citizens and interpret causes and potential solutions to the problems. Their decisions about what and whom to cover can convey powerful messages about who counts as full citizens of the society.

Practicing Integrative Leadership

As noted in Chapter 8, the work of integrative leadership is linking and integrating diverse constituencies—along with resources, processes, and structures—in sustainable arrangements for remedying a complex public problem or responding to a "grand challenge." (The Center for Integrative Leadership describes a grand challenge as "novel, emergent, highly complex, and beyond the resources or knowledge of a single discipline, organization, or sector to address. Grand challenges [such as climate change] do not lend themselves to simple or technical solutions. Single-sector actions to address these challenges often precipitate unanticipated and unintended consequences. Grand challenges are sometimes described in the literature as wicked problems or social messes.") Any particular case of successful integrative leadership is likely to include multiple leaders from all sectors (government, business, nonprofit, community, and media) drawing on democratic virtues and skills. As suggested earlier, however, government officials and administrators have special responsibility for ensuring that these collaborative efforts actually achieve the common good.

Understanding the Common Good

In just a moment I will describe in some detail the practices of integrative leadership, but for now I want to focus on the meaning of the common good. When John Bryson and I, in the early 1990s, first formulated our definition of leadership as "the inspiration and mobilization of others to undertake collective action in pursuit of the common good," we chose common good as an accessible shorthand for what we call "regimes of mutual gain." It also signaled our agreement with James MacGregor Burns that leadership was by definition aimed at serving the needs and aspirations of followers and fostering their moral development. We realized, however, that we needed a deeper understanding of how philosophers and other scholars thought about the common good. We developed a reading list and organized faculty seminars to explore traditional and contemporary views of the common good and related concepts like the public interest and the good society. Ultimately, we identified four basic dimensions of ideas about the common good:

- A focus on the relation of individuals and society
- A concern for the well-being of a defined group of people (whose common good?)
- Content of the common good
- Processes for achieving the common good

Regarding the first dimension, John Bryson and I note that "any conception of the common good rests on an understanding of the connection between the welfare of the individuals and the society of which he or she is a part" (Crosby and Bryson, 2005,183). Different societies (and individuals within them) see that connection as resting somewhere on a continuum anchored by individualism on one end and collectivism on the other. At the individualist end is a focus on individuals who have diverse goals and interests best served by a high degree of personal freedom. Government's main function is to protect personal freedom and keep one person's actions from hurting another. At the collectivist end is a focus on society and the belief that the well-being of individuals is thoroughly enmeshed and possibly even the same as societal well-being. Government would have multiple functions: supplying public goods, fostering continuation of the society, and ensuring that individuals harmonize their actions with societal norms and traditions. An exercise for helping groups explore their views of the relation of individual and society is in Chapter 12.

The second dimension of the common good directs attention to the groups whose well-being is of paramount concern. The group of concern could be one's family, a team, an organization, a professional, geographic, or other type of community. Even though one may care most about a particular group, there are both pragmatic and ethical reasons for expanding concern to other groups as well. Pragmatically, it is often impossible to separate the well-being of one group from those that exist alongside it and even from those in distant parts of the world. Ethically, individuals have obligations to care for people outside their own group and even for the natural world.

The third dimension—the content of the common good—has been debated by philosophers for centuries. A nondemocratic version of what constitutes the common good is the assumption that what is good for a ruler or an elite group is good for everyone else. Some philosophers find the common good in connection to God or communal traditions. Marxists see the common good as a classless society, in which wealth and status are distributed evenly among all citizens. Philosophers with a liberal democratic bent share some of Marx's egalitarian views of human beings, but believe the common good characterizes a society in which individual freedom and equal opportunity (rather than equality of outcomes) are prime values. Other well-developed views of the content of the common good include utilitarianism (the greatest good for the greatest number), the caring community, and stewardship of the earth.

The fourth dimension—the means of achieving the common good—overlaps somewhat with the third. If one accepts that the common good is an extension of elite interests, an authoritarian state would serve the purpose. If the common good requires a fairly equal distribution of wealth, people might turn to more socialist or communist governing processes. If common good is equated with freedom and equality of opportunity, markets will have a strong role. If the common good is wrapped up with a religious tradition, the means of achieving it may be a religious regime. Here are other main means societies have used to achieve the common good: representative government, expert judgment, informed public, citizen engagement, mobilization of the less powerful, and some local autonomy.

The Leadership for the Common Good framework ties the four dimensions to the work of tackling shared public problems. John and I believe a prime goal of society should be the well-being of individuals, and that individuals, in turn, have a responsibility to care for others. As for whose common good should be the focus of problem solving, that depends on the problem. We argue that key stakeholders—that is, those most affected, those with responsibility for responding to the problem, and those with needed resources—must be involved in the effort and ways must be found to develop shared understanding of the problem and solutions that are acceptable to all. Attention to the well-being of future generations also makes sense. Democratic decision-making processes (including, for example, representative assemblies, consensus building, negotiation, and protection of minority interests) are most likely to achieve outcomes acceptable to the group and to the broader society. Our general prescription for the outcome of these processes is a regime of mutual gain, "a set of principles, laws, norms, rules, and decision-making procedures that achieve lasting benefit at reasonable cost and tap and serve the stakeholders' deepest interests in, and desire for, a better world for themselves and those they care about" (187).

Diagnosing the Context for Integrative Leadership

Three integrative leadership practices are essential at the outset of an effort to tackle a complex public problem or "grand challenge." They are:

- Shaping and taking advantage of a window of opportunity
- Building strategic cross-boundary relationships
- Deploying personal assets on behalf of desired change

To identify or shape *a window of opportunity*, leaders help constituents understand the context of the problem or challenge that concerns them. What political systems are involved? What are the social, political, economic, technological, and ecological conditions contributing to the problem? How are conditions changing in ways that increase the urgency for tackling the problem and the prospects for achieving good results? Perhaps a new political party has taken over the presidency with a mandate for change. Perhaps the economy is expanding after a downturn. Perhaps the problem most severely affects a population group that is growing. Perhaps an emerging technology offers promise for reducing the cost of remedying the problem of concern.

Leaders also help constituents make sense of the problem: How urgent is it? How likely is it that efforts to tackle the problem can be successful? Why should we care?

To build *strategic cross-boundary relationships* that will be necessary for launching a cross-sector collaboration, leaders and their constituents as a planning group should consider who besides themselves has a stake in the problem. Asking this question for all the sectors—government, business, nonprofit, community, and media—may be helpful. The planning group can use stakeholder analysis techniques like power-versus-interest grids and influence diagrams to develop ideas of what coalitions may be possible and needed, which sponsors and champions might participate, and what preexisting relationships might be tapped in order to launch a cross-sector collaboration.

Ultimately, some sponsors and champions must be willing to *deploy their personal assets*—e.g., formal and informal authority, energy, and connections—on behalf of the change effort. Their actions and words will communicate the message that the time is right to act on an urgent problem and that those who participate are engaged in a worthy endeavor that has hope of succeeding.

Developing Inclusive Processes And Structures

The crucial work of cross-sector collaborations occurs in interrelated processes and structures. Inclusive processes help collaborating partners bridge differences, build inclusive and functional structures, plan effectively, and manage power imbalances. Inclusive structures, in turn, provide governance for the collaboration, include diverse stakeholders, and help the collaboration implement its decisions. The leadership practices associated with collaborative processes and structures are:

- Designing and using formal and informal forums
- Designing and using governance structures (arenas) and decision-making processes for the collaboration
- Influencing and authorizing decision makers in key arenas outside the collaboration
- Enforcing and reinforcing formal and informal rules and norms in courts
- Maintaining structural flexibility in order to respond to shifts in funding streams, participating organizations, and the political environment, and in order to match the demands of different collaboration phases

Since the design and use of forums, arenas, and courts has been discussed in Chapter 8, I will focus here on how to make these settings more inclusive and thus more democratic. In their book, *Free Spaces: The Sources of Democratic Change in America* (1992), Sara Evans and Harry Boyte give particular attention to the settings (such as church halls, settlement houses, union meetings, and schools) in which citizens begin to build understandings of a shared public problem, or opportunity, and commit to a reform effort. Evans and Boyte argue that these settings, or "free spaces," should be evaluated on their effectiveness as schools for democracy—that is, settings which offer "new opportunities for self-definition, for the development of public and leadership skills, for a new confidence in the possibility of participation, and for wider connections between the movement and other groups and institutions" (xix).

An excellent resource is *Public Participation for 21st Century Democracy* (2015) by Tina Nabatchi and Matt Leighninger. These two civic engagement experts advise "participation leaders" from any sector on how to use online and face-to-face forums to maximize citizen participation in public problem solving. Focusing on the U.S., but noting implications for societies around the world, they review the history of public participation in the U.S. and highlight shortcomings of conventional modes (such as public hearings) of providing information and gathering input from citizens. They provide evidence that the most effective modes (such as facilitated town hall meetings, public budgeting processes, civic journalism, and conversations about racial justice) use methods such as those outlined in the Chapters 5 and 6 of this book to recruit diverse participants, build relationships, and develop shared understandings of a public problem and commitment to solutions. Nabatchi and Leighninger approvingly call these methods "thick participation," but they also note their downside—chiefly that they require considerable time and resources. "Thin participation" engages individuals rather than groups via online surveys, fundraising campaigns, petition drives, and opportunities to report local problems. The benefits of thin participation are low cost and convenience (for those with access to the Internet); certainly this type of participation is a valuable complement to more time-intensive methods.

From local to global issues, well-organized citizen participation can have multiple benefits, according to Nabatchi and Leighninger. It can prompt citizen action to solve problems, generate new ideas, help citizens find resources and allies, develop new leadership, and encourage cross-sector collaboration.

Nabatchi and Leighninger advise participation leaders to answer the following four strategic questions at the outset of their efforts:

- Who should participate and how should they be recruited?
- How will participants interact with each other and with decision makers?
- What information do participants need?
- How will participation impact policy decisions, problem-solving efforts, or other kinds of public action? (244)

The answers to these questions should guide the design of the participation process, and Nabatchi and Leighninger offer extensive, practical design guidelines. Of particular importance is clarity about how citizen input will be used by policy makers as they carry out their responsibilities, whether as elected officials, corporate board members, department heads, or the like. The benefits of participation will be significantly undermined if citizens believe their work will affect policy decisions and they find that in reality the policy makers have ignored their input. Of course, as Nabatchi and Leighninger note, citizens whose advice is ignored can and often do rise up and insist that policy makers rethink.

Kathy Quick and Martha Feldman (2014) describe three key practices that can foster successful collaboration across or even through the boundaries separating groups, sectors, regions, and cultures. They are: translating across differences (for example, by "adopting another language or way of expressing understandings to create a new, shared domain" [677]); aligning among differences (by "accepting differences and using them as a basis for pursuing new, shared interests" [678]); and decentering differences (for example, by groups' creating [cross-]boundary objects, such as plans or maps, that capture their areas of agreement and possibly disagreement).

Attending to Outcomes and Accountabilities

When diverse individuals, groups, and organizations join in a collaborative effort that crosses sector, cultural, and geographic boundaries, keeping track of outcomes and holding the partners accountable for achieving the common good can be challenging. Accordingly, successful integrative leaders engage in the following practices:

- Explicitly identifying and seeking immediate, intermediate, and long-term outcomes

- Building an accountability system that tracks inputs, processes, and outcomes; uses a variety of methods for gathering, interpreting, and using data; and uses a results-management system built on strong relationships with key political and professional constituencies
- Demonstrating resilience in the face of setbacks and engaging in regular reassessments

(Crosby and Bryson, 2012)

Examples of more immediate outcomes are: creation of social, intellectual, and political capital; high-quality collaboration agreements; and innovative strategies. Intermediate outcomes occur when a collaboration is well under way and include new partnerships, coordination and joint action, implementation of agreements, and changes in practices and perceptions. Long-term outcomes might include new institutions, language, and norms related to addressing public problems. A useful accountability system would incorporate the desired outcomes, assign responsibility for achieving them, and track resources devoted to the process. As John Bryson and I have noted, integrative leaders should collect and organize evidence about the outcomes of collaboration in ways that can appeal to diverse constituencies. When the evidence reveals setbacks and failures, leaders should help collaborating partners reassess and adjust their strategies. To foster resilience in the face of setbacks, they help the partners sustain a focus on the vision that animates their work.

Additional Work on Integrative Leadership

Besides the work of scholars at the Center for Integrative Leadership, several other scholars and practitioners have contributed to the theory of integrative leadership and guidance for leading across sector, cultural, and geographic boundaries. Several contributed to the *Leadership Quarterly* special issue on public integrative leader published in April 2010. A group of consultants from Booz Allen Hamilton published *Megacommunities: How Leaders of Government, Business and Nonprofits Can Tackle Today's Global Challenges* (Gerencser, Van Lee, Napolitano, and Kelly, 2008). They defined megacommunities as "a public sphere in which organizations from three sectors—business, government, and civil society—deliberately join together around compelling issues of mutual importance, following a set of practices and principles that make it easier for them to achieve results without sacrificing their individual goals" (53). They conducted interviews and drew on their own experience to describe particular megacommunities and develop guidance for forming and sustaining trisector networks. To build a megacommunity, participants must strive for "megacommunity thinking"—that is, move away from unilateralism and command-and-control modes of operating and toward shared power and optimization, rather than maximization, of localized benefits. Partners must listen and learn from each other, which requires "sensing across borders" (172) with the aim of understanding the different logics, language, and governance structures that characterize the different sectors.

The initiators of megacommunities, the authors say, should be clear about their own interests, be convinced that a megacommunity actually is needed, and have relationships and credibility that can help launch the network. Initiators are likely to come from organizations that value innovation—and those would most likely be businesses, in the authors' view. Essential characteristics of a megacommunity leader include a spirit of inclusiveness, trisector exposure, a nonimperial approach, presence and passion, adaptability, and long-term thinking. These leaders also should have strong communication skills, be technologically savvy, and good at developing other integrative leaders (212).

In *Boundary Spanning Leadership* (2011) Chris Ernst and Donna Chrobot-Mason report on the results of an ambitious research project conducted by a Center for Creative Leadership team in several regions of the world. The researchers sought to understand how leaders bridged serious divides between groups "in service of a higher vision or goal" (5). Ernst and Chrobot-Mason present a model composed of three strategies: managing boundaries, forging common ground, and discovering new frontiers.

The leadership practices associated with each practice are presented in Figure 11.1. Buffering refers to "defining boundaries to create safety in groups" (9). To do this, facilitators help groups strengthen their sense of identity and cohesion as a group—for example, by giving them opportunities to focus on what makes the group distinctive. In reflecting, facilitators help groups consider how they are different from and similar to other groups that share a stake in an issue.

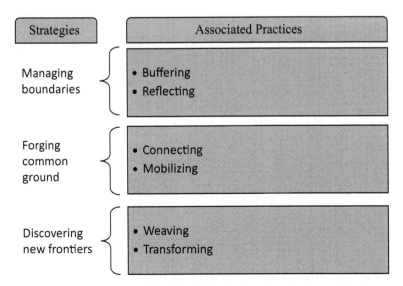

FIGURE 11.1 Ernst and Chrobot-Mason's Model of Boundary Spanning Leadership

This involves "sensitizing each group to the other's needs, values, beliefs, and preferences" (108). Ernst and Chrobot-Mason cite advice from Chuck Palus and David Horth (2002), who urge facilitators to ask the groups to answer powerful questions that "invite exploration, resist easy answers and invoke strong passions" (115). The work of connecting begins when groups begin to see similarities between each other's fears and hopes and when facilitators give individuals from different groups chances to connect informally and one-on-one. Mobilizing includes developing a common vision and creating a "new and larger identity that is inclusive of all group members" (156). (This resonates with Ganz's move to the story of us and the story of now.) Weaving involves creating an interdependent network that can align different groups while capitalizing on differences. Transforming involves seeing the borders between groups as frontiers where the groups can "unlock new and emergent opportunities" (205).

★★★

This chapter has highlighted the work of scholars who firmly tie leadership to citizenship, democracy, and public problem solving. We have considered "habits of the heart," public narratives, and public work as important means by which citizens can build their individual and collective power, shoulder more responsibility for their societies, and become leaders themselves. We have explored what several scholars have to say about the democratic virtues and skills that leaders in different sectors should exhibit. The special responsibility of public officials and managers for upholding public values has been highlighted. Finally, the chapter has explored different views of the common good and described the integrative leadership practices that foster democratic problem solving across sector, cultural, and geographic boundaries. The next chapter will focus on practical exercises for heightening attention to citizenship in leadership development and encouraging democratic problem solving.

References

Ansell, C. K. (2011). *Pragmatist democracy: Evolutionary learning as public philosophy*. New York: Oxford University Press.

Boyte, H. C. (2004). *Everyday politics: Reconnecting citizens and public life*. Philadelphia: University of Pennsylvania Press.

Boyte, H. C. (2015). Creating public value: Contributions of the new civic politics. In J. M. Bryson, B. C. Crosby, & L. Bloomberg (Eds.), *Creating public value in practice: Advancing the common good in a multi-sector, shared-power, no-one-wholly-in-charge world* (pp. 49–66). New York: Taylor & Francis.

Boyte, H. C., & Finders, M. J. (2016). "Liberation of powers": Agency and education for democracy. *Educational Theory, 66* (1–2), 127–145.

Boyte, H. C., & Kari, N. N. (1996). *Building America: The democratic promise of public work*. Philadelphia: Temple.

Burns, J. M. (2003). *Transforming leadership: The pursuit of happiness*. New York: Atlantic Monthly Press.

Crosby, B. C., & Bryson, J. M. (2005). *Leadership for the common good: Tackling public problems in a shared-power world*. San Francisco: Wiley.

Crosby, B. C., & Bryson, J. M. (2012). Integrative leadership and policy change: A hybrid relational view. In M. Uhl-Bien & S. Ospina (Eds.), *Advancing relational leadership research: A dialogue among perspectives* (pp. 303–334). Charlotte, NC: Information Age.

Crutchfield, L. R., & Grant, H. M. (2008). *Forces for good: The six practices of high-impact nonprofits*. San Francisco: Jossey-Bass.

Ernst, C., & Chrobot-Mason, D. (2011). *Boundary spanning leadership*. New York: McGraw Hill.

Evans, S. M., & Boyte, H. C. (1992). *Free spaces*. Chicago: University of Chicago Press.

Ganz, M. (2011). Public narrative, collective action, and power. In S. Odugbeni, & T. Lee (Eds.), Accountability though public opinion: From inertia to public action (pp. 273–289). Washington, DC: The World Bank.

Gardner, H. (1995). *Leading minds*. New York: Basic Books.

Gerencser, M., Van Lee, R., Napolitano, F., & Kelly, C. (2008). *Megacommunities: How leaders of government, business and non-profits can tackle today's global challenges together*. New York: Palgrave Macmillan.

Kellerman, B. (2010). *Leadership*. New York: McGraw Hill.

Luke, J. S. (1998). *Catalytic leadership: Strategies for an interconnected world*. San Francisco: Jossey-Bass Publishers.

Maak, T., & Pless, N. M. (2006). Responsible leadership: A relational approach. In T. Maak & N. M. Pless (Eds.), *Responsible leadership* (pp. 33–53). London and New York: Routledge.

Nabatchi, T., & Leighninger, M. (2015). *Public participation for 21st century democracy*. Hoboken, NJ: Wiley.

Ospina, S. M., & Saz-Carranza, A. (2010). Paradox and collaboration in network management. *Administration & Society, 42*, 404–440.

Palmer, P. J. (2011). *Healing the heart of democracy: The courage to create a politics worthy of the human spirit*. San Francisco: Jossey-Bass.

Palus, C. J., & Horth, D. M. (2002). *The leader's edge: Six creative competencies for navigating complex challenges*. San Francisco: Jossey-Bass.

Quick, K. S., & Feldman, M. S. (2014). Boundaries as junctures: Collaborative boundary work for building efficient resilience. *Journal of Public Administration Research and Theory, 24*, 673–695.

Ruscio, K. P. (1999). The connections between democratic theory and leadership theory: The case of public reason. *Selected Proceedings 1999 Annual Meeting, International Leadership Association*, Atlanta, GA.

Ruscio, K. P. (2004). *The leadership dilemma in modern democracy*. Cheltenham, UK: Edward Elgar.

Scherer, A. G., & Palazzo, G. (2007). Toward a political conception of corporate responsibility: Business and society seen from a Habermasian perspective. *Academy of Management Review, 32*(4), 1096–1120.

Schutz, A. (2011). Power and trust in the public realm: John Dewey, Saul Alinsky, and the limits of progressive democratic education. *Educational Theory, 61*(4), 491–512.

Van Wart, M. (2011). *Dynamics of leadership in public service: Theory and practice* (2nd ed.). Armonk, NY: M.E. Sharpe.

Van Wart, M. (2012). *Leadership in public organizations* (2nd ed.). New York: Taylor & Francis.

Waddock, S. (2007). Leadership integrity in a fractured knowledge world. *Academy of Management Learning & Education, 6*(4), 543–557.

Woodward, B., & Bernstein, C. (1974). *All the President's men*. New York: Simon & Schuster.

12

STRENGTHENING CITIZENSHIP AND THE HANDS

Leadership educators use a variety of exercises, assignments, and learning experiences to help participants in our workshops and courses integrate leadership with citizenship and democracy. These range from inclusive recruitment and session design to attention to democratic virtues and public values to cross-sector leadership projects. Inclusive recruitment and session design have been explored in previous chapters, so they receive attention here only in reference to democratic values. First I will consider assignments and exercises designed to foster democratic habits of the heart and attention to public work; then I will focus on democratic values; and finally, on integrative leadership.

Paying Attention to Citizenship

As a first step in exploring leaders' responsibilities for strengthening democracy, I encourage participants in my classes to acknowledge the importance of citizenship in democratic leadership. I often ask participants in my classes to consider three questions:

1. What does it mean to be a citizen of your state or country?
2. What does it mean to be a citizen of the world?
3. How might organizations be good citizens?

After allowing some time for participants to jot down answers individually, I might invite them to talk about their answers in small groups and then facilitate a large group conversation. Answering the first question is typically easier since people can come up with a list of well-defined rights and responsibilities: for example, voting, paying taxes, obtaining certain services, obeying the law, and serving in the military. Some people will point out that they are denied full citizenship in their country because of their religion, race, gender, or ethnicity; others may be seeking to become citizens in a new country. The second question usually is more puzzling, since no unitary world government sets out expectations and requirements for global citizenship. Answers might include freedom of travel across national borders, responsibility for the well-being of people in all parts of the world, or stewardship of the planet's scarce resources. Participants who are familiar with the U.N.'s Universal Declaration of Human Rights and other human rights documents might cite, for example, the right to basic needs such as housing or food, the right to due process, or the prohibition against torture. The third question may not even make sense to some participants, since they associate citizenship with government or intergovernmental agreements. Still, organizational citizenship is a label that scholars and some practitioners have applied to employees' or volunteers' sense of stewardship for their organizations or networks. (Organizational citizenship also may include a sense of at least informal entitlement to some rights within the organization.)

As an educator, my goals in this conversation include reminding participants of their citizenship and its frequently taken-for-granted character. I encourage them to see citizenship as a bundle of rights and responsibilities that are variably enforced and enacted. (I may record answers to the questions in two columns, headed by rights and responsibilities.) I raise questions about how those rights and responsibilities were established, which will inevitably reveal examples of political and movement leadership. I often note the importance in a democratic system of protecting minority rights and providing plenty of opportunities for those who lose a policy battle to win in future rounds.

I might accompany this exercise with readings about how citizen movements defended, expanded, or restricted rights and responsibilities of citizenship—for example, I might assign chapters from Sara Evans and Harry Boyte's *Free Spaces: The Sources of Democratic Change in America* (1992). Harry Boyte's (2004) book *Everyday Politics: Reconnecting Citizens and Public Life* or his chapter in *Creating Public Value in Practice* (2015) are other supportive readings. In order to explore citizenship behavior of business organizations I might assign Klaus Schwab's (2008) article "Global Corporate Citizenship."

Jodi Sandfort and Gary DeCramer assigned Parker Palmer's *Healing the Heart of Democracy* in their leadership course at the Humphrey School in order to acknowledge growing mistrust in U.S. public institutions and concern over the level of rigid partisanship in legislative bodies. I certainly agree with them that Palmer's call for developing democratic habits of the heart is an important leadership challenge for this country and others. Yet, Jodi and Gary found that many participants felt Palmer's critique of contemporary U.S. politics was too harsh and left-leaning. Thus, if this book is assigned, instructors should add contrasting perspectives or make room for them in class discussion.

Marshal Ganz provides students with a worksheet for constructing a public narrative: http://marshallganz.usmblogs.com/files/2012/08/Public-Narrative-Worksheet-Fall-2013-.pdf. A short version adapted from his paper "What is Public Narrative?" (2008) is in Inset 12.1.

INSET 12.1   CREATING A PUBLIC NARRATIVE

Marshall Ganz (2008) emphasizes the power of public narrative to mobilize citizen action. The narrative has three aspects: the story of self, the story of us, and the story of now. All stories, he emphasizes, involve plot, character, and moral, and are affected by the setting in which they are told. The engine of a story is its plot—that is, depiction of a challenge, the choices of individuals or groups in response, and an outcome. To be effective, the central character or characters of the story must be people with whom the listeners can identify. Finally the moral is a heartfelt teaching—"emotionally experienced understanding, not only conceptual understanding, and a lesson of the heart, not only the head" (8).

Here are some questions to help you put together an interconnected story of self, us, and now:

1. Telling your *story of self*—tell about key choice points that have deeply affected the course of your life. How did those choices (by your parents, yourself, or others) shape you? How do they affect you now in your chosen work?
2. Telling your *story of us*—link your story to the story of your community (geographic, professional, or affiliative), the group you seek to call to action. What key choices has that community made? What values have been elevated or reinforced by those choices? What is the moral of the story?
3. Telling the *story of now*—what urgent challenge confronts your group at this time, what values are at stake, and what are the risks and sources of hope? The story should include a "credible vision" of how to get from the current situation to a desired better future.

Now consider a setting in which you might communicate the narrative. Reshape the language, add detail that can help you reach the audience in that particular setting. What are the most effective ways of conveying the narrative—speeches, songs, documentaries? Refine the story through the actual telling and learning from that experience.

As a complement to the public narrative assignment, leadership educators may ask course or workshop participants to write their economic and political autobiographies, either as separate or integrated essays. Guidance for drafting separate essays is in Insets 12.2 and 12.3 and is adapted from an exercise developed at the Humphrey School's Reflective Leadership Center.

INSET 12.2 WRITING YOUR ECONOMIC AUTOBIOGRAPHY

This essay is a reflection on the economic status of your original family and on major economic influences on your life trajectory and worldview. It is an opportunity to consider connections among work, education, property ownership, personal and public investment, and public values. The essay should be about five double-spaced pages; it could be a letter to a significant person in your life. Here are some guiding questions:

1. What was your economic and social status as a child? What did your mother and father (or guardians) do for a living? What unpaid work did they perform? What property did they own? In what ways did they save and invest (if they did)? How did your family's status affect you?
2. What is your own history of paid and unpaid work? What have been the economic effects of major life events like marriage, divorce, illness, or becoming a parent? How has your socioeconomic status changed (or not) over time? How has investment (personal and public) benefited or harmed you?
3. What is your philosophy of charitable giving?
4. What key economic values have you acquired from your family and life experience?

INSET 12.3 WRITING YOUR POLITICAL AUTOBIOGRAPHY

This essay is a reflection on your original family's involvement in public life and on major political influences on your life trajectory and worldview. It is an opportunity to consider connections among party affiliation, political advocacy, and public service. The essay should be about five double-spaced pages; it could be a letter to a significant person in your life. Here are some guiding questions:

1. What were the political affiliations (if any) of your original family? What were your parents or guardians' attitudes toward politics, public life, and community service?
2. What is your own political history? How and why has your political perspective changed (or not) over time?
3. How do you view the desirable roles of government and citizens? How do you practice citizenship?

You may want to assign these essays as homework and then invite participants to share what they wish in one-to-one or small-group conversations in a class or workshop session. You might note that the essays are yet another effort to deepen self-awareness, but also are aimed at helping us reflect on how we have been affected by forces (some of which are the result of political decision making) that have shaped many of our fellow citizens. They may reveal often-hidden rules or practices that advantage or disadvantage us. The essays also can uncover sources of our public values, and they may help us understand why we identify with some groups rather than others. You may want to provide your own essays to provide a model for the participants.

Attending to Democratic Virtues and Values

Some consideration of democratic virtues and values is likely to surface in any conversation about citizenship. A "virtuous" citizen would be one who carries out responsibilities of citizenship and supports the granting of rights to his/her fellow citizens. A "virtuous" leader would be one who provides encouragement, incentives, and organizing knowledge to help citizens carry out their responsibilities and claim their rights. Such a leader also is accountable to citizens for the authority they have granted him/her. In simplest terms, the mark of virtuous leaders and citizens in democratic settings is that they uphold democratic values.

To foster additional attention to democratic virtues, I might assign Kenneth Ruscio's 1999 paper or simply present his view that in a liberal democracy, the three central virtues that public officials should uphold are civility, tolerance, and respect. I would direct attention to the assumptions that underlie these virtues— chiefly a reliance on public reason, the creation of trust in the political system, and a belief in the possibility of achieving the common good. As part of the discussion of Ruscio's ideas, I would ask participants to identify any virtues missing from his scheme. They are likely to add words like: fair behavior, respect for differences, tolerance, personal integrity, commitment to the most vulnerable people, stewardship of the environment, compromise, and efficient use of public resources.

Alternatively, I might assign both Ruscio's paper and an essay that Harry Boyte has written about public work and ask participants to identify the leaders' and citizens' democratic virtues that emerge from the two readings. If time permits, I might assign additional readings or concepts from Chapter 11 that highlight democratic virtues of leaders in governmental and nongovernmental settings. In discussion of these readings, I might draw attention to the connection with values that the group itself has highlighted as they set ground rules for working together.

In order to call attention to the tensions inherent in enacting democratic virtues and values, I have used Deborah Stone's *Policy Paradox* (2012) to help participants in my courses understand varying interpretations of the central democratic values of efficiency, equity, security, liberty, and human welfare. Reading all of her book (or the first six chapters) underscores the need, for democratic leaders especially, to understand politics as the means of working through the different views of advocates who will use every tool at their disposal to shape laws, policies, and social norms.

Using films, poems, paintings, or other art forms can be an effective way to spark conversations about democratic virtues and values. For example, I have assigned Steven Spielberg's *Lincoln*, which portrays Abraham Lincoln's high-minded, yet wily efforts to win congressional passage of the Thirteenth Amendment to the U.S. Constitution. We can ask what democratic virtues seem to characterize the drama's main actors—Lincoln, Mary Todd Lincoln, Thaddeus Stevens, Francis Preston Blair, William Seward, and others—and what democratic values were at stake. We can ask what virtues seemed to outweigh others in the choices that the actors made and whether some values (such as transparency) were sacrificed in service to other values (such as justice for enslaved citizens).

My colleagues and I have used Martin Ritt's *Norma Rae* to highlight the virtue of courage to confront injustice. As a textile mill worker experiencing oppressive working conditions, the title character steps up, at considerable personal risk, to support a unionizing campaign. With this act of engaged citizenship she becomes a leader, modeling resistance for her fellow workers.

Practicing Integrative Leadership

Attention to democratic virtues and values and related tensions lays the groundwork for focusing on the common good and integrative leadership. Since achieving the common good is the aim of integrative leadership, I often begin by helping course or workshop participants explore the meaning of common good. A possible reading is chapter 5 of *Leadership for the Common Good* (Crosby and Bryson, 2005), which links the common good to leadership over the course of a policy change cycle.

In a face-to-face session I might provide a handout or PowerPoint slides identifying and possibly elaborating on the main dimensions of the common good. An exercise for understanding the first dimension (the relation of individuals and society) is presented in Inset 12.4.

INSET 12.4   CLARIFYING YOUR VIEW OF
THE RELATION OF INDIVIDUAL AND SOCIETY

In your small group, share honestly your understanding of human nature, especially the connection of individuals to society. Each person should jot down brief responses to the following questions:

- Are people mainly self-interested, mainly concerned with and about others, or some mixture?
- Are people fundamentally equal?

- Is human life sacred? Are individual human beings sacred?
- How does or should the community enhance individual development?
- What is the society's responsibility for the welfare of the individual and the individual's responsibility to society?

Ask one group member to record answers as group members share them, question by question, in a round-robin process. The group member who serves as the recorder can then make a general report on the responses once all small groups have joined as one.

In the large group debriefing exercise, the instructor can ask what the answers imply for achieving the common good.

Once I have given participants a chance to review and raise questions about the other dimensions of the common good, I ask them to apply the dimensions to their own cases, an individual leadership project, or a team action learning experience. Alternatively, I might ask the group to focus on a current public problem, such as the high cost of higher education. The exercise I use is in Inset 12.5.

INSET 12.5 ACHIEVING THE COMMON GOOD IN YOUR CASE

This exercise is designed to help you, or your group, develop your approach to enacting the common good in a particular case. We begin, though, with general questions.

1. Answer these general questions about the first dimension of the common good:

   a. How do you view the connections of individual and society, citizen and government?

   b. How is the well-being of a citizen tied to the well-being of the society as a whole?

2. Now focus on the problem or challenge that concerns you and answer the following questions:

   a. Whose common good is foremost?

   b. What is your idea of what the common good might be in this case?

   c. What methods would you use to achieve the common good?

3. Drawing on your answers to the preceding questions, identify concrete steps will you take to achieve the common good in your case.

To introduce the practices of integrative leadership I typically assign participants in my courses a reading like the chapter on public integrative leadership in the *Oxford Handbook of Organizational Leadership* (Crosby and Bryson, 2014). I might direct participants to the website of the Center for Integrative Leadership (www.leadership.umn.edu), which presents other research and case studies related to integrative leadership.

Since integrative leadership at the societal level includes leading across boundaries at the personal, team, and organizational levels, courses and workshops on integrative leadership typically include attention to these levels as well—and previous chapters in this book have offered resources and guidance for integrating diverse aspects of the self, diverse team members, organizational units, and even multiple organizations with the aim of leading for the common good.

The semester-long integrative leadership course offered at the University of Minnesota includes modules devoted to all four levels, though the heart of the course is analysis of several cases of integrative leadership for remedying complex public problems (such as unemployment in Minneapolis, endemic polio in countries throughout the world, or sex trafficking).

Integrative Leadership Workshop or Short Course

A challenge for leadership teaching is being able to give different audiences practice grappling with key concepts and their application in a variety of formats. As a leadership educator I must be able to design learning opportunities that last an hour, a day, or a week, a semester, or longer. I have presented integrative leadership concepts and practices in most of these time frames, and where feasible I do much of this in an online presentation so that more democratic, more effective learning can occur via a "flipped" classroom in which participants are engaged mainly in grappling with and applying leadership concepts rather than listening to instructor lectures. Here I offer the design of a one-day, for-credit workshop that requires preparation prior to the six-hour face-to-face session and includes a reflection paper submitted after the class. The syllabus is in Inset 12.6.

On the day of the workshop, I ensure that the classroom is welcoming and conducive to learning (see Chapter 6), and I post a general agenda or include it in a handout. I also prepare and post a flip chart sheet with learning objectives from the syllabus.

INSET 12.6 LEADING ACROSS BOUNDARIES FOR THE COMMON GOOD: A WORKSHOP IN INTEGRATIVE LEADERSHIP

Instructor: Dr. Barbara C. Crosby, associate professor, Humphrey School of Public Affairs

9:00 a.m.–3:00 p.m., 1 credit

Integrative leadership—the work of leading across multiple kinds of boundaries—is becoming increasingly necessary in a world in which societal problems and potential solutions often involve multiple organizations, cultures, and levels of government, from local to global. The goal of this workshop is to help people from multiple organizational, professional, and artistic backgrounds understand integrative leadership and key integrative leadership practices, and apply them to their own work.

Understanding and practicing integrative leadership can be useful for people at many levels of organizational and community life. For example, a human services professional who wants to transform her county's approach to homelessness will need to understand how to bring together disparate groups—from business owners and employees, to religious congregations, to government agencies, to nonprofits, to grassroots groups involving homeless people—if she is to help her community develop systemic solutions to homelessness. She will need to understand the ways that boundaries between these groups contribute to the problem and how to reshape these boundaries in ways that foster shared commitment to moving beyond the status quo. She will need to understand the unique contributions that different sectors, organizations, cultures, and communities can make to developing sustainable solutions. She will need to understand how to use her own formal and informal authority as well as draw on the authority of others.

Faculty at the Center for Integrative Leadership at the University of Minnesota have begun formulating a theory of integrative leadership and have identified a number of leadership practices that contribute to successful efforts to collaborate across sectors, cultures, and communities. This workshop will offer an introduction to the theory of integrative leadership, then will focus on two cases of integrative leadership in order to illustrate integrative leadership practices. The cases will focus on Heading Home Hennepin, an initiative to end homelessness in Hennepin County, and on Juxtaposition Arts' work in using arts to foster youth employment and community regeneration. At least one of the cases will be presented in multimedia format.

Participants will focus on their current or future work in order to discern where integrative leadership would be most helpful and consider how integrative leadership practices are and might be enacted. They also will consider barriers to integrative leadership. As a follow-up to the workshop, participants will write a reflective paper detailing one or more efforts to put integrative leadership into practice.

Learning Objectives

- Able to define integrative leadership
- Knowledgeable about integrative leadership practices
- Able to discern these practices in particular cases
- Prepared to enact integrative leadership practices in current or future work

Preparation

Before the workshop, please read "Public Integrative Leadership" by Barbara C. Crosby and John Bryson and focus on the practices of integrative leadership starting on p. 63. Additionally, read Kathryn Quick and Martha Feldman's "Boundaries as Junctures: Collaborative Boundary Work for Building Efficient Resilience" and focus on "boundary work practices" described starting on p. 5. The readings are available through the course website.

Come to the workshop prepared to discuss the enactment of (and ask questions about) the practices described in the articles. Also think about how these practices might apply to complex problems or challenges that you are concerned about—say, for example, ensuring affordable access to higher education! You also may wish to refer to these articles in the reflective paper you write for the class.

Please review "Heading Home Hennepin," a multimedia case that we will discuss in class: http://www.hubertproject.org/hubert-material/201/. A supplemental reading, "Integrative Leadership and the Creation and Maintenance of Cross-Sector Collaborations," by Crosby and Bryson also is available through the course website.

Homework and Reflective Paper

The reflective paper should be 7 to 10 pages, doubled spaced, 12 pt. type. It must draw on at least three sources from the bibliography or other scholarly articles or books about integrative leadership. It will be due two weeks after the workshop.

References

Akkerman, S. F., & Bakker, A. (2011). Boundary crossing and boundary objects. *Review of Educational Research, 81*(2), 132–169.

Bryson, J. M., Crosby, B. C., & Stone, M. M. (2006). The design and implementation of cross-sector collaborations: Propositions from the literature. *Public Administration Review, 66*(s1), 44–55.

Carlile, P. R. (2004). Transferring, translating, and transforming: An integrative framework for managing knowledge across boundaries. *Organization Science, 15*(5), 555–568.

Crosby, B. C., & Bryson, J. M. (2010). Integrative leadership and the creation and maintenance of cross-sector collaborations. *Leadership Quarterly, 21*(2), 211–230.

Crosby, B. C., & Bryson, J. M. (2014). Public integrative leadership. In D. V. Day (Ed.), *Oxford handbook of leadership and organizations* (pp. 57–72). New York: Oxford University Press.

Ernst, C., & Chrobot-Mason, D. (2011). *Boundary spanning leadership*. New York: McGraw Hill.

Gerencser, M., Van Lee, R., Napolitano, F., & Kelly, C. (2008). *Megacommunities: How leaders of government, business and non-profits can tackle today's global challenges together*. New York: Palgrave Macmillan.

Martin, R. (2002). Integrative thinking: A model takes shape. *Rotman Management, Fall*, 8–11.

Morse, R. (2010). Integrative public leadership: Catalyzing collaboration to create public value. *Leadership Quarterly, 21*(2), 231–245.

Nelson, M. C. (2008). *How we lead matters: Reflections on a life of leadership*. New York: McGraw-Hill.

Pittinsky, T. L. (Ed.). (2009). *Crossing the divide: Intergroup leadership in a world of difference*. Boston, MA: Harvard Business Press.

Quick, K. S., & Feldman, M. S. (2014). Boundaries as junctures: Collaborative boundary work for building effective resilience. *Journal of Public Administration Research and Theory, 24*, 673–695.

Senge, P. M., Smith, B., Schley, S., & Laur, J. (2008). *The necessary revolution: How individuals and organizations are working together to create a sustainable world*. New York: Doubleday.

Waddock, S. (2007). Leadership integrity in a fractured knowledge world. *Academy of Management Learning & Education, 6*(4), 543–557.

Agenda

9:00 a.m.	Introductions
9:45	Plan for the day & learning objectives
	(Snow cards—what I want to learn as a result of this course)
10:00	Theory of integrative leadership
	Levels of integrative leadership Personal, group, organizational, societal
10:15	Break
10:30	Personal integration Exercise from StrengthsQuest

11:00	Practices of integrative leadership at societal level
	Case examples
	Small group exercise
12:00	Break for lunch
1:00	Boundary work practices in forums
1:20	Creating maps as (cross)boundary objects
	Small groups map
2:45	Barriers to integrative leadership
	Application in my work
3:00 p.m.	Wrap

I prepare an instructor's guide (see Inset 12.7) that fleshes out the agenda, connects to the PowerPoints or Prezi I will use, and notes key points and exercise directions. The guide is organized by main topic and includes class materials and slide descriptions.

INSET 12.7   INSTRUCTOR'S GUIDE FOR ONE-DAY WORKSHOP, LEADING ACROSS BOUNDARIES FOR THE COMMON GOOD

Needed materials: Flip chart sheets, ovals or large sticky notes, masking tape, pencils, and markers. Strategy map from a previous workshop to post on the classroom wall.
Handouts: Practicing Personal Integration, Oval Mapping.

9:00   *Introduction.* Say a bit about myself and integrative leadership (its roots in Leadership for the Common Good). Emphasize centrality of leading across boundaries.

> Title slide: Leading Across Boundaries for the Common Good

> Slide 2 Integrative leadership
> Integrative leaders are adept at *fostering collective action* across boundaries to advance the common good and address the grand challenges of our time.

The boundaries can be between sectors, cultures and generations, or regions.

> Slide 3 with images of types of boundaries and questions for participant introductions: When were you required to cross a significant boundary? What did it feel like? What did you learn?

Directions to participants: Discuss your answers to these questions in dyads and prepare to introduce your partner to the larger group.
As introductions proceed, record feelings and lessons on flip chart or whiteboard. When everyone has been introduced, ask for general comments re feelings and lessons.

9:45   *Plan for the day.* Go over agenda briefly. Note learning objectives.
Exercise: Use snow cards to elaborate on learning objectives. Have participants record their answers to this question: What do I want to learn as a result of this course?

10:00 *Theory of integrative leadership.*
Exercise: Participants jot down ideas and images in response to question, What is leadership? I record responses as participants call them out.

Next question: What does integrative mean to you? Turn to someone you haven't talked to so far and share your answers.

Elicit some ideas from participants after pairs talk a bit.

> Slide 4 with four overlapping circles labeled individual, group/team, organizational, and societal

Note that integrative leadership lies within the area of intersection of all four circles. Refer to some of the participants' answers.

10:15 *Break*

10:30 *Personal integration.* Tell the story of the founding of Juxtaposition Arts in North Minneapolis—how three good friends drew on their skills and passion to develop a successful nonprofit that teaches art and entrepreneurial skills to young people from a low-income neighborhood. Scroll through timeline on Juxta's website, http://juxtapositionarts.org/about/our-story/.

Directions to participants: Individually record your answers to the questions in the handout entitled "Practicing Personal Integration" (see Inset 12.8).

Once the participants have finished, invite them to share some responses to the final two questions.

11:00   *Practices of integrative leadership at the societal level*

> Slide 5 superimposes word "Practice" over photo of a conductor and orchestra.

I note that a focus on practice (as in an orchestral performance) involves numerous other people and instruments, and also the development and refinement of particular ways of doing things.

> Slide 6 includes logos and some key information for three cases of integrative leadership: Heading Home Hennepin; the effort to create a geographic information system, called MetroGIS, for the Minneapolis-St. Paul region; and PolioPlus, Rotary International's global campaign to eradicate polio. These cases are featured in the preparatory assignments for the workshop.

Briefly remind participants of key aspects of each case. Introduce first set of integrative leadership practices. What practices are important at the outset of developing a cross-boundary collaboration to tackle complex public problems or grand challenges? The first is *shaping and taking advantage of windows of opportunity.*

> Slide 7 titled Starting Places shows a window opening onto the words Political, Social, Economic, Technological, and Ecological Conditions and Trends; Tangible and Intangible Assets.

Provide examples from cases of how leaders shaped and took advantage of windows of opportunity resulting from conditions and trends. Note the tangible and intangible assets that they preserved as they were seeking major change.

The second key practice is *building strategic cross-boundary relationships.* Note the importance of using stakeholder analysis, especially influence diagrams, to do this. Define stakeholders and strategic relationships.

Slide 8 shows image conveying interconnection of people or groups.

The third key practice is *deploying personal and organizational assets* on behalf of policy change. Identifying sponsors and champions is crucial part of this. Define sponsors and champions and give examples from the cases.

Small group exercise: Discuss how these three practices were enacted in similar or different ways in the cases. Raise questions.

Debrief small-group exercise.

Turn to next set of practices: Developing collaborative processes and structures.

Slide 9 labeled Developing Collaborative Processes and Structures includes images of group meeting and Capitol building or courthouse.

Note that these processes help collaborators bridge differences, build inclusive and functional structures, plan effectively, and manage power imbalances. These structures include diverse stakeholders, provide governance for the collaboration, and help the collaboration implement its decisions.

The first practices in this set are connected to the design and use of formal and informal forums. They are:

- *Inclusive convening*—getting the system in the room. You may need many rooms, and many different meetings. Of course, there's a chance that some people can't be in the room together. So you may need to be creative about getting the input of all key stakeholders. (Offer examples from a case)
- *Fostering dialogue and deliberation*—Dialogue, which includes opportunities to fully listen to diverse perspectives, is absolutely essential to developing sound and politically acceptable solutions. Deliberation is the process of using dialogue to craft workable policies, making choices among solutions. Note Iceberg Exercise described in required Crosby and Bryson reading as example of fostering dialogue and deliberation and promoting systems thinking.
- *Framing and reframing the challenge* (vision)—Often those who want to make headway on a significant problem have to change the way people think about, or see the problem.

Consciously plan forums to be boundary experiences, in which diverse participants move to shared understanding and possibly shared identity. Boundary objects, such as stakeholder maps, can help. (Offer examples from a case.)

We will talk further about these practices after lunch and how a particular tool—strategy maps—can support these practices.

Next comes the main practice connected to the design and use of formal and informal arenas (governance structures for the collaboration as well as policy-making settings outside the collaboration). This practice is *influencing and authorizing decision makers*—partners in a collaboration must develop an inclusive, but functional means of governing the collaboration and relating to policy makers that control crucial resources. (Offer examples from a case.)

The final practice in this set, *enforcing and reinforcing rules and norms*, is connected to the design and use of formal and informal courts. (Offer examples from a case.)

Exercise: In small groups discuss how forums were effectively designed and used, especially in the Heading Home Hennepin (HHH) case.

Some points to make or reinforce in large-group debrief about the design and use of forums in the case:

- Good example of design and use of forums in HHH was the commission and the 100-day limit that helped reassure over-committed people. The working groups also provided ways for more people to be involved around particular areas of concern or expertise.
- In the HHH case, Cathy ten Broeke, Commissioner Dorfman, Mayor Rybak, and their collaborators reframed homelessness as something that *could* be eliminated. And through events and visual images and reports, they helped people see that many types of people were either experiencing or were threatened by homelessness. They have also highlighted the benefits of prevention.

Add examples of design and use of arenas and courts:

- Leaders in HHH also gave attention to arenas. HHH is staffed by the Office to End Homelessness, a cross-departmental team of county and city employees. Executive Committee chaired by Rybak, Dorfman, and Rev. Gertmenian. Other coordinating structures have formed—especially important is a network called Downtown Congregations to End Homelessness.
- Cathy ten Broeke and others have paid attention to courts. They have worked with tenants to understand and claim their legal rights.

The next set of practices are aimed at sustaining collaborative process and structure. They keep diverse stakeholders and projects working together.

> Slide 10 is titled Sustaining Collaborative Processes and Structure and has image of multihued tree with many branches and long roots.

These practices are:

- *Navigating hierarchical and collaborative structures over time.* Collaboration is about inclusion and participatory decision making, but many partners will themselves be hierarchical organizations; additionally, some will have more control over crucial resources than others. So integrative leaders must stay alert to power dynamics and be able to foster collaboration in the shadow of hierarchy and keep structures flexible in response to changing conditions. (Offer examples from a case.)
- *Managing the blend of diversity and unity within collaborative groups.* One way to do this is to have numerous initiatives within a collaboration; groups work on what they are most interested in, or most adept at. (Offer examples from a case.)

The final set of practices are aimed at achieving outcomes and managing accountabilities.

> Slide 11 is titled Attending to Outcomes and has image of accounting tools.

The practices are:

- *Staying attuned to vision of success.* (Offer examples from a case.)
- *Assessing outcomes and managing results.* HHH has done research to track outcomes and highlight the benefits of this work; researchers found, for example, that housing people and preventing homelessness are far less expensive than having people live on the streets or in shelters or in detox.

Exercise: New small groups discuss how assessing outcomes and managing results was enacted in similar or different ways in the cases. Raise questions.

Debrief exercise, respond to questions.

12:00   *Lunch*

1:00   *Boundary work practices in forums.* The assigned Quick and Feldman article focuses on the value in thinking of boundaries (between organizations, sectors, professions, etc.) as opportunities for connection rather than as barriers.

They describe three practices that can be woven into the dialogue and reframing work in forums.

- Translating across differences—helping groups develop a common language
- Aligning differences—for example, by building partnerships among different groups
- Decentering differences—rendering difference inconsequential

Slide 12 shows hands putting together puzzle pieces consisting of the three boundary practices.

Question to the class: Where have you been able to do this kind of boundary work?

1:20   *Creating strategy maps as cross-boundary objects.* This technique can help translate across differences and decenter differences and lay groundwork for aligning differences. It is described in the oval mapping handout (Inset 12.9).

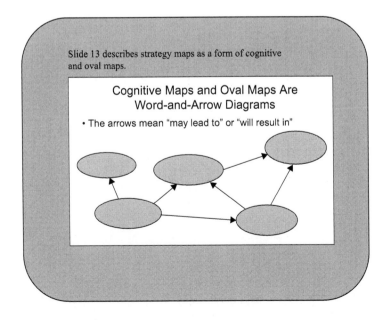

Slide 13 describes strategy maps as a form of cognitive and oval maps.

Cognitive Maps and Oval Maps Are Word-and-Arrow Diagrams

• The arrows mean "may lead to" or "will result in"

Slide 14 To work down a chain of arrows:

- Keep asking, "How would I do that?" or "What would it take to do that?"
- The arrows should lead *from* "how" you would do something *to* what you want to accomplish.

To work up a chain of arrows:

- Keep asking, "What would happen if I did that?" or "What would the consequences be if I did that?"

Slides 15 Preparing ovals:

- The arrows should go *from* what you might to do *to* the consequences of doing it
- Begin with a verb: do, create, fund, talk . . .
- 5–7 words
- Avoid "and" & "or" (one idea per oval)
- More abstract or general ideas higher on the map
- Cluster like ideas together

Slides 16–18 show photos from a strategy mapping process at a MetroGIS workshop.

Direct attention to a previously constructed strategy map on the wall. Say to the class: Now it's your turn. Divide into three groups and develop strategy maps that respond to one of the following questions:

How do we combat sex trafficking in Minnesota?
How do we make the University of Minnesota a carbon-neutral campus?
How do we make higher education affordable?

I will give each group flip chart sheets, ovals or sticky notes, markers, pencils, and tape and I will walk you through the mapping process.

2:45   *Barriers to integrative leadership.* Ask the group for ideas.
Requires commitment, patience, willingness to accept messiness.

Application. Where can you apply integrative leadership? Which integrative leadership challenge will I choose for my reflective paper?

2:55   Field final questions and wish class good luck in their integrative leadership work.

3:00   Conclude

INSET 12.8   PRACTICING PERSONAL INTEGRATION

1. Heart: What do you love, feel passionate about?
2. Soul: What inspires you, what makes you feel alive?
3. Mind: What do you like to think about? What are your deepest beliefs?
4. Strength: What key capabilities and talents do I have?

After answering these questions consider two more:

1. How are you integrating heart, soul, mind, and strength?
2. How might you do more of this?

   (The first four questions are adapted from Clifton and Anderson, 2004.)

INSET 12.9   OVAL MAPPING

Oval mapping is a process that captures a group's shared vision, or "group mind." Visionary leaders can use the process in small-scale forums to define public problems and begin searching for solutions or to provide a framework for action.

The process facilitator guides participants in brainstorming solutions to a problem posed as a question. Participants write their ideas on ovals, or egg-shaped cards (Post-its can be used instead). The ovals are then displayed on a wall and participants cluster them into groups and then work with the clusters to identify goals and priority actions. Here is an outline of the process, which is described more fully in John M. Bryson's book, *Strategic Planning for Public and Nonprofit Organizations* (3rd ed.). San Francisco: Jossey Bass, 2004.

1. The basic requirements are as follows:

---

a group consisting of no more than 12 people (7 is optimal) a facilitator (ideally from outside the group) a large wall	flip chart sheets masking tape black markers pencils with erasers	paper ovals (in yellow or another light color), approximately 7.5" long and 4.5" wide, 20 per person

---

1. The flip chart sheets should be taped together on the wall to make a rectangular backdrop for the ovals. The rectangle should be 4–6 sheets wide and 2–3 sheets high, depending on the size of the group.

2. The facilitator asks each group member to think of solutions or responses to the problem being considered and write those ideas on the ovals, one idea per oval, using the black markers.

The process assumes that participants can read and write the same language. If participants do not, an alternative process would be drawing pictures that represent possible actions. The pictures can be displayed to serve as a visual backdrop for talking about the actions.

For example, if the problem were female illiteracy, the facilitator might pose the question, "What should we do to increase female literacy?"

The facilitator directs the group to express their solutions as imperatives, for example, "Have reading materials with female heroes." The idea should be expressed in no more than 10 words. Group members put a tape roll or other adhesive on the back of their ovals and place them on the flip chart-covered wall when they are finished.

3. The facilitator then leads participants in clustering the ovals according to common themes or subjects. Within the clusters, the more general, abstract, or goal-oriented are moved toward the top and the more concrete, specific, and detailed clusters toward the bottom. The facilitator asks participants to name the clusters and places a new oval with a name above each cluster. (The group may also decide that an existing oval is the cluster title.)

4. The facilitator works with participants to pencil in arrows indicating linkages within and between clusters. An arrow pointing upward from oval A to oval B indicates that the action described on oval A causes, influences, or precedes the action described on B; conversely the action on oval B is an effect, outcome, or follow-up to the action on A. Once the group agrees on the placement of the arrows, they can be drawn in permanently with a marker.

5. The group now has a map of clusters in which specific actions or options are located toward the bottom and more goal-oriented statements toward the top. The facilitator then encourages the group to think further about what they hope to achieve by carrying out the actions on the map. The responses, or "higher" goals can be placed on new ovals at the top of the map, and arrows drawn from ovals that would contribute to those goals.

6. Finally, the group may want to prioritize the actions and goals on the map. The facilitator might give everyone five red dots to place on the five ovals considered most vital. This process can be much more elaborate, but the simple version presented here is adequate for constructing a preliminary vision of what the group should be doing about a problem and why.

The map produced can be preserved as is, translated into an outline, or reproduced using computer graphics. A helpful computer program is Decision Explore produced by Banxia Software (http://www.banxia.com).

Obviously, a one-day workshop even with preliminary and follow-up assignments cannot properly explore integrative leadership. Still, it can convey an overarching framework, examples, and practice that help empower people who otherwise would consider work on complex public problems something that is far beyond their capabilities and something that must be left to the "authorities." The ethos of the workshop is profoundly democratic in the methods used (e.g., attention to each person's capabilities, and participatory mapping), the assumption that responsibility for public problems is everyone's business, and the framework's emphasis on inclusive processes and structures. The framework, however, can apply in a range of political systems, since it emphasizes the importance of connecting to (or possibly circumventing) governmental and nongovernmental policy makers, whether or not they operate in a democratic fashion.

★★★

Whether in online or face-to-face classrooms, leadership educators can draw on a variety of readings, exercises, and art forms to link leadership and citizenship. This chapter presented guidance for helping participants explore the meaning of citizenship and the role of leadership in protecting human rights and inculcating the responsibilities of citizenship. Associated exercises focused on creating public narratives and writing economic and political autobiographies.

The chapter also offered ways to explore the virtues and values that sustain democracy. The virtues typically highlighted in my courses and workshops are fair behavior, respect for differences, tolerance, personal integrity, commitment to the well-being of others, collaboration, and compromise. Finally, this chapter presents exercises and a class plan for practicing integrative leadership—that is, bringing diverse people, organizations, and resources together in sustainable arrangements to tackle complex public problems and achieve the common good.

The next part of this book turns to the practice of assessing leadership (including evaluation of leadership education), along with coaching and mentoring. Ideally, assessing, coaching, and mentoring attend to the other four leadership practices covered so far.

References

Boyte, H. C. (2004). *Everyday politics: Reconnecting citizens and public life.* Philadelphia: University of Pennsylvania Press.

Boyte, H. C. (2015). Creating public value: Contributions of the new civic politics. In J. M. Bryson, B. C. Crosby, & L. Bloomberg (Eds.), *Creating public value in practice: Advancing the common good in a multi-sector, shared-power, no-one-wholly-in-charge world* (pp. 49–66). New York: Taylor & Francis.

Clifton, D. O., & Anderson, E. C. (2004). *Strengths quest: Discover and develop your strengths in academics, career, and beyond.* Washington, DC: The Gallup Organization.

Crosby, B. C., & Bryson, J. M. (2005). *Leadership for the common good: Tackling public problems in a shared-power world* (2nd ed.). San Francisco: Jossey-Bass.

Crosby, B. C., & Bryson, J. M. (2014). Public integrative leadership. In D. V. Day (Ed.), *Oxford handbook of leadership and organizations* (pp. 57–72). Oxford, UK: Oxford.

Evans, S. M., & Boyte, H. C. (1992). *Free spaces.* Chicago: University of Chicago Press.

Ganz, M. (2008). "What is public narrative?" Cambridge, MA: Kennedy School of Government.

Ruscio, K. P. (1999). The connections between democratic theory and leadership theory: The case of public reason. *Selected Proceedings 1999 Annual Meeting, International Leadership Association,* Atlanta, GA.

Schwab, K. (2008). Global corporate citizenship: Working with governments and civil society. *Foreign Affairs, 87*(1), 107–118.

Stone, D. (2012). *Policy paradox: The art of political decision making.* New York: W.W. Norton & Company.

PART V

Assessing, Coaching, Mentoring

These three leadership development practices are linked together because they are all aimed at helping ourselves and others achieve desirable goals—whether it is improving our emotional intelligence, building productive teams, or eradicating malaria. Assessment may be informal, such as completing the leadership highs and lows exercise described in Chapter 3, or formal, such as the Multifactor Leadership Questionnaire or a 360-degree performance assessment. As educators, we are being informally assessed every time we conduct a workshop or class session, and we also use formal assessments to determine to what extent learning objectives are being met and how sessions might be improved.

We may also work with coaches and mentors to interpret assessments of our leadership in and outside of the classroom, and we are likely to provide (or require) coaching and mentoring opportunities for participants in our programs. The work of coaching and mentoring overlaps, but I see coaching as focused on accomplishing a set of specific goals over a relatively short time frame and perhaps limited to a particular project. Mentoring tends to involve more long-term support for the mentee, as well as provision of tacit knowledge about a profession or social systems.

In Chapter 13, the leadership educators featured in this book will describe how we have been coached and mentored and what we have learned about coaching and mentoring. We also note important lessons we have learned about receiving and providing feedback.

Chapter 14 will consider more thoroughly the effectiveness of different assessment methods in leadership development. It also will examine frameworks, theories, and research findings about the role of coaching and mentoring in leadership development.

Chapter 15 will provide practical guidance for incorporating leadership assessments in workshops and courses and for responding to assessments of our own teaching. Additionally, the chapter will present guidance for effective coaching and mentoring in leadership development.

13

ASSESSING, COACHING, MENTORING, AND THE HEART

The aim of assessment in leadership development is less about checking on how well participants in courses or workshops are able to regurgitate theories and research findings and more about assisting participants in closing the gap between their existing and desired leadership capabilities. It is a process of providing feedback on participants' progress in applying theories, concepts, and practical guidance in their own workplaces and communities. In a for-credit course, the process will include graded assignments. Whether or not grades are involved, the most effective feedback processes will be developmental, which is where coaching and mentoring come in. Coaches and mentors help leadership learners make sense of feedback contained in assessments (including the coaches' and mentors' observations) and decide how to use that feedback in reaching developmental goals.

In this chapter, my colleagues and I first describe the ways that we have been coached and mentored and how we incorporate coaching into our courses and workshops. We offer examples of our best and worst experiences as mentors and offer some lessons based on those experiences. Finally, we reflect on the feedback process as a fundamental part of coaching and mentoring.

Being Coached and Mentored

My colleagues and I have been coached and mentored by many types of people—family members, high school and college teachers, spiritual guides, scout leaders, colleagues, supervisors, students, and actual executive coaches. In the first chapter of this book, Lars Leafblad and Gill Hickman acknowledged the role modeling (a form of mentoring) provided by their mothers. Spouses have also mentored and coached. Long ago, I was severely challenged by the high-pressure environment within the governor's office where I worked. I often faced the workday with anxiety and a certain amount of dread that threatened to overwhelm my enthusiasm for being at the center of government. My husband continually reminded me that I had the intelligence and skill to succeed there. In our subsequent academic careers he and I have often mentored each other. Sonia Ospina says, "My husband is a great mentor. I have gaps in the history, geography, language of this country. He was also an academic before I was. Now he asks me for advice about academic matters. We help each other."

Georgia Sorenson mentioned a high school teacher "who thought I could write well" and a Zen teacher, in addition to James MacGregor Burns. Rick Morse cited Gary Bryner, his undergraduate faculty adviser, "who spent a lot of his life advocating for environmental causes." This professor was Morse's mentor throughout his public policy studies at Brigham Young University. Later, another professor would help him decide to pursue a Ph.D.

Colleagues were important for several of us. Gill Hickman turned to her much older, white male supervisor when she was a young woman who had just begun working in the central office of the California state college system. She also acquired a second mentor, a black woman who had recently left the office. "I introduced myself because people had said good things about her."

Gill Hickman was 26 when she came to the central office for California state colleges. The head of the office was a 64-year-old white man. "People were terrified of him. He was one of those people who ruled with an iron hand in a lot of ways. When I got into the Ph.D. program, I realized it was full-time. I took this guy to lunch. I said, 'I love my job, but I can't stay if I can't get flexibility.' He became my mentor. He said, 'I've been hoping somebody would want to do this and I can be your mentor.'" The man introduced her to high-level meetings and sent her to conferences. "He and his number two person threw me a huge graduation party. By the time I went to my first director position, I was so well prepared."

Sonia Ospina was mentored by two colleagues at New York University (NYU). "Early on I had no idea what I was doing and I was feeling very isolated. I didn't understand my colleagues." An older faculty member invited Ospina and her husband to her home, where the woman talked with Ospina about her work. "When she died," Ospina says, "I realized how much I valued her. This leads me to be more generous with my time." The second NYU mentor was Ellen Schall, who had been a public administrator before joining the faculty. "We became good friends. Whenever I have an issue I can go to her. We understand that we each have different strengths." Ospina was able to mentor Schall regarding academic life and Schall offered insight about the world of practice.

Rick Morse was mentored by Kurt Thurmaier, the professor who hired him at Iowa State. "Even after I left, he has continued to be a mentor. He modeled the way, not just teaching about public issues, but being engaged as a community leader." Like Ospina, Morse was also mentored by someone who had been a top public administrator before coming to academia. "He took me under his wing. We did projects with citizen engagement; he showed me how to lead."

My own most significant mentor was Robert Terry, who welcomed me into the intellectual quest to build more satisfying frameworks for leadership education. He gave me opportunities to test my teaching wings as well. Other people have provided more short-term professional mentoring—from the crusty city editor in my first reporting job to a veteran speechwriter in the Minnesota governor's office. Usually, mentors have been a least a decade older than I, but I also have been mentored by younger co-teachers. I think especially of a fellow instructor in the leadership minor at the University of Minnesota. I observed how she enlivened the classroom and focused directly on undergraduates' interests and concerns, something I hadn't had to do previously because I had mainly taught midcareer students.

Like Gill Hickman, Lars Leafblad didn't wait for mentors to seek him out. He said, "If I were to draw a chart of my career, there would be a mentor linked to every stage. I've benefited greatly from the wisdom and acumen of a wide range of people I've reached out to. Many have said they were absolutely willing to help. Many have been sounding boards." Leafblad also recently turned to an executive coach to provide guidance as he went through a professional transition. Likewise, Sonia Ospina began working with a coach as she was winding down the leadership center that she had built and nurtured over a decade. The experience, she said was "terribly helpful. It allowed me to articulate my concerns in a way that another person can understand." As someone not involved in Ospina's professional and personal circles, the person could be a more objective guide, someone who wasn't invested in particular outcomes.

For the first time in my life when I was at the Bush Foundation, I worked with an executive coach. We had formal monthly sessions. Mentors are more personal. There's an ebb and flow, wisdom extended when asked for. A coach holds you accountable.

I decided to drink the medicine I'd been espousing. [The search firm where he worked before coming to Bush had provided the candidates they placed a leadership coach for the first 90 days in their new job.] I was leading a team larger than I'd ever led and adjusting to the transition from being an owner operator to being a staff member of a large organization.

—Lars Leafblad

Providing Coaching and Mentoring for Others

Several of us incorporate individual coaching into our courses and workshops. In the community leadership program that Valerie Shangreaux directs, each participant meets with a leadership coach for 90 minutes to talk about his/her learning, MBTI results, and the participant's work. "People get a lot out of that," says Shangreaux. Bob Denhardt coaches individual participants in his courses about needed improvements in their leadership skills. "I might say, Brian, you talk too much. Morgan, you don't talk enough. You're a bright guy, get your ideas out there. In one course a woman was extremely shy and nervous about public speaking. She started Toastmasters and by end of semester did a great job." Brad Jackson offers an entire class aimed at coaching participants in their leadership practice. "In our leadership class we got people pumped up and realized we needed to support them afterward. So we created a coaching class right after the leadership class."

In the leadership course for people beginning the midcareer master's program at the Humphrey School, we offer face-to-face faculty coaching sessions for participants as they design and carry out an Action Learning Project. The project must be explicitly designed to develop their leadership skills. As coaches, the faculty help participants clarify what skills they want to develop in a context in which they are uniquely able to exercise leadership. We help them set goals and check their progress through follow-up meetings, online reports, and other communication. In her integrative leadership course, Kathy Quick has tried peer coaching, but feels a need to make it more effective. The coaching vignettes in Inset 13.1 describe several typical scenarios I have encountered in coaching sessions incorporated in my leadership courses. While typical, these are fictionalized accounts, and student descriptions have been altered to protect their privacy.

INSET 13.1   COACHING VIGNETTES

In coaching sessions, my questions will be designed to elicit information about a person's strengths, areas of desired development, and the context for leading. In most cases, I seek to increase the person's sense of self-efficacy and potential. Occasionally, I might try to rein in someone's conviction that he or she is the most competent person in every context. Here are five vignettes that illustrate how I adapt my coaching approach to different types of participants.

The Eager Leader

A man comes to the coaching session and within minutes has repeated at least five times, "I want to be a leader." I let him know that aspiration is great and say I want to learn more about his experience and what he wants to lead about. Then I say, "First, however, please tell me what insights you gained from the leadership assessments you have done either in our course or previously." We talk about the strengths that emerge from those assessments—perseverance, resilience, a supportive spouse. Then I ask about his experience, though some details have already emerged in talking about the assessments. "Now," I say, "tell me more about the context in which you want to lead at this time. Who is involved?" After that we explore additional questions: "What goals do you want to accomplish? How will this build on your strengths, possibly develop them further, and add new skills to your portfolio? What benchmarks will you set for yourself?" I may offer some resources—for example, contacts or readings—that I think will be helpful as he works on his goals and we agree that he will provide reports about his progress at different points in the semester.

The Reluctant Leader

A woman comes to the coaching session and says, "I'm not sure I want to be a leader, but my company is going through a huge change and I think I have good ideas for what we should do next. It's really a scary time because a new CEO has been hired with a mandate for change and that is going to require laying off some good people. She is interviewing all of the long-term managers (including me) one at a time, and I have to meet with her soon. How can I present my ideas and have some impact?" I ask her to tell me more about how she sees the future of the organization and how her skills contribute to that. I reflect back to her that her passion and competence really shine through her account. She agrees to rehearse for the meeting so that her new boss will also see her commitment to the organization, know a bit about her previous contributions, and understand her ideas for renewing the organization's mission.

A week later, the woman reports back that she has met with the new CEO and it went so well that the CEO is asking her to head up a team that will work on redesigning a major part of the organization. "Now what do I do?" she says. "I know this will mean eliminating the jobs of several good friends. What if I fail? I don't really like the limelight." We agree that she will bring her dilemma to the next face-to-face session of our class.

At the class session, she gives some background of her work situation, her opportunity to lead, and openly describes her fears and worries. Class members ask questions and offer new ideas for her discernment process. "What really excites you about this possibility?" is a typical question. "What would you feel like if you pass up this opportunity?" causes her to pause and think. "How could you ensure that the lay-off process is fair and humane?" The probing is serious and at times humorous.

Ultimately, the student chooses to accept the new assignment. When she reports her decision and thanks everyone for listening to her case, class members applaud and wish her a successful outcome.

Thwarted Leaders

An energetic man with a winning smile tells me that our leadership course supplies him with great ideas and appealing methods for helping people tackle organizational and community challenges. "It's all wonderful," he says, "but none of it would work in my organization. Nobody wants to change. The culture is all about doing things the way we always have, complying with the rules, not rocking the boat." So I could simply advise this man to find other leadership venues that would be more receptive to change. Instead I ask questions about the man's history in the organization and what he would like to change. I suggest that he do some fact-finding to check out his assumptions about his co-workers. "Maybe," I say, "you will surprise yourself by finding potential allies there."

I tell him a personal story about a time when I found myself in a somewhat similar situation. Working in a governor's press office, I was really stimulated by being at the heart of the policy-making process, learning about the inner workings of government, and interacting with veteran Capitol reporters. At the same time, I hated the frenzied, often harsh atmosphere in which we worked. I could see lots of ways in which we could be more efficient, less frenzied, and more humane. Everybody else in the governor's office just seemed to take the conditions for granted, but gradually my frustration led me to talk to others at my level. I learned that they were as frustrated and had their own good ideas about how to improve our environment.

Finally, I summoned the courage to speak to my own supervisor and one or two other senior staff. For the most part, these men had no idea that so many midlevel staff (mostly women) were unhappy. They expressed willingness to consider some of the ideas we had for improvement. A big change in the press office was that the entire staff agreed to start going out for Friday lunch and planning the week ahead—an innovation that created a friendlier atmosphere and reduced frenzy.

So, I say to my student, "I have learned to find out more about the barriers that I see between me and my goals." We identify three of his colleagues who seem more receptive than others to change and we agree that he will find time in the next two weeks to meet with them and get a more accurate idea of the potential for instigating change in the organization.

In another coaching session, a woman says I know I have a lot to offer, but I think sometimes people don't take my ideas seriously because of my ethnicity. I ask her to tell me more about her specific experiences. I acknowledge the demoralizing effects of suspecting one is being judged unfairly. I encourage her to brainstorm ways that she could counter those judgments, but I also remind her of the usefulness of assembling "exit cards," as we have discussed in class. She agrees to create three exit cards that offer alternative paths for having more impact in an organization or her community.

The Disillusioned Leader

In our coaching session, a student tells me he has been mainly a hands-on dad for several years, but has come to graduate school because he is starting to feel ready to provide leadership in his community. Still, he remembers the bad experiences he had in his early career, which left him disillusioned about public service. I ask him about the leadership strengths that have emerged in the assessments we have done so far, and urge him to talk more about why he feels ready to lead at this point. He talks about the strength of his belief in democratic politics and about the connections he has made as he worked on various community change projects in recent years. We consider possibilities for building on those connections and using the tools he is acquiring in the course to become a more effective change agent and counter his remaining cynicism. He makes a plan for acquiring a mentor who knows the community networks well and has been successful in building coalitions for change.

The Overwhelmed Leaders

I have encountered these people among undergraduates as well as graduate students. They come to our coaching sessions complaining that they simply have agreed to too many leadership responsibilities or they have several competing commitments that keep them from doing a good job at any one. As I ask them to describe their situation further, they may reveal that they simply don't trust that someone else can do the leadership tasks they have taken on. They may have a hard time saying no. They may be doing some things mainly to keep their scholarship or earn money and then agreeing to too many more attractive responsibilities.

In our sessions, I might reflect back to the person what I hear him saying about the ill effects of having too many responsibilities. I might ask him what would happen if he decided to devote his energies to only one or two of the competing commitments. If that exploration causes him to brighten up, I encourage him to lay plans for shedding the things that are least appealing and giving more energy to one or two of the things that remain.

Because our courses and workshops typically last no more than a semester, we are usually unable to serve as a full-blown mentor to participants. More likely we provide mentoring for colleagues and graduate students. Sonia Ospina says, "Where I've done the best mentoring is with doctoral students, helping them feel they're not alone, that they have an ally and resource they can use. They can be vulnerable."

When I was a brand-new faculty member I got a grant to work with communities in Iowa around citizen engagement. I had a couple of grad students who were very different in talent and dispositions. I saw them both blossom. I gave them responsibilities, opportunities to facilitate public meetings, etc. Both went on to good careers. It's gratifying to play a tiny role in developing these students.

—Rick Morse

Chuck Palus says his best mentoring experience has been with an African colleague in the Leadership Beyond Boundaries program. Even though they are usually on different continents, they have frequent email communication to the point that the colleague told Palus, "It feels like you're in my head all the time." Palus said, "We're deeply collaborative about a lot of things. He's taken some of the things I've written and used them. The idea that I'm one of the voices in your head—it's funny. He says it's okay."

Gill Hickman says, "I love mentoring my students and other people as an administrator. It's a privilege to give back." She remembers a couple of mentees in particular. One was the daughter of an administrator on campus. "Her mother said, 'I'm turning my daughter over to you.' We developed a close bond and mentorship. She pursued a double major in leadership studies and pre-med. Her mother said I'd ruined her. Now she wanted to be a do-gooder. Today she heads a nonprofit focused on infertility and adoption." The second mentee was an African American student that she spotted standing with his parents in the corner of a room on parents weekend. "I said, 'I haven't met you—I want you in my office in the next week.' The parents smiled. He was from a privileged background, but not doing well. . . . He came with a lot of baggage. He had been in private schools and was trying to fit in. I said, 'You're a lot like me. You're very privileged like me. You have a responsibility to do something.' He continued to come to my office. We pushed till he graduated. He went for a year to Hungary to teach and the next thing I know he's teaching in Saudi Arabia. Now he has a great job in D.C. It brings me joy when I see him."

Georgia Sorenson has found that mentees can become colleagues and even mentors themselves. She notes James (Jim) MacGregor Burns's argument that leaders become transformational in response to their followers. She says, "I know I'm a much better person because of students. I want to be thoughtful because I know they're watching. I don't want to fail in their eyes. Jim and I became colleagues and that taught me students and teachers can become colleagues." She often remains involved in her students' lives after they leave her campus.

Not all of our experiences with mentoring have been positive. Sometimes we are approached by people who would like us to be a mentor, but we know that we aren't the best fit for them, or as Gill Hickman found out once, we may be assigned a mentee who isn't ready. As part of a campus mentorship program she was asked to mentor a young black male student. "I had to hunt him down. We had a few meetings. I couldn't get to the heart of who he was. I tried to let him know somebody cared about him, but he was very closed down."

Sonia Ospina regrets that she has had little time to develop mentoring relationships with master's students in her department. Partly that was due to the structure of their program, but also to the demands of the promotion process she was going through. She plans to do more now.

Lars Leafblad watched a former mentor succumb to early onset dementia. "He was a very successful entrepreneurial type. Our correspondence decreased over the years. We had a final mentor-mentee lunch. His mind was clearly not whole, and it was painful that he could no longer recall our shared story."

Drawing Lessons From Our Experiences

Our experience with mentoring and being mentored gives us several insights into acquiring and working with mentors. Gill Hickman sees value in obtaining at least one mentor who is like you and one who is quite different. Georgia Sorenson recommends finding multiple mentors, since no single mentor "can provide everything you need." Lars Leafblad advises young professionals to find mentors in civic engagement and turn to coaches as needed. Recruiting mentors and coaches "can never be too early. It doesn't have to be a crisis. The idea is to help your professional and civic self achieve full potential." Sonia Ospina counsels leadership educators to "be active in terms of finding mentors and mentoring others." She would like more recognition of the value of mentoring in university pay and performance guidelines.

Georgia Sorenson has found that in good mentoring relationships, the exchange of support and guidance begins to equalize over time. "There's benefit for both sides." She also warns against relying on mentors to deal with the kinds of challenges that are best dealt with in therapy or personal introspection. "You have to do your own work."

Chuck Palus and Sonia Ospina offer additional advice about how to be a good mentor. "The best mentoring you can do is to be yourself," says Palus. "Do not hold yourself up as the best example, but claim your territory." Ospina adds: "It's not all about I know best. It's about being a companion on the journey. Over time, over the long run, lots of conversations can help people see and trust they can get to the other side of whatever challenges or difficulties they are facing."

Using Assessment and Feedback in Leadership Development

I must admit that I've never really liked the term feedback. Maybe it sounds a little too close to "feedbat" to me. At least in my early years as a professional, whenever someone said to me that he was going to give me some feedback I knew I was on the way to getting beat up over something I had done wrong. Since then I've learned to view feedback as a more neutral term, and even potentially very beneficial. Crucially, I have learned that some means of giving and receiving feedback are more effective than others, and I have learned to ask for feedback in forms that I can best absorb. I remember very early in my leadership teaching career concluding a seminar and sitting down with colleagues to debrief the experience. The most senior person in the group made fun of a habitual nervous gesture I made during my presentations, and I felt a hot surge of shame. Later, I went to this person to say, please give me feedback in a more constructive way. Tell me what you think I've done well, and then how I might improve. In this way I won't feel shamed and defensive and will be better able to absorb recommendations for improvement.

Lars Leafblad urges everyone to be willing to ask for feedback, though he acknowledges that people may fear it will illuminate their weaknesses. He counsels: "Think of feedback as data that informs how you might make a decision or alter your course of action." He asks people if they are open to his feedback before providing it. He also recognizes that giving honest feedback is a bit countercultural in Minnesota. "I need to continue to seek, hear, and share feedback in my ongoing personal development."

> *In giving feedback, I try to always start with something I appreciate so the person can open up. I try to be careful about wording so it comes from more generous place. I may try to speak from my most generous self rather than my most judgmental self. I realize feedback threatens one's sense of competence. I try to not be defensive and try not to make others defensive.*
>
> —Sonia Ospina

Tracey Manning advises, "Be as vulnerable as you can. Be open to feedback but with high confidence that you can be a facilitator of learning. This is not the idea that students run the whole thing and you abdicate. It's a juggling act."

Feedback may be useful both when it contradicts how you see your actions and when it reinforces your own view, says Ospina. When she receives insights that are very different from what she expected, she reads and thinks about them. She asks, "What does this mean for what I need to do next?" When the feedback validates her views, it "helps me be grounded, helps me get more ideas. I feel more competent."

Like many of us, Yvonne Cheek elicits feedback in a number of ways. She says, "Sometimes I do evaluation or quick feedback forms. Other times I just ask people at the end of a meeting, What worked well? What surprised you? I have also asked people indirectly about how they feel when I'm leading a learning event." She has had to self-consciously manage her reaction to the resulting responses. "My initial reaction might be, Oh no, that's not me."

That can be true whether the response is complimentary or critical. She has learned to move beyond the initial reaction and own the behavior that is being reflected back to her. "Maybe I tweak my style. Maybe I say this is an extraordinary compliment and realize I need to drink it in."

As noted in Chapter 7, Brad Jackson continually seeks feedback about the level of tension in the class. "I want to know is there enough tension, too much tension. I say to the class, if you are feeling really content, and have it all sorted out, I've done a lousy job."

As leadership educators, we seek feedback not only on our own style and conduct in virtual and face-to-face classrooms, but on the design of our courses and workshops. Ideally, we have a systematic way of collecting and analyzing responses, so that we can note patterns and avoid reacting to the one participant who is very unhappy or the one who has heaped extravagant praise on the course. Also useful is remembering that every iteration of a course or workshop will be distinctive because a new group of people will participate in a new time in local and world events. We should avoid the temptation to redesign the instructional experience so that it perfectly fits the last group of participants!

We may benefit from having more than one means of collecting systematic feedback about courses and workshops. For example, in addition to formal evaluations we may keep a teaching journal in which we keep track of key events, trends, or dilemmas in the classroom. In the journal we may also record our reactions to those things. We can review the journal periodically to discern patterns in our practice or consider changes in course or workshop design. The quality of projects carried out by participants can supply information about teaching success. Valerie Shangreaux's community leadership program conducts alumni surveys and other forms of assessment to discern the program's lasting effects and gather ideas about how to improve the program.

> Just recently I was in a community having a listening session. I asked alumni and others, What do you love about your community? One woman said, "I have to tell about my cohort [in the Blandin community leadership program]." She was fairly new to the community. She was an emerging leader when she came to our program. Shortly after, she found herself as a single mom. She said she had to think deeply about whether to stay in the community or move to be near her parents. It was the cohort that surrounded her and said if you stay we will support you.
>
> —Valerie Shangreaux

Giving Regular Feedback to Participants in Our Courses and Workshops

Many of the exercises described in earlier chapters provide feedback to participants about their mastery of certain leadership skills and their progress in their leadership journey. Monty Van Wart's Leadership Action Cycle demonstrates how assessment can be a spur to continuous leadership learning.

My personal framework is the Leadership Action Cycle, which starts with assessment, takes account of traits and basic skills, seeks to expand one's style range, and reviews the ranges of behaviors one needs in getting things done, working through people, and making sure that systems are in alignment. Of course, it ends with figuring out how well you are doing, what you need to be better at, which leads you back to the beginning of the cycle—assessment.

—Montgomery Van Wart

In our for-credit courses, grading is a regular way that we give feedback. It can also be a cause of considerable fear and loathing, both on the part of instructors and students. For instructors the process can be time-consuming and boring; for students it can be a game of trying to figure out what an instructor wants and coping with anxieties about measuring up. Fortunately, leadership educators have ways to reduce the fear and loathing that accompanies grading. Assignments do not have to be boring, and we can manage the time we devote to the process. To alleviate student anxieties, we can establish transparent criteria for grading and provide clear feedback, as well as opportunities, for improvement.

Still, grading may always be an uncomfortable process. Leadership courses that aim to improve participants' self-awareness, capacity for deep reflection, and impact within their teams, organizations, and communities do not lend themselves to multiple-choice exams. As instructors we are always making subjective evaluations of student reflections, progress reports, reading analyses, presentations, and other products. We may supplement our evaluations with feedback from others; we may require peer evaluations of some assignments, ask team members to assess the contributions of each other, or consider feedback from outside participants in student projects. Ultimately, however, we make grading decisions, and that gives us a good deal of power, since grades are the currency of the academic system.

I advocate developing a philosophy of grading. Here is mine: My job is to use the grading process to help students become more self-aware, more confident in exercising leadership skills, more attuned to multiple perspectives, and better equipped to handle the leadership challenges that confront them now and in the future. I want to help everyone obtain A's in my courses, and the corollary is that I must clearly mark out the path to receiving an A and coach students along the path. At the same time, not everyone will receive an A; some students by choice or lack of ability will simply not demonstrate the levels of skill or analysis that I require. I rarely give A+'s.

When Monty Van Wart reviews assignments and does not see "comments that demonstrate real management insights and genuine intent to improve their leadership and management competencies," he concludes, "I am not doing my job. The challenge of teaching leadership is that people are interested in learning about different things, and ready for different deep learning insights. That means that I must craft my assignments in such a way that people have flexibility to learn what they need to learn for the level and situation that they are at."

I recognize this view is counter to the idea that higher education should serve as a winnowing machine that separates the top students from everybody else. Perhaps because I teach in a land-grant university I have been infected by the notion that I should help every student strive for excellence and that most of them can rise to high standards. I have sat through many a faculty meeting in which yet another colleague bemoans rampant "grade inflation" in higher education. For the most part, these conversations seem to be a waste of time. Of course, instructors should not be "dumbing down" standards so that everyone can make high grades. What I question is some assumptions lurking in the grade inflation debate: chiefly, that abilities follow a bell-curve distribution and that good instructors will ensure that grades match the bell curve.

Students deserve to know what our philosophy of grading is and what criteria we will use to assess their performance. When we make our philosophy and criteria clear and provide developmental feedback, students are more likely to consider the grading system fair and beneficial rather than a necessary evil. Typically, I will take time early in a course to discuss my grading approach and directly acknowledge the power differential that is inherent in the process. While I emphasize my commitment to helping students improve their leadership practice, I also remind them that they are responsible for their own learning (something Georgia Sorenson does as well).

Because I am firmly convinced that clear and persuasive communication is a vital leadership skill, I give special attention to how well students convey their ideas orally, visually, or in writing. Partly because of my editing background I habitually give detailed feedback on written assignments. At a high level, I focus on the organization of material: In formal essays or reports, is the writer providing a helpful overview or roadmap early on? Are ideas presented clearly and coherently? Do topic sentences adequately convey the focus of a paragraph? Are transitions between sentences, paragraphs, or sections adequate? Are examples and evidence provided? Does the language hold my attention, is it vivid, is it apt? Are appropriate conclusions drawn and summaries provided? At a finer level, when I have time I will highlight grammatical or formatting mistakes that are likely to detract from the ease of reading or credibility of the document. When I see that someone needs more assistance than I can provide, I recommend a writing coach.

For oral presentations, I provide feedback about "stickiness" of the key ideas, time keeping, audience engagement, and nonverbal signals. Did you capture audience attention with stories and vivid images? Did you appeal to the emotions? Did you convey with words, body language, or visual aids that you care about the topic? Did you provide support for your argument? In what ways did you engage the audience? Were your conclusions clear? What would improve the presentation? When participants make presentations in face-to-face sessions, I often distribute a feedback sheet to all audience members, so they too can identify strengths and possible improvements in the presentation.

Often my course websites suggest resources like Strunk and White's venerable *Elements of Style* (1999). I frequently post the explanation entitled "Why I Scribble on Your Papers" (see Inset 3.7). Of course, these days I am more likely to provide feedback in "track changes" and insert comments on Word documents than I am to scribble on actual copies.

Preparing Coaches and Mentors

In my courses and workshops I often assert that a high calling for leaders is the development of others' leadership potential. I encourage them to use concepts and tools that have been introduced earlier in this book and I provide suggestions (as I also have done in the "hands" chapters) about how to introduce the concepts and use the tools most effectively.

Where feasible I also offer guidance for being a good coach and mentor to those engaged in leadership development. Some of that guidance has already been presented in this chapter, but I will pull it together here. First of all, convey your authentic interest in the other person's development through inquiry and attentive listening. Demonstrate vulnerability and trust to encourage the same in him or her. Assist the person in gathering and reflecting on feedback on his/her leadership via formal and informal assessments. Help her/him set goals and arrange ways to report on progress. Ask how the person prefers to receive your feedback. If you are able to have a longer-term mentor relationship, actively connect the person to networks and opportunities to which you have access. Publicly recognize his or her achievements.

★★★

The practice of assessing, coaching, and mentoring is probably the most delicate work that leadership educators do. If our aim is to help individuals become more adept in applying their unique talents to the leadership challenges they confront, we will employ our expertise, not so much as judges of performance levels, but as partners in a mutual endeavor. We will give undivided attention, we will inquire, we will acknowledge pain and resistance, we will offer realistic hope and point to alternative possibilities, and we will suggest helpful resources.

This chapter has considered the multiple ways that leadership educators have been coached and mentored in our work and how we have coached and mentored others. We talk about some difficulties with mentoring and we offer advice for securing mentors and being a good one. The chapter has given extensive consideration to the assessment, or feedback, process that underlies coaching and mentoring. Leadership educators explain how we use feedback to improve our teaching as well as instructional design. We talk about using feedback to help participants achieve their learning and leadership goals. Grading is an especially sensitive type of feedback that we provide as part of for-credit instruction, and we should develop explicit philosophy and criteria doing it. I describe my own grading philosophy and explain how I provide feedback on written and oral assignments. Finally, the chapter emphasizes the importance of helping participants in our courses and workshops become good coaches and mentors themselves.

The next chapter will consider theory and research about the practice of assessing, coaching, and mentoring for leadership development. We will learn more about how to gear this practice to different individuals and groups.

Reference

Strunk Jr., W., & White, E. B. (1999). *The elements of style* (4th ed.). New York: Longman.

14

ASSESSING, COACHING, MENTORING, AND THE HEAD

Leadership assessment methods and instruments (many of which have been introduced in earlier chapters) abound. As leadership educators, which ones we choose will be based on what aspect of leadership we want to develop and how useful the assessments have proven to be. Fortunately, a good deal of research now exists about the best use of the assessments, and—for the formal instruments—extensive reporting of their validity and reliability is available. Researchers also offer findings about the best ways of assessing the effectiveness of leadership education itself. This chapter will examine research on the effectiveness and usefulness of the assessment methods that can be incorporated into coaching and mentoring for leadership development.

Certainly coaching, which relies on formal and informal assessment, has received considerable attention by popular and scholarly writers. This chapter will present insights from coaching practitioners and findings about the use of feedback in fostering leadership development. Beginning with the appearance of Mentor in the *Odyssey*, writers and researchers also have probed the role of mentors in developing a person's capabilities and courage to change. This chapter will report research findings pertinent to the mentor-mentee relationship in leadership development.

Assessing Leadership Assessments

Both informal and formal assessments can give leadership educators and those we teach valuable insights about personal, team, organizational, and societal leadership. Informal modes include observation and reflection, journaling, storytelling, therapy and personal growth programs, informal conversations, reading fiction and nonfiction, attending plays or other performances, watching films, and consulting research studies. I have described several examples (such as the leadership highs and lows exercise and Narrative of Commitment) in the previous chapters.

Formal assessments are of two types—those that are overtly about leadership and those that can be used in leadership development even if they don't present themselves explicitly as serving that purpose. The Myers-Briggs Type Indicator is a prime example of the second type, and I will give some attention here to the research on its validity and reliability. Numerous formal leadership assessments, frequently focused on organizational leadership, are available; some, however, have a much more solid grounding in leadership theory and have been more thoroughly validated than others. In this category, the Multifactor Leadership Questionnaire (MLQ) is exemplary.

MBTI

I have highlighted the usefulness of Myers-Briggs for leadership development in Chapter 3. Crucially, it promotes awareness of how personal orientation to the world and habitual ways of understanding and judging events in the world can affect our communication and collaboration with others, clearly a fundamental aspect of leadership practice. CPP (formerly Consulting Psychologists Press) is the publisher of this instrument and offers extensive information on the MBTI's reliability and validity. (See https://www.cpp.com/Products/mbti/mbti_info.aspx.) Additional research backing and discussion of the instrument's ethical use is available through the Center for Applications of Psychological Type (CAPT), established by Isabel Briggs Myers and Mary McCauley, a psychologist and academic. For example, CAPT reports that MBTI reliability scores are "quite good across age and ethnic groups, although reliabilities on some scales with some groups may be somewhat lower. The T-F scale tends to have the lowest reliability of the four scales." The center has several publications that report extensively on the MBTI's reliability and validity (http://www.capt.org/mbti-assessment/reliability-validity. htm). The center also provides a detailed "Code of Ethics: For using the MBTI." For example, administrators of the instrument are to provide results "in a way that is personal and allows for questions, clarification and interaction with the respondent" and "use terms and descriptors that are nonjudgmental and describe type attributes as tendencies, preferences, or inclinations rather than as absolutes" (http://www.capt.org/mbti-assessment/ethical-use.htm).

Critiques of the MBTI often focus on its misuse. For a fairly balanced consideration, see John Lloyd's (2012) article "The Myers-Briggs Type Indicator® and Mainstream Psychology: Analysis and Evaluation of an Unresolved Hostility."

Other Assessments Not Focused Explicitly on Leadership

In Chapter 2, I introduce assessments designed to reveal the strengths of various personality traits and intelligences linked to leadership. I recommend these assessments because the purveyors make clear the theories and research behind them and usually note their limitations. Similarly, in Chapter 6 I recommend the Intercultural Development Inventory, which is taken as part of training aimed at assessing and developing one's skills in navigating cultural differences. A similar assessment is the Intercultural Effectiveness Scale developed by the Kozai Group (http://www.intercultural.org/kozai.php). I also have frequently used the Thomas-Kilmann Conflict Mode Instrument, which has the shortcoming of relying on self-report, though the creators attempted to reduce "socially desirable response bias" in constructing it (http://www.kilmanndiagnostics.com/catalog/thomas-kilmann-conflict-mode-instrument).

MLQ

The Multifactor Leadership Questionnaire (MLQ) is based on the "full-range" leadership framework developed by Bernard Bass and Bruce Avolio (see Chapter 8). It is one of several leadership assessment tools sold by Mindgarden (http://www.mindgarden.com/46-leadership). Extensive information about the theory and administration of the instrument and its validity is published in the *Multifactor Leadership Questionnaire Manual* (http://www.mindgarden.com/multifactor-leadership-questionnaire/238-mlq-manual.html). The MLQ assesses leadership behaviors and outcomes in one's work life and is most accurate in its 360-degree version (that is, a combination of self, peer, supervisor, and supervisee reports). The report of a person's results includes information about effective leadership behaviors (based on reviews of leadership studies) and guidance about how one might improve in each behavioral area. The "Actual versus Ought" version of the MLQ is useful when a 360-degree assessment is not feasible. In this version, an individual assesses his/her own transformational, transactional, and passive/avoidant leadership behaviors, and rates his/her ideal leader on the same behaviors. The report of a person's results then reveals the gap between his/her ideal behaviors and actual practice (or at least, what s/he thinks that practice is). Mindgarden also offers a team version of the MLQ (http://www.mindgarden.com/149-team-multifactor-leadership-questionnaire).

A major strength of the MLQ is that it is based on a well-articulated leadership framework and has been thoroughly tested. Its limitations include its incorporation of a fairly hierarchical (and business-oriented) view of organizations and a minimalist version of leadership outcomes: extra effort on the part of followers; individual, unit, and organizational effectiveness; and followers' satisfaction with their leader.

Other 360-Degree or Multi-Rater Instruments

The Center for Creative Leadership offers several 360-degree assessments (http://www.ccl.org/leadership/assessments/assessment360.aspx), including the Global6, designed for use in different global contexts. Global6 emphasizes the leadership dimensions derived from the GLOBE study (see Chapter 5) and provides helpful feedback for people who must lead across national boundaries.

As with the MLQ, other multi-rater leadership assessments are usually intended to be used in particular organizational contexts. Manuel London, James Smither, and Thomas Diamante (2007) offer guidance for constructing an organization-specific 360 leadership assessment that would focus on leader characteristics and behavior tied to the organization's needs. They outline a comprehensive process (including structured interviews and other methods in addition to 360 surveys) designed for recruiting and developing senior organizational leaders. I use the London, Smither, and Diamante chapter in my short course on leadership capacity assessment because it demonstrates how 360-degree assessment can be used in the organizational context and it highlights some of the limitations of such assessments (see Inset 14.1).

INSET 14.1   SOME LIMITATIONS OF 360-DEGREE LEADERSHIP ASSESSMENTS

Manuel London, James Smither, and Thomas Diamante (2007) note, "The popularity of 360 feedback has led some organizations to implement it haphazardly without adequate development, explanation of its purpose, or involvement of raters and ratees in writing items and formulating the administration and feedback process. . . . Human resource experts argue that multisource feedback should be used for development alone, not for administrative decisions, such as compensation or promotion." London, Smither, and Diamante point to the likelihood of rater bias and insist that 360-degree feedback "should be viewed as part of a long-term performance management process, not a one-time event. The results should be used to set goals for performance improvement, and development, perhaps in consultation with an executive coach or discussions with one's supervisor or other coworkers" (59).

Another limitation of multi-rater leadership assessments is the cost of investing in either off-the-shelf or customized instruments and accompanying feedback processes. Especially in small organizations, the anonymity of raters will be hard to preserve.

Robin Ely, Herminia Ibarra, and Deborah Kolb (2011) have found that 360-degree feedback can be especially useful for participants in women's leadership development programs. One reason, they note, is that "women tend to receive less—and less candid—feedback than men" (480). A 360-degree assessment can provide often surprising feedback that reveals how different groups (supervisors, peers, and supervisees) see their performance. Working with peers and coaches in a women's leadership program, participants can think about the role of stereotypes and contradictory expectations in shaping the ratings and develop action plans for altering raters' perceptions. "The contradictory feedback can leave women puzzling over how to strike just the right balance between two seemingly opposing styles; being told to soften a hard-charging style that has heretofore been effective can be heard as a charge to be more feminine." In conversation with peers and coaches, these women can "consider how they may have implicitly bought into the culture's dominant construction of leadership by choosing 'competence' in the competence-likability tradeoff and to see how advancing their leadership goals often requires relational skills as well" (481).

The Peculiar Form of Assessment Known as Grading

As noted in the previous chapter, part of the assessment in for-credit courses occurs via graded assignments. While grading has a certain taken-for-granted quality in higher education, leadership educators have an obligation to match our grading system to our understanding of the leadership learning process. We are not in the business of certifying the leadership of participants in our courses, but rather assessing the extent to which participants have acquired or demonstrated certain knowledge, self-awareness, new perspectives, skills, and behaviors (Van Velsor, 1998). We construct assignments that we will judge on the basis of criteria associated with each of these elements. For example, I might assign a reflective essay on participants' experience practicing conflict management in their workplaces. The assignment includes the following criteria for grading:

- demonstrates knowledge of the Thomas-Kilmann framework and other conflict management guidance presented in class (knowledge)
- shows awareness of own thinking, feeling, and behavior in conflictual situations (self-awareness)
- offers evidence of changed or more expansive thinking (new perspective)
- offers evidence of more skillful application of conflict management tools (skill and behavioral development)
- graduate-level writing (well-organized, grammatically sound, sources cited appropriately)

I explain that essays will receive letter grades as follows: A (all criteria well satisfied), A- (four criteria well satisfied), B+ (three criteria well satisfied), B (two criteria well satisfied), B- (1 criteria well satisfied or all five adequately demonstrated), C+ (adequate demonstration of four criteria), C (adequate demonstration of three criteria), C- (adequate demonstration of two criteria), D+ (adequate demonstration of one criterion), D (no criterion satisfied).

Because grades can have such significant impact, our grading system must be fair and transparent (and we should encourage students to suggest ways to make it so).We also should remember Ken Bain's finding in *What the Best College Teachers Do* (2004) that the most effective teachers offer students lots of feedback on their assignments and opportunities to revise based on the feedback.

Assessing Leadership Education

In addition to using assessments that can help individuals improve their leadership practice, we leadership educators want to know what aspects of our courses and workshops are achieving desired results and which should be altered.We can always use standard post-experience assessments that ask participants to indicate their level of satisfaction with key aspects of the course of workshop. For example, my university requires that students fill out a survey at the end of every course. The survey asks students to rate the class and instructor on a number of dimensions, such as how much was learned in comparison to other courses or the degree to which the instructor showed respect for diversity.

Fortunately, we have access to multiple additional modes of assessing the impact of our leadership courses and workshops. At the informal end of the spectrum are our own and others' observations.We can keep teaching journals in which we record reflections on key events, concerns or learning about participant progress, and our instructional style.We can describe what happened in a particular event, examine how we reacted, and suggest how this might affect what we do in the future.We can invite other educators to observe and offer feedback, and we can take time at the end of any exercise, session, or series of sessions to ask participants for quick, informal feedback.We can require students to keep learning journals, though as Ellen Van Velsor (1998) of the Center for Creative Leadership points out, participants may self-censor when they know an instructor will see their entries.

More formally, we may develop a questionnaire that asks participants to report on their learning in areas that match the course objectives. For example, in her book *Student Leadership Competencies Guidebook* (2014) Corey Seemiller offers templates designed to evaluate the development of a range of leadership competencies that are likely to be emphasized in undergraduate curricular and co-curricular programs.The competencies were derived mainly from the Relational Leadership Model developed by Susan Komives and colleagues, the Social Change Model of Helen and Alexander Astin, and James Kouzes and Barry Posner's Five Practices of Exemplary Leadership. Instructors can use the templates to build their own questionnaires and may then review the completed questionnaires to identify themes in learning that happened (or did not).As Van Velsor (1998) notes, questionnaires from different offerings of a course or workshop can be compared to assess changes in reported learning over time.

Leadership educators may also ask participants to complete a questionnaire (a pre-test) at the beginning of a course and then administer the same questionnaire as a post-test at the end of the learning experience. The comparisons, however, can be hard to interpret at times. A person's self-rating may drop by the end of a workshop, not because he or she has actually gotten worse at a skill, but because s/he understands more thoroughly what is involved in the skill. One way to overcome this shortcoming is to use a "post-then" assessment, in which a person fills out a questionnaire following the course or workshop but assesses his/her behavior or attitudes at two points in time: just before the learning experience and at the present time (which could be weeks or months after the experience).

At the formal, most sophisticated end of the assessment spectrum are combined survey questionnaires (ideally of the post-then variety) and structured interviews that ask participants and those who work with them (or know them well) to identify changes in the participants' leadership practice in the weeks or months following the development experience. Additional guidance for assessing leadership education are in Jennifer Martineau and Tracy Patterson's chapter in the *Center for Creative Leadership Handbook of Leadership Development* (Van Velsor, McCauley, and Ruderman, 2010).

Some leadership development programs are aimed ultimately at improving the performance of organizations or strengthening communities. Stephanie Lott and Scott Chazdon (2009) offer a model of assessment based on the theory that leadership development programs can accomplish these aims by first affecting individual knowledge, skills, and attitudes, which in turn lead to changes in participants' leadership behavior, including taking on new or more expansive leadership roles and responsibilities. As participants become more engaged in leading their organizations and communities, they are able to have several types of impacts (social, political, financial, built environment and natural resources, cultural, and health). Using a protocol based on this theory, Lott and Chazdon conducted semi-structured interviews of people who had completed leadership programs organized by University of Minnesota Extension. Questions they asked about organizational and community outcomes are in Inset 14.2.

INSET 14.2 QUESTIONS FOR ASSESSING ORGANIZATIONAL AND COMMUNITY IMPACT OF LEADERSHIP DEVELOPMENT PROGRAMS

General

- Did your experience in the leadership program help to expand or deepen your personal, social, or professional connections? Did your experience in the leadership program encourage you to strengthen networks among people and organizations in your community?
- Since completion of the program, have you shared the knowledge and learning gained from your experience with others (this could be formal sharing

such as making presentations or informal sharing such as discussions or conversations with family, friends, and coworkers)?

Political

- Since completion of the program, are you more comfortable voicing your opinion to political or public leaders?
- Since completion of the program, have you become involved or increased your participation in organizational or community decision making?
- Since completion of the program, have you run or considered running for political office?

Financial

- Since completion of the program, have you become involved or been more successful with fundraising efforts or grant-writing projects for the benefit of your community or organization?
- Do you feel more knowledgeable about where to find information about financial resources available to the public after completing the program?

Built environment

- Since completion of the program, have you become involved or increased your participation in projects that focused on enhancing or preserving the built environment (such as historic preservation, community beautification projects, park and recreation projects or infrastructure development)?

Natural environment

- Since completion of the program, have you become involved or increased your participation in conservation efforts aimed at protecting natural resources?

Cultural

- Since completion of the program, have you become involved or increased your participation in community cultural events such as theater and music events, festivals, celebrations, or county fairs?
- Since completion of the program, have you become involved or increased efforts to promote diversity in your community or organization (e.g., people of different ages and of different cultural and economic backgrounds)?

Health

- Since completion of the program, have you become involved in or increased efforts to promote the physical and mental well-being of your community or organization (such as tobacco reduction, drug prevention, or wellness and nutrition efforts)?

— Lott and Chazdon, 2009

Reprinted with permission from Lott, S., & Chazdon, S. (2009). *The effects of leadership development: Individual outcomes and community impacts*. St. Paul: University of Minnesota.

Coaching and Mentoring for Leadership Development

Coaching can occur in three main ways in leadership education:

- as part of an assessment process, in which the coach helps a participant make sense of assessment results, develop a plan for acting on the results, and report on progress in implementing the plan
- in connection with a specific Action Learning Project that is part of an extended leadership program
- as an opportunity for each participant to meet with an instructor or professional coach to review the participant's leadership history, current challenges, and develop and monitor strategies for effectively responding to the challenges

James Flaherty's approach, described in his book *Coaching: Evoking Excellence in Others* (2010), offers valuable guidance for engaging in all three coaching assignments, though he focuses more on the third one. Flaherty, who combines work in coaching and leadership development, describes coaching as "a way of working with people that leaves them more competent and more fulfilled so that they are more able to contribute to their organizations and find meaning in what they are doing" (3). The hallmarks of excellent coaching, in his view, are long-term excellent performance, self-correction, and continuous improvement.

His philosophy of coaching is based in a pragmatist perspective that rejects absolute truths and finds value in activities that have "power to alleviate human concern, lessen human suffering, improve how we live together, and free people to take action" (17). He offers five guiding principles for coaching practice:

- relationship based on mutual respect, trust, and freedom of expression
- focus on practical outcomes
- mutual learning
- recognition that participants are already in the midst of their lives and come to the experience with existing "views, commitments, possibilities, and concerns" (11)
- recognition that *techniques* don't work

The bulk of his book describes each of the five stages that make up the coaching process: relationship, an opening due to a change in the participant's routine, assessment (including participant competencies, interpretive structure, and the array of relationships, projects, and practices that make up the participant's life), enrollment, and coaching. Examples of coaching conversations are sprinkled throughout.

Flaherty urges coaches to pay particular attention to language. He agrees with philosopher Martin Heidegger that "language uses us, in the sense that language provides for us the horizon of possible actions, experiences, relationships, and meanings" (23). The astute coach listens closely in order to find out how a participant is interpreting the world, and she monitors her own use of language as she reflects those interpretations back to the participant, suggests alternative interpretations, and reveals some of her own relevant experiences. Flaherty emphasizes the need for coaches to stay attuned to the readiness (including mood) of people we are coaching.

If a participant is getting stuck at some point in the coaching process, Flaherty urges the coach to shake up the process in some way. For example, coach and participant might do a "forensic review" of the conversations that the two have had so far. The coach might discern that the conversations have largely focused on emotions and sense the time has come to switch to a cognitive emphasis; conversely, more attention to feelings might be needed because the conversations have been too "heady." As another example, the coach might realize she needs to examine and perhaps alter her own emotional reactions to the participant. Other possibilities are noted in chapter 10 of Flaherty's book.

Candice Frankovelgia and Douglas Riddle (2010) sum up the functions of coaching as assessment, challenge, and support. They emphasize the importance of working with coachees to set development goals "with the right amount of challenge. Too small a challenge minimizes growth; too much challenge can overwhelm and discourage the coachee" (128).

Virginia E. Bianco-Mathis, Lisa K. Nabors, and Cynthia Roman, three experienced pracademics, have developed a coaching model of leadership described in their book *Leading From the Inside Out* (2002). They offer advice for finding a leadership coach and for being more coach-like in your leadership practice—that is, becoming a coaching leader. Such leaders, they say, "communicate powerfully, help others to create desired outcomes, and hold relationships based on honesty, acceptance, and accountability" (4).

To those seeking a suitable coach, they recommend interviewing candidates. "You should explore everything from the coach's philosophy and background to his or her fees and policies" (19). They emphasize the importance of assessing your own readiness to be coached, and offer a series of questions that should be answered affirmatively before proceeding. Especially important examples are:

- Am I willing to make the coaching process a top priority in my life?
- Am I willing to have an honest relationship with a coach?
- Am I willing to change my attitudes and behaviors? (18)

Giving and receiving feedback is a vital skill in coaching relationships. If we leadership educators follow the advice of Bianco-Mathis, Nabors, and Roman about receiving feedback, we must be open to hearing discrepancies between our own perceptions and what others are observing in our behavior. We can then consider what those discrepancies suggest we do differently. When we give feedback to an individual or a team, Bianco-Mathis, Nabors, and Roman advise us to:

- Put the feedback in context
- Highlight strengths and positive areas
- Provide support in working through difficult-to-hear feedback
- Generate and evaluate options
- Answer questions
- Provide focus and balance
- Keep the process moving
- Role-model coaching behaviors (98)

They remind us that all parties in a coaching relationship must guard against barriers erected by ego, fear, and impatience. They quote Robert Staub's comment in *The Heart of Leadership* (2000): "Ego makes us unwilling to learn from others, and even from our own mistakes. Fear can cause us not to give or receive needed feedback—it prevents us from acting. Impatience is the unwillingness to allow events and processes to mature and unfold" (25).

Coaches also should be prepared to help participants cope with the fall-off in performance that may accompany the shift to new behaviors, a phenomenon noted by Day, Harrison, and Halpin (2009).

Scholars view mentoring as a more general, often longer-term relationship between a more experienced role model and a mentee. It may include coaching behaviors as evident in the description by Richard Cotton, Yan Shen, and Reut Livne-Tarandach (2011). They say,

> Both theoretical and empirical research has shown that mentors usually provide two kinds of support functions: (1) career functions, which include *sponsorship, coaching, protection, challenging assignments, and exposure,* and (2) psychosocial functions, which include *acceptance and confirmation, counseling, friendship, and role modeling.*
>
> *(18)*

Linda Grooms and Kathaleen Reid-Martinez (2011, 417) offer a more detailed list of mentoring functions:

- acceptance/support/encouragement
- advice/guidance
- access to resources

- challenge
- clarification of values and goals
- coaching
- information
- protection
- role modeling
- social status
- socialization
- sponsorship
- stimulation of knowledge acquisition
- training/instruction
- visibility/exposure

Because of the long-term nature of mentorship, mentors must also assist mentees in moving on to new mentors, when the time comes (Kram, 1983). Perhaps the mentee has reached the point that he or she has mastered all the original mentor can offer, or the mentor is no longer able to devote adequate time to the relationship.

Frankie Weinberg and William Locander (2014) emphasize the spiritual side of mentoring. In their view, spirituality encompasses "meaningful life, wholeness and interconnectedness with others" (391). Spiritual mentors, they say, contribute

> to a protégé's personal growth and development by providing a context that nourishes the protégé's individual spirit through recognition of his or her inner life and by providing or suggesting meaningful work appealing to the protégé's own sense of calling and thus promotes an experience of transcendence through the work process.
>
> *(394)*

At the outset, they say, spiritual mentors appreciate their own inner life and bring their authentic selves to the mentoring relationship. They then engage in conversations with their mentees about purpose and co-reflect on the spiritual nature of workplace activities. Mentors should be sensitive to mentees' stage of spiritual development. For example, a mentee may still be striving to align his/her ego with collective interest or well along in dedication to serving others.

The effectiveness of coaching and mentoring in leadership development has been studied mainly in organizational contexts. Gro Ladegard and Susann Gjerde (2014) cite studies showing that 360-degree feedback combined with coaching had positive impacts on participants' development. Their own experimental study focused on middle and upper-level managers working with leadership coaches trained in "Co-Active Coaching," and they found the managers' "leader-role efficacy" and trust in subordinates increased compared with a control group. Paul Lester, Sean Hannah, P.D. Harms, Gretchen Vogelsang, and Bruce Avolio (2011) reported clear impacts of a mentorship program that was part of leadership training instruction for West Point cadets. The program probably aligned more with the way I have described coaching, in that participating cadets selected a mentor from West Point staff and faculty; mentee and mentor then engaged in at least six structured diagnostic and goal-setting sessions. Lester and colleagues found that participation in the mentorship program increased mentees' leader efficacy and performance, compared to a control group. They also found that mentees' preferences for feedback and trust in the mentor moderated the effects of the program. Similarly, Dugan, Kodama, Correia, & Associates (2013) found mentoring relationships were among the high-impact practices in undergraduate leadership programs.

Finally, Cotton, Shen, and Livne-Tarandach (2011) remind us that coaching and mentoring come from a variety of sources throughout our lives. Their study of major league baseball hall of famers directs attention to a person's "development network" that may consist of family members, professional peers, formal mentors, coaches, personal heroes, and teachers, among others. Their results suggest that rich developmental networks are advantageous in career success.

★★★

Formal and informal assessments can help us leadership educators and participants in our programs clarify the attitudes, skills, and aspirations we bring to our leadership work and check our progress toward developmental goals. Informal assessments, such as the Narrative of Commitment, are described more fully in previous chapters. This chapter examined several formal assessments and emphasized the importance of understanding the theoretical framework behind the assessments as well as the research on their validity and reliability and their limitations. Among the assessments that are not explicitly related to leadership, I have given most attention to the popular Myers-Briggs Type Indicator, but also discussed the Thomas-Kilmann Conflict Mode Instrument. Among formal assessments based on a leadership model, I have highlighted strengths and limitations of the Multifactor Leadership Questionnaire and other 360-degree assessments.

Since much of leadership education is provided in the form of for-credit college courses at the graduate or undergraduate level, I also have considered the peculiar form of assessment known as grading. I noted the importance of relating graded assignments to the leadership knowledge, self-awareness, perspectives, skills, and behaviors we are seeking to develop. Grading criteria should be clear, and students should have opportunities to revise, based on extensive feedback.

In addition to offering assessment to the participants in our courses and workshops, we seek information about the effectiveness of these leadership development experiences. This chapter examines a range of methods for doing this, from teaching and learning journals, to follow-up surveys and structured interviews. I also describe the approach used by Minnesota Extension to evaluate the organizational and community impact of three community leadership programs.

The usefulness of the information provided by assessments can be amplified by trusted and adept coaches and mentors. I have noted several ways that coaching can be used in leadership education and described exemplary approaches. A vital skill in coaching relationships is giving and receiving feedback, and coaching experts featured in this chapter offer guidance for improving this skill. Mentoring encompasses coaching practices, but usually is a more extensive, longer-term relationship. Among the additional functions that mentors play are role modeling and socialization into a profession. I also describe a "spiritual mentoring" approach that helps mentees find meaningfulness in their work.

In the next chapter, I will explore practical aspects of conducting leadership assessments highlighted in this chapter and make suggestions for using evaluations of our workshops and courses as we design new versions. Additionally, I will highlight considerations for incorporating coaching and mentoring into our leadership development programs.

References

Bain, K. (2004). *What the best college teachers do*. Cambridge, MA: Harvard University Press.

Bianco-Mathis, V. E., Nabors, L. K., & Roman, C. H. (2002). *Leading from the inside out: A coaching model*. Thousand Oaks, CA: Sage Publications.

Cotton, R. D., Shen, Y., & Livne-Tarandach, R. (2011). On becoming extraordinary: The content and structure of the developmental networks of Major League Baseball hall of famers. *Academy of Management Journal, 54*(1), 15–46.

Day, D. V., Harrison, M. M., & Halpin, S. M. (2009). *An integrative approach to leader development: Connecting adult development, identity, and expertise*. New York: Routledge.

Dugan, J. P., Kodama, C. M., Correia, B., & Associates. (2013). *Multi-institutional study of leadership insight report: Leadership program delivery*. College Park, MD: National Clearinghouse for Leadership Programs.

Ely, R. J., Ibarra, H., & Kolb, D. M. (2011). Taking gender into account: Theory and design for women's leadership development programs. *Academy of Management Learning & Education, 10*(3), 474–493.

Flaherty, J. (2010). *Coaching: Evoking excellence in others* (3rd ed.). New York: Routledge.

Frankovelgia, C. C., & Riddle, D. D. (2010). Leadership coaching. In E. Van Velsor, C. D. McCauley, & M. N. Ruderman (Eds.), *The center for creative leadership handbook of leadership development* (3rd ed., pp. 125–146). San Francisco: Jossey-Bass.

Grooms, L. D., & Reid-Martinez, K. (2011). Sustainable leadership development: A conceptual model of cross-cultural blended learning program. *International Journal of Leadership Studies, 6*(3), 412–429.

Kram, K. E. (1983). Phases of the mentor relationship. *Academy of Management Review, 26*(4), 608–625.

Ladegard, G., & Gjerde, S. (2014). Leadership coaching, leader role-efficacy, and trust in subordinates: A mixed methods study assessing leadership coaching as a leadership development tool. *Leadership Quarterly, 25*(4), 631–646.

Lester, P. B., Hannah, S. T., Harms, P. D., Vogelsang, G. R., & Avolio, B. J. (2011). Mentoring impact on leader efficacy development: A field experiment. *Academy of Management Learning & Education, 10*(3), 409–429.

Lloyd, J. (2012) The Myers-Briggs Type Indicator® and mainstream psychology: Analysis and evaluation of an unresolved hostility. *Journal of Beliefs and Values, 33*(1), 23–34.

London, M., Smither, J. W., & Diamante, T. (2007). Best practices in leadership assessment. In J. A. Conger & R. E. and Riggio (Eds.), *The practice of leadership* (pp. 41–63). San Francisco: Jossey-Bass.

Lott, S., & Chazdon, S. (2009). *The effects of leadership development: Individual outcomes and community impacts.* St. Paul: University of Minnesota.

Seemiller, C. (2014). *Student leadership competencies guidebook.* San Francisco: Jossey-Bass.

Staub, R. (2000). *The heart of leadership.* Provo, UT: Executive Excellence Publishing.

Van Velsor, E. (1998). Assessing the impact of development experiences. In C. D. McCauley, R. S. Moxley, & E. Van Velsor (Eds.), *The center for creative leadership handbook of leadership development* (pp. 262–288). San Francisco: Jossey-Bass.

Van Velsor, E., McCauley, C. D., & Ruderman, M. N. (2010). *Center for creative leadership handbook of leadership development.* San Francisco: Jossey-Bass.

Weinberg, F. J., & Locander, W. B. (2014). Advancing workplace spiritual development: A dyadic mentoring approach. *Leadership Quarterly, 25*(2), 391–408.

15

ASSESSING, COACHING, MENTORING, AND THE HANDS

The practice of assessing, coaching, and mentoring may be the most sensitive work we do as leadership educators. It gives us access to other people's deepest concerns and their highest aspirations. We see and rate their accomplishments and we glimpse their failures. We prompt them to let down their ego defenses and ask that they examine their lives with open minds and a willingness to change. At times during the years, I have wondered if my leadership courses should come with a warning, something like, "Be careful, all who enter here. You may be at risk of major life changes; some others who have engaged in the self-examination and learning offered by this experience have quit their jobs, divorced their spouses, and challenged authorities. These may actually have been positive and healthy changes, but you should know what you are getting into."

This concern certainly should motivate us to be as grounded, open, and caring as we possibly can be in this work. It means that we should have engaged in the same kind of self-examination and development that we are offering the participants in our courses and workshops.

This chapter will explore the practicalities of including assessments, coaching, and mentoring in leadership development programs. The section on assessment will also consider how we redesign courses and workshops in response to participant feedback.

Assessing for Learning

The good news, as noted in the previous chapter, is that we have plenty of informal and formal assessments to choose from. The important thing is to match the assessment to the practice we are seeking to develop and to choose formal assessments that are based on coherent leadership theory and have been validated in a transparent way.

When I ask students to identify their favorite form of leadership assessment, using the exercise in Inset 15.1, they typically select one of the informal modes—journaling, observation, conversation, and the like. The cause may be that the informal modes often have a more relational quality or engage head and heart more than filling out a questionnaire does. At the same time, many participants also appreciate the chance to take formal assessments, since these offer a more objective analysis and give participants a chance to compare themselves with others. These responses have led me to include both types of assessments in many of my courses and workshops and to include relational debriefing for the formal assessments. By relational debriefing I mean the chance to talk with other participants or a coach about your results.

INSET 15.1   USING PERSONAL ASSESSMENT METHODS

Methods for understanding yourself and others include:

- Observation and reflection
- Journaling
- Storytelling
- Formal assessments
- Therapy and personal growth programs
- Informal conversations
- Reading fiction and nonfiction, attending plays, watching films
- Consulting research studies

1. What are your preferred methods of learning about yourself and others?
2. What do you like about those methods?
3. How would you go about exploring other approaches? What is keeping you from doing so?
4. What is your greatest strength connected with understanding self and others? Where do you encounter difficulties understanding self and others?

Whether I am using a formal or informal assessment, I usually emphasize that participants will be asked to choose what results to share. This honors participants' privacy and may diminish the understandable tendency to choose the more socially acceptable responses. I also emphasize that no particular assessment is likely to provide a comprehensive view of one's leadership practice and, therefore, basing judgments on multiple assessments is best.

At times, I may ask participants to engage in an exercise that reveals something about their assessment results. For example, to help participants understand the different perspectives and behaviors associated with Myers-Briggs dichotomies, I may ask all the people who have Extraversion in their MBTI type to go to one side of the room and the people who have Introversion to go to another side; I instruct each group to prepare questions for the other group. I consider revealing one's MBTI type to be fairly low-risk, since I have reminded everyone that the MBTI is just one source of information about one's personality and warned against type-casting.

Another example of a low-risk assessment is the role-model exercise that my colleagues and I have used to explore ethical leadership (see Inset 15.2). Note: An instructor may or may not decide to define ethical leadership in introducing the exercise. I typically do not supply a definition and, if asked for one, I encourage participants to answer based on their own definition. Usually, once participants have filled out the assessment, I ask them to share the results with a partner or small group, and I may ask for volunteers to talk about insights from the small group discussion.

INSET 15.2   IDENTIFYING ETHICAL ROLE MODELS AND OVERCOMING BARRIERS TO ETHICAL LEADERSHIP

Complete and discuss with group:

1. Who are your role models for ethical leadership?
2. What ethical principles do they espouse or live out?
3. What draws you to these people?
4. What are the main barriers to practicing ethical leadership?
5. How can you overcome these barriers?

Action planning provides an important overlay for assessment, since it is a concrete way for participants to decide what to do about the information they glean from an array of assessments. An action plan could list commitments for changed behavior or for improving existing strengths. Typically, I ask participants to engage in action planning near the end of a course or workshop. They complete the exercise in Inset 15.3 and then talk with other participants to refine the plan.

INSET 15.3   ACTION PLANNING

1. What six things will you do in the next six months to implement your ideas about leadership?
2. What barriers do you expect and how will you overcome them?

3. What cultural dimensions are important in your work and how will you address them?

4. Leadership for the common good calls for many talents and capacities. Since none of us has them all, how will you develop this collective phenomenon?

For many years I have taught a two-day course called Assessing Leadership Capacity. The plan for the course is in Inset 15.4. I prepare an instructor's guide that provides notes for each part of the agenda and describes accompanying PowerPoints or Prezi presentation (see Inset 15.5).

INSET 15.4   ASSESSING LEADERSHIP CAPACITY

Instructor: Dr. Barbara C. Crosby

Description: Participants will explore several methods of assessing personal, team, organizational, and community leadership. Formal instruments, such as the Myers-Briggs Type Indicator, the Keirsey Temperament Sorter, and the Multifactor Leadership Questionnaire, will be introduced, along with elder narrative, 360-degree feedback, and assets inventories.

Participants will design and analyze a leadership capacity assessment tool.

Learning outcomes

- Ability to identify purposes of leadership capacity assessment
- Ability to develop (or adapt) leadership assessment tools suited to group, organizational, or community needs
- Ability to assess usefulness and reliability of leadership assessment tools
- Deeper understanding of personal leadership commitments and enactments

Course website: [access information]
Readings will be posted on the course website. They are:

Murphy, Susan E., & Johnson, Stephanie, K. (2011). The benefits of a long-lens approach to leader development: Understanding the seeds of leadership. *Leadership Quarterly, 22*(3), 459–470.

Shamir, Boas, & Eilam, Galit. (2005). What's your story? A life-stories approach to authentic leadership development. *Leadership Quarterly, 16*, 395–417.

Crosby, Barbara C. (1999). *Leadership for global citizenship*: *Building transnational community*. Thousand Oaks, CA: SAGE, Chapter 3.

Wheelan, Susan E. (2005). Creating effective teams (2nd ed.). Thousand Oaks, CA: SAGE, Chapter 6.

London, Manuel, Smither, James W., & Diamante, Thomas. (2007). Best practices in leadership assessment. In Jay A. Conger, & Ronald E. Riggio (Eds.), The practice of leadership (pp. 41–63). San Francisco: Jossey-Bass.

Kretzmann, John P., & McKnight, John. (1993). Building communities from the inside out: A path toward finding and mobilizing a community's assets. Chicago: ACTA Publications, intro and pp. 109–111.

Wallis, Allan. (2003). Building leadership capacity in a socially emerging community. In J. Gastil & P. Levine (Eds.), The deliberative democracy handbook. San Francisco: Jossey-Bass.

University Resources: [some standard language about student services and academic honesty]

Course Preparation: Enrolled participants will receive instructions for completing the online Multifactor Leadership Questionnaire (MLQ) Actual-Ought before the class begins. Individual MLQ reports will be distributed in class. Readings that will receive extensive attention during the class are Crosby (*Leadership for Global Citizenship*) and Kretzmann and McKnight. The others are resources that will be referenced in class. Participants may wish to get started on the homework due before the second day of class.

Agenda

Day 1

1:00–2:00	Introduction
	Leadership—What is it? Why assess leadership capacity?
	Overview of course
2:00–2:35	Personal leadership—understanding self and others
	Formal instruments Myers-Briggs, Keirsey Recommended reading: Murphy and Johnson
2:35–2:45	Break
2:45–3:45	Multifactor Leadership Questionnaire
3:45–4:00	Personal narrative
	Recommended reading: Shamir and Eilam

4:00–4:15   Break
4:15–5:00   Exercise—"Using Personal Assessment Methods"
5:00–5:30   Review and preparation for Day 2

Homework:
Read Chapter 3, Leadership for Global Citizenship
Prepare an outline of a personal leadership assessment based on the "Additional Resources" section (starting on p. 40)

Complete the following exercises:
    "Exploring Personal Highs and Lows"
    "Creating a Personal Credo"
    "Analyzing Social Group Membership"

Note: Bring outline, exercises (& commentary), self-addressed stamped envelope to class the next morning. Be sure writing is legible.

Day 2

8:00–9:00   Personal Leadership continued

Small group reflection
    What did you learn about your leadership capacity from in-class and homework exercises?

9:00–10:00   Group project

10:00–10:15 Break

10:15–11:15 Team Leadership—mini lecture

Team Practices Inventory—Kouzes and Posner
Team Leadership Checklist
(Small groups—How would you assess team leadership capacity?)
Recommended reading:
Wheelan: Creating Effective Teams

11:15–11:30 Fill out Leadership Action Assessment
11:30–12:30 Lunch
12:30–1:30   Organizational Leadership

360-degree Feedback
Recommended reading:
London, Smither, and Diamante

	Leadership Action Assessment
	Organizational Leadership Checklist
	(Mini-lecture followed by small group evaluation of each method)
1:30–1:45	Break
1:45–2:15	Community Leadership
	Assets inventories (read Kretzmann and McKnight intro, identify main points, talk about in small groups)
2:15–3:00	Civic Leadership tool (University of Minnesota and Zobius)
	Guest: University of Minnesota Extension educator Participants evaluate Civic Leadership tool Strengths and weaknesses, modifications to improve
3:00–3:15	Break
3:15–3:30	Portfolio idea
	Elder narrative Recommended reading: Wallis
3:30–4:30	Small groups develop strategies for assessing community leadership capacity
4:30–5:00	Wrap/Evaluation

Final assignment

Prepare a five-page, double-spaced analysis of one of the assessments discussed in class. Or create your own.

- Briefly describe the assessment. How does it assess leadership or leadership-related behavior? For what audiences is it intended?
- Describe the theory of leadership or human behavior that guided (or seemed to guide) developers of the assessment. What assumptions seem to underlie the theory? What research supports the theory? Reference at least two books or scholarly articles describing the research.
- Identify strengths and weaknesses of the theory and of the assessment. Where possible, cite research on the assessment's validity and reliability.

- Explain how the instrument might be used in leadership development programs, possibly in your own organization or community. Suggest modifications of the assessment for different audiences.

If you design your own assessment, you may benefit from focusing on assessing the leadership of specific groups, organizations, or communities.

Bibliography should be included. APA style for in-text citations and for bibliography preferred. Submit through course website by *[date]*. If for some compelling reason, this due date cannot be met, students must have a written contract with the professor for completion.

Your submission will be reviewed through Turnitin, an antiplagiarism software adopted by the university. This program identifies matches between your submission and other written documents on file. I recognize that many matches do not indicate plagiarism and will review each match.

Grading

The final grade is based on class participation (30%), homework assignment (20%), and final assignment (50%).

- The class participation grading is based on attendance (15 points) and in-class work (15 points).
- Homework will be graded on an A- to A+ scheme.
- Grading for the final assignment is based on the five components listed above, organization, and strength of writing (clarity, grammar, etc.).

Note: The syllabus is accompanied by an extensive bibliography of leadership assessment resources.

INSET 15.5 INSTRUCTOR'S GUIDE FOR ASSESSING LEADERSHIP CAPACITY

Needed materials: Flip chart sheets, name tags, tape, CD/iPod player, slides, markers, clicker.

Handouts: syllabus, MBTI profile of U.S. and U.K. groups, organizational leadership assessment, Terry's Action Wheel

Preparation: Room set up in tables of 5–6 participants. Write my leadership definition on covered flip chart. Call up Keirsey temperaments website.

Day 1

1:00   *Introduction.* Note importance of being clear about leadership definitions and purpose of assessment.

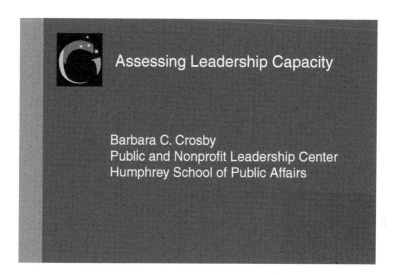

Overview of course. Emphasize learning lab approach, importance of backing for instruments and adaptation for particular uses.

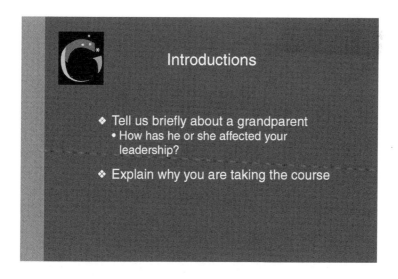

(Be sure participants say their names when speaking.)
Brief review of syllabus. Note availability of excellent papers.

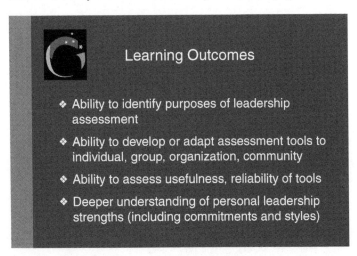

Definitions of leadership. Ask everyone to jot down words or images they associate with leadership. Collect via round robin and write on flip chart or whiteboard. Reveal my own definition from covered flip chart when all have been recorded.

Ask why a person or organization might wish to assess leadership. Jot down answers on a flip chart or whiteboard.

Note connections of leadership and followership; both might be assessed.

2:00   *Personal leadership.* This is about understanding the people involved in the leadership work and deploying your personal assets on behalf of a collective initiative.

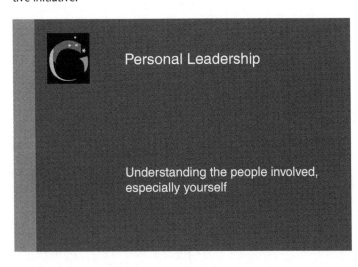

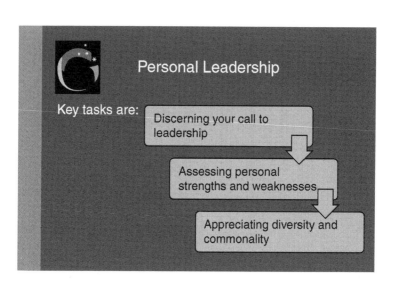

Personal Leadership

Key tasks are:

- Discerning your call to leadership
- Assessing personal strengths and weaknesses
- Appreciating diversity and commonality

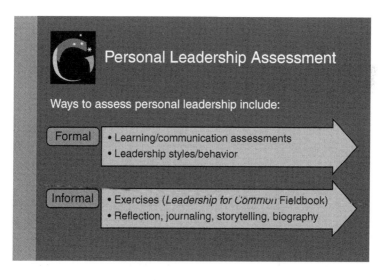

Personal Leadership Assessment

Ways to assess personal leadership include:

Formal
- Learning/communication assessments
- Leadership styles/behavior

Informal
- Exercises (*Leadership for Common* Fieldbook)
- Reflection, journaling, storytelling, biography

These assessments can help people discern their call to leadership via identifying and assessing their public passions, assessing other strengths and weaknesses, and understanding how individual passions, experiences, and characteristics connect and separate people.

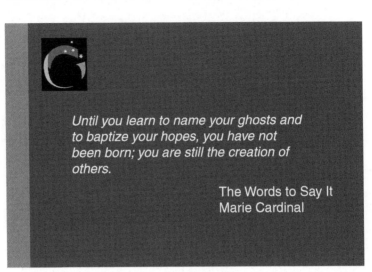

> *Until you learn to name your ghosts and to baptize your hopes, you have not been born; you are still the creation of others.*
>
> The Words to Say It
> Marie Cardinal

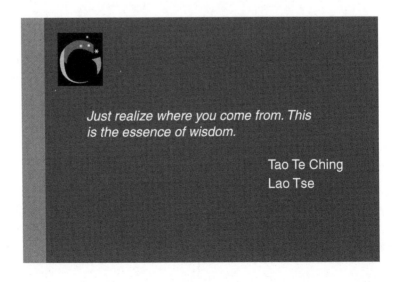

> *Just realize where you come from. This is the essence of wisdom.*
>
> Tao Te Ching
> Lao Tse

Formal instruments can be mainly or secondarily about leadership. In the secondary category are instruments like MBTI and Keirsey Temperament Sorter. (There are at least 2,500 personality tests.) Ask who has taken MBTI and how many of those remember their four-letter type. Explain MBTI.

Myers-Briggs Personality Type Indicator

❖ Tool for personal leadership development
  • Understanding self and others
  • Foundation for other aspects of leadership

❖ Provides insights into our preferred ways of doing things

❖ Advantages
  • No type is better than another
  • Very widely used

Explain type theory and background of MBTI.

Type Preference Theory

❖ Explains much behavior

❖ Reveals preferences, not abilities

❖ Argues that most individuals have access to all preferences

❖ Is dynamic
  • Ideal trajectory: Becoming best possible version of self

Provide historical information about work of Katherine Briggs and Isabel Briggs Myers.

Overview of MBTI dichotomies

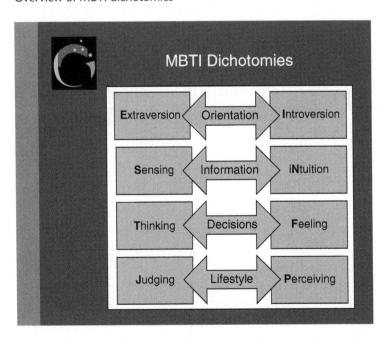

Implications for learning and work styles

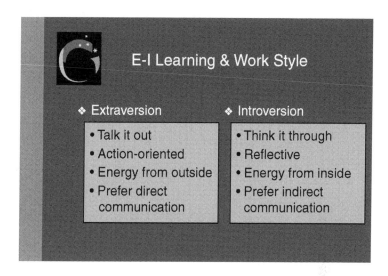

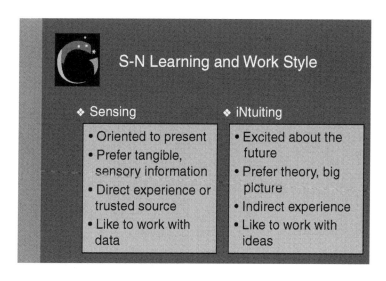

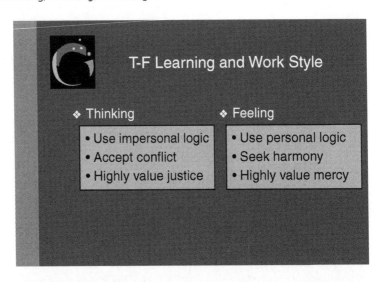

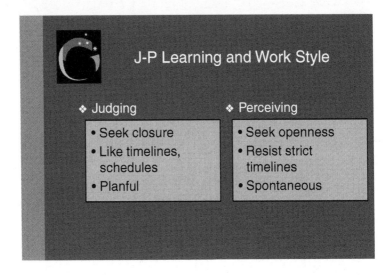

Handout: MBTI profiles. Note some difference among racial groups.
Exercise: In dyads talk about: How might MBTI be used to assess personal leadership?
Debrief.
Discuss reliability and validity in context of MBTI.

Reliability and Validity

❖ Reliability – Does the test measure people consistently?

❖ Validity – Does the test measure what it claims to measure? Can it be used for stated purposes?
  • Face validity
  • Content validity
  • Construct validity
  • Criterion-related validity

Note Habermas's idea of intersubjective validity; London, Smither, and Diamante mention predictive validity.

Review Keirsey website. Temperaments overlap with Myers-Briggs dichotomies. Urge participants to take Keirsey Temperament Sorter. Note strengths and weaknesses.

Other assessments: StrengthsFinder (34 common talents identified from Gallup Polls on human strengths; message to leaders—help others develop their strengths)

Big Five personality traits—extraversion, openness/intellect, agreeableness, conscientiousness, neuroticism/emotional stability

Note importance of genetics, early experiences in leadership development (see Murphy & Johnson reading).

2:35 Break

2:45 Formal instruments primarily about leadership. Prime example is Multifactor Leadership Questionnaire. Hand out participant MLQ reports at break.

Describe the full-range leadership model and the way the MLQ measures each component and outcomes.

Multifactor Leadership Questionnaire

- ❖ Based on "full range leadership" model
  - Bernard Bass and Bruce Avolio
- ❖ Leadership styles (differing outcomes and influence processes)
  - Transformational
  - Transactional
  - Passive-Avoidant

Transformational Style

- ❖ Idealized attributes and behaviors
- ❖ Inspirational motivation
- ❖ Intellectual stimulation
- ❖ Individualized consideration

Transactional and Passive – Avoidant Styles

- ❖ Transactional
  - Contingent reward
  - Management by exception (active)

- ❖ Passive-Avoidant
  - Management by exception (passive)
  - Laissez-faire

MLQ Outcome Measures

- ❖ Extra effort
- ❖ Individual, unit, and organizational effectiveness
- ❖ Satisfaction with leadership

Note other formal leadership assessments, such as Lipman-Blumen's Achieving Styles instrument.

3:45   Informal leadership assessment

Exercise: Writing a personal narrative
Directions: Write a paragraph or two answering the questions on the slide.

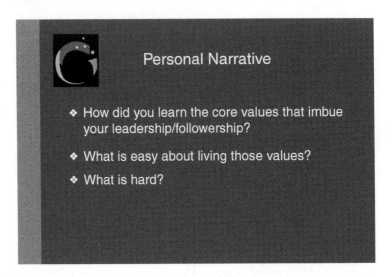

Talk about your paragraph with someone from another table than your own.

4:00   Break

4:15   Debrief personal narrative exercise in large group. Note Shamir and Eilam reading.

Assessment preferences
Exercise: "Using Personal Assessment Methods"
Debrief in large group.
Mention other assessments such as Emotional Intelligence, Authentic Happiness. Ask if participants have candidates.

5:00   Review and preparation for Day 2

Ask: What stands out for you from today?
Explain homework, note that food will be available in the morning.

5:30   Conclude

Day 2

8:00   *Reflection*. Note importance of doing this.

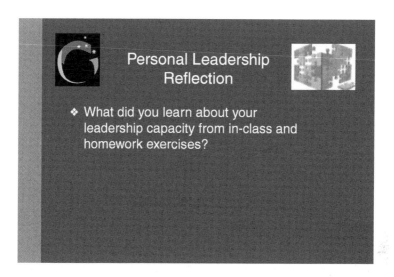

Add anything that seems to be missing—for example, storytelling that links courage and leadership.
Ask for questions about final assignment.

9:00   Group project on personal leadership

Each table compiles a personal leadership assessment based on outlines developed as homework. Outline on flip chart sheets.

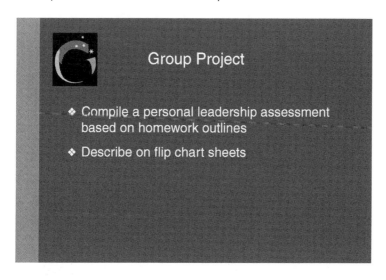

A spokesperson for each group presents the assessment and describes implications for personal leadership development.

10:00 Break

10:15 *Team Leadership*
Mini-lecture on definition and tasks of team leadership

Team Leadership

Team leaders pay attention to group maintenance, member satisfaction, and task accomplishment by:

❖ Skillful recruitment of team members

❖ Effective communication

❖ Empowerment of team members

❖ Leadership development of team members

❖ Development of trust and spirit

Skillful Recruitment

❖ People with common concern

❖ People with knowledge, contacts, skills, other resources

❖ Key stakeholders

❖ Balance of unity and diversity

❖ Manageable size

Effective Communication

- ❖ Art of listening and sending messages
- ❖ Verbal and nonverbal messages
- ❖ Dialogue as well as discussion
- ❖ Conflict management
- ❖ Seriousness and playfulness
- ❖ Setting
- ❖ Cultural influences
- ❖ Group needs

Effective Communication

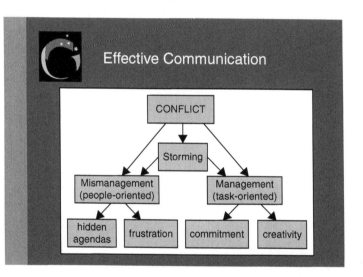

 Empowerment

- ❖ Stages of group development
- ❖ Clear mission and goals
- ❖ Decision-making procedures, rules, roles, norms
- ❖ Strategies, action plan, evaluation methods

Leadership Development

- ❖ Successors
- ❖ Shared responsibilities
- ❖ Training sessions
- ❖ Leadership development program

Trust and Spirit

- ❖ Live your values and standards
- ❖ Trust and keep promises
- ❖ Be open and sensitive to others' needs
- ❖ Demonstrate competence
- ❖ Blend challenge and support
- ❖ Learn from defeat and difficulty
- ❖ Laugh

Leadership is people taking the initiative, carrying things through, having ideas and the imagination to get something started, and exhibiting particular skills in different areas.

Charlotte Bunch

Team Practices Inventory (Kouzes and Posner, 1992)

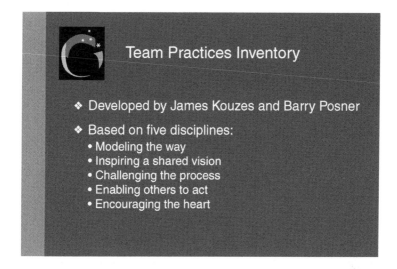

Mention Wheelan's stages of team development and checklist, Team MLQ, team leadership assessment from *Leadership for the Common Good* (LCG) (Crosby and Bryson, 2005).

Small group exercise: How would you assess team leadership capacity? Distribute Leadership Action Assessment (Booth, Ayers, and Dein, 1999) and ask participants to complete it for their organization before reconvening.

11:30 Lunch break

12:30 *Organizational Leadership*

Elements of organizational leadership from LCG

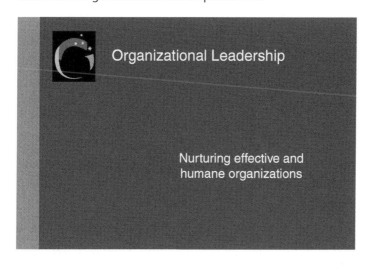

Organizational Leadership

Organizational leaders pay attention to organizational design by:

- ❖ Creating mission and philosophy statements
- ❖ Developing goals and strategies
- ❖ Constructing inspiring visions embodying organizational goals and key strategies
- ❖ Aligning design with organizational purpose
- ❖ Being a role model

Organizational Leadership

Organizational leaders adapt to internal and external change by:

- ❖ Constantly monitoring environment
- ❖ Emphasizing different operating values at different stages in organization's life cycle
- ❖ Being entrepreneurial and experimental
- ❖ Overseeing management routines and details
- ❖ Emphasizing collaboration and team building
- ❖ Planning for change

Organizational Leadership

Organizational leaders build inclusive community inside and outside organizations by:

- ❖ Caring for self and others
- ❖ Facilitating communal problem definition and resolution
- ❖ Providing resources, including knowledge of group process

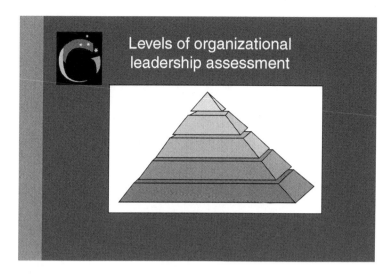

Debrief Leadership Action Assessment in large group. What did you find out about organization's challenges?

Handout: Terry's Action Wheel (Terry, 2001). Explain Terry's leadership categories embedded in the "Action Wheel." Note his finding that groups tend to try to resolve problems by moving counterclockwise on the wheel, when real resolution more likely by moving clockwise.

Note that some assessments are designed for board leadership. Resource in bibliography.

Note importance of a supportive culture for any needed change revealed by assessments.

Exercise: Complete Organizational Leadership checklist from LCG. (Fill out individually and discuss in small groups.)

Assessment of individual leadership in organizations

360-degree Feedback

MLQ

See London, Smither, Diamante reading, focused on senior executives.

Ask class members to identify pros and cons of 360-degree feedback.

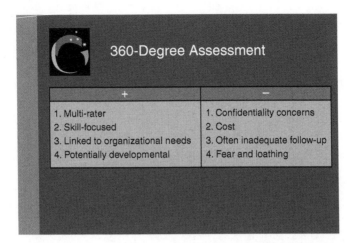

Note Hogan, Curphy, and Hogan's (1994) article in bibliography—best way to forecast (organizational) leadership is combo of cognitive ability, personality, simulation, role play, and multi-rater assessment instruments. Any questions about organizational leadership?

1:30   Break

1:45   *Community Leadership*

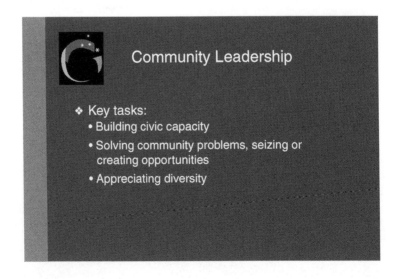

Note variety of communities—geographic, socioeconomic, ethnic, professional.
Assets inventories (read Kretzmann and McKnight intro and pp. 109–119)
Discuss Kretzmann and McKnight in small groups.

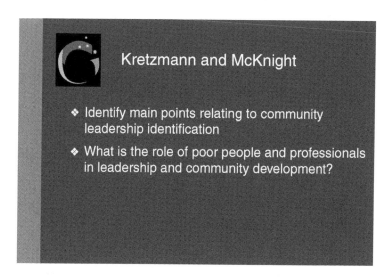

Draw out insights from each group; put the Kretzmann and McKnight approach into context of shift to assets rather than deficit/needs perspective.

2:15 Civic leadership tool based on Terry's Action Wheel or community capitals assessment
Introduce Extension educator, who will lead exercise using the tool.
Ask participants to assess strengths and weaknesses of the tool and suggest modifications to improve it.

3:00 Break

3:15 Other community assessments

Mapping social networks, Blandin Foundation categories, community portfolios (similar to community capitals)
Gastil and Levine idea—map differing levels of community or circles; identify people who can move across boundaries
Elder narrative—project recruited school children to interview community elders about their lives; put together a musical performance based on the interviews and invited the community

3:30 Small group exercise identifying preferred strategies for assessing community leadership

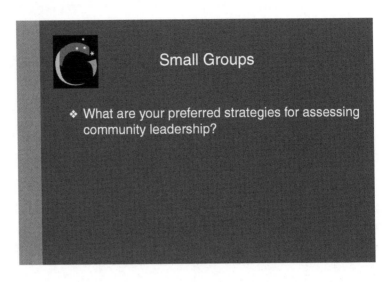

Different ideas of leadership in different communities
Wallis chapter—community is affiliative or interest-based
Collaborative approach to leadership development; designed new program for civic sector leadership

- personal development
- team building
- organizational skills
- communication and outreach

Personal assessment by leader
Shows how individual assessment and development can be used to build community leadership capacity, focuses on outcomes

4:30   Wrap/Evaluation

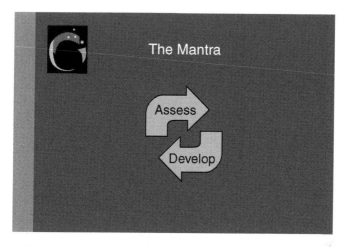

What stood out for you today? (round-robin responses)
Any questions about the final paper?

5:30   Go forth and assess leadership!

Grading

As noted in the previous chapter, the foundation of a formal grading process is the instructor's understanding of her grading philosophy. Ideally, that philosophy will be clear in the syllabus section explaining how grades will be apportioned among assignments. It can also be communicated verbally in face-to-face sessions. Grading criteria for each assignment can be specified in the syllabus or in separate documents. I frequently use the criteria to construct a grading rubric on which I comment on how well a student fulfilled each criterion.

Providing feedback aimed at helping students improve their communication skills, reflection, analysis, creativity, self-efficacy, and other leadership skills is the heart of the grading process. Thus, I strive to be specific in my comments and grade assignments within a week of submission. (If the grading will take longer, I let students know.) I frequently offer students a chance to revise assignments that receive anything below 90 points out of 100.

In my feedback on writing and visual and oral presentations, my aim is always to help students express their ideas more effectively. In order to help students write more clearly and persuasively, I offer suggestions for reorganizing, pruning, and choosing more apt language. I sometimes offer line edits to demonstrate how sentences or paragraphs can be improved. My main tactic, however, is to ask questions about missing information or unclear references. I focus my feedback on oral presentations both on what is said and on body language—for example, facial expression, stance, gestures, and tone of voice. I note whether or not a presenter has used visuals effectively. For example, I may point out that he had too much information on slides or on a poster. I may remind him to avoid reading material on the slides.

An especially thorny question is how to assess team projects. Do we give everyone the same grade for the project, regardless of the person's contribution? If we want to reward according to contribution, how do we really know who did what? My approach typically has been to give all team members the same grade for the project, but to base part of the class participation grade on what mandatory, confidential team evaluations tell me about member contributions. A sample team evaluation form is in Inset 15.6.

INSET 15.6 TEAM EVALUATION

Team Name/Topic _____ (please print)
Your Name _____ (please print)

1. How well did you live up to the team's contract (on a scale of 1–5, where 5 is complete fulfillment of the contract)? ___

    COMMENTS:

2. Team Member Name _____(please print)

    How well did he or she live up to the team's contract (on a scale of 1–5, where 5 is complete fulfillment of the contract)? ___
    COMMENTS:

3. Team Member Name _____(please print)

    How well did he or she live up to the team's contract (on a scale of 1–5, where 5 is complete fulfillment of the contract)? ___
    COMMENTS:

4. Team Member Name _____(please print)

    How well did he or she live up to the team's contract (on a scale of 1–5, where 5 is complete fulfillment of the contract)? ___
    COMMENTS

5. Team Member Name _____(please print)

    How well did he or she live up to the team's contract (on a scale of 1–5, where 5 is complete fulfillment of the contract)? ___
    COMMENTS

6. Who displayed particularly helpful leadership in your team and what was effective?

7. Who displayed particularly helpful followership in your team and what was effective?

This evaluation is based on development of a contract or initial agreement among team members at the outset of their project. In deciding how much participation credit to give a team member, I pool the judgments offered by all the other team members. I confess to continual amazement at how differently team members can perceive a fellow team member's performance!

Assessing and Redesigning Our Own Programs

The previous chapter discussed several methods for assessing the extent to which a course or workshop is achieving desired learning outcomes in the near term and beyond. Leadership educators also use these assessments to discern which content and teaching methods seem to be most effective and which ones should be improved or discarded. (By continuing to collect ideas from our fellow educators and other sources we can always have new material or approaches to try when old ones are wearing thin.)

As we redesign, we sometimes share our syllabi and participant feedback with colleagues and ask for their advice. We consider whether tweaks or radical change make sense given previous responses to a program, so that we are not in danger of overreacting to a particular group. If we have just begun a program, we may want to continue the basic design for three iterations, since many of us find that the third time we offer a class or workshop is when we really have realized the design's potential.

Coaching and Mentoring for Leadership Development

The organizers of some leadership development programs can afford to hire professional coaches. In other cases, leadership educators will do this ourselves. For example, Kevin Gerdes, Jodi Sandfort, and I act as coaches for the Action Learning Project (see Inset 15.7) that each learner undertakes as part of the foundational leadership course in the Master of Public Affairs program at the Humphrey School. Each learner is assigned to one of us for coaching, and we schedule an initial coaching session with our "coachees" after they have completed some leadership assessments early in the fall semester. In the session we review information from the assessments and listen to the learner's initial ideas for the Action Learning Project. We ask questions and make suggestions designed to help the learner develop a statement of intent, or project plan, which is submitted to the course website a week later. The statement briefly describes the project, the student's motivation for undertaking it, benchmarks of success, and desired results. It includes ideas for how the project will develop the learner's leadership skills and how that development will be tracked. Finally, it describes how the learner will develop a personal learning network to support the project.

INSET 15.7 ACTION LEARNING PROJECT

This assignment is the cornerstone of the Public Affairs Leadership cohort. You will identify a real problem confronting your workplace, volunteer site, or community that you are uniquely positioned to help address. Throughout the program, you will apply course learning, readings, and writing to this problem. In this way, you will reflect on your own behavior and interaction with others, while implementing new practices in your particular context. You will work in a small group (an Action Learning Circle), using a process informed by Parker Palmer's Circles of Trust. These circles will work to enable deeper learning about your opportunities for refining your leadership practice presented in the Action Learning Project. Written reflection assignments will supplement circle meetings.

Using online forums and face-to-face meetings, learners report on their progress and seek guidance from their Action Learning Circles and their faculty coach during fall and spring semesters. Near the conclusion of fall semester, learners give their faculty coach a formal interim report on how the project is progressing and how it is integrated with course readings and class discussion. The project concludes with a 15-minute presentation to the learner's Action Learning Circle and a final report to the instructors. The final report summarizes project process and outcomes, including the learner's leadership development, and considers results and sustainability.

As coaches, instructors must help learners define projects that can be accomplished in two semesters and help them overcome anxieties about trying out new leadership behaviors. Some learners will need encouragement to slow down and others must be nudged to speed up their process. I keep notes on everyone's project so that I can offer timely guidance and recommend resources. My fellow coaches and I experience a sense of gratitude that we are trusted with learners' heartfelt desires to improve their organizations, communities, and entire societies. We hear their fears and frustrations, their ah-has and triumphs. We in turn receive gratitude— often learners are glad that someone has pushed them out of their comfort zones, and helped them see their progress. At their most basic, the coaching and Action Learning Circle process is about giving each student undivided, caring attention at various times over the course of several months, and that is a gift for all involved.

Candice Frankovelgia and Douglas Riddle (2010) offer helpful guidance for adapting coaching practices to different cultural backgrounds and for using coaching in leadership development initiatives embedded in organizations.

To work effectively in a cross-cultural context, coaches must be aware of their own cultural assumptions and have the ability to adapt coaching practices to the cultural context. If coaches are unaware of cultural differences and do not attempt to adapt, they risk losing credibility, offending their hosts, and neutralizing the power of coaching.

—Candice Frankovelgia and Douglas Riddle

They advise coaches to adapt their practice to accommodate the following cultural differences:

- Varying degrees of formality, closeness and spontaneity expected in a coaching relationship
- Differing levels of comfort with multi-rater assessments, which have an egalitarian and quantification bias. Frankovelgia and Riddle suggest using interviews and observation to gather feedback when such assessments are a bad fit.
- Differences in willingness to take risks and accept challenges beyond the mastery level
- Differences in responsiveness to "pushy" coaching behavior
- Individualistic versus collectivist focus. When the cultural context is more collectivist, a coach should highlight especially the connection of individual and group development.

Turning to the use of coaching in organizations, Frankovelgia and Riddle offer a five-stage model (see Inset 15.8) that indicates how coaching might be linked to leadership development in an increasingly integrated and systematic way. They note that moving from one stage to another will require investment of organizational resources.

INSET 15.8 FRANKOVELGIA AND RIDDLE'S FIVE-STAGE MODEL OF COACHING FOR LEADERSHIP DEVELOPMENT IN ORGANIZATIONS

Stage 1. Ad hoc coaching. Formal coaching is not a key feature of the organization's leader development system; it may be used for "high-potential, transitioning, or struggling leaders" (134).

Stage 2. Organized coaching. Standards and policies are set for coaching and external coaches made available.

Stage 3. Extended coaching. Coaching is incorporated into a leadership development system and managers are trained in coaching skills.

Stage 4. Coaching culture. Everyone is "expected to engage in coaching behaviors" and leaders "model a coaching mind-set" (135).

Stage 5. Coaching as driver of business strategy. "Coaching is explicitly used as an accelerator of the organizational changes needed to adapt to emerging industrial and market trends" (135).

As noted in the previous chapter, mentoring and coaching practice have similarities, but a mentoring relationship tends to be longer term and aimed more at helping the mentee master organizational systems, advance in a profession, or craft a life path. In coaching sessions with participants in leadership programs, I sometimes recommend that a participant find a mentor who has deep knowledge of her organization or profession and can provide needed advice and support. I also have been a formal mentor for participants in my university's emerging leaders program; these mentees mainly sought guidance about how to balance work and family responsibilities. I helped them think longer term about their careers (as a mentor had once done for me) and helped them identify some trade-offs they might consider.

Two aspects of mentoring may require special sensitivity and determination. They are giving the mentee visibility and experience in your own circles and helping the mentee move on to another mentor as needed. Thus, if I am mentoring a less-seasoned leadership educator, I ideally will give the mentee a chance to take a visible role in a program or course that I am coordinating, just as Bob Terry once did for me. I may secretly think I could do the job better and know that I'm accountable for program quality, so I have to squelch my desire to handle the whole thing myself. Winding down a mentoring relationship also can be challenging. As the mentee matures, he or she is likely to become more of a peer than mentee or need mentoring in a new field or at a new organizational level. The mentoring relationship may evolve into friendship, as has been the case for Georgia Sorenson and her students at times; regardless, a mentor may have to accept that the time has come for the mentee to find another mentor and give permission for the shift. A mentee may have to take the initiative here and let the mentor know that he or she is grateful for the mentor's support and is ready to move forward on her own or with the help of a new mentor. Scheduling a lunch or other special occasion is a way both to honor the relationship and give it some closure.

★★★

Leadership educators can choose from an array of formal and informal assessments for leadership development. We can even design our own. The important thing is to match assessments to purpose and to combine formal and informal assessments. Also important for formal assessments is choosing those based on a coherent leadership theory and accompanied by research on their reliability and validity.

In for-credit courses, we also will give feedback via grades and accompanying comments. We should make this process as clear, fair, and developmental as possible. In assessing our own courses and workshops, we will systematically collect feedback and use it to improve the learning experience.

Assessments are most useful when they are part of a coaching process, and coaches can be peers, professional coaches, or instructors. In helping participants interpret assessments, make development plans, and monitor progress, leadership educators should be guided by tried-and-true coaching frameworks. At the same time, the essential element will always be the individualized, caring attention that a coach gives a participant, and the way that is done must be attuned to the participant's personality, stage in life, cultural assumptions, and other characteristics. Mentoring usually includes elements of coaching, but it often has a longer-term support function and can include opening up leadership opportunities for the person being mentored.

References

Booth, D. M., Ayers, J., & Dein, C. (1999). *Leadership action assessment: A way to identify elements contributing to or limiting purposeful action.* Minneapolis: BI Performance Services and Robert Terry.

Crosby, B. C., & Bryson, J. M. (2005). *Leadership for the common good: Tackling public problems in a shared-power world.* San Francisco: Jossey-Bass.

Frankovelgia, C. C., & Riddle, D. D. (2010). Leadership coaching. In E. Van Velsor, C. D. McCauley, & M. N. Ruderman (Eds.), *The center for creative leadership handbook of leadership development* (3rd ed., pp. 125–146). San Francisco: Jossey-Bass.

Gastil, J., & Levine, P. (Eds.). (2005). *The deliberative democracy handbook: Strategies for effective citizen engagement in the 21st century.* San Francisco: Jossey-Bass.

Hogan, R., Curphy, G. J., & Hogan, J. (1994). What we know about leadership: Effectiveness and personality. *American Psychologist, 49,* 493–504.

Kouzes, J. M., & Posner, P. L. (1992). *Team leadership practices inventory.* San Francisco: Pfeiffer.

Terry, R. W. (2001). *Seven zones for leadership: Acting authentically in stability and chaos.* Palo Alto, CA: Davies-Black Publishing.

Wallis, A. (2003). Building leadership capacity in a socially emerging community. In D. D. Chrislip (Ed.), *Collaborative leadership fieldbook* (pp. 230–245). Amherst, MA: Wiley.

CONCLUSION

As I was completing this book in November 2015, a spate of terrorist bombings shook Baghdad, Beirut, and Paris. The bombings were one more reminder of the need for millions of leadership acts to create a more just and peaceful planet. They also were a reminder that some people—Jean Lipman-Blumen would call them toxic leaders and James MacGregor Burns would call them demagogues—fulfill human desires to follow seemingly heroic figures who promise a better world, but only after apostates and undesirables are purged. People like me, who are in the business of educating leaders and global citizens, have our work cut out for us if we are to foster beneficial leadership by all kinds of people at many levels and if we are to counter the attraction of toxic leaders and demagogues.

I assume that you have read this book because you want to be or already are engaged in this vital work. By now you are quite aware that we have a lot of rich theory, extensive research, practical methods, and tools to deploy as we work with participants in a variety of leadership programs aimed at developing individual leaders and engaged citizens, as well as fostering more humane organizations and thriving communities.

In this book you have heard from numerous talented leadership educators—people I admire for their reflective practice, their contributions to leadership studies, and their inclusive, democratic approach to leadership development. In selecting conversation partners for this book, I intentionally chose seasoned leadership educators from diverse backgrounds—people who are based in universities as well as people who operate mainly as consultants, coaches, and program directors outside the academy. All of these people have helped me flesh out the five main practices of leadership development, wherever it occurs:

- Using personal narrative to foster self-understanding and commitment
- Hosting and hospitality

- Tackling organizational and societal problems
- Strengthening citizenship
- Assessing, coaching, and mentoring

The order in which the first four practices are presented loosely follows the progression from personal to group or team, to organizational, to societal levels; the final practice circles back to personal development but also focuses on evaluation of leadership programs themselves. The practices not only build on each other, but they overlap, so that attention to leader identity or context, as examples, shows up in more than one part of the book.

My overarching aim has been to help people who are just getting started as leadership educators prepare themselves for this arduous and rewarding work, but also to provide opportunities for more seasoned educators to reflect on their own leadership journeys, situate themselves in the arc of contemporary leadership studies, and collect some additional ideas, tools, and guidance for their ongoing work.

One way to think about our journeys as leadership educators is that we aim to help participants in our courses and workshops move along a spectrum ranging from novice to expert leader, even as we ourselves are moving along the same spectrum. As my conversation partners for this book, I have chosen people who can remember their experiences as novices and who provide insights about how they have moved a lot closer to the expert end of the spectrum. As novices we were far more likely than now to think that our job was to master (or develop) the most compelling theories and research findings and be sure our knowledge was transferred to participants in our programs. Many years later, we are more likely to see ourselves in the business of designing appropriate learning experiences based on particular purposes, audiences, and context. We know the most potent learning experiences combine socio-emotional, cognitive, and behavioral components (mirroring the heart, head, hands theme of this book).

Throughout this book, you have been offered a generous collection of leadership theories and frameworks, exercises, and methodologies. I have even supplied a couple of syllabi and instructor guides. However, as noted at the beginning, this is by no means a leadership cookbook or instruction manual. Rather, it is an organized guide to practice, suggesting a number of design principles. Some of the principles are tied to the five main practices featured in the book and others are more general.

Using Personal Narrative to Foster Self-Understanding and Commitment

The design principle tied to this practice is: *Ensure that participant experiences enhance their capacity to develop and communicate a leader (and follower) identity.* The principle can be carried out through chances to examine formative experiences, crucible experiences, critical incidents or decisions; to clarify values and commitments;

to acknowledge shortcomings and vulnerabilities; to focus on sources of joy and support; and to analyze personal assets and liabilities. Participants can tell their life stories in a variety of ways, from written essays, to one-on-one conversations, to video talks.

Hosting and Hospitality

The key design principle for this practice is: *Ensure that the learning environment is welcoming and inclusive for people in all their diversity (belief, ethnicity, nationality, physical ability, learning styles, class, gender, etc.).* To carry out this principle, leadership educators attend to participants' and our own needs. We arrange physical space, food, music, and cultural symbols, and we introduce processes to facilitate the building of relationships among participants and between ourselves and participants.

Tackling Organizational and Societal Problems

Two design principles are tied to this practice. The first is: *Ensure that featured leadership theories and research are relevant for the organizational and societal challenges the participants are facing.* Leadership educators can carry out this principle by helping participants locate their own implicit leadership theories in the array of scholarly views and help them identify how different theories may provide insights for their own work. Educators can engage participants in analyzing examples and cases that are similar to participants' challenges, and we can assign the Action Learning Project and organize simulations or role plays.

The second principle is: *Foster habits of mind and skills that help participants develop socio-emotional, cognitive, and behavioral complexity.* The habits of mind include awareness of leadership potential in almost everyone; respect for different views; continuous inquiry; compassion for self and others; tolerance of paradox, uncertainty, tension, and adversity; flexibility; and learning from failure. Skills include deploying personal strengths and compensating for shortcomings, convening diverse colleagues, diagnosing context, building productive teams and sustainable organizations, and wisely designing and using forums, arenas, and courts.

Strengthening Citizenship

The key design principle is: *Make your program an exercise in democratic education.* Begin with recruitment of diverse participants. Use inclusive processes like small-group problem solving, peer circles, and student-led dialogue. Give participants opportunities to reflect on their citizenship within organizations, communities, and countries. Ask them to write their economic and political histories and parse the common good. Help them apply integrative leadership practices to complex public problems.

Assessing, Coaching, and Mentoring

For assessment, the chief design principle is: *Ensure that assessments are helping participants move from the novice end of the leader spectrum toward the expert end.* Leadership educators can draw on numerous formal and informal assessments that help participants analyze their leadership styles, skills, and other strengths. These are most effective when combined with adept coaching and mentoring. For coaching, the chief design principle is: *Ensure the coaching relationship is focused on the well-being and development of the person being coached, and the person has a suitable combination of assessment, challenge, and support.* The extent of coaching will vary according to program resources. For mentoring, the chief design principle is: *Mentoring is promoted as a process that can help leaders develop over their lifespan.* Ideally, leadership educators will use these principles to ensure participants in our programs receive useful assessment, coaching, and mentoring and prepare to be good coaches and mentors themselves. As coaches and mentors, our focus must be on our relationship with those being coached and mentored. We will convey our deep interest in their development and demonstrate vulnerability and trust. We will help them gather and reflect on feedback they obtain from formal and informal assessments and help them set goals and report on their progress. Especially when we have longer-term mentor relationships, we will connect mentees to our professional networks and give them opportunities to shine.

Some General Design Principles

These principles mainly are about ensuring that leadership development programs fit the needs of participants and context. They are:

- *Leadership programs should be flexible enough to accommodate the diverse situations and talents of participants.*
- *Leadership programs should have cross-cultural appeal and embrace different learning modes.*
- *Leadership programs should take advantage of, and respond to, the information-rich environment of the Internet age.*
- *Leadership programs should provide opportunities for participants to interpret their experiences and challenges in light of theories and research findings, reflect on implications for future practice, and return to practice in an iterative fashion.*

Wrapping Up

I will end this book where I began, by inviting you to spend some time on your own leadership assessment. If you haven't done so already, craft your Narrative of Commitment. Describe your experiences with hosting, including attention to your social identities. Write your relational leadership narrative and your economic and political autobiographies. Think about what these exercises reveal about what you bring to leadership education and what you want to accomplish in the future. May you bring your whole self—heart, head, and hands—to this vital endeavor.

In closing, I want to highlight the comments of several of the educators you have met in this book.

Commitment to stay the course and move forward in the face of evil is leadership.
—*Lars Leafblad*

You need to contribute to leadership wherever you are—academic, professional, and geographic communities.
—*Yvonne Cheek*

Democracy and citizenship require constructive thought and constructive participation. To me that comes from what leadership requires and what leadership education should nurture: understanding of self, meaningful relationships with others, and commitment to action.
—*Ronnie Brooks*

Leadership arises at the intersection of personal passions and public needs.
—*Barbara Crosby and John Bryson*

APPENDIX A

Methodology

Teaching Leadership has developed somewhat organically from my own experience as a leadership educator and researcher based at the Humphrey School of Public Affairs at the University of Minnesota for the past 30 years. I have taught primarily master's level courses, but also at the undergraduate and Ph.D. level; I have designed and conducted leadership programs for public managers, university administrators, nonprofit groups, business people, senior citizens, and international fellows, mainly in U.S. settings, but also in the United Kingdom, Poland, and Ukraine. I began formulating ideas for the book while on sabbatical in London in 2009–2010; the break in my normal responsibilities gave me the chance to document my own experiences with teaching, but also to do more research into the kind of teaching that helps people, individually and collectively, grapple with the leadership challenges they encounter in their organizations and communities. Ultimately, I decided to write a book that would emphasize the integration of passion and commitment (heart), theory and research (head), and practical application (hands). I envisioned shifting attention from the question of how to teach leadership to the question of how one prepares oneself to teach leadership, which encompasses the question of how to lead.

Because I wanted to benefit from the wisdom of other leadership educators, I also engaged in numerous informal conversations with colleagues and conducted formal semi-structured interviews with 25 leadership educators. In developing my list of interviewees, I sought to include seasoned educators who view leadership as a relational process, rather than the exercise of influence or control tactics by powerful individuals. I wanted diversity in the type of leadership teaching they do—thus, I included educators mainly from the academic world, but also people who work mainly with community or foundation leadership programs. I sought diversity in age, discipline, ethnicity, gender, and nationality. I asked 10 of the interviewees to engage in a lengthy interview, using Protocol A, and the remainder to answer the questions on the much shorter Protocol B. Most of the interviews were in person, several were conducted via Skype, and a few by telephone. As noted in the Preface, Jodi Sandfort and Gary DeCramer were especially important contributors to the book. Our working sessions in 2012 shaped much of the book's framework.

Teaching Leadership Interview Protocol A

Part 1: Using Personal Narrative

What commitments inspire you in your leadership development work?
What makes you care about this work?
> Tell me about a time you felt born to teach.
> Tell me about a teaching experience when you wish you'd never been born.
What key challenges have you faced in your life that affect your approach to teaching or developing leadership?
Talk about your leadership and followership journey:
> In what ways have you been called to lead in your family, organizations, or communities?
> What "crucible experiences" or critical moments have been important?
> How have you dealt with failure and the persistence of evil in the world?
> How has your own view of leadership and followership evolved?

Part 2: Hosting and Hospitality

What's different about teaching different groups of people?
How have your gender, racial/ethnic, class, national, sexual, and religious identities been an asset or a hindrance in working with diverse groups of people?
How have your families and friendships affected your skills and attitudes toward hosting?
When have you struggled to welcome the stranger, to provide hospitality for people not like you?
What lessons have you taken to heart?

Part 3: Linking Leadership Theory and Practice

Tell me about key habits of mind, frameworks, skills that inform or guide your practice, whether it's field and program building or course design and instruction.
What ideas, frameworks, and skills do your students say have been most useful to them?

Part 4: Strengthening Citizenship

In what ways do you help participants in your courses, workshops, and programs link their leadership to citizenship in their organizations, communities, country, and in the world?

Do you see your work as strengthening democracy? How?

Tell me about how you came to see yourself as a public person.

What is your economic and political history?

Part 5: Assessing, Coaching, and Mentoring

How have you been mentored or coached in your work?

What have been some of your best experiences as a mentor?

What have been some of the worst experiences as a mentor?

What lessons would you draw from those experiences?

How do you use feedback to improve your own and others' practice?

Teaching Leadership Interview Protocol B

What frameworks, ideas, skills, or methods do participants in your leadership courses and workshops find most helpful?

What advice would you give to people who seek to be better leadership educators?

What feedback from students has changed your teaching?

In what ways does leadership education, as you practice it, contribute to democracy and citizenship?

APPENDIX B

Teaching Leadership Glossary

Action Learning Circles (a variation on peer circle process)—small groups of learners that focus on members' leadership practice and allow each person to share his/her own leadership actions and aspirations with the group. The aim is not to solve each other's problems, but to listen deeply to each other, and respond with inquiry and insights.

Appreciative inquiry—a strengths-based approach to investigating organizational or societal issues.

Arenas—the settings in which policy makers debate and decide on competing policy proposals and oversee implementation of adopted policies.

Courts—the settings in which leaders and followers rely on ethical principles, laws, and norms to sanction conduct and adjudicate competing claims related to the policies adopted in arenas.

Critical incidents—specific times when people's values are tested, when they have to summon the courage to persist despite self-doubts, pushback from the authorities, and no guarantee of success.

Crucible experiences—trying situations that change a person in some fundamental way.

Exit cards—strategies for getting out of a threatening or toxic job or assignment.

Forums—the settings in which stakeholders develop shared understanding of a public problem or challenge, evaluate potential solutions or responses, and craft proposals for specific policy changes, programs, and projects.

Integrative leadership—the work of linking and integrating diverse constituencies—along with resources, processes, and structures—in sustainable arrangements for remedying a complex public problem or responding to a "grand challenge."

Narrative of Commitment—an extended essay about how a person enacts his/her values.

Open Space—a method that allows groups to shape their own agendas. For example, group members are invited to propose topics, the proposers then take a stand by a sign proclaiming their topic, and other group members "vote with their feet" by gravitating to the topic they like best.

Peer circle process—derives from long-standing traditions that invite participants to sit together in a circle and take turns speaking, possibly using a talking stick or other object. The person who has the object is the one who speaks.

Policy regime—the system of policies, programs, laws, rules, and norms for handling a particular public issue.

Role plays—a structured exercise in which participants act out assigned or chosen roles as they confront organizational and societal challenges.

Round-robin process—each participant takes a turn contributing an idea.

Snow cards—half sheets of typing paper, 5" x 7" index cards, or sticky notes, on which participants write their ideas. Once they are arranged on a wall in clusters or columns of similar ideas, they resemble a "blizzard" of ideas, thus the name snow cards.

World Café—consists of multiple rounds of table conversations on one or more focal questions. Table hosts stay at their assigned tables and participants circulate to different tables as the rounds proceed. Hosts pose a question to participants, facilitate the conversation, and collect participant ideas in a form that can be shared with other participants in the next round.

APPENDIX C

Guidance for Transforming Public Policy Teams

The team project is a type of *action research* and *action learning*. You are undertaking research in order to produce action on a public problem, need, or opportunity that you care about. You will be learning amidst the action of working in a team to develop a report, poster, and presentation that makes your best case for policy change.

You will be constructing a report that constitutes a policy proposition supported by facts and values. Policy analysis and synthesis are not exact sciences, though scientific evidence is crucial. As you gather evidence and examine arguments, we encourage you to take both an appreciative and critical stance. As you engage in analysis and develop your own persuasive arguments, you will exercise your own judgment and appeal to the good judgment (and emotions) of others. You should establish credibility of your sources, probe and reveal their assumptions, and draw on multiple, independent sources from more than one discipline.

You will need to deal with what Herbert Simons (2001) calls "stock issues." Is change needed? Do proposed solutions fit the problem? Are proposed solutions the best available? We encourage you to use the three forms of evidence cited by Simons: stories, statistics, and testimony.

As you begin to construct your report, focus on your audience. Is it a client organization? Policy makers? Citizens? A combination of these?

We also encourage you to publish the results of your research. For example, give the report to an interested organization or policy maker, or publish your op-ed essay.

The remainder of this memo offers guidance for each phase of the project. Please let the instructors know where you need additional information.

Initial Meeting

Designate temporary facilitator. Share strengths and experiences that each team member brings to policy making and to group work. Agree on group norms and develop plan for how the team will work together.

Brainstorm project ideas. Projects should be broadly defined at this point, but capable of being turned into a manageable inquiry.

Projects should:

- Be inherently interdisciplinary
- Ultimately result in a clear and achievable institutional design or policy change objective(s)
- Be geographically specific

The "Project Topic Worksheet" (attachment 1) may be helpful.

Begin fashioning initial agreement focusing on:

General project idea and possible ways of developing it
Norms
Team member roles (e.g., coordinator, editor, agenda keeper)

You may use the resource "Creating a Project Work Plan" (see attachment 2) to develop the work plan that is part of the initial agreement.

Initial Agreement

The initial agreement consists of the proposed project idea, including work plan and group norms. (No more than five pages, double-spaced.) Be sure to designate someone on the team to check the IRB (human subjects) informed consent requirements for this course (see IRB folder). The plan and norms, plus updates, will constitute the team contract.

Problem Formulation Section

Submit a hard copy of your problem statement (about 10 double-spaced pages) that includes:

- Background of the problem, need, opportunity
- A summary of the literature (include bibliography) regarding the policy area; include at least 20 articles, books, websites
- Discussion of several ways to frame problem
- Solution search strategy plus sample solutions and how key stakeholders might react to those solutions

Attach stakeholder analyses (maps, diagrams).

See "Problem Formulation Additional Guidance" on the course website for further information about problem formulation and the literature review. You may also want to look at "Examples of Good Literature Reviews" on the course website.

Solution Assessment Section

Submit a hard copy of the report so far: The revised problem formulation section and a new section that identifies and elaborates on options for addressing the problem or need. Assess stakeholder support and opposition for each option. Articulate what it would take to pursue each option and what would be gained by doing so. Consider preparing an action-oriented causal map. (The new section should be no more than five pages. By this point, you may wish to prune earlier material—for example, by adding some of it to appendices.)

Policy Proposal Formulation Section

Submit a hard copy of the report so far, now with the addition of recommendations for addressing the problem or need. Include strategies for implementing the recommendations and show how you would garner sufficient stakeholder support. Attach solution criteria grid. (The new section should be no more than five pages.)

Draft Final Report and Op-Ed

Submit a 20–25 page draft report plus appendices that includes:

- executive summary
- a refined statement of the policy issue
- recommended solutions
- the rationale and design considerations behind the recommendations
- a strategy for adopting, implementing, and evaluating each recommendation (each strategy should be technically and administratively workable, politically acceptable, and legally and ethically defensible)
- an explanation of why the recommendation is acceptable to key stakeholders and thus is adoptable and implementable. If it is not politically feasible, explain why you are still supporting the recommendation.
- attention to who (and which organizations) can or should provide visionary, political, and ethical leadership needed to adopt and implement the solutions

Reference all tables, figures, and appendices in the text.

The op-ed essay should be aimed at policy makers and general readers and be about 500 words.

Poster and Presentation

Prepare a display and presentation that summarizes the team's report and transmits its most important content in a succinct, persuasive, and visually pleasing manner.

Think of the poster and oral presentation as an "executive summary" of your full paper. Pull the key points from each of the sections of your paper into abbreviated points. Consider including your most cogent charts, graphs, maps, etc., that synthesize information well.

Your oral presentation can talk us through the main points. It is to be 15 minutes long, with 10 minutes for questions. The class might be interested in hearing your biggest "ah-has" as you incorporated class material into your topic.

Please create handouts to accompany the presentation; we encourage you to include PowerPoint slides. The goal of your presentation is to provide enough information about your analysis and recommendations so that the class understands what type of further information is in your paper. Your paper will be available from the instructors so that if you pique class members' interest, they can read it.

PowerPoint or another useful software program can help you prepare the posters. PowerPoint is an easy program and the instructors encourage everybody to use it.

Final Report

The final report should draw together the team's previous work and present it in a cogent and persuasive way. The body of the paper should be 20 to 25 double-spaced pages (12-point type), not including bibliography, appendices, and attachments.

Incorporate comments from the instructors and feedback from class participants and others into a final report that leaves people stunned by your brilliance and persuasiveness!

Reference

Simons, H. W. (2001). *Persuasion in society*. Thousand Oaks, CA: SAGE.

Attachment 1 Project Topic Worksheet

Possible Topics	Why Interested	Benefits	Resources Available

Attachment 2 Creating a Project Work Plan

1. Identify your clients.
2. Clarify the purpose of your project.
3. Brainstorm all likely tasks needed to fulfill the purpose.
4. Put each task on a separate snow card.
5. Cluster snow cards and develop a descriptive heading (for example, report production, team building, team meetings, celebrations).
6. Prepare an Excel sheet, or a GANTT chart on an easel sheet:

   a. List the task headings on the left.
   b. Divide the project timeline into appropriate periods (for example, weeks) and use these as column headers.
   c. Note when tasks need to be completed and who will be responsible for completion.

APPENDIX D

Storify Assignment

PA5103, LS/IS 5100 Team Action Research Project *

Purpose

To practice leadership for the common good by:

1. Reflecting on and synthesizing information about an innovation your team cares about
2. Honing content "curation" skills—seeking, making sense of, and effectively sharing various social media content online via a story about the future
3. Sharing examples with your classmates of how you have begun to apply course learnings
4. Nudging beneficial change via your story about the future
5. Building a high-performing team

Preparation:
    Watch:
    Storify Guided Tour
    Getting Started in Storify
    How to Make a Storify
    Example 1

General Directions

1. Teams will be formed through an "open space" process during the face-to-face session on [date] (Week 4).
2. In your initial team meeting, develop a plan of action and assign initial roles and responsibilities. Select a coordinator. One person should be the "Storify"

lead. He or she will set up an account on storify.com and be responsible for entering material and links on the team's webpage. Other team members may select particular media to follow.

3. Team members will identify several social media "assets" from Twitter, Facebook, Google+, YouTube, Instagram, or other sources. The group will decide which assets to include in their "story about the future." It is important to build a seamless, analytical narrative.

4. The group will agree on a title for the story and a few paragraphs that frame the story and elicit responses or other actions. See the grading rubric below for expectations related to number of assets, engagement with course concepts/readings, and narrative impact.

5. With guidance from the team, the Storify lead will complete the draft story and the team will review it.

6. Throughout, practice team leadership by nurturing relationships, building on individual strengths, using methods of dialogue and deliberation, honoring timelines and other commitments, and having fun.

Specific Guidance

To the Storify Lead

Once you have set up an account, click on new story icon at upper right of your page and enter a story title. You can either call it "Explorations in PA5103 & LS/IS 5100" or get creative with the title as long as you include "PA5103 & LS/IS 5100." This is so your classmates and I—in the spirit of peer learning—can find your story by searching for PA5103 & LS/IS 5100.

To the Team

The story also must have an informative **headline.** The headline should be more than just a two- or three-word label. It should be similar to the headline of a news story or a press release. It should have a subject and verb. It should make sense to the casual reader. Keep in mind that the headline is what would show up in Google search results, so think in terms of keywords and search engine optimization.

In addition to the headline, the story should include **introductory text** (directly underneath the headline), **at least two subheadings** (use the "Header" button in the toolbar of the Storify editor), and **at least three paragraphs of transition/explanatory text**.

- **Selection of appropriate social media content:** Don't just use any tweets, Facebook posts, videos, etc. Be a curator, not just an aggregator. Find **good** content that **adds informational value**. Make sure the social media content is coming from credible sources.

- **Organization:** The Storify story is a **narrative**. It should "flow." There should be a logic to the order in which the information is presented. For some topics, a **chronological** approach might work best. For others, an **"inverted pyramid"** approach (most important information at the top) might be best. For still others, a **thematic** approach, in which information is grouped by theme or subtopic, might be most appropriate.
- **Solid writing, with background and context:** Write strong passages to tie together the social media content and provide any necessary background and context to the reader. Pay attention to spelling, grammar, and punctuation.

To the Storify Lead

You can save the story as a draft and return to it. Once you have completed it, be sure to "publish." Copy the link for the story and paste it into the homework submission space on the Moodle course site.

Project Grading Rubric (15 points—15%)

Attributes	Above Standard	At Standard	Still a Goal	Points Earned
Comprehensiveness	Includes at least 10 assets from at least 3 different sources (e.g., Twitter, Facebook, Google+, YouTube, Instagram, Flickr, other external articles/resources). 5	Includes at least 5 assets from 2 different sources (e.g., Twitter, Facebook, Google+, YouTube, Instagram, Flickr, other external articles/resources). 3	Includes at least 2 assets from at least 1 source (e.g., Twitter, Facebook, Google+, YouTube, Instagram, Flickr, other external articles/resources) 1	/5
Depth of engagement with course concepts & readings/resources	Connects with course readings and resources provided. Shows that student pursued additional information around his or her questions. 5	Shares synthesis of concepts from 2–3 sessions and lingering questions. Ties back to readings/resources provided. 3	Shares synthesis of concepts from 1–2 sessions and lingering questions. 1	/5
Exemplifies learning & application	Summary shows ongoing in-class and out-of-class experimentation and exploration over the period of the course related to each week's concepts and tools. Includes examples of how course learnings have already begun to be applied in professional and/or personal setting or plans for application in the near future. 5	Summary shows in-class engagement with course concepts and tools, but little to no application or experimentation outside of class. 3	Summary shows little to no application or engagement with course concepts and tools. 1	/5
Total Points				/15

*Definition of Action Research

- Undertaken in order to guide action
- Stakeholders involved in the research
- Shaped by a theory of action and change that can also emerge from the research

INDEX

Taylor & Francis eBooks

Helping you to choose the right eBooks for your Library

Add Routledge titles to your library's digital collection today. Taylor and Francis ebooks contains over 50,000 titles in the Humanities, Social Sciences, Behavioural Sciences, Built Environment and Law.

Choose from a range of subject packages or create your own!

Benefits for you

» Free MARC records
» COUNTER-compliant usage statistics
» Flexible purchase and pricing options
» All titles DRM-free.

Benefits for your user

» Off-site, anytime access via Athens or referring URL
» Print or copy pages or chapters
» Full content search
» Bookmark, highlight and annotate text
» Access to thousands of pages of quality research at the click of a button.

REQUEST YOUR **FREE** INSTITUTIONAL TRIAL TODAY

Free Trials Available
We offer free trials to qualifying academic, corporate and government customers.

eCollections – Choose from over 30 subject eCollections, including:

Archaeology	Language Learning
Architecture	Law
Asian Studies	Literature
Business & Management	Media & Communication
Classical Studies	Middle East Studies
Construction	Music
Creative & Media Arts	Philosophy
Criminology & Criminal Justice	Planning
Economics	Politics
Education	Psychology & Mental Health
Energy	Religion
Engineering	Security
English Language & Linguistics	Social Work
Environment & Sustainability	Sociology
Geography	Sport
Health Studies	Theatre & Performance
History	Tourism, Hospitality & Events

For more information, pricing enquiries or to order a free trial, please contact your local sales team:
www.tandfebooks.com/page/sales

Routledge
Taylor & Francis Group

The home of
Routledge books

www.tandfebooks.com

Printed in Great Britain
by Amazon